# THE HEBREW BIBLE IN SOCIAL PERSPECTIVE

Series Editor

Francesca Stavrakopoulou
University of Exeter, UK

Forthcoming titles in the series:

*Life and Death: Social Perspectives on Biblical Bodies*, edited by Francesca Stavrakopoulou

# SCRIBES AND SCRIBALISM

*Edited by Mark Leuchter*

BLOOMSBURY ACADEMIC
LONDON • NEW YORK • OXFORD • NEW DELHI • SYDNEY

T&T CLARK

Bloomsbury Publishing Plc

50 Bedford Square, London, WC1B 3DP, UK
1385 Broadway, New York, NY 10018, USA
29 Earlsfort Terrace, Dublin 2, Ireland

BLOOMSBURY, T&T CLARK and the T&T Clark logo are trademarks of Bloomsbury Publishing Plc

First published in Great Britain 2021
This paperback edition published in 2022

Copyright © Mark Leuchter and contributors, 2021

Mark Leuchter has asserted his right under the Copyright, Designs and Patents Act, 1988, to be identified as Editor of this work.

Cover design: Charlotte James
Cover image © www.BibleLandPictures.com / Alamy Stock Photo

All rights reserved. No part of this publication may be reproduced or transmitted in any form or by any means, electronic or mechanical, including photocopying, recording, or any information storage or retrieval system, without prior permission in writing from the publishers.

Bloomsbury Publishing Plc does not have any control over, or responsibility for, any third-party websites referred to or in this book. All internet addresses given in this book were correct at the time of going to press. The author and publisher regret any inconvenience caused if addresses have changed or sites have ceased to exist, but can accept no responsibility for any such changes.

A catalogue record for this book is available from the British Library.

A catalog record for this book is available from the Library of Congress.
Library of Congress Control Number: 2020942345

| ISBN: | HB: | 978-0-5676-5974-3 |
|---|---|---|
| | PB: | 978-0-5676-9700-4 |
| | ePDF: | 978-0-5676-9617-5 |
| | ePUB: | 978-0-5676-9616-8 |

To find out more about our authors and books visit www.bloomsbury.com and sign up for our newsletters.

# CONTENTS

Abbreviations — vii
Notes on Contributors — xi
Series Editor's Preface — xiii

Introduction:
The Scholarly Context for the Study of Scribes and Scribalism
*Mark Leuchter* — 1

## Part One
### Praxis and Materiality

Influential Inscriptions:
Resituating Scribal Activity during the Iron I–IIA Transition
*Sarah Malena* — 13

The Media and Materiality of Southern Levantine Inscriptions:
Production and Reception Contexts
*Madah Richey* — 29

Scribes and Scribalism in Archaic Crete
*Anselm C. Hagedorn* — 41

## Part Two
### Power and Status

Scribes, Schools and Ideological Conflict in Ancient Israel and Judah
*Brian Rainey* — 63

Ecclesiastes and the Problem of Transmission in Biblical Literature
*Jacqueline Vayntrub* — 79

Textualization and the Transformation of Biblical Prophecy
*Heath D. Dewrell* — 95

Reorientation in Responsibility of Levites Taking Care of the Ark:
The Levites' Role in Samuel–Kings in Relation to Deuteronomistic Expressions
Concerning Interpretation of the Law
*Antje Labahn* — 107

## Part Three
## Between Ideology and Authority

Writing in Three Dimensions:
Scribal Activity and Spaces in Jewish Antiquity
*Laura Carlson Hasler* 125

Rejecting "Patriarchy":
Reflections on Feminism, Biblical Scholarship, and Social Perspective
*Shawna Dolansky* 133

BIBLIOGRAPHY 149
INDEX OF REFERENCES 174
INDEX OF AUTHORS 179

# ABBREVIATIONS

| | |
|---|---|
| AA | *American Archivist* |
| AAAS | *Annales archéologiques arabes syriennes* |
| AASOR | Annual of the American Schools of Oriental Research |
| AB | Anchor Bible |
| ABS | Archaeology and Biblical Studies (Society of Biblical Literature) |
| *ADAJ* | *Annual of the Department of Antiquities of Jordan* |
| ADPV | Abhandlungen des Deutschen Palästina-Vereins |
| *AHw* | *Akkadisches Handwörterbuch*. Wolfram von Soden. 3 vols. Wiesbaden, 1965–81 |
| AIL | Ancient Israel and Its Literature (Society of Biblical Literature) |
| *AJA* | *American Journal of Archaeology* |
| ALASP | Abhandlungen zur Literatur Alt-Syrien-Palästinas |
| AnBib | Analecta biblica |
| ANEM | Ancient Near Eastern Monographs |
| ANESSup | Ancient Near Eastern Studies Supplement |
| *AnSt* | *Anatolian Studies* |
| AOAT | Alter Orient und Altes Testament |
| ATD | Das Alte Testament Deutsch |
| AYB | Anchor Yale Bible |
| *BARev* | *Biblical Archaeology Review* |
| *BASOR* | *Bulletin for the American School of Oriental Research* |
| BASORSup | Bulletin of the American Schools of Oriental Research Supplements |
| BBB | Bonner biblische Beiträge |
| BBVO | Berliner Beiträge zum Vorderen Orient |
| *BCH* | *Bulletin de correspondence héllenique* |
| BEATAJ | Beiträge zur Erforschung des Alten Testamentes und des antiken Judentum |
| BETL | Bibliotheca Ephemeridum Theologicarum Lovaniensium |
| *BH* | *Book History* |
| BibInt | Biblical Interpretation |
| BibOr | Biblica et Orientalia |
| *BiOr* | *Bibliotheca Orientalis* |
| BJS | Brown Judaic Studies |
| BWANT | Beiträge zur Wissenschaft vom Alten Testament |
| BZAR | Beihefte zur Zeitschrift für Altorientalische und Biblische Rechtsgeschichte |
| BZAW | Beiträge zur Zeitschrift für die alttestamentliche Wissenschaft |
| BZNW | Beihefte zur Zeitschrift für die neutestamentliche Wissenschaft |
| CAD | *The Assyrian Dictionary of the Oriental Institute of the University of Chicago.* Chicago: The Oriental Institute of the University of Chicago, 1956–2010 |
| CB.OT | Coniectanea biblica: Old Testament Series |
| *CBQ* | *Catholic Biblical Quarterly* |

| | |
|---|---|
| CBQMS | Catholic Biblical Quarterly Monograph Series |
| CC | Continental Commentaries |
| CHANE | Culture and History of the Ancient Near East |
| DJD | Discoveries in the Judaean Desert |
| DMOA | Documenta et Monumenta Orientis Antiqui |
| *EHLL* | Geoffrey Khan et al., eds., *Encyclopedia of Hebrew Language and Linguistics*. Leiden: Brill, 2013 |
| EdF | Erträge der Forschung |
| FAT | Forschungen zum Alten Testament |
| FRLANT | Forschungen zur Religion und Literatur des Alten und Neuen Testaments |
| *HeBAI* | *Hebrew Bible and Ancient Israel* |
| HSM | Harvard Semitic Monographs |
| HSS | Harvard Semitic Studies |
| *HUCA* | *Hebrew Union College Annual* |
| *IC* | M. Guarducci (ed.), *Inscriptiones Creticae Vol. I-IV*. Rome 1935–50 |
| ICC | International Critical Commentary |
| *ICS* | O. Masson, *Inscriptions Chypriotes Syllabique*, Études Chrypriote 1, 2nd ed, Paris, 1983 |
| *IE* | H. Engelmann and R. Merkelbach (eds.), *Die Inschriften von Erythrai und Klazomenai Teil 1 (Nr 1–200)*, Inschriften griechischer Städte aus Kleinasien 1, Bonn, 1972 |
| IECOT | International Exegetical Commentary on the Old Testament |
| *IEJ* | *Israel Exploration Journal* |
| *IG* | *Inscriptiones Graece*, Berlin, 1897– |
| *IvO* | K. Dittenberger and W. Purgold, *Die Inschriften von Olympia*, Berlin, 1896 |
| *IMSA* | *Israel Museum Studies in Archaeology* |
| *JANER* | *Journal of Ancient Near Eastern Religions* |
| *JANES* | *Journal of the Ancient Near Eastern Society* |
| *JAOS* | *Journal of the American Oriental Society* |
| *JBL* | *Journal of Biblical Literature* |
| *JCS* | *Journal of Cuneiform Studies* |
| *JHS* | *Journal of Hebrew Scriptures* |
| *JNES* | *Journal of Near Eastern Studies* |
| *JNSL* | *Journal of Northwest Semitic Languages* |
| *JQR* | *Jewish Quarterly Review* |
| JSJSup | Journal for the Study of Judaism Supplements |
| *JSOT* | *Journal for the Study of the Old Testament* |
| JSOTSup | Journal for the Study of the Old Testament Supplements |
| *JSS* | *Journal of Semitic Studies* |
| *JTS* | *Journal of Theological Studies* |
| *KAI* | *Kanaanäische und Aramäische Inschriften*. Ed. Herbert Donner and Wolfgang Rollig. Wisebaden, 1962; 5th ed. 2002 |
| KAT | Kommentar zum Alten Testament |
| *KTU/CAT* | *Keilalphabetische Texte aus Ugarit/Cuneiform Alphabetic Texts from Ugarit* |
| LAPO | Littératures anciennes du Proche-Orient |
| LCL | Loeb Classical Library |
| LHBOTS | The Library of Hebrew Bible/Old Testament Studies |
| *LSCG* | F. Sokolowski, *Lois sacrées des cités greque*, Paris, 2nd ed., 1969 |

| | |
|---|---|
| MdB | Le Monde de la Bible |
| MIFAO | Mémoires de Institut français d'archéologie orientale |
| ML | R. Meiggs and D. Lewis, *A Selection of Greek Historical Inscriptions to the End of the Fifth Century BC*, rev. ed. Oxford 1999 |
| Mn.S | Mnemosyne Supplements |
| NEB | Neue Echter Bibel |
| NICOT | New International Commentary on the Old Testament |
| *Nomima* I-II | H. van Effenterre and F. Ruzé (eds.), *Nomima. Receuil d'inscriptions politiques et juridiques de l'archaisme grec I-II*, Collection de l'École française de Rome 188, Rome 1994/1995 |
| OAC | Orientis Antiqui Collectio |
| OBO | Orbis Biblicus et Orientalis |
| *Or* | *Orientalia* (NS) |
| OTL | Old Testament Library |
| *PEFQS* | *Palestine Exploration Fund Quarterly Statement* |
| RBS | Resources for Biblical Study |
| *RÉS* | *Répertoire d'épigraphie sémitique.* Paris: Imprimerie nationale, 1900– |
| RSO | Ras Shamra – Ougarit |
| SAA | SAA State Archives of Assyria |
| SAAS | State Archives of Assyria Studies |
| SBL | Society of Biblical Literature |
| SBLSymS | Society of Biblical Literature Symposium Series |
| SEG | Supplementum Epigraphicum Graecum |
| *Sem* | *Semitica* |
| *SJOT* | *Scandinavian Journal of the Old Testament* |
| STDJ | Studies on the Texts of the Desert of Judah |
| *TA* | *Tel Aviv* |
| TAD | Bezalel Porten and Ada Yardeni, *Textbook of Aramaic Documents from Ancient Egypt.* 4 vols. Jerusalem: Hebrew University, 1986–99 |
| ThB | Theologische Bibliothek |
| *Transeuph* | *Transeuphratène* |
| *TSSI* | *Textbook of Syrian Semitic Inscriptions* |
| *UF* | *Ugarit-Forschungen* |
| UISK | Untersuchungen zur indogermanischen Sprach- und Kulturwissenschaft |
| *VT* | *Vetus Testamentum* |
| VTSup | Supplements to Vetus Testamentum |
| WAW | Writing from the Ancient World: Society of Biblical Literature |
| WMANT | Wissenschaftliche Monographen zum Alten und Neuen Testament |
| *ZAR* | *Zeitschrift für Altorientalische und Biblische Rechtsgeschichte* |
| *ZAW* | *Zeitschrift für die alttestamentliche Wissenschaft* |
| ZBK.AT | Zürcher Bibelkommentare Altes Testament |
| *ZDPV* | *Zeitschrift des deutschen Palästina-Vereins* |
| *ZPE* | *Zeitschrift für Papyrologie und Epigraphik* |

# NOTES ON CONTRIBUTORS

Heath D. Dewrell is Assistant Professor of Old Testament at Princeton Theological Seminary, USA.

Shawna Dolansky is Associate Professor at Carleton University, Canada.

Anselm C. Hagedorn is Professor of Old Testament and Ancient Judaism at Osnabrück University, Germany.

Laura Carlson Hesler is Alvin H. Rosenfeld Chair in Jewish Studies, Assistant Professor of Jewish Studies and Religious Studies at Indiana University Bloomington, USA.

Antje Labahn is Extraordinary Associate Professor, Faculty of Theology, North-West University, South Africa.

Mark Leuchter is Associate Professor of Religion and Director of Jewish Studies at Temple University, USA.

Sarah Malena is Assistant Professor of History at St Mary's College of Maryland, USA.

Brian Rainey is Assistant Professor of Old Testament at Princeton Theological Seminary, USA.

Madadh Richey is Humanities Teaching Fellow at the University of Chicago, USA.

Jacqueline Vayntrub is Assistant Professor of Hebrew Bible at Yale University, USA.

# SERIES EDITOR'S PREFACE

It is a pleasure to publish *Scribes and Scribalism* in the Hebrew Bible in Social Perspective series—a new collection of multi-authored volumes addressing major themes integral to the academic study of the Hebrew Bible. Despite the divine origins and influences they have often been ascribed, religious texts do not simply descend from the heavens, nor are they set in stone. They are human creations, variously reflecting and transforming those who made, read, heard, and curated them, and those who continue to engage them today. As such, the texts and traditions of the Hebrew Bible are both social products and social agents, and it is this sociality this series aims to take seriously. Comprising specially commissioned pieces from some of the most innovative scholars in the field, each volume offers stimulating, cutting-edge insights into the social worlds of the Hebrew Bible, whether past or present. These exciting volumes will both refresh and revitalize key debates and tricky issues clustering within and around the Hebrew Bible—and in doing so, tell us something new about the people caught up in its social worlds.

In this book, Mark Leuchter has assembled a stellar cast of scholars to explore the social diversities and dynamics of scribalism in ancient Israelite, Judahite and early Jewish cultures. Interrogating topics ranging from the materialities and economies of writing to the shifting roles of power, embodiment and imagination within scribal communities, the essays collected in this volume offer exciting new trajectories in our understanding of ancient writers and the ways in which we continue to read their work.

Francesca Stavrakopoulou
Series Editor

# Introduction

## The Scholarly Context for the Study of Scribes and Scribalism

MARK LEUCHTER

Since the mid-1990s, scholars have devoted increased attention to the centrifugal role of scribes and scribal culture in the creation of not only texts and traditions but of social identity in ancient Israel/ancient Judaism as evidenced in the biblical record and beyond.[1] Whereas earlier approaches to the study of biblical texts saw scribes either as incidental transmitters of valuable material or as hindrances to recovering the original contours of such material, contemporary approaches recognize that scribes did not simply textualize tradition but profoundly shaped it and even served as its fundamental architects.[2] Likewise, scribal culture—the universe of ideas that provided context for understanding texts and the very process of their production and preservation—has emerged more prominently in recent years as a fundamental feature of ancient Israelite/Judahite and Jewish social identity in relation to the biblical record. It is clear to most scholars now that scribes were not simply literate elites sequestered away in the depths of a temple or palace and given to composing strictly esoteric or theoretical literature. Scribal works were reflections on, reactions to, and foundations for larger trends in the societies surrounding them. The texts they created were not simply witnesses to identity claims and boundaries within ancient Israelite/ancient Jewish communities, but often the very forces by which those claims and boundaries were formed and delineated.[3]

Looking back at a century or more of modern critical biblical scholarship, one might inquire as to why the serious study of scribes and scribalism in ancient Israel and ancient Judaism has only emerged as a vanguard area in relatively recent years. The comparative evidence from other ancient Near Eastern cultures has long been available, and archaeology throughout much of the twentieth century provided a sufficient yield of epigraphic artifacts to allow for more careful and detailed scrutiny of the biblical record. Yet for most of this time, scholarship in both Europe and North America labored under the shadow of certain priorities and assumptions dating from the nineteenth

---

[1] For the sake of convenience, I use the phrase "ancient Israel" here to refer to the cultures of pre-monarchic Israel and the pre-exilic Israelite states/monarchies. By contrast, I use the phrase "ancient Judaism" to refer primarily to the post-exilic culture of Yehud in the Persian period and the Jewish writers active in the Hellenistic period. The dividing line between these categories is, to my mind, the experience of exile and forced migration that characterized Israelite and Judahite populations in the neo-Babylonian period, but a fuller discussion is well beyond the narrow scope of this introductory essay.

[2] The bibliography over the last two decades related to this topic is exhaustive. Prominent examples include David W. Baker, "Scribes as Transmitters of Tradition," in *Faith, Tradition & History: Old Testament Historiography in Its Near Eastern Context*, ed. A. R. Millard et al. (Winona Lake: Eisenbrauns, 1994), 65–77; Philip R. Davies, *Scribes and Schools: The Canonization of the Hebrew Scriptures* (Louisville: Westminster John Knox, 1998); David M. Carr, *Writing on the Tablet of the Heart: Origins of Scripture and Literature* (New York: Oxford University Press, 2005); idem, *The Formation of the Hebrew Bible: A New Reconstruction* (Oxford: Oxford University Press, 2011); Karel van der Toorn, *Scribal Culture and the Making of the Hebrew Bible* (Cambridge, MA: Harvard University Press, 2007).

[3] I examine this in greater detail in my recent monograph *The Levites and the Boundaries of Israelite Identity* (New York: Oxford University Press, 2017), especially in Chapters 5–7.

century regarding what dimensions of the biblical record were worthy of serious scrutiny and what were ancillary or even tertiary in importance. The recovery of an "original" tradition embedded in a text—be it the ostensible *ipsissima verba* of a prophet or the kerygma of a hinterland liturgy—was prioritized far above the manners or mechanisms whereby older sources or motifs were set in their received literary contexts. This approach was characterized by a theological romanticization of the sources: the search for the original traditions represented the search for the inspired divine word. Anything else was, effectively, a distraction.[4]

Attitudes regarding the merits of sources that earlier scholars tended to overlook evolved throughout the latter half of the twentieth century, but scholarship continued to labor under the weight of inherited biases. At the same time, a rising tide of pushback to these assumptions began to surface as well, though this too brought with it a number of complicating factors. The case of Jeremiah studies in the 1980s is a telling example. The early twentieth-century source-critical models of Bernard Duhm and Sigmund Mowinckel continued to inform how most scholars categorized the material in the book of Jeremiah, with the poetry largely reflecting the prophet's own words and teachings and the prose passages deriving from a secondary set of scribal hands.[5] Various advocates of this view offered (significant) adjustments and qualifications, while others rejected it altogether, opting instead for the view—championed most prominently by Robert Carroll—that nothing in the book should be seen as "authentic" and is purely a work of much later scribal imagination.[6] Thus even among scholars who did not see an historical prophet's words preserved in the book, the very concept of "authenticity" (if one defines the term as something directly connected to an historical experience or individuals to which the principal contents and contours of a tradition should be credited) thereby remained somehow remote from the scribal process that produced it.

Other approaches, however, began to conceive of a different and more tenable understanding of the role of scribes in the formation of the book of Jeremiah. Jack Lundbom's work into the literary topography of the book did much to challenge the strict partitions of sources based on formal criteria, and went on to situate the book's rhetorical features within the conventions of ancient Near Eastern scribal praxes.[7] As a result, the role of scribes within the book emerged not simply as a relic of its transmission history but as a central feature of its message and purpose; Lundbom even argued that the prophet himself possessed scribal training, a view that has gained support for different reasons in later investigations of the book.[8] From this perspective, the natures of prophetic performance and scribal performance emerge as far more inter-connected—a view that receives support from the study of relatively contemporaneous Mesopotamian prophecy.[9]

---

[4] And this, to no small degree, was accompanied by an anti-Jewish ethos that distinguished between authentically sacred Israelite tradition as early and pristine, with the degeneration of that sanctity over time leading to "un-inspired" Jewish scribalism steeped in mechanical literary transmission and fossilized legalism. See further J. W. Rogerson, *Old Testament Criticism in the 19th Century: England and Germany* (Minneapolis: Fortress, 1985), 79–90.

[5] Bernard Duhm, *Das Buch Jeremia* (Tübingen: Mohr, 1901); note that Duhm is explicit about his anti-Jewish ethos regarding scribalism at the very outset of his commentary (p. xviii); Sigmund Mowinckel, *Der Komposition des Buches Jeremia* (Kristiania: Dybwad, 1914).

[6] The most prominent example of the latter view is Robert Carroll's *Jeremiah: A Commentary*, OTL (Philadelphia: Westminster, 1986), 47 and passim.

[7] Jack R. Lundbom, *Jeremiah: A Study in Ancient Hebrew Rhetoric* (Missoula: Scholars Press, 1975). See more fully Lundbom's later commentaries, *Jeremiah 1–20*, AB 21A (New York: Doubleday, 1999); *Jeremiah 21–36*, AB 21B (New York: Doubleday, 2004); and *Jeremiah 37–52*, AB 21C (New York: Doubleday, 2004).

[8] Jack R. Lundbom, "Baruch, Seraiah, and Scribal Colophons in the Book of Jeremiah," *JSOT* 36 (1986): 89–114; see further Leuchter, *The Levites*, 193–96.

[9] Karel van der Toorn, "Mesopotamian Prophecy between Immanence and Transcendence: A Comparison of Old Babylonian and Neo-Assyrian Prophecy," in *Prophecy in Its Ancient Near Eastern Context: Mesopotamian, Biblical, and Arabian Perspectives*, ed. Martti Nissinen, SBLSymS (Atlanta: Society of Biblical Literature, 2000), 71–87. See also the essay by Dewrell in the present volume.

Previous categorical distinctions required significant adjustment, as it became clear that the search for "authentic" prophecy was not simply a matter separating poetry from prose. The concept of a scribal product lacking "authenticity" could thus no longer be sustained, since scribalism was revealed as an essential sacral concept within the book.

Similar changes in the understanding of scribal roles accompanied the study of the book of Deuteronomy. The influential theory of Gerhard von Rad from the mid-twentieth century stipulated that Deuteronomy was principally the legacy of inspired northern Levites; Judahite scribes involved in its textual transmission occupied a lower hierarchical rung.[10] This was challenged by the work of Moshe Weinfeld, whose 1972 monograph on Deuteronomy placed the Judahite scribes who wrought it as its primary intellectual and theological architects.[11] Weinfeld's examination of Deuteronomic scribalism relied heavily on comparisons with the types of ancient Near Eastern genres with which only learned scribes among the elites of Jerusalem would have had sufficient familiarity to create Deuteronomy and its related texts. Weinfeld thereby emphasized that scribes were not merely copyists or stenographers but creative and profoundly influential thinkers fully conversant with a dizzying range of international and Israelite traditions.[12]

But even Weinfeld's contribution to the discussion (which cannot be over-valued) carried with it a number of limiting suppositions regarding scribes, literacy, and textuality in the Israelite world that produced Deuteronomy. Weinfeld's tenable reconstruction of an elite Jerusalemite scribal culture was, to be sure, a sufficient basis upon which one could seriously challenge von Rad's earlier model. But his full dismissal of Levites as major contributors to Deuteronomy's contents assume that literary facility and sophistication could only be harnessed by royal sage-scribes of Jerusalem, or that a sophisticated scribal tradition fostered by Levites was not feasible.[13] Neither position is easily defended as subsequent studies have pointed to the problems with this assumption on both textual and anthropological grounds.[14] Furthermore, archaeological evidence points to textual resources and scribal facility well beyond Jerusalem, and recent historical-critical studies of the biblical sources support a deep ethos of decentralization of power and textuality characterizing Iron IIA-B Israelite society.[15] Weinfeld was correct to highlight to essential nature of scribal culture in the production of Deuteronomy, but he did not adequately consider the possibility (and, indeed, likelihood) that the authors of Deuteronomy could well be Levites of northern Israelite heritage who sustained their own highly sophisticated, non-Jerusalemite scribal tradition. The social context in which scribes could and did operate in the production of Deuteronomy moved well beyond the strictures of Weinfeld's model, further challenging the constructed categories of convention, language, and group identity that informed earlier scholarly concepts of scribal function and authority.

The contemporary shift in attitude regarding the importance of scribes in the aforementioned social contexts has to do with several important innovations in the field of biblical studies and the study of Israelite/Jewish antiquity. First and foremost among these is the recognition that older models for conceiving of substantial scribal activity were significantly challenged by subsequent research, but even that subsequent research was itself subjected to significant qualification over the last two decades of investigation. Scholars in the mid-twentieth century adopted a model of a massive uptick in literary sophistication and productivity during the early to mid-tenth century

---

[10] Gerhard von Rad, *Studies in Deuteronomy* (London: SCM, 1953), 66–67.
[11] Moshe Weinfeld, *Deuteronomy and the Deuteronomic School* (Oxford: Clarendon, 1972), 177–78.
[12] Ibid., 158–78.
[13] Ibid., 53–58.
[14] Leuchter, *The Levites*, 155–61. See also Jeffrey C. Geoghegan, *The Time, Place and Purpose of the Deuteronomistic History: The Evidence of "Until This Day"*, BJS (Providence: Brown University Press, 2006), 139–64.
[15] Daniel Fleming, *The Legacy of Israel in Judah's Bible* (New York: Cambridge University Press, 2012), 172, 309–10.

BCE (von Rad's so-called Solomonic Enlightenment).[16] According to this model, various Pentateuchal sources, old liturgical poems, prophetic narratives and even wisdom texts were assigned to learned scribes of the early courts of Jerusalem (or, later, Samaria) whose work was widely disseminated, taught, and digested among the spiritually and intellectually advanced Israelite and Judahite hinterland populations. This model eventually came under serious fire when more methodologically advanced examinations revealed that the majority of the Israelite and Judahite populations had severely limited resources for obtaining literacy beyond elite circles.[17] The influential 1991 study of David W. Jamieson-Drake on scribal resources and state-formation in Israel and Judah served as the point of departure for many scholars in putting to rest the un-nuanced concept of a widespread literary "enlightenment" anytime before the mid- to late eighth century BCE.[18] Even then, substantial literary production remained socially limited in scope and restricted to a limited circle of literati and was not experienced much beyond this circle.

But while Jamieson-Drake and the scholars who followed his lead introduced mitigating factors that are necessary for reconstructing the reach of scribalism and textuality in ancient Israel, this more restrictive model has received criticism and adjustments in the intervening years. Jamieson-Drake's proposal addressed one model of state formation but did not consider others that have since emerged. These models align well with the archaeological evidence from pre-eighth-century BCE contexts that attests to early states that could indeed support scribal activity in the tenth century BCE.[19] The critique of a widespread interest in or access to texts and literacy remains sound, but this does not nullify the likelihood that at least some notable scribal activity took place among a limited but powerful group of elites in the tenth and ninth centuries BCE in Israel and Judah.[20] It would be in such nascent states, forged during eras of turbulence and cultural transition, that text production would have served stabilizing purposes, reinforcing new and evolving concepts of authority while situating that authority within much earlier traditions and social conventions. The production and regulation of authoritative texts among the new elite castes established new ways for these infrastructural innovations to interact with deep-seated clan and village-based forms of social organization.[21] This is not to suggest that rural corners of a subsistence-level economic society possessed access to these written works, but the contents of such written compositions created a baseline of elite self-perception and culture that, through the mechanisms of a forming state, would intermingle with older forms of discourse.[22]

New understandings of the categories of orality and literacy are essential to the reconstruction of the aforementioned dynamic. Earlier concepts either pitted orality against textuality or assumed a sort of linear progression from the latter to the former. To be sure, there remain some limited

---

[16] Gerhard von Rad, "Beginnings of Historical Writing in Ancient Israel," in *From Genesis to Chronicles* (Minneapolis: Fortress, 2005 [original, 1944]), 125–53.
[17] See further Carr, *Writing on the Tablet of the Heart*, 115–16; Ian M. Young, "Israelite Literacy: Interpreting the Evidence," *VT* 48 (1998): 239–53, 408–22.
[18] David W. Jamieson-Drake, *Scribes and Schools in Monarchic Judah: A Socio-Archaeological Approach*, The Social World of Biblical Antiquity Series 9; JSOTSup 109 (Sheffield: Sheffield Academic, 1991).
[19] See Daniel I. Master, "State Formation Theory and the Kingdom of Ancient Israel," *JNES* 60 (2001): 117–34; Lawrence E. Stager, "The Patrimonial Kingdom of Solomon," in *Symbiosis, Symbolism and the Power of the Past*, ed. W. G. Dever and S. Gitin (Winona Lake: Eisenbrauns, 2003), 63–73. The social conditions that Master and Stager observe appear to persist all the way down to the end of the Judahite monarchy; see Aren Maeir and Itzhaq Shai, "Reassessing the Character of the Judahite Kingdom: Archaeological Evidence for Non-Centralized, Kinship-based Components," in *From Sha'ar Hagolan to Shaaraim: Essays in Honor of Prof. Yossi Garfinkel*, ed. Saar Ganor et al. (Jerusalem: Israel Exploration Society, 2016), 323–40.
[20] See most recently the compelling argument by Matthieu Richelle, "Elusive Scrolls: Could Any Hebrew Literature Have Been Written Prior to the Eighth Century BCE?," *VT* 66 (2016): 556–94.
[21] Seth L. Sanders, "Writing and Early Iron Age Israel: Before National Scripts, Beyond Nations and States," in *Literate Culture and Tenth-Century Canaan: The Tel Zayit Abecedary in Context*, ed. Ron E. Tappy and P. Kyle McCarter (Winona Lake: Eisenbrauns, 2008), 108–9.
[22] This seems to be the very purpose of the composition of an early Exodus narrative in the late tenth century BCE in the nascent northern state. See further Leuchter, *The Levites*, 120–25.

grounds for retaining aspects of these earlier understandings. For example, sociolinguistic presuppositions embedded in a text may indicate that an author was addressing social factors where writing and textuality were valued to greater of lesser degrees.[23] Furthermore, the rise in resources for literacy and writing does seem to increase over the course of the Iron II period down to (and through) the Persian period in different ways.[24] Yet neither of these examples supports the view that scribalism and textuality were ever separated from hinterland society throughout the Iron Age (or later) or that oral traditions and written traditions developed in discrete categories. Recent studies have suggested just the opposite: learned scribal texts were directly influenced by oral tradition and culture well beyond a royal scriptorium or temple library/workshop, and influenced oral discourse and culture in turn.[25] The relationship is far more complex than what is permitted by previous bifurcations and polar categories, which demands a more carefully tuned recognition of the place that scribes occupied in such an environment.

Of great importance, too, are advances in the study of both cultural memory and individual memorialization in the formation of biblical texts and traditions. The former provides scholars with an arsenal of methods whereby the contents of a text reflect not only the intentions of the scribe/author behind it but the assumptions and expectations, deliberate and inadvertent, of the culture in which the scribe operates.[26] A scribal work encodes information about an historical past as remembered by the scribe's immediate social group but also the society to which it contributes. Such a work thus encodes information about the scribe's own contemporaneous world that is preserved, transmitted, and interpreted by later scribes and their audiences. This information ranges from explicit archival or annalistic details to ethical norms and social and even linguistic conventions from diverse eras, requiring contemporary scholars to approach questions of sources, dating, and purpose with great caution. Yet this also provides scholars with a new set of questions regarding how cultures conceive of history and their place within it, as well as the mechanisms through which events, personalities, and ideas are passed along across time.

Individual memorization is in some ways a microcosm of the foregoing issues. Recent research makes clear that ancient scribes learned their craft through copying material texts but also by memorizing them.[27] Scribes were required to digest a curriculum of textual work and become enculturated in the linguistic vernacular of these works and their ideologies—and, therefore, the worldviews of the earlier scribes who wrought these earlier texts. The process of memorization, however, invariably led to transformation of the sources they memorized. In his detailed study of scribal methods of memorization, David Carr has shown that the reproduction of Text A was regularly affected by memorization of details from Text B; scribes enculturated in a given linguistic and

---

[23]Frank M. Polak, "Style is More than the Person: Sociolinguistics, Literary Culture, and the Distinction between Written and Oral Narrative," in *Biblical Hebrew: Studies in Chronology and Typology*, ed. Ian Young, JSOTSup 369 (London: T&T Clark, 2003), 38–103, though additional factors must be considered when using this criteria to establish a possible date for a text. The sociolinguistic features Polak discusses could pertain to types of populations (elite literati versus groups less enculturated in textual traditions) rather that particular temporal circumstances or settings, though the complex prose he analyzes is best seen—as he suggests—as a function of the encounter with foreign imperialism in the late monarchic and post-monarchic periods.
[24]A convenient overview is provided by William Schniedewind, *How the Bible Became a Book: The Textualization of Ancient Israel* (Cambridge: Cambridge University Press, 2004), 64–117, 165–94, though I part ways with Schniedewind on the dearth of creative scribal activity in the Persian period.
[25]Dalit Rom-Shiloni, "'How can you say, "I am not defiled…"?' (Jeremiah 2:20-25): Allusions to Priestly Legal Traditions in the Poetry of Jeremiah," *JBL* 133 (2014): 774–75; Laura Quick, *Deuteronomy 28 and the Aramaic Curse Tradition* (Oxford: Oxford University Press, 2018), 161–85; Carr, *Formation of the Hebrew Bible*, 25–34.
[26]See *inter alia* Ronald S. Hendel, *Remembering Abraham: Culture, Memory and History in the Hebrew Bible* (New York: Oxford University Press, 2005). See also the introductory chapter by Diana V. Edelman in *Remembering Biblical Figures in the Late Persian and Early Hellenistic Periods: Social Memory and Imagination*, ed. Diana V. Edelman and Ehud Ben Zvi (Oxford: Oxford University Press, 2013), xi–xxiv.
[27]Carr, *Writing on the Tablet of the Heart*, passim.

ideological tradition allowed for terms and features of that tradition to influence the transmission of textual sources beyond it.[28] These changes and variants are often minor, and scholars are still able to identify distinct scribal traditions and modalities in texts that carry unique features of expression (for example, P vs. H. vs. D in the Pentateuchal literature). Nevertheless, and over time, the cross-pollination of terms and motifs across sources created new paradigms for subsequent scribes to understand their own inherited curriculum.

Lastly, the sociology of power has emerged as a major feature of the study of scribalism in Israelite and Jewish antiquity. Scholars have recognized that in ancient Israel (and ancient Judaism) scribalism was a resource of the powerful, and many scholars have argued that this was primarily a feature either of royal authority, priestly authority, or both. While this is certainly true, the sociology of power involving scribes and scribal works is more multifaceted than just the aforementioned assignments. As noted above, the archaeological evidence for writing in Iron Age Israel and Judah shows textuality as a decentralized phenomenon.[29] Of course, writing and texts were genetic components of royal and priestly establishments at palaces and sanctuaries, but texts were also part of life in rural contexts among different types of elites, sacral and non-sacral alike. Levites, warlords, local chieftains, and high-ranking military officers represent the diversity of social groups wherein literary works were forged or transmitted.[30] Prophecy, too, becomes a primarily literary enterprise—not only in the book of Jeremiah (as previously discussed) but also in the characterization of other prophets as reliant upon the materiality of textual resources and methods.[31]

The sheer variety of social groups that are represented in the prophetic literature reveals that multiple loci and types of social authority that cannot be reduced solely to temple-based or royal contexts. The prophetic tradition in the biblical record traces its roots to Judahite ranchers and village elders (Amos and Micah),[32] Aaronide priests (Ezekiel and possibly Zechariah), Levites of Ephraimite heritage (Jeremiah and Hosea, and possibly the author of the Malachi oracles), hinterland disciples of shamanistic figures (Samuel and Elisha) and other groups as well.[33] In light of the variety of outlets for literary production, it strains credulity that the earliest written sources for all of these traditions resulted solely from the pen of royal and/or temple scribes in Jerusalem. The caveat, of course, is that these Jerusalemite scribes became the trustees of these sources as history marched forward, and their importance as mediators of tradition was amplified in the face of encroaching foreign imperialism from the late eighth century BCE onward. It would be during this era that text production became a vehicle for both mimetic emulation of and resistance to authority emanating from external cultures and administrative hierarchies. But it is also in the shadow of foreign imperialism that the sociology of power weighs even more heavily upon the self-perception of scribes, who found themselves at the nexus between native anchors of identity (the literary relics from generations past) and those imposed by the prevailing forces surrounding them. The social locations and self-perception of scribes in Mesopotamian and later Persian intellectual culture became genetic

---

[28] Carr, *Formation of the Hebrew Bible*, 11–101.

[29] Fleming, *Israel in Judah's Bible*, 309–10; Sanders, "Writing and Early Iron Age Israel."

[30] Young, "Israelite Literacy," 408–22. See further Ryan C. Byrne, "The Refuge of Scribalism in Iron I Palestine," *BASOR* 345 (2007): 1–31.

[31] One thinks especially of the presentation of Elijah in 2 Chr 21:12 via letter. Part of this, to be sure, is an attempt to funnel a northern prophet into an historiographic work mostly concerned with Judahite geographic and social space. But it also sees fit to present the convention of letter-writing as a suitable vehicle for revelation characteristic of the Chronicler's late-Persian socio-religious worldview. Antecedents in the neo-Babylonian period are evident in Jeremiah 29, where a series of letters form the basis for prophetic discourse, the materiality of the scroll consumed by Ezekiel in Ezek 2:9–3:1, and Zechariah's vision of a material scroll (replete with measure physical dimensions) in Zech 5:1–2.

[32] On Micah as a village elder, see Stephen L. Cook, *The Social Roots of Biblical Yahwism* (Atlanta: SBL, 2004), 170–80.

[33] Robert D. Miller, "Shamanism in Early Israel," in *Wiener Zeitschrift für die Kunde des Morgenlandes*, vol. 101, ed. Claudia Römer (Vienna: Department of Oriental Studies, 2011), 335–37.

components of Israelite and ancient Jewish modes of textual production and literary expression.[34] Scholars have long recognized that it is impossible to mine these texts for information without recognizing their (subordinate) place within an imperial world and the inescapability of imperial influence upon them.

* * *

The essays in the present volume attempt to address the way in which the foregoing panoply of issues are taken up in contemporary approaches to scribalism, literacy, and textuality in the study of the biblical sources and the worlds that produced them. The first contribution, by Sarah Malena ("Influential Inscriptions: Resituating Scribal Activity During the Iron I–IIA Transition"), takes a broad look at the social topography of populations in Canaan in the era that produced Emergent Israel. Malena provides an overview of the shifting tides of power and economy in the rocky move from the Late Bronze Age socio-political situation to that of the early Iron Age and the implications of this move for the survival of groups of scribes and the outlets available to them for the practice of their craft. Malena evaluates the epigraphic evidence from this period (and relevant inscriptions from subsequent periods) to determine the social function of material texts in pre-monarchic Israel, comparing their contribution to the formation of social hierarchies to international parallels of the era. Emerging from Malena's study are possibilities for better understanding the manner in which pre-monarchic Israel and the foundational years of the early monarchies are characterized by biblical writers looking back at this formative time.

The essay by Madadh Richey ("The Media and Materiality of Southern Levantine Inscriptions: Production and Reception Contexts") looks to the range of media on which inscriptions from the Iron Age southern Levant were written, suggesting a restriction of literate professionals to the authorship of ink inscriptions and drafts for monumental stone texts. Yet the minimal attestation of cuneiform in the Iron Age southern Levant suggests a restriction of this training; this is corroborated by the limited genres for which cuneiform was used in this period, i.e. mainly economic and juridical texts. The types of texts that were eventually collected and transmitted as important works of literature and/or history are known from numerous media. Texts similar to the lengthy historical narratives of Kings, for example, are found chiseled into monumental stones, but most often in the kingdoms neighboring Israel and Judah. The unique amulets from Ketef Hinnom show that professionals produced apotropaic texts similar to biblical invocations—in this case Num 6:24–26—and that users were interred with and perhaps wore such pieces for beneficence and protection. Based on scribal practices elsewhere in the Near East and in later periods in the southern Levant itself, it seems likely that literary and/or historical texts would have been written in ink on papyrus and/or parchment. Evidence for the use of these media in the Iron Age southern Levant remains, however, mostly indirect, namely from bullae, especially those with papyrus imprints, and texts describing Iron Age Judahite scribal practice (e.g. Jer 36). Even with such gaps in the evidence, attention to the manufacture and use contexts of texts in these multiple media illustrates the complex interplay of power and praxis operative in the histories of all textual artifacts.

The next essay, by Anselm Hagedorn ("Scribes and Scribalism in Archaic Crete"), looks to conventions of old Greek scribal culture for informative parallels that relate to dimensions of scribalism in the biblical record. Hagedorn draws crucial attention to the Greek awareness that their scribal tradition was firmly rooted in Phoenician praxes; Greek traditions claiming the origins of the scribal craft as a native innovation wrestled with the persistent memory that Greek scribalism

---

[34] Seth L. Sanders, *From Adapa to Enoch*, FAT (Tübingen: Mohr Siebeck, 2017), 228–29. See also Mark Leuchter, "The Aramaic Transition and the Redaction of the Pentateuch," *JBL* 136 (2017): 249–68.

possessed a foreign heritage. Hagedorn devotes most of his critical attention to the role of Crete in the formation of a distinctively Greek scribal culture, and observes that the power/influence of scribes as trustees and mediators of Greek identity itself became a matter of contention in some Cretan communities. Scribalism was an office meant to serve the polis rather than a position that preserved narrow access to elite status and power, even as the preservation of that narrow elitism among some families safeguarded the history and character of a given community. Hagedorn concludes with the observation that like the scribes of Crete, the scribes behind the biblical sources likely evolved as the work they produced took on new meaning as written materials initially pertaining to social organization were reworked to take on theological dimensions.

Brian Rainey's contribution ("Scribes, Schools, and Ideological Conflict in Ancient Israel and Judah") examines how divergent ideological perspectives might have been transmitted concretely within scribal institutions in ancient Israel and Judah. If the temple and palace were loci for scribal training and transmission, how would ideologies be passed down and disseminated within those institutions? Would these institutions be able to accommodate a variety of ideological traditions at the same time, and in the same place? Did influential scribal families or individuals play a role in the creation of dominant ideologies within ancient Israel and Judah? The essay assesses four possible, theoretical modes of ideological transmission within ancient Israelite scribal culture: the "school," the "household," the institution, and the individual. When looking at the "school" model, the idea that Holiness or Deuteronomic "schools" might have transmitted these ideological traditions is compared with existing information about the *é-dub-ba-a*/*bīt tuppi* in Mesopotamia. With respect to the "household" model, the portrayal of the Shaphan family is also compared with evidence from Mesopotamia. When dealing with institutions, the evidence for the connection of scribes to the temple and palace is analyzed, especially with respect to priestly scribal traditions in the Hebrew Bible, as well as the composition of the Ezekiel corpus. Finally, the potential role of individuals in shaping a tradition is assessed, with a special focus on Baruch and the Jeremiah corpus.

Turning to the issue of textual authority and transmission, Jaqueline Vayntrub's essay ("Ecclesiastes and the Problem of Transmission in Biblical Literature") examines the importance of the *nefesh*—understood in Israelite antiquity as the physical organ that sustains life, communicates instruction, and offers blessing—in the transmission of traditions in disembodied textual contexts. Can the authority of a tradition be retained across generations when disembodied and cast in written form? In contrast to the way this question is addressed in the Pentateuchal sources, Vayntrub notes that Ecclesiastes frames the issue in a dramatically different manner. The mortality of an originating speaker becomes the fundamental question in Ecclesiastes, highlighting the veracity and authority of its written contents far beyond the power claims or social location of an authorizing figure who first (physically) voiced them. In treating para-biblical sources and extra-biblical memorial inscriptions, Vayntrub builds the case that the transition of spoken words into written form is intimately bound to the anxiety surrounding death but, also, its rhetorical potency. In a variety of texts within the biblical record, this potency becomes a *topos* upon which scribes seized in order to reinforce the authority of their textualized discourse through the invocation of a (deceased) authorizing name, but Ecclesiastes moves in the opposite direction through obscuring the identity of its (ostensible) authorizing figure and destabilizing that figure's rhetorical claims. Yet, as Vayntrub argues, through destabilizing the message of the authorizing "speaker" the metaliterary dynamics of Ecclesiastes perfectly convey what that speaker sought to express: that textual transmission is an inherently unstable vehicle, and always has been.

The essay by Heath Dewrell ("Textualization and the Transformation of Biblical Prophecy") continues this direction of thought by addressing the conceptual implications of the move from oral-centered to text-centered prophecy. Near Eastern prophecy was originally an oral phenomenon. Prophetic oracles were initially only committed to writing for the purpose of conveying their content to an interested party who was not physically present for the delivery of the oracle. During the Neo-Assyrian period, however, both in Mesopotamia and in the Levant, there was a move not only to write down prophetic oracles but also to gather these written oracles into collections, apparently to allow for them to be consulted in the future. While the fall of the Neo-Assyrian empire ended the development of this tradition in Mesopotamia, it continued on in the Levant and its results are attested in collections of the writing prophets of the Hebrew Bible. This textualization of Israelite prophecy led to shift from a focus on what had been the original primary audience, i.e., the audience present for the oral delivery of the oracles, to what earlier had only been a secondary audience, i.e., those who would read those oracles as text in the future. This shift from a focus on a present listening audience to a future reading audience may explain some of the shifts in theme and content as one moves from earlier to later prophetic collections in the Hebrew Bible. Features that one might attribute to the textualization of prophecy include an ambiguity of referents in later prophetic oracles, as well as a concern for the end of time.

Antje Labahn's essay ("Reorientation in Responsibility of Levites Taking Care for the Ark: The Levites' Role in Samuel–Kings in Relation to Deuteronomistic Expressions concerning Interpretation of the Law") provides a companion argument to Dewrell's discussion by observing the changes in the presentation of Levites in narrative sources in the Deuteronomistic literature and Chronicles. Within the books Samuel–Kings, the Levites appear just three times: 1 Sam 6:15; 2 Sam 15:24; 1 Kgs 8:4. In these rare occurrences, the Levites are active in carrying the ark. Such a statement is quite surprising since in these contexts this appears to be the duty of other personnel. Diachronic analyses show that these three little remarks originated somewhat later and were secondarily redacted into their surroundings. According to such a late Deuteronomistic portrait, the Levites took over the role that once belonged to other people. The reason for this, however, is due to a reorientation in responsibility for the ark and its contents. As the ark becomes a symbol of written torah, the Levites are placed in closer and more intimate proximity to it due to the scribal re-conception of Levite duties vis-à-vis the teaching of authoritative sacred texts. Labahn analyzes the role of the Levites in reflecting on nomistic implications which were linked with the group in various traditions, noting that the social location of Levites and the shape of the literature addressing their duties underwent discernible stages of development at the hands of writers who re-conceived of their own social functions and authority.

Turning to the issue of textual collections, Laura Carlson Hasler's essay explores the methodological opportunities of approaching Second Temple scribalism in spatial context ("Writing in Three Dimensions: Scribal Activity and Spaces in Jewish Antiquity"). Carlson Hasler asks how scribal practice endeavors to rebuild vital social spaces and how that might re-wire our expectations for composition and citation. The essay also addresses how one may think beyond coherence and linearity as authoritative aesthetics in this period. To what degree do texts associated with specific spaces and institutions (e.g., temple, archive, treasury…to the extent that those spaces can be separated) contribute to the construction of ideas regarding those spaces within their own literary boundaries? That is—how does viewing ancient Jewish texts as archives reframe some of the assumptions scholars often bring to the study of a text's characteristic topography? In what way do the scribes behind these texts challenge conventions on the level of form and genre by constructing literary works, themselves, as archives? Thinking about space alongside scribal practice and viewing scribal constructs as textual iterations of spatial institutions demands that concepts such as "canon" be viewed in a different light, with more intricate sociological implications veering from earlier critical concepts of normativity or authority.

In the final essay ("Rejecting 'Patriarchy': Reflections on Feminism, Biblical Scholarship, and Social Perspective"), Shawna Dolansky addresses the way in which the study of scribes and writing in the biblical record interfaces with the evolving area of feminist biblical scholarship. Dolansky notes that the term "feminist scholarship" has developed a variety of meanings in relation to the study of the Hebrew Bible. Some feminist scholars are theologians, seeking to redeem the biblical text for modern faith communities; others are literary critics, many of whom attempt to subvert the authority of what they see as a biblically mandated patriarchy in the present. A third category of feminist scholars is historians interested in what the text might reveal about women and men in the world that produced the Bible. Many have recently widened their feminist lens to a gender-critical perspective in an attempt to understand the intersectional nature of society, status, and power. Dolansky's contribution advocates for a gender-critical historiography that contextualizes biblical writings within the androcentric and elite circles within which they were produced, in an attempt to avoid reading modern categories and concepts such as "patriarchy" into the biblical text. A gendered and historically focused literary analysis investigates the narrative's own internal explanations and word choices, and thereby reveals the heterarchical and interdependent nature of power, autonomy, and personhood in ancient Israel. The story of Dinah and Shechem in Genesis 34 serves as a case study in how scribal products from antiquity should be approached in contemporary social contexts.

The variety of issues and methods represented by the essays in this volume indicates the need for ongoing study of biblical scribes and scribalism not simply as features of a literary tradition but as part of experienced social milieus of the past. Critical scholars can (and should) view the biblical record as a trove of hermeneutical and theological richness, but those reflexes can be more thoroughly unpacked and studied when social factors informing the creation/transmission of these written artifacts are taken into consideration. No text is produced in a void, and no writer functions without a network of resources. These resources are varied and range from the material objects required to compose and preserve a written work (papyrus, parchment, a pen and ink, storage jars or bookshelves) to the economic and administrative outlets through which such objects or resources could be secured to the cultural and spatial vehicles for supporting and authorizing these works (ritual settings, public squares, royal courts, messenger networks, etc.).

In each case, the component was constructed, cultivated or valued with an eye to its role within the social composite as a whole. In the same way, the production of written works and the sustenance of a class of literati capable of engaging in this enterprise can only be conceived as part of a larger social context. The study of biblical literature has periodically been characterized by a privileging of its contents beyond such social categories, with a concept of the biblical material as a unique witness to antiquity. But to maintain this concept without due consideration to the economic, political, anthropological, material, and even physical aspects of the universe that produced the scribes who penned these texts is to rob the material of the detailed attention it so richly deserves. The present volume seeks to contribute to the scholarly work that continues to expand the boundaries of what can be said about the groups, individuals, processes, and ideologies that stand behind the sources under consideration.

PART ONE

# Praxis and Materiality

# Influential Inscriptions

## *Resituating Scribal Activity during the Iron I–IIA Transition*

SARAH MALENA

Epigraphic discoveries have made the last decade very exciting for those interested in the development of linear alphabetic scripts and the emergence of Iron Age states in the southern Levant. Excavations throughout the region have yielded new inscriptions from the transition between the Iron I and IIA periods (or roughly the late eleventh and tenth centuries BCE).[1] With each new discovery, scholars race to propose the definitive reading or identify the missing link in our histories of the early Levantine kingdoms. My contribution to this wave of discovery has very little to do with paleography in the traditional sense of forms, stances, readings, and reconstructions. Rather, I am concerned with the historical and social contexts of the creation and possession of inscribed objects, viewing them as akin to other rare or luxury goods such as imported wares. Our limited corpus makes clear that the creation of inscriptions during this period was in fact a rarity. At the same time, there is sufficient evidence of the demand for a scribe's service, at least in certain circles. My discussion explores what it meant to commission or acquire an inscription and proposes social and political explanations for the apparent increase in scribal activity around the tenth century BCE. In short, I argue that it was regional elites who created the demand for inscriptions and supported the work of scribes.

My interest in the early Iron Age documents stems from my research into how the Levant changed in the centuries between the Late Bronze Age and the emergence of local kingdoms, particularly how intercultural interactions impacted social and political change.[2] My research suggests that those who possessed inscriptions sought membership in an elite network linked to the greater eastern Mediterranean world. Contemporary evidence from the better-attested regions of Byblos and Egypt shows parallel developments. While these polities were obviously of different complexity compared to Levantine elites, they provide important comparisons for the role of inscriptions in the processes of political reorganization, eventual stabilization, and interregional activity.

---

[1] This essay generally follows the Modified Conventional Chronology proposed by Ahimai Mazar, augmented by "Early Iron IIA" (second half of the tenth century) and "Late Iron IIA" (most of the ninth century) distinctions. See Hayah Katz and Avraham Faust, "The Chronology of the Iron Age IIA in Judah in Light of Tel 'Eton Tomb C3 and Other Assemblages," *BASOR* 371 (2014): 103–27; Amihai Mazar, "The Iron Age Chronology Debate: Is the Gap Narrowing? Another Viewpoint," *Near Eastern Archaeology* 74, no. 2 (2011): 105–11; Ze'ev Herzog and Lily Singer-Avitz, "Sub-Dividing the Iron Age IIA in Northern Israel: A Suggested Solution to the Chronological Debate," *Tel Aviv* 33, no. 2 (2006): 163–95; Ze'ev Herzog and Lily Singer-Avitz, "Redefining the Centre: The Emergence of State in Judah," *Tel Aviv* 31, no. 2 (2004): 209–44.

[2] Sarah Malena, "Fertile Crossroads: The Growth and Influence of Interregional Exchange in the Southern Levant's Iron Age I–IIA Transition, Examined through Biblical, Epigraphic, and Archaeological Sources" (PhD diss., University of California, San Diego, 2015).

# THE NATURE OF THE EVIDENCE AND SCHOLARLY DEBATES

Although the recent wave of discoveries has more than doubled the corpus of early Iron Age inscriptions, a sober look at the evidence reminds us that compared to the Late Bronze Age or later phases of the Iron Age, there is very little to work with regarding the late eleventh and tenth centuries.[3] Our epigraphic evidence consists of short inscriptions and ostraca plus a number of inscribed arrowheads (nearly all unprovenanced).[4] Not one of the inscriptions is monumental in character. The most promising news is, in contrast to what was known of this period a few decades ago, the majority of the evidence aside from the arrowheads now comes from stratigraphically sound discoveries. With this new wealth of material—relatively speaking—there is renewed discussion of the significance of this evidence.

Some scholarly trends have had considerable influence on how we view the relationships between scribal activity and social complexity. The most critical is related to the tension between the extrabiblical and biblical evidence regarding centralized states. One school of thought, rooted in the work of David Jamieson-Drake, maintains that centralized kingdoms could not operate without supporting scribal activity (of both administrative and monumental character).[5] These arguments rest in certain assumptions about the constellation of entities that support a state, things like a standing military, public and private spheres apparent through city plan and architecture, and government bodies that might include, for example, scribes. Another aspect of this issue is the influential biblical claim that premonarchic Israel was relatively egalitarian and slow to diversify in power. Historians who are particularly loyal to (or swayed by) the biblical history attribute the advent of administrative offices (other than the priesthood) to Solomon's reign, with its dramatic transition to centralized administration (1 Kgs 4). It would be more realistic, however, to expect a less dramatic, less punctuated transition.

---

[3] This essay focuses on inscriptions, but for a fuller picture one must also consider seals and clay bullae, which testify to the existence of scrolls and the demand for scribes. For a recent summary of this evidence, see Matthieu Richelle, "Elusive Scrolls: Could Any Hebrew Literature Have Been Written Prior to the Eight Century BCE?," *VT* 66 (2016): 1–39. See also Seth L. Sanders, *The Invention of Hebrew* (Urbana: University of Illinois Press, 2009), 108, 212 n. 6; Othmar Keel and Amihai Mazar, "Iron Age Seals and Seal Impressions from Tel Reḥov," *Eretz-Israel* 29 (2009): 57*–69*.

[4] There are more than sixty now known. They have been found and purchased throughout the Levantine region, in Lebanon, Israel/Palestine, and Jordan. Only one from Ruweiseh, Lebanon was found in a secure (albeit disturbed) archaeological context. Many may be forgeries, but there is a consensus that *some* are authentic and thus the practice of inscribing arrowheads can be situated in the late eleventh–tenth centuries. See most recently André Lemaire, "Levantine Literacy ca. 1000–750 BCE," in *Contextualizing Israel's Sacred Writing: Ancient Literacy, Orality, and Literary Production*, ed. Brian B. Schmidt (Atlanta: SBL, 2015), 13–14; André Lemaire, "From the Origin of the Alphabet to the Tenth Century B.C.E.: New Documents and New Directions," in *New Inscriptions and Seals Relating to the Biblical World*, ed. Meir Lubetski and Edith Lubetski (Atlanta: Society of Biblical Literature, 2012), 1–20. For a discussion of their social significance, see Sanders, *The Invention of Hebrew*, 55, 106–8.

[5] David W. Jamieson-Drake, *Scribes and Schools in Monarchic Judah: A Socio-Archaeological Approach*, The Social World of Biblical Antiquity Series 9; JSOTSup 109 (Sheffield: Almond, 1991). Jamieson-Drake has been a favorite among the so-called minimalist scholars. His approach has strengths in proposing ways to measure cultural activities and in his warnings about the nature of the evidence. It does not, however, provide a framework for making meaning of *all* of the results, especially more subtle changes and in discussions of the eleventh to eighth centuries. In addition, Jamieson-Drake assumes that literacy should have been widespread or "democratic" in order to recognize social change, which obscures important trends in his evidence. I maintain a very different premise, that scribal activity would have been a tool of the elite in the process of social change and not easily acquired or readily available to a broader population (see further discussion and references below). With this model, we should expect small numbers of inscriptions and other "luxury items" for some time, which produces a better correlation between the data and interpretation. As Jamieson-Drake admits, "If a datum must be interpreted in an unnatural way in order to fit into our model, we must consider modifying or overhauling the model" (p. 149). In this case, it is the model regarding literacy that needs to be changed.

To make this point, we can focus on writing or scribal activity, often considered to be among the hallmarks of statehood—and for good reason. Writing is extremely useful in the operations of a state. Its applications range from basic record keeping necessary for taxes to more elaborate applications like court histories, monumental inscriptions, or propaganda, but these uses come at an advanced stage of a state. We should not necessarily expect them in the formative stages (e.g., in the eleventh and tenth centuries). Ryan Byrne proposes a more nuanced relationship with attention to different stages of both the state's and writing's development, concluding, "The state facilitates the alphabet's segue from a curiosity to the sine qua non."[6] The development of both institutions, alphabetic writing and the state, influenced each other. Based on his evaluation of southern Levantine, Ugaritic, and Byblian evidence, Byrne argues that we should not expect standardization in scribal institutions before an established state and not even at the early stages of a state system. This perspective eases pressures to fit the limited epigraphic material into any particular depiction of political organization.

## INSCRIPTIONS FROM THE SOUTHERN LEVANT

Local, southern Levantine inscriptions that date from the late eleventh and tenth centuries now number at least fifteen, not counting the arrowheads (see Table 1).[7] They are all written in linear alphabetic script, and most appear to be in Northwest Semitic languages (most likely Hebrew, Phoenician, or Aramaic) with a notable, possible exception from Tell eṣ-Ṣafi (Gath).[8] By far the most common type of inscription is the name formula, used to mark possession or dedication of an object, but there are also examples of educational or scribal exercises (e.g., Gezer calendar and Tel Zayit abecedary) and others whose readings cannot yet be classified (e.g., Khirbet Qeiyafa ostracon). The inscriptions come from ten sites: Kefar Veradim, Tel ʿAmal, Tel Reḥov, the Ophel/Jerusalem, Gezer, Tel Batash, Beth-Shemesh, Khirbet Qeiyafa, Tell eṣ-Ṣafi (Gath), and Tel Zayit.[9] Of these, eight have produced one inscription from the Iron I–IIA transition period. Tel Reḥov and Khirbet Qeiyafa are exceptional in yielding numerous inscriptions from controlled excavations. Tel Reḥov boasts ten dating to the Iron IIA (tenth-ninth centuries); three to five of these fall within the Iron

---

[6] Ryan Byrne, "The Refuge of Scribalism in Iron I Palestine," *BASOR* 345 (2007): 23. Note that the state precedes a large-scale scribal institution here, rather than the reverse. This reconstruction better fits our archaeological evidence.
[7] There continues to be significant debate about the chronology of the late Iron I and Iron IIA, and the archaeological and historical periodization may not correspond well to paleographic developments. Finkelstein and Sass, using the low chronology and corresponding paleographic considerations, differ in their classification of Late Iron I and Early Iron IIA inscriptions ("The West Semitic Alphabetic Inscriptions, Late Bronze II to Iron IIA: Archeological Context, Distribution and Chronology," *Hebrew Bible and Ancient Israel* 2 [2013]: 149–220). Other recent discussions of the corpus may be found in Richelle, "Elusive Scrolls"; Gordon J. Hamilton, "Two Methodological Issues Concerning the Expanded Collection of Early Alphabetic Texts," in *Epigraphy, Philology, and the Hebrew Bible: Methodological Perspectives on Philological and Comparative Study of the Hebrew Bible in Honor of Jo Ann Hackett*, ANEM 12 (Atlanta: SBL, 2015), 127–56; Shmuel Aḥituv and Amihai Mazar, "The Inscriptions from Tel Rehov and Their Contribution to Study of Script and Writing During the Iron Age IIA," in *"See, I Will Bring a Scroll Recounting What Befell Me" (Ps 40:8): Epigraphy and Daily Life—From the Bible to the Talmud Dedicated to the Memory of Professor Hanan Eshel*, ed. Esther Eshel and Yigal Levin, Journal of Ancient Judaism Supplements 12 (Göttingen: Vandenhoeck & Ruprecht, 2014), 39–68; Chris A. Rollston, *Writing and Literacy in the World of Ancient Israel: Epigraphic Evidence from the Iron Age* (Atlanta: Society of Biblical Literature, 2010).
[8] For discussions of distinctions in script and language, see Christopher A. Rollston, "The Phoenician Script of the Tel Zayit Abecedary and Putative Evidence for Israelite Literacy," in *Literate Culture and Tenth-Century Canaan: The Tel Zayit Abecedary in Context*, ed. Ron E. Tappy and P. Kyle McCarter (Winona Lake: Eisenbrauns, 2008), 61–96, and, in the same volume, Seth L. Sanders, "Writing and Early Iron Age Israel: Before National Scripts, Beyond Nations and States," 97–112; Sanders, *The Invention of Hebrew*.
[9] A recent find from Megiddo may need to be added to the Iron I–IIA transition group. Sass and Finkelstein published a linear alphabetic inscription from Megiddo, stratum VB/VA-IVB, which they date to the ninth century ("The Swan-Song of Proto-Canaanite in the Ninth Century BCE in Light of an Alphabetic Inscription from Megiddo," *Semitica et Classica* 9 [2016]: 19–42). Considering their use of the low chronology, this inscription may be contemporary to those included here.

I–IIA transition period.[10] Excavations at Khirbet Qeiyafa have uncovered three from the Iron I–IIA transition.[11] Tel Reḥov, Beth-Shemesh, and Tell eṣ-Ṣafi (Gath) have yielded multiple inscriptions from the larger span of the Iron I and IIA periods combined, which helps to illustrate the fairly continuous use of linear alphabetic scripts in the southern Levant in the early Iron Age.[12]

Table 1. Southern Levantine Inscriptions from the Iron I–IIA Transition

| Site | Object Description | Reading | Personal Name |
|---|---|---|---|
| Kefar Veradim[13] | engraved bronze bowl | ks psḥ bn šmʿ | psḥ bn šmʿ |
| Tel ʿAmal[14] | hippo storage jar | lnmś | nmś |
| Tel Reḥov[15] | No. 1: storage jar, inscribed near base (str. VI, Area C) | ʿy | ? |
| | No. 2: narrow storage jar, inscribed twice with the same inscription (str. VIB, Area C) | mtʾ \| | mtʾ |
| | No. 3: inner side of a storage jar (str. VI, Area C) | l | ? |
| | No. 4: storage jar (str. VI, Area B) | lnḥm? or lnbʾ? | nḥm? |
| | No. 5: hippo storage jar (str. V, Area C, apiary) | lnmś | nmś |
| Ophel/Jerusalem[16] | neckless pithos | ḥ]mr lḥnn[ | ḥnn |
| Gezer[17] | calendar/writing exercise on limestone | Describes agricultural activity of different months | ʾbyh |
| Tel Batash[18] | ceramic bowl body sherd | n\|ḥnn | [b]n\|ḥnn |

---

[10]Ahituv and Mazar, "The Inscriptions from Tel Reḥov." An additional sherd, typically dated to the Iron I was found out of context in 1939. Finkelstein and Sass date it to early Iron IIA (partly out of a determination that any linear alphabetic inscription found outside of Philistia must be later than the Iron I) ("West Semitic Alphabetic Inscriptions," 160–61, 177, 186, 209).

[11]Yosef Garfinkel et al., "The ʾIšbaʿal Inscription from Khirbet Qeiyafa," BASOR 373 (2015): 217–33; Haggai Misgav, Yosef Garfinkel, and Saar Ganor, "The Ostracon," in Khirbet Qeiyafa. Vol. 1, Excavation Report 2007–2008, ed. Yosef Garfinkel and Saar Ganor (Jerusalem: Israel Exploration Society; Institute of Archaeology, Hebrew University of Jerusalem, 2009), 243–57; Ada Yardeni, "Further Observations on the Ostracon," in Khirbet Qeiyafa. Vol. 1, Excavation Report 2007–2008, ed. Yosef Garfinkel and Saar Ganor (Jerusalem: Israel Exploration Society; Institute of Archaeology, Hebrew University of Jerusalem, 2009), 259–60.

[12]These discoveries are compiled by Finkelstein and Sass, but note that their chronologies and paleographic dating are typically low and do not represent the consensus ("West Semitic Alphabetic Inscriptions").

[13]Yardenna Alexandre, "A Canaanite-Early Phoenician Inscribed Bronze Bowl in an Iron Age IIA-B Burial Cave at Kefar Veradim, Northern Israel," Maarav 13, no. 1 (2006): 7–41, 129–32.

[14]F. W. Dobbs-Allsopp et al., Hebrew Inscriptions: Texts from the Biblical Period of the Monarchy with Concordance (New Haven: Yale University Press, 2005), 3.

[15]Ahituv and Mazar, "The Inscriptions from Tel Reḥov."

[16]Eilat Mazar, David Ben-Shlomo, and Shmuel Aḥituv, "An Inscribed Pithos from the Ophel, Jerusalem," IEJ 63 (2013): 39–49.

[17]W. F. Albright, "The Gezer Calendar," BASOR 92 (1943): 16–26; Dobbs-Allsopp et al., Hebrew Inscriptions, 155–65.

[18]George L. Kelm and Amihai Mazar, "Tel Batash (Timnah) Excavations: Third Preliminary Report, 1984–1989," BASORSup 27 (1991): 47–67; Dobbs-Allsopp et al., Hebrew Inscriptions, 113–14.

| Beth-Shemesh[19] | game board fragment | ḥnn | ḥnn |
| Tell eṣ-Ṣafi (Gath)[20] | ceramic bowl rim sherd | ʾlwt\|wlt[ | ʾlwt\|wlt[ Philistine? names Alyattes and Oletas[21] |
| Khirbet Qeiyafa[22] | ostracon | Not yet definitive | possible (Phoenician) names include bdmlk, ʿbd', špṭ, grbʾl, nqmy, ʾltṣ[23] |
| | storage jar | ʾšbʿl \|ʿbnʾ\|bdʿ | ʾšbʿl \|ʿbnʾ\|bdʿ |
| | additional inscription | Not yet published | ? |
| Tel Zayit[24] | abecedary on stone | above abecedary: ʿzr line 1: ʾ b g d w h ḥ z ṭ y l k m n ʿs ʿpʾ ⌈ʿ⌉ ⌈ṣ⌉ line 2: ⌈q⌉ ⌈r⌉ š ⌈t⌉ | ʿzr |
| Various locations[25] | bronze arrowheads | various | various |

Since my interest lies in cultural contexts and interactions, it is necessary to be oriented to the geographic distribution of the finds. The inscriptions are mostly concentrated in two areas, easily divided into a northern and a southern group (see Map 1). In the south, there is a cluster of sites in the Shephelah, primarily in the contact zones between Philistia and the hill country. Some sites can be characterized fairly easily. Tell eṣ-Ṣafi (Gath) was Philistine; Khirbet Qeiyafa was part of the emerging hill country culture. Some others, however, seem to be border communities with diverse populations and cultural contacts, such as Beth-Shemesh.[26] The southern group also includes Jerusalem. Although it was outside of the border region, it was closely connected by major roads and can be considered part of a larger interaction unit. The frequency of epigraphic finds in an area that according to both archaeological and historical research was an intense contact zone between emerging cultures suggests that the intensification in interactions corresponded to an increase in scribal activities.

---

[19]Shlomo Bunimovitz and Zvi Lederman, "Beth-Shemesh: Culture Conflict on Judah's Frontier," *BARev* 23, no. 1 (1997): 42–49, 75–77.
[20]A. Maeir et al., "A Late Iron Age I/Early Iron Age II Old Canaanite Inscription from Tell eṣ-Ṣâfi/Gath, Israel: Palaeography, Dating, and Historical-Cultural Significance," *BASOR* 351 (2008): 39–71.
[21]Hamilton has a slightly different reading of the first name: ʾḥwt; interpreting it as West Semitic name ("From the Seal of a Seer," 12).
[22]Garfinkel et al., "The ʾIšbaʿal Inscription"; Misgav, Garfinkel, and Ganor, "The Ostracon"; Yardeni, "Further Observations on the Ostracon."
[23]Edward M. Cook, "Olive Pits and Alef-Bets: Notes on the Qeiyafa Ostracon," *Ralph the Sacred River*, March 14, 2010, http://ralphriver.blogspot.com/2010/03/olive-pits-and-alef-bets-notes-on.html.
[24]Ron E. Tappy et al., "An Abecedary of the Mid-Tenth Century B.C.E. from the Judaean Shephelah," *BASOR* 344 (2006): 5–46; Rollston, "The Phoenician Script of the Tel Zayit Abecedary and Putative Evidence for Israelite Literacy."
[25]For examples, see Josette Elayi, "Four New Inscribed Phoenician Arrowheads," *Studi Epigrafici e Linguistici* 22 (2005): 35–45; Finkelstein and Sass, "West Semitic Alphabetic Inscriptions," 163, 210–12; Lemaire, "From the Origin of the Alphabet," 1–20; Lemaire, "Levantine Literacy ca. 1000–750 BCE," 13–14.
[26]Bunimovitz and Lederman, "Beth-Shemesh."

Map 1. Sites with Inscriptions from the Iron I–IIA Transition Period

The other concentration of inscriptions is in the north. Rather than being clustered together, these sites are all related to routes that led to and from the Mediterranean ports. Kefar Veradim, where an exceptional example of an engraved bronze bowl was found in a burial deposit, was closely connected to the Achzib and Acco port regions. It is clear from the quality of the engraved bowl (the object as well as the inscription) and the associated finds that the family who used the burial cave was not only wealthy but also well integrated into the growing Mediterranean exchange systems of the time. The other northern sites where inscriptions have been found, Tel 'Amal and Tel Reḥov, essentially guarded the intersection of the eastern extension of the Jezreel Valley highway (i.e., the Harod Valley) and the Jordan Valley corridor. This crossroads witnessed north–south traffic along the Jordan Valley, which would have included activity from the Transjordanian metallurgical trade, travelers using the Jezreel to pass through the hill country between the Mediterranean and Transjordan, or those seeking access to the Great Trunk Road linking Egypt and Syria/Mesopotamia. All of these routes were well traveled during the Iron I–IIA transition period.[27] As in the south, the sites where inscriptions have been found correspond to areas that saw more exchange and cultural interaction.

The contexts of the epigraphic finds indicate that they should be considered in the class of trade and prestige goods.[28] Many of the possession inscriptions have been found on large storage jars indicating that scribes were employed to mark collected or commercial goods. Most sites (eight of ten) where inscriptions have been found have also produced evidence of imported pottery, usually from the Mediterranean.[29] Some sites provide more comprehensive evidence of the potential for wealth at this time. Kefar Veradim's burial assemblage, including the engraved bowl, testifies to a family of extraordinary wealth that had the means to make use of a scribe, possess imported goods, and use these valuable items in a burial deposit, eliminating them from the activities of the living. Remains of a smithy's workshop, another specialized and high-value industry, have been uncovered at Beth-Shemesh.[30] Finally, excavations at Tel Reḥov have brought to light evidence of an elaborate elite culture. In addition to inscriptions and Mediterranean imports (including from the Aegean), there is evidence of feasting and a large apiary.[31] Overall, the evidence is adding up that the use of scribes in the late eleventh and tenth centuries coincided with uncommon wealth and status and that writing was used to demonstrate ownership or patronage of some kind.

These connections are underscored by the fact that nearly every inscription from this period documents personal names. In the majority of cases, the purpose of the inscription was to signify ownership, for example, the owner/producer of goods in storage jars or the identity of a lord or patron, as on the arrowheads. Even in the texts that would not fall in the category of a possession inscription, however, we find the inclusion of names. The Tel Zayit abecedary and the Gezer calendar each appear to have a name inscribed near the primary text, and the Khirbet Qeiyafa ostracon, according to some readings, may be a list of names, rather than a narrative composition.[32] According to the current body of evidence, a significant aspect of the scribe's work was documenting personal names. Assuming the knowledge of a specialist was required, we have a growing list of individuals or families who employed scribes (on at least one occasion) or even the names of some of the scribes themselves (see Table 1). There was a varied application of this practice. Names accompany commercial goods (e.g., storage jars), personal items (e.g., Beth-Shemesh game board), grave goods (e.g., Kefar Veradim bronze bowl), symbols of power (e.g., bronze arrowheads), and possibly intellectual material as well (e.g., scribal exercises).

---

[27] David A. Dorsey, *The Roads and Highways of Ancient Israel*, ASOR Library of Biblical and Near Eastern Archaeology (Baltimore: The Johns Hopkins University Press, 1991), 93–116.

[28] Jamieson-Drake argues well why inscriptions should be viewed as prestige goods (*Scribes and Schools in Monarchic Judah*, 107–35).

[29] These include Kefar Veradim, Tel 'Amal, Tel Reḥov, Gezer, Beth Shemesh, Tell eṣ-Ṣafi (Gath), Khirbet Qeiyafa, and the Ophel/Jerusalem.

[30] Trade in copper and iron was important in the Iron I–IIA and involved both of the areas where epigraphic discoveries have been most intense. In the south, metallurgical evidence has been found at Tell eṣ-Ṣafi (Gath), Beth-Shemesh, and the City of David excavations in Jerusalem, as well as in the north at Megiddo. The source areas for metal production sites were in Transjordan at Tell Hammeh (iron) and the Faynan/Khirbat en-Nahas (copper). For a discussion of how these different areas may have interacted, see Malena, "Fertile Crossroads," 80–85.

[31] See references below.

[32] Cook, "Olive Pits and Alef-Bets"; Matthieu Richelle, "Quelques Nouvelles Lectures Sur L'ostracon de Khirbet Qeiyafa," *Semitica* 57 (2015): 147–62.

In two cases, we have repetition of a name in more than one location. We must note upfront that it is possible that these instances represent multiple, unrelated individuals who happened to share a common name.[33] At the same time, it is worth exploring possible connections among the occurrences. The name *ḥnn* was written on the side of a bowl from Tel Batash (Timnah) and on the game board discovered at Beth-Shemesh (as well as on an Iron I ostracon also from Beth-Shemesh).[34] The name has also been proposed in readings of Jerusalem's Ophel inscription.[35] In addition, the place name Elon-Beth-Ḥanan follows Beth-Shemesh in the description of the Solomon's second district in 1 Kgs 4:9.[36] The find locations were connected by a road that led from Jerusalem to the Mediterranean via the Soreq Valley, and Tel Batash and Beth-Shemesh are only about 7.5 km apart on that route.[37] While the name *ḥnn* and variations of it were common (e.g., Jehu son of Ḥanani in 1 Kgs 16; the "false" prophet Ḥananiah in Jer 28), the geographic and chronological proximity of the *ḥnn* finds is intriguing.[38] We cannot help but wonder, was there a prominent *ḥnn* family in the Soreq Valley in the early Iron Age?[39] We cannot say conclusively that these references all belonged to one family, but if they were related, we would have an excellent case for exploring regional leadership of an elite lineage.

A parallel situation exists in the northern Jordan Valley. The personal name *nmš* is attested on the Tel ʿAmal sherd and on two inscriptions at Tel Reḥov, one of which was found in the apiary, as well as in later periods on an inscription, several seals, and in the Hebrew Bible (e.g., Jehu's family, 2 Kgs 9).[40] Multiple *nmš* inscriptions in close proximity (also about 7.5 km apart) compels us to consider whether they could be related. Like *ḥnn*, *nmš* was not an uncommon name, but the inscribed vessels (all storage jars) are similar and were part of comparable ceramic assemblages. In addition, there is some epigraphic affinity between the sites.[41] Shmuel Aḥituv and Amihai Mazar venture that, indeed, these are all related and that the "Nimshi clan" was a prominent, elite family in the region, with Tel Reḥov as their hometown "just before and during the reign of Jehu."[42] As with the Soreq Valley connections, we will need additional evidence to be sure, but the connections provide an opportunity to explore ideas about prominent individuals or families and their leadership in local networks.

---

[33] Regarding *ḥnn*, see Hamilton, "Two Methodological Issues," 151 n. 41.

[34] Bunimovitz and Lederman, "Beth-Shemesh," 42–49, 75–77.

[35] Aaron Demsky, "The Jerusalem Ceramic Inscription," Sidebar in "Artifact Found Near Temple Mount Bearing Canaanite Inscription from the Time before King David," *Foundation Stone*, July 7, 2013, http://www.foundationstone.org/mazar/; Hamilton, "Two Methodological Issues."

[36] Frank Moore Cross, "The Origin and Early Evolution of the Alphabet," *Eretz-Israel* 8 (1967): 8\*–24\*; Bunimovitz and Lederman, "Beth-Shemesh."

[37] Dorsey, *Roads and Highways*, 186–89.

[38] On the commonness of *ḥnn*, see Hamilton, "Two Methodological Issues," 151 n. 41.

[39] This possibility was first entertained by Amihai Mazar, who excavated Tel Batash ("The Northern Shephelah in the Iron Age: Some Issues in Biblical History and Archaeology," in *Scripture and Other Artifacts: Essays on the Bible and Archaeology in Honor of Philip J. King*, ed. Michael D. Coogan et al. [Louisville: Westminster John Knox, 1994], 255). See also Koert van Bekkum, "'The Situation Is More Complicated': Archaeology and Text in the Historical Reconstruction of the Iron Age IIA Southern Levant," in *Exploring the Narrative: Jerusalem and Jordan in the Bronze and Iron Ages: Papers in Honour of Margreet Steiner*, ed. Noor Mulder-Hymans, Jeannette Boertien, and Eveline van der Steen, LHBOTS 583 (London: Bloomsbury T&T Clark, 2014), 233 n. 31; Shlomo Bunimovitz and Zvi Lederman, "The Early Israelite Monarchy in the Sorek Valley: Tel Beth-Shemesh and Tel Batash (Timnah) in the 10th and 9th Centuries BCE," in *"I Will Speak the Riddles of Ancient Times": Archaeological and Historical Studies in Honor of Amihai Mazar on the Occasion of His Sixtieth Birthday*, ed. Aren M. Maeir and Pierre De Miroschedji (Winona Lake: Eisenbrauns, 2006), 422 n. 10.

[40] Dobbs-Allsopp et al., *Hebrew Inscriptions*, 3.

[41] Amihai Mazar, "Three 10th–9th Century B.C.E. Inscriptions from *Tēl Reḥōv*," in **Saxa Loquentur**: *Studien zur Archäologie Palästinas/Israels. Festschrift für Volkmar Fritz*, ed. Cornelis G. Den Hartog, Ulrich Hübner, and Stefan Münger, AOAT 302 (Münster: Ugarit Verlag, 2003), 171–84; Aḥituv and Mazar, "The Inscriptions from Tel Reḥov," 43–44, 64.

[42] Aḥituv and Mazar, "The Inscriptions from Tel Reḥov," 64.

## THE ASSERTION OF ELITE STATUS THROUGH WRITING

While it is a fairly common notion that literacy would have been limited in the ancient world, there have been some persistent assumptions in conflict with this understanding regarding literacy in the southern Levant. Seth Sanders and Christopher Rollston draw our attention to the predominance of the scholarly view that becoming fluent in the Semitic alphabetic scripts would have been a swift and simple process.[43] This kind of thinking might lead to the idea that anyone would easily become literate in ancient Israel and that writing was not a limited or privileged activity. Such a notion conforms well with another assumption about early Israel, that it was relatively egalitarian (and therefore the antithesis of urbanized and elite Canaanite society). In this idyllic depiction, we might imagine a classless society where the cultural wisdom, including literacy, passed to all members of small, peaceful hamlets. More recent investigations, however, demonstrate that many settlements were culturally complex, and the material evidence shows diversity in wealth and status. We can no longer hold to the earlier views that Iron II Israel developed from an egalitarian and homogenous Iron I existence.

Ryan Byrne argues convincingly for the use of alphabetic writing as a status statement in this transitional period:

> The survivability of the alphabetic *haute couture* in the centuries after the ebb of Canaanite cuneiform ironically hinged on its own irrelevance, i.e., in its relevance to those who could afford the *luxury*. Perhaps this illuminates a peculiar pericope about the primordial monarchy. In each of David's entourage lists (2 Sam 8:16-18; 20:23-26), the king boasts a single scribe (Seraiah and Sheva, respectively). Some have taken this to represent a larger bureaucracy (or worse still, an Egyptian derivative), but the text makes more sense at face value. David retains a scribe when scribes are curiosities. The narrative is less interested in the hint of a chancery (certainly an anachronism) than the accentuation of a status retainer fashionable for the time. These scribes were less administrators than hagiographers.[44]

In this depiction, one's employment of a scribe conveyed one's ability to "afford the luxury," which would, in turn, convey distinction and power. When we see conspicuous consumption, even in a way that appears subtle compared to monumental creations like structures or statuary, we should expect that it arose in response to others' similar behavior or an accepted model for elite behavior. The elite retainer would have been emulating well-known models of power and competing with more localized individuals or groups. For this point, it is important to keep in mind the appropriate cultural context. In the southern Levant at this time, the employment of a scribe may have been quite distinguishing. Rather than view the few inscriptions that we know of as anomalous or insignificant in being "only a name," we can posit that they indicate rising elites who were competing for recognition as the region was transitioning through economic and cultural

---

[43] Propagated by Albright, Cross, and others; see Seth L. Sanders, "What Was the Alphabet For? The Rise of Written Vernaculars and the Making of Israelite National Literature," *Maarav* 11, no. 1 (2004): 34–42; Rollston, "The Phoenician Script of the Tel Zayit Abecedary and Putative Evidence for Israelite Literacy," 67–70. More recently, Alan Millard has also asserted that, since the Khirbet Qeiyafa inscription does not appear to be by a skilled hand, writing must have been widespread ("The Ostracon from the Days of David Found at Khirbet Qeiyafa," *TynBul* 62, no. 1 [2011]: 1–13). Similarly, George Hamilton suggests that the newer discoveries (from Middle Bronze through Iron Age) indicate "the use of alphabetic scripts along a spectrum from formal to informal levels of writing" and "among people of various social classes" ("From the Seal of a Seer to an Inscribed Game Board: A Catalogue of Eleven Early Alphabetic Inscriptions Recently Discovered in Egypt and Palestine," *The Bible and Interpretation*, February 2010, 24, http://www.bibleinterp.com/PDFs/Seal_of_a_Seer.pdf).

[44] Byrne, "The Refuge of Scribalism," 23; emphasis in the original.

disruption from the end of the Late Bronze Age, withdrawal of Egypt, and arrival of new population groups.[45]

The excavations at Tel Reḥov provide an interesting test case for both the relationships among writing, elites, and exchange and the role of scholarly expectations. Amihai Mazar, director of the project, has interpreted the wealth of inscriptions from the site as a general increase in literacy in society and as evidence against the proposal that the amount of inscriptions from a society correlates to the presence of state-level organization. In various publications, Mazar stresses that the early inscriptions in general, and the Tel Reḥov finds particularly, are evidence of: "everyday use of writing," "writing on everyday objects," and "the spread of literacy in daily activities" and "for routine purposes."[46] He is building a case for the possibility of a complex state prior to evidence of major institutions of writing such as royal administrations and monumental inscriptions. In his effort to demonstrate that there is enough evidence of writing to support the advent of monarchy, he rules out another important interpretation.

Mazar acknowledges but downplays the possibility that writing should be viewed as an elite activity at Tel Reḥov. His initial comment to this effect is tucked away in the final footnote of his 2003 report on the first three inscriptions discovered at the site. It was prompted by comments from Diana Edelman that the ninth-century inscriptions came from what might be a public building and should be attributed to elite, not common, use of writing.[47] Mazar responds,

> …the general argument against literacy before the 8th century is that it either did not exist at all or was limited to the royal court. Even if the *Tēl Reḥōv* inscriptions are related to elite activity, this was a local elite of priests, merchants, etc. Thus, the inscriptions should signify the spread of literacy to a broad spectrum of Israelite society.[48]

A critical assumption here is that "local elite" were part of "a broad spectrum" who presumably received their knowledge through a relationship to a centralized (i.e., Davidic) state. Literacy, in Mazar's implied argument, emanated from a central Israelite power.

In addition, his response to the nature of the archaeological context glossed over critical information about the site. The assemblages corresponding to the inscriptions speak to *un*common wealth and connections, even at the time of the 2003 publication. In addition to evidence of scribal activity and significant wealth, Aegean ceramic imports were discovered at Tel Reḥov in the same periods as the inscriptions (i.e., in tenth- and ninth-century contexts). It is notable that, at present, eight of the ten inscriptions found during the excavations and three of eight imported Greek sherds were found in Area C.[49] In addition, most of the inscriptions were found on storage vessels, including hippo

---

[45] Paul Ash is dismissive of the value of the tenth-century inscriptions for conveying information about social status or change in this period. For example, he refers to the Tel Batash inscription as "a potter's name" and the Tel 'Amal inscription as "only a personal name" and "graffito" ("Solomon's? District? List," *JSOT* 67 [1995]: 72 n. 22).

[46] Mazar, "Three 10th–9th Century B.C.E. Inscriptions"; Amihai Mazar, "Rehob," in *The Oxford Encyclopedia of Bible and Archaeology*, ed. Daniel M. Master et al. (New York: Oxford University Press, 2013), 226; Ahituv and Mazar, "The Inscriptions from Tel Reḥov," 63.

[47] Their debate implicitly references Jamieson-Drake's arguments about scribal schools appearing no earlier than the eighth century. The two sides have in common the assumption that literacy was accessible and had to be widespread, which is also derived from Jamieson-Drake's arguments although he is somewhat inconsistent on the matter (Jamieson-Drake, *Scribes and Schools in Monarchic Judah*, 148–53).

[48] Mazar, "Three 10th–9th Century B.C.E. Inscriptions," n. 16. It is notable that although he refers to a "scribe" when discussing the character of the inscriptions, Mazar does not acknowledge or consider those who would have such knowledge necessarily to be in or employed by an elite group.

[49] Nicolas Coldstream and Amihai Mazar, "Greek Pottery from Tel Rehov and Iron Age Chronology," *IEJ* 53 (2003): 29–48; Ahituv and Mazar, "The Inscriptions from Tel Reḥov."

jars, which may have been part of an organized, commercial operation in the region.⁵⁰ In Mazar's 2003 interpretation, he ruled out the possibility that local elite groups were important, independent players in regional and longer-distance interactions. Since that report, excavations have uncovered a unique apiary complex (Area C), an elite "patrician" house (Building F in Area C), an ivory statuette (Area C, near Building F), and zooarchaeological evidence of feasting at the site.⁵¹ This additional evidence of economic stratification and interregional exchange changes the characterization of the site during the Iron IIA period. The importance of a well-established elite group (probably not exclusively "Israelite") is now acknowledged.⁵² Even so, Mazar continues to stress that inscriptions were found in mundane contexts throughout the site, ruling out exclusively elite activities.⁵³

Sanders has argued for a more nuanced understanding of the scribal enterprise at this time, emphasizing that writing need not be confined to the category of a state bureaucracy:

> The simplest explanation for the persistence of the linear alphabet between the Late Bronze Age collapse and the Iron IIB renaissance of writing is that writing was a small-scale luxury craft… The goal of these scribes' work was to signify local powers such as the king of Amurru (witness the arrowheads bearing his name) but through inscriptions on portable luxury items such as engraved weapons, not monuments. The linear alphabet's durability was tied to a small-scale, adaptable craft tradition serving elites but free of allegiance to any specific dialect or regime.⁵⁴

This alternate sphere of activity and influence creates a space in which the late Iron I–early Iron IIA inscriptions can be situated. There is no need to force the characterization of a state system or reconstruct a court-sponsored scribal education that made these texts possible. Elite patronage seems a more likely explanation. The inscriptions and their corresponding evidence (i.e., ceramic assemblages, geographic locations, long-term history of the sites) suggest that elite families become visible in these eleventh- and tenth-century remains. Even the diversity of contexts in which the Tel Reḥov inscriptions have been found fits this interpretation. The scribal activity may have been sponsored by the elite leadership, whose reach went beyond specialized residences or structures. It seems plausible that those who emerged in status at this time came from entities (whether it be families or locales) that weathered the economic and cultural transitions better than most. Still others may have filled niches that translated into local status, for example, a person in a position of leadership over a border zone (e.g., Beth-Shemesh, Tel Zayit) or a major traffic area (e.g., Tel Reḥov), or an émigré who retained connections to another region (e.g., Tell eṣ-Ṣafi).⁵⁵

---

⁵⁰Yardenna Alexandre, "The 'Hippo' Jar and Other Storage Jars at Hurvat Rosh Zayit," *Tel Aviv* 22, no. 1 (1995): 77–88; Leore Grosman et al., "Archaeology in Three Dimensions: Computer-Based Methods in Archaeological Research," *Journal of Eastern Mediterranean Archaeology & Heritage Studies* 2, no. 1 (2014): 62.
⁵¹Amihai Mazar, "An Ivory Statuette Depicting an Enthroned Figure from Tel Reḥov," in *Bilder Als Quellen, Images as Sources: Studies on Ancient Near Eastern Artefacts and the Bible Inspired by the Work of Othmar Keel*, ed. Susanne Bickel et al., OBO (Fribourg: Academic Press; Göttingen: Vandenhoeck & Ruprecht, 2007), 101–10; Amihai Mazar and Nava Panitz-Cohen, "It Is the Land of Honey: Beekeeping at Tel Reḥov," *Near Eastern Archaeology* 70, no. 4 (2007): 202–19; Nimrud Marom et al., "Backbone of Society: Evidence for Social and Economic Status of the Iron Age Population of Tel Rehov, Beth-Shean Valley, Israel," *BASOR* 354 (2009): 1–21; Mazar, "Reḥob"; Aḥituv and Mazar, "The Inscriptions from Tel Reḥov."
⁵²Mazar, "Reḥob."
⁵³Aḥituv and Mazar, "The Inscriptions from Tel Reḥov," 63.
⁵⁴Seth L. Sanders, "From People to Public in the Iron Age Levant," in *Organization, Representation, and Symbols of Power in the Ancient Near East: Proceedings of the 54th Rencontre Assyriologique Internationale at Würzburg 20–25 July 2008*, ed. Gernot Wilhelm (Winona Lake: Eisenbrauns, 2012), 106.
⁵⁵Despite the anachronistic language, the Iron I period was a time of widespread displacement and migration. We should expect that not all connections were lost even across long distances.

## CROSS-CULTURAL MATERIAL: BYBLOS AND EGYPT

We can turn to neighbors of the southern Levant, Byblos and Egypt, for a comparison of how writing and scribes were employed in the early Iron Age. Admittedly, comparing Egypt and Byblos on the one hand and the southern Levantine sites on the other is not a simple issue. The nature of the Byblian and Egyptian evidence is distinct from the southern Levant; we have monumental royal inscriptions as well as a contemporary Egyptian narrative source, the Report of Wenamun. In addition, these cultures have dramatically different histories from the smaller, and typically younger, southern Levantine sites, but all locations sought new directions in the wake of the Late Bronze collapse. Not surprisingly, Byblian and Egyptian inscriptions of this time stress the power and legitimacy of new leadership. Elites used scribes and inscriptions to promote their authority, legitimacy, and distinction from others. While we cannot transfer all of this information unaltered to the southern Levant, we can see similar trends in the evidence, albeit on a different scale.

Four royal inscriptions from Byblos illustrate how new rulers used scribes as a part of their campaigns for legitimacy during the Iron I–IIA period.[56] These are the Aḥiram sarcophagus, commissioned by son 'Ittoba'al (late eleventh/tenth century); the Abiba'al inscription (second half of the tenth century); and inscriptions by Yeḥimilk and his son Eliba'al (tenth to early ninth century).[57] In general, these documents paint a picture of emerging status, but not necessarily of overwhelming power. The inscriptions document the rulers' good deeds and successes in carrying out quintessentially royal duties, especially the creation of and care for monuments, which we should understand as a method for establishing authority. With the exception of the sarcophagus, the texts describe dedication to Byblos' patron goddess, Ba'alat Gebal, the Mistress of Byblos—again cultivating legitimacy.[58] At the same time, the inscriptions hint at political instability. Aḥiram's sarcophagus contains warnings to future rulers against disturbing the burial (ironic since the tomb and possibly also the sarcophagus were reused for Aḥiram).[59] Yeḥimilk's inscription lacks a statement of a hereditary claim to the throne, instead asserting that he is "the legitimate and rightful king" of Byblos, a description fitting of a usurper.[60] Abiba'al and Eliba'al placed their inscriptions on statues of pharaohs (Shoshenq I and Osorkon I, respectively). While the monuments of early Twenty-second Dynasty kings in Byblos stand as a testimony to renewed relations between the two states, and Byblian participation in that exchange appears to have been meaningful for supporting a king's

---

[56]This discussion follows the conventional scheme for the early Phoenician rulers and their approximate dates. Benjamin Sass has argued for a dramatic down-dating of the inscriptions that seems unnecessary (*The Alphabet at the Turn of the Millennium: The West Semitic Alphabet ca. 1150–850 BCE: The Antiquity of the Arabian, Greek and Phrygian Alphabets* [Tel Aviv: Emery and Claire Yass Publications in Archaeology, 2005]; Finkelstein and Sass, "West Semitic Alphabetic Inscriptions," 181–83). For a detailed critique of Sass, see Christopher A. Rollston, "The Dating of the Early Royal Byblian Phoenician Inscriptions: A Response to Benjamin Sass," *Maarav* 15, no. 1 (2008): 57–93.

[57]For a general review of the inscriptions, see John C. L. Gibson, *Textbook of Syrian Semitic Inscriptions III: Phoenician Inscriptions Including Inscriptions in the Mixed Dialect of Arslan Tash* (Oxford: Clarendon, 1982), 12–24. See also W. F. Albright, "The Phoenician Inscriptions of the Tenth Century B. C. from Byblus," *JAOS* 67, no. 3 (1947): 153–60; *TSSI* 3:12–18; Yitzhak Avishur, *Phoenician Inscriptions and the Bible: Select Inscriptions and Studies in Stylistic and Literary Devices Common to the Phoenician Inscriptions and the Bible* (Tel Aviv: Archaeological Center Publication, 2000), 103–4; Marilyn J. Lundberg, "Editor's Notes: The Ahiram Inscription," *Maarav* 11, no. 1 (2004): 81–93.

[58]Most translations of Yeḥimilk's inscription emend *b'l gbl* to *b'lt gbl* because of the frequency of the latter and infrequency of the former. For an argument against the emendation, see Aaron Schade, "The Syntax and Literary Structure of the Phoenician Inscription of Yeḥimilk," *Maarav* 13, no. 1 (2006): 119–22.

[59]Matthew James Suriano, "The Formulaic Epilogue for a King in the Book of Kings in Light of Royal Funerary Rites in Ancient Israel and the Levant" (PhD diss., University of California, Los Angeles, 2008), 152.

[60]Eliba'al's text (and his son Shipitba'al's) establishes his legitimacy through Yeḥimilk.

authority, we should give thought to why these kings chose Egyptian statuary for their declarations.[61] Were they not in command of enough resources to have their own monuments crafted? Or were the Byblian kings asserting themselves over their Egyptian contemporaries? In either case, their scribes served in a powerful role as the agents of appropriation and monument creation, particularly when the rulers may have felt limitations in their authority.

The Egyptian evidence is more plentiful although still scant compared to other periods in Egyptian history. Even so, rulers and officials left significant evidence of their activities in inscriptions.[62] Tenth-century rulers Siamun, Shoshenq I, and Osorkon I recorded their accomplishments, including relations with the Levant.[63] Their documents illustrate a more fully realized exhibition of power through inscribed monuments. In emulation of classic New Kingdom displays of power, Siamun and Sheshonq I depicted campaigns against foreigners in monumental inscriptions, the first since the end of the Ramessides.[64] The use of this convention, which relied on professional artists and scribes, makes the claim that they were worthy and powerful kings, rightfully situated alongside their great predecessors. In the same vein, Shoshenq and Osorkon recorded tribute, temple gifts, and offerings, drawing attention to their abilities to amass a significant amount of wealth and dominate other regions.[65] Perhaps the most impressive for this period is the epigraphic evidence of these kings outside of Egypt. As we have noted Shoshenq and Osorkon gave statues to the Mistress of Byblos, long associated with the Egyptian goddess Hathor.[66] A stele fragment found in Megiddo bears Shoshenq's name, presumably installed as a reminder of his Levantine campaign,[67] and a

---

[61] John Gibson suggests that these inscriptions on Egyptian monuments served to elevate the reputation and status of the Byblian king to the level of a pharaoh (*TSSI* 3:22). The Report of Wenamun, however, presents a power reversal, where Egyptian authority was not well respected by Levantine rulers (see below). Does the Byblian kings' defacing/appropriating of these statues corroborate the Egyptian tale? Rather than interpret the act as a resourceful way for a king to "create" a monumental inscription, we could also view it as a type of dominance, Byblos over Egypt, where the king appropriates the status object and presents it to the goddess under his name.

[62] An Egyptian official, "Pa-di-iset, the justified, son of Apy," "the only renowned one, the impartial envoy of Philistine Canaan," had himself immortalized by removing the inscription from a Middle Kingdom official's statue and replacing it with his own. Pa-di-iset may have served a Twenty-second Dynasty king (the inscription is often dated to the tenth century), but there is not enough evidence to pin down a more precise date. The inscription's character fits the model of reuse and assertion that we have seen, though this combination is not exclusive to the period by any means. See Georg Steindorff, "The Statuette of an Egyptian Commissioner in Syria," *JEA* 25, no. 1 (1939): 30–33, plate VII; "Translation, Walter's Art Gallery," http://art.thewalters.org/viewwoa.aspx?id=33246; Itamar Singer, "Egyptians, Canaanites, and Philistines in the Period of the Emergence of Israel," in *From Nomadism to Monarchy: Archaeological and Historical Aspects of Early Israel* (Jerusalem: Biblical Archaeology Society, 1994), 330.

[63] Egyptian chronology of this period is also debated. See Kenneth Kitchen, "Establishing Chronology in Pharaonic Egypt and the Ancient Near East: Interlocking Textual Sources Relating to C. 1600–664 BC," in *Radiocarbon and the Chronologies of Ancient Egypt*, ed. Andrew J. Shortland and Christopher Bronk Ramsey (Oxford: Oxbow, 2013), 1–18; Andrew Shortland, "Shishak, King of Egypt: The Challenges of Egyptian Calendrical Chronology in the Iron Age," in *The Bible and Radiocarbon Dating: Archaeology, Text and Science*, ed. Thomas E. Levy and T. Higham (London/Oakville: Equinox, 2005), 43–54; John Taylor, "The Third Intermediate Period (1069–664 BCE)," in *The Oxford History of Ancient Egypt*, ed. Ian Shaw (Oxford: Oxford University Press, 2002), 330–68.

[64] Kenneth A. Kitchen, "Egyptian Interventions in the Levant in the Iron Age II," in *Symbiosis, Symbolism, and the Power of the Past: Canaan, Ancient Israel, and Their Neighbors from the Late Bronze Age through Roman Palaestina. Proceedings of the Centennial Symposium, W.F. Albright Institute of Archaeological Research and American Schools of Oriental Research, Jerusalem, May 29/31, 2000*, ed. William G. Dever and Seymour Gitin (Winona Lake: Eisenbrauns, 2003), 118–19, 121–25. For Siamun's relief, see P. Montet, *La Nécropole Royale de Tanis*. Vol. 1, *Les Constructions et le Tombeau d'Osorkon II à Tanis* (Paris, 1947), plate 9A. For Shoshenq's Karnak inscription, see Anson F. Rainey and R. Steven Notley, *The Sacred Bridge: Carta's Atlas of the Biblical World* (Jerusalem: Carta, 2006), 185–89.

[65] James H. Breasted, *Ancient Records of Egypt: Historical Documents from the Earliest Times to the Persian Conquest*, vol. 4 (Chicago: University of Chicago Press, 1906), secs. 723, 729–37.

[66] Susan Tower Hollis, "Hathor and Isis in Byblos in the Second and First Millennia BCE," *Journal of Ancient Egyptian Interconnections* 1, no. 2 (2009): 1–8.

[67] Robert S. Lamon and Geoffrey M. Shipton, *Megiddo I: Seasons of 1925–1934, Strata I–V*, Oriental Institute Communications 42 (Chicago: University of Chicago Press, 1939), 60–61, fig. 70. The choice of Megiddo for such a display of power must have been related to the international traffic that passed through the site. The logistics of this are intriguing: were

Shoshenq scarab was found in the Faynan region in Jordan, possibly a result of the campaign or of Egyptian involvement in the region's copper trade.[68]

Finally, the Report of Wenamun, probably best characterized as a work of historical fiction, follows an Egyptian official on a journey along the Levantine coast to acquire cedar for the Barque of Amun in Karnak.[69] The story, set in the early eleventh century and composed in the eleventh or tenth century, provides a glimpse at changes in elite status and exchange relations across the eastern Mediterranean at the turn of the millennium.[70] In the tale, former vassals no longer treat Egypt with the deference that was customary in previous years. Instead, centers like Dor and Byblos assert new-found authority. The tale is also a rich resource for attitudes about the authority of the written word in establishing one's bona fides and negotiating international relations. At the beginning of the text, Wenamun shows his papers in northern Egypt in order to outfit himself for his journey, but his lack of papers in Byblos (because he left them in Egypt) causes great hardship when trying to do business with the Byblian prince, Zakar-Baal. Wary of the undocumented Wenamun, the prince consults royal annals that preserve a history of relations between Byblos and Egypt. Eventually, the men arrive at a solution, and Zakar-Baal calls on his scribe to provide new papers for Wenamun's return. Within the narrative and from the perspective of the author, we see that scribes and written documentation provided evidence of identification and authority in what is characterized as a very chaotic and confusing time in international relations. Notice that the author draws a stark contrast between Wenamun, lacking official papers or a means to produce new ones (i.e., a scribe), and Zakar-Baal, who both retains a scribe and has access to the authority of written precedents.

An examination of these contemporary records situates Egypt as the most established in the use of scribes, which included the creation of new monumental works, but we also know from both historical and archaeological sources that Egypt was not the world power it was previously and that stable, familial dynasties were not the norm. New rulers had to vie for their position and legitimacy through visible and powerful means: construction, conquest, and conspicuous inscriptions. The Report of Wenamun suggests that authority and legitimacy accompanied the possession of written documents and that one who could produce such items held significant power. In both Egypt and Byblos, new rulers and dynasties declared their status through inscriptions. Egypt provides the best evidence of elites both creating monuments and documenting power on them. In contrast, Byblian leaders added their statements to preexisting objects, but these illustrate this same sentiment. They employed scribes in order to establish their status, even if they could not secure the wealth and authority required to commission original works. If other luxuries were lacking, one could "make a statement" through an inscription. This practice puts a spin on the association between monumental inscriptions and complex states—Byblian elites "created" monumental inscriptions through graffiti and associated themselves with recognized elites, thereby elevating themselves in their sphere of influence.

---

Egyptian scribes part of the campaign and left to commemorate it? Was the stele later shipped from Egypt? And what was the impact of this monumental inscription on the scribes of the southern Levant's elites?

[68] Stefan Münger and Thomas E. Levy, "The Iron Age Egyptian Amulet Assemblage," in *New Insights into the Iron Age Archaeology of Edom, Southern Jordan: Surveys, Excavations and Research from the University of California, San Diego & Department of Antiquities of Jordan, Edom Lowlands Regional Archaeology Project (ELRAP)*, ed. Thomas E. Levy et al., Monumenta Archaeologica 35 (Los Angeles: The Cotsen Institute of Archaeology Press, 2014), 748–49, 758.

[69] The account probably relied on real-life experiences of travel in the region; see Miriam Lichtheim, *Ancient Egyptian Literature: A Book of Readings*. Vol. 2, *The New Kingdom* (Berkeley: University of California Press, 1973), 224, 229–30.

[70] The tale is typically understood to date to the eleventh century. Edward F. Wente Jr. and Benjamin Sass have, separately, proposed arguments for the tenth century: Wente proposing authorship during the Twenty-first Dynasty ("The Report of Wenamun," in *The Literature of Ancient Egypt: An Anthology of Stories, Instructions, Stelae, Autobiographies, and Poetry*, ed. William Kelly Simpson [New Haven: Yale University Press, 2003], 116); Sass argues for Shoshenq I's reign ("Wenamun and His Levant–1075 B.C. or 925 B.C.?," *Egypt and the Levant* 12 [2002]: 247–55) Sass's arguments are not as convincing, but the historical situations of either the eleventh or tenth centuries are plausible settings for the story's creation.

## CONCLUSIONS

We return now to the southern Levantine inscriptions. The examples from Byblos or Egypt cannot be compared without qualification. Instead of expecting the same scale from the southern Levant, we should look for indications of relative forms of distinction. New pharaohs modeled themselves and their inscriptions on the greats of Egyptian history. Byblian and southern Levantine elites were engaged in similar emulation processes but in ways relative to their respective locations and wealth.[71] Individuals were documenting their status on materials that may have already testified to their elevated social positions. In the southern Levant, name formulae appear on prestige items: a fine bronze bowl, bronze arrowheads, a game board, or a dedication vessel. In other cases, names were placed on storage vessels, likely documenting the status of the producer. In the context of limited literacy, it is not so much the content of the written word that mattered but its presence, its conspicuousness.

In all regions, the apparent increase in epigraphic finds corresponds to the rise of new elite groups and intensifying cultural interactions. The new leaders promoted their status through inscribed objects and other luxury goods in order to gain prominence within their emerging territories and in their competition for regional power. This image of various, competing elites contradicts the biblical image of a lack of diversity in wealth in pre-Solomonic eras. The Bible recounts that outstanding individuals like the Judges, Saul, or David were plucked from a common mass, with dynastic succession endorsed only after David proved his piety. The history conspicuously denies hereditary status or dynastic succession for anything but the priesthood or Davidic line. Despite these efforts, the illusion is not completely successful. Elite status is apparent in minor characters like the wealthy Nabal (1 Sam. 25) or wealthy and influential Barzillai (2 Sam. 19). If we overlook the biblical argument regarding wealth, the emergence of regional leadership is apparent in the inscribed materials and other testaments to elevated status.

The scribes who were employed by these elites played a significant role in drawing a line between an emerging class of power players and everyone else, the common people of the land. While there remains the view that a range of social classes participated in writing and literacy, when we resituate the inscribed artifacts in the contexts where they have been found and in the relative contexts of how inscriptions were being used in the late eleventh and tenth centuries, I find the depictions of Byrne and Sanders to be the more likely characterizations of who the scribes were and how they operated. They made themselves first useful and later necessary to those who were involved in rapidly intensifying cultural, commercial, and political interactions. By doing so, they furthered their own distinction and aligned with the future ruling classes.

---

[71]Other studies have shown that emulation was an important factor in the growth of Iron Age leadership in the region. See Carolyn R. Higginbotham, *Egyptianization and Elite Emulation in Ramesside Palestine: Governance and Accommodation on the Imperial Periphery*, CHANE 2 (Leiden: Brill, 2000); Alexander H. Joffe, "The Rise of Secondary States in the Iron Age Levant: Archaeological and Historical Considerations," in *Excavating Ancient History: Interdisciplinary Studies in Archaeology and History*, ed. Norman Yoffee and Bradley L. Crowell (Tucson: University of Arizona Press, 2006), 67–112.

# The Media and Materiality of Southern Levantine Inscriptions

## *Production and Reception Contexts*

MADADH RICHEY

Inscriptions from the Iron Age southern Levant, including ancient Israel and Judah, were written with and on a range of media, most commonly ink on various surfaces and clay and stone incised using various techniques.[1] Although the media in and on which inscriptions were written are a vital part of their manifestation and the production processes of inscribed artifacts profoundly influenced both their form and their content, the physical properties of Hebrew and other Northwest Semitic inscriptions remain a generally under-explored field. There are signs of a more inclusive and object-grounded orientation in recent studies of epigraphic materiality,[2] and the present contribution participates in this turn by exploring a select set of media-related topics that yield immediate and important insights for biblical studies.[3] These are (1) the manufacture of inscribed

---

[1] The most comprehensive, detailed, and reliable edition of Iron Age inscriptions in Hebrew and/or from the territories of Israel and Judah is Johannes Renz and Wolfgang Röllig, *Handbuch der althebräischen Epigraphik*, 4 vols. (Darmstadt: Wissenschaftliche Buchgesellschaft, 1995–2003). Two other epigraphic compilations are commonly cited: Shmuel Aḥituv, *Echoes from the Past. Hebrew and Cognate Inscriptions from the Biblical Period* (Jerusalem: Carta, 2008); and F. W. Dobbs-Allsopp et al., *Hebrew Inscriptions: Texts from the Biblical Period of the Monarchy with Concordance* (New Haven: Yale University Press, 2005)—as is Christopher A. Rollston's introductory guidebook, *Writing and Literacy in the World of Ancient Israel*, ABS 11 (Atlanta: SBL, 2010). An excellent recent response to this last volume and summary of the field of Iron Age Northwest Semitic epigraphy is Andrew R. Burlingame, "Writing and Literacy in the World of Ancient Israel: Recent Developments and Future Directions," *BiOr* 76 (2019): 46–74. Phoenician, Aramaic, and some other inscriptions are often referenced below and elsewhere following their numeration in Herbert Donner and Wolfgang Röllig's selective compilation *Kanaanäische und aramäische Inschriften*, 2nd ed. in 3 vols. (Wiesbaden: Harrassowitz, 1966–69; hereafter *KAI*), with a substantive update to the first volume of transcriptions only in the 2002 5th ed. Moabite inscriptions are at present most comprehensively treated in Erasmus Gass, *Der Moabiter: Geschichte und Kultur eines ostjordanischen Volkes im 1. Jahrtausend v. Chr.*, ADPV 38 (Wiesbaden: Harrassowitz, 2009), 5–101. Ammonite inscriptions are collected in Walter E. Aufrecht, *A Corpus of Ammonite Inscriptions*, 2nd ed. (University Park: Eisenbrauns, 2019). No Edomite inscriptions are discussed below; the most careful delineation of that corpus—to which some recent additions must be made—is David S. Vanderhooft, "The Edomite Dialect and Script: A Review of the Evidence," in *You Shall Not Abhor an Edomite, for He Is Your Brother: Edom and Seir in History and Tradition*, ed. Diana V. Edelman, ABS 3 (Atlanta: Scholars Press, 1995), 137–57.

[2] See, e.g., the contributions to *Maarav* 23.1 (2019), a special issue titled "Communicating through the Material in the Ancient World," guest edited by Emily Cole and Alice Mandell, some essays from which are cited below; along with Alice Mandell, "Reading and Writing Remembrance in Canaan: Early Alphabetic Inscriptions as Multimodal Objects," *HeBAI* 7 (2018): 253–84; Alice Mandell and Jeremy D. Smoak, "Reading beyond Literacy, Writing beyond Epigraphy: Multimodality and the Monumental Inscriptions at Ekron and Tel Dan," *Maarav* 22 (2018): 79–112; idem, "Reconsidering the Function of Tomb Inscriptions in Iron Age Judah: Khirbet Beit Lei as a Test Case," *JANER* 16 (2016): 192–245; Brian B. Schmidt, *The Materiality of Power: Explorations in the Social History of Early Israelite Magic*, FAT 105 (Tübingen: Mohr Siebeck, 2016); and idem, ed., *Contextualizing Israel's Sacred Writings: Ancient Literacy, Orality, and Literary Production*, AIL 22 (Atlanta: SBL, 2015), from which several essays are cited below.

[3] Notably, there are ways in which the foregrounding of palaeographic questions is also object-centered rather than content-centered, since palaeography studies developments in the graphic morphologies of letters and, often, the material and other exigencies that produce these developments, usually with relatively minimal regard for content. A collection of palaeographic approaches to Northwest Semitic texts, several of which attend to materiality, is Jo Ann Hackett and Walter E. Aufrecht, eds., *"An Eye for Form": Epigraphic Essays in Honor of Frank Moore Cross* (Winona Lake: Eisenbrauns, 2014). The first global

monuments, with a focus on a previously unremarked media particularity of Hebrew monumental inscriptions; (2) the widely known problem of Iron Age Hebrew papyri disintegration, including how this manifests in the archaeological record; and (3) the surprising variety of media on which texts similar to those of the Hebrew Bible are preserved. Taken together, these foci move beyond the traditionally linguistic emphases of Northwest Semitic epigraphy and bring new material-centered questions into dialogue with the conservative fixation on texts.

## 1. MAKING A MONUMENT

The process by which inscriptions were produced might seem simple at first thought. A scribe sets reed pen to papyrus, and an inscription is born. But even the most straightforward epigraphic praxis involves multiple preconditions, individuals, and preparatory steps. All tools and surfaces go through more and less complex processes of manufacture, and there is a parallel process of formation for literate professionals. Even when no southern Levantine sources reveal these processes directly, the outlines of material manufacture and education can be extrapolated from comparison with data from elsewhere in the ancient Near East and Mediterranean as well as from anthropological studies. There have been, for example, many studies on the manufacture of writing tools[4] and clay tablets.[5] The training of literate professionals has likewise been the topic of much work aimed at describing ancient Israelian and Judahite education.[6]

But arguably the most elaborate process of textual production, namely stone monument incision and display, has gone under-theorized in Hebrew epigraphic studies. This is in part because public

---

treatment of Iron Age Hebrew palaeography has now been published: Ada Yardeni, *The National Hebrew Script up to the Babylonian Exile* (Jerusalem: Carta, 2019). Extensive palaeographic discussions treating particular genres and corpora are Heather Dana Davis Parker, "The Levant Comes of Age: The Ninth Century BCE through Script Traditions" (PhD diss., The Johns Hopkins University, 2013); and Christopher A. Rollston, "The Script of Hebrew Ostraca of the Iron Age: 8th–6th Centuries BCE" (PhD diss., The Johns Hopkins University, 1999). An excellent article that combines media with palaeographic considerations is Reinhard G. Lehmann, "Calligraphy and Craftsmanship in the Aḥīrōm Inscription: Considerations on Skilled Linear Flat Writing in Early First Millennium Byblos," *Maarav* 15 (2008): 119–64.

[4] Most such tools are discussed by Philip Zhakevich, "The Tools of an Israelite Scribe: A Semantic Study of the Terms Signifying the Tools and Materials of Writing in Biblical Hebrew" (PhD diss., University of Texas at Austin, 2015); and/or Aaron J. Koller, *The Semantic Field of Cutting Tools in Biblical Hebrew*, CBQMS 49 (Washington, DC: Catholic Biblical Association, 2012).

[5] Material aspects of writing on clay tablets are explored recently in several essays in Eva Cancik-Kirschbaum and Babette Schnitzlein, eds., *Keilschriftartefakte: Untersuchungen zur Materialität von Keilschriftdokumenten*, BBVO 26 (Gladbeck: PeWe-Verlag, 2018); and, on the treatment of tablets as objects in Assyriology, Julian Reade, "The Manufacture, Evaluation, and Conservation of Clay Tablets Inscribed in Cuneiform: Traditional Problems and Solutions," *Iraq* 79 (2017): 163–202. Laurie E. Pierce discusses the use of and rhetoric around other cuneiform media, especially precious stones, in "Materials of Writing and Materiality of Knowledge," in *Gazing on the Deep: Ancient Near Eastern and Other Studies in Honor of Tzvi Abusch*, ed. Jeffrey Stackert, Barbara Nevling Porter, and David P. Wright (Bethesda: CDL, 2010), 167–79. In keeping with the suggestion in n. 3, above, that palaeography is fundamentally an endeavor of materiality, see recently Elena Devecchi, Gerfried G. W. Müller, and Jana Mynářová, eds., *Current Research in Cuneiform Palaeography: Proceedings of the Workshop Organized at the 60th Rencontre Assyriologique Internationale, Warsaw 2014* (Gladbeck: PeWe-Verlag, 2015).

[6] Early work on Israelian and Judahite education often extrapolated historical praxis from biblical depictions. More recently, scholars have attempted to deduce both education and literacy from certain types of inscriptions (especially abecedaries), the prevalence of inscriptions, and comparison with neighboring and contemporary (but much larger) societies in which educational processes are more transparent, especially Egypt and Mesopotamia. Two recent global expositions are William M. Schniedewind, *The Finger of the Scribe: How Scribes Learned to Write the Bible* (Oxford: Oxford University Press, 2019), and Aaron Demsky, *Literacy in Ancient Israel*, The Biblical Encyclopedia Library 28 (Jerusalem: Bialik, 2012 [Hebrew]), and see also Rollston, *Writing and Literacy*, 91–135. Three recent summaries with good bibliography are William M. Schniedewind, "Scribal Education in Ancient Israel and Judah into the Persian Period," in *Second Temple Jewish Paideia in Context*, ed. Jason M. Zurawski and Gabriele Boccaccini, BZNW 228 (Berlin: de Gruyter, 2017), 11–28; Christopher A. Rollston, "Scribal Curriculum during the First Temple Period: Epigraphic Hebrew and Biblical Evidence," in Schmidt, ed., *Contextualizing*, 71–102; and Anat Mendel-Geberovich, "Literacy: Biblical Hebrew," *EHLL* 2 (2013): 552–58.

monumental inscriptions are poorly attested in the territories of ancient Israel and Judah despite extensive use in neighboring, contemporary, and sociologically comparable polities.[7] Stone monuments from the northern and southern Levant were generally incised in basalt, a mafic igneous rock with a hardness of 7 on the Mohs scale.[8] Basalt monuments are found in the southern Levant exclusively east of the Jordan, within the spheres of Moabite and Ammonite influence. Moabite monumental inscriptions in basalt are the Mesha stele from Ḏībān (*KAI* 181),[9] along with a further tiny fragment from the same site,[10] the el-Kerak statue fragment,[11] and the large "Captives of Moab" fragment of unknown provenance, now in the Israel Museum.[12] The Ammonites, to the north, are known to have produced one monumental inscription in basalt, namely the ʿAmmān Theater inscription.[13] With few exceptions (see below), other stones were not generally used for such inscriptions among these groups, Israel and Judah's most immediate neighbors. Basalt was the lithic material of choice in the Aramean states of modern-day Syria and Turkey,[14] and the Luwians

---

[7] I emphasize "public" in agreement with recent work on monumentality that stresses this accessibility aspect of an installation or inscription as crucial for its social significance. An introduction to monumentality theory in Near Eastern archaeological context is James F. Osborne, "Monuments and Monumentality," in *Approaching Monumentality in Archaeology*, ed. James F. Osborne (Albany: SUNY, 2014), 1–19; and recent applications to Northwest Semitic epigraphic texts include Jeremy D. Smoak and Alice Mandell, "Texts in the City: Monumental Inscriptions in Jerusalem's Urban Landscape," in *Size Matters—Understanding Monumentality Across Ancient Civilizations*, ed. Federico Buccellati et al., Histoire 146 (Bielefeld: Transcript, 2019), 309–43; Jeremy D. Smoak, "Inscribing Temple Space: The Ekron Dedication as Monumental Text," *JNES* 76 (2017): 319–36. In his dissertation ("The Eternal Monument of the Divine King: Monumentality, Reembodiment, and Social Formation in the Decalogue" [PhD diss., UCLA, 2019]) and several recent articles, Timothy Hogue has extended these observations by examining ways in which the biblical Decalogue functions as a monumental text. Epigraphs like the eighth-century Hebrew Siloam Tunnel inscription (*KAI* 189; Ahituv, *Echoes*, 19–25; Dobbs-Allsopp et al., *Hebrew Inscriptions*, 499–506; Renz and Röllig, *Handbuch*, I/178–89), hidden in a water conduit, are therefore less usefully described as monumental. Hebrew tomb inscriptions were accessible but were less "public" in their creation, that is, likely commissioned by private individuals. Such inscriptions are recently summarized by Matthew J. Suriano, *A History of Death in the Hebrew Bible* (Oxford: Oxford University Press, 2018), 98–127; with some additional details in Jody Washburn, "The Family Tomb as an Inscribed Artifact: Toward an Integrative Analysis of the Beit Lei Inscriptions," *Maarav* 23 (2019): 93–113.
[8] Basalt is discussed in mineralogical terms throughout R. W. Le Maitre, ed., *Igneous Rocks: A Classification and Glossary of Terms*, 2nd ed. (Cambridge: Cambridge University Press, 2002), esp. 30–32, 36–39, 60–61.
[9] The Mesha inscription is most comprehensively treated by and most easily accessed via J. Andrew Dearman, ed., *Studies in the Mesha Inscription and Moab*, ABS 2 (Atlanta: Scholars Press, 1989); a recent comprehensive text edition is Gass, *Moabiter*, 5–65; see also Ahituv, *Echoes*, 389–418.
[10] First edition: Roland E. Murphy "A Fragment of an Early Moabite Inscription from Dibon," *BASOR* 125 (1952): 20–23; further discussion in Gass, *Moabiter*, 65.
[11] First edition: William L. Reed and Fred V. Winnett, "A Fragment of an Early Moabite Inscription from Kerak," *BASOR* 172: 1–9; further discussion in Dennis Pardee, "Moabite Compositions," in *The Context of Scripture*. Vol. 4, *Supplements*, ed. K. Lawson Younger (Leiden: Brill, 2017), 89; Gass, *Moabiter*, 66–69; and Ahituv, *Echoes*, 387–89. Heather Dana Davis Parker and Ashley Fiutko Arico ("A Moabite-Inscribed Statue Fragment from Kerak: Egyptian Parallels," *BASOR* 373 [2015]: 105–20) have studied this inscription recently with a focus on its formal and media features, especially its Egyptian statuary parallels.
[12] First edition: Shmuel Ahituv, "A New Moabite Inscription," *IMSA* 2 (2003): 3–10; further discussion in Pardee, "Moabite Compositions," 89–90; Gass, *Moabiter*, 76–83; and Ahituv, *Echoes*, 421–23. Gass has also studied the inscription in some detail recently; see his "New Moabite Inscriptions and Their Historical Relevance," *JNSL* 38 (2012): 45–78, here 47–60.
[13] First edition: R. W. Dajani, "The Amman Theater Fragment," *ADAJ* 12–13 (1967–68): 65–67 and pl. 39, with a more accessible study based on autopsy in William J. Fulco, "The Amman Theater Inscription," *JNES* 38 (1979): 37–38. See also the entries in Aufrecht, *Corpus*; and Ahituv, *Echoes*, 367–70.
[14] Early Aramaic monuments in basalt include the Bar Hadad stele (*KAI* 201), the Zakkur stele (*KAI* 202), the monumental inscriptions from Zincirli (*KAI* 214–21; Josef Tropper, *Die Inschriften von Zincirli*, ALASP 6 (Münster: Ugarit-Verlag, 1993], 54–150)—including the KTMW inscription (Dennis Pardee, "A New Aramaic Inscription from Zincirli," *BASOR* 356 [2009]: 51–71) and three fragments found in the University of Chicago Neubauer excavations (Samuel L. Boyd, Humphrey H. Hardy II, and Benjamin D. Thomas, "Two New Inscriptions from Zincirli and Its Environs," *BASOR* 356 [2009]: 73–80; forthcoming edition of a third fragment by Pardee and the present author)—the Sefire stelae (*KAI* 222–24; Joseph A. Fitzmyer, *The Aramaic Inscriptions of Sefire*, BibOr 19/A, 2nd ed. [Rome: Pontifical Biblical Institute, 1995]), and the Tel Dan stele (George Athas, *The Tel Dan Inscription: A Reappraisal and a New Interpretation*, JSOTSup 360 [London: Sheffield Academic, 2003], esp. 18–23), along with several others.

likewise tended to use basalt for their monuments.[15] As Alice Mandell and Jeremy Smoak have recently pointed out, the use of basalt therefore conveyed not only technical skill and political power but also "coordinated the inscription with other basalt stelae and monuments"[16] thereby signifying the responsible ruler's membership in an elite group.

Not only have Israel and Judah yielded few stone monuments in general, but all four that are presently known were incised in limestone, a stone that is much softer than basalt (Mohs scale 3) and therefore somewhat easier to incise.[17] Limestone use for monumental inscriptions is attested in the single known Philistian monument—the Ekron dedicatory inscription[18]—in the ʿAmmān Citadel inscription,[19] and in a few early Phoenician inscriptions.[20] It is, however, not otherwise very common in the ancient Near East. The four Old Hebrew monumental inscriptions are all fragmentary and from the territorial capitals of Samaria and Jerusalem. The single Samaria fragment reads simply {ʾšr . }, probably the relative complementizer "which, that,"[21] while one fragment from the Ophel[22] and two from the City of David[23] are more extensive but contain few complete words among them.

---

[15]The Luwian or "Neo-Hittite" situation is summarized in James F. Osborne, "Monuments of the Hittite and Neo-Assyrian Empires During the Late Bronze and Iron Ages," in *Mercury's Wings: Exploring Modes of Communication in the Ancient World*, ed. F. S. Naiden and Richard J. A. Talbert (Oxford: Oxford University Press, 2017), 87–105; with editions of inscriptions themselves in John David Hawkins, *Corpus of Hieroglyphic Luwian Inscriptions*, 3 vols., UISK 8 (Berlin: de Gruyter, 2000).

[16]Mandell and Smoak, "Multimodality," 110.

[17]A recent palaeographic study of these inscriptions is David S. Vanderhooft, "Iron Age Moabite, Hebrew, and Edomite Monumental Scripts," in Hackett and Aufrecht, ed., *"Eye for Form"*, 107–26. Both Mandell and Smoak ("Multimodality," 110) and Kyle H. Keimer ("The Impact of Ductus on Script Form and Development in Monumental Northwest Semitic Inscriptions," *UF* 46 [2015]: 189–212, here 190–94) note the lithic contrast between basalt and limestone mentioned here, but neither discuss the striking geographic restrictions delineated below.

[18]First edition: Seymour Gitin, Trude Dothan, and Joseph Naveh, "A Royal Dedicatory Inscription from Ekron," *IEJ* 47 (1997): 1–16. Smoak ("Inscribing") repeatedly mentions the limestone medium but does not draw direct conclusions from this lithic fact nor from the contrast with basalt monuments (cf. esp. p. 329).

[19]First edition: Siegfried H. Horn, "The Ammān Citadel Inscription," *BASOR* 193 (1969): 2–13. In addition to the entry in Aufrecht, *Corpus*, see Aḥituv, *Echoes*, 357–62. The most recent study of this inscription, with excellent photographs, comprehensive bibliography, and a close study of line 5, is Andrew Burlingame, "Line Five of the Amman Citadel Inscription: History of Interpretation and a New Proposal," *BASOR* 376 (2016): 63–82.

[20]Both the Yeḥimilk (*KAI* 4) and Shipiṭbaal (*KAI* 7) inscriptions from Byblos (tenth century BCE) are in limestone, as are the Persian-period inscriptions of the "Son of Shipiṭbaal" (*KAI* 9) and Yeḥawmilk (*KAI* 10), suggesting continuity of lithic tradition. This media consideration has rarely been foregrounded even in extensive work on early Byblian palaeography, e.g., Benjamin Sass, "The Emergence of Monumental West Semitic Alphabetic Writing, with an Emphasis on Byblos," *Sem* 59 (2017): 109–41; Maria Giulia Amadasi Guzzo, "'Alphabet insaisissable'. Quelques notes concernant la diffusion de l'écriture consonantique," *Transeuph* 44 (2014): 67–86. This is true also of my own recent summary: Madadh Richey, "Inscriptions," in *The Oxford Handbook of the Phoenician and Punic Mediterranean*, ed. Carolina López-Ruiz and Brian Doak (Oxford: Oxford University Press, 2019), 223–40, esp. 224–25 for illustration of the Yehimilk inscription and discussion of the Byblian epigraphic context.

[21]First edition: Eleazar L. Sukenik, "Note on a Fragment of an Israelite Stele found at Samaria," *PEFQS* (1936): 156, with several subsequent studies (in the handbooks, Aḥituv, *Echoes*, 257; Dobbs-Allsopp et al., *Hebrew Inscriptions*, 497; Renz and Röllig, *Handbuch*, I/135). Naʿama Pat-El ("Israelian Hebrew: A Re-Evaluation," *VT* 67 [2017]: 227–63, here 231) has recently noted that this {ʾšr} occurrence complicates dialectal reconstructions according to which the Israelian North used *šæ* as opposed to *ʾăšær* as its relative complementizer.

[22]First edition: Joseph Naveh, "A Fragment of an Ancient Hebrew Inscription from the Ophel," *IEJ* 32 (1982): 195–98. Later treatments are confined to the handbooks: Rollston, *Writing and Literacy*, 55; Aḥituv, *Echoes*, 30–32; Dobbs-Allsopp et al., *Hebrew Inscriptions*, 226–27; Renz and Röllig, *Handbuch*, I/189–90). The collocations {mtḥt . l}, "underneath" (l. 1'), and {byrkty}, "in the back of" (l. 3'), may suggest that this is a building inscription.

[23]The first fragment from the City of David was published by Joseph Naveh, "Hebrew and Aramaic Inscriptions," in *Excavations at the City of David 1978–1985 Directed by Yigal Shiloh*. Vol. 6, *Inscriptions*, ed. Donald T. Ariel, Qedem 41 (Jerusalem: Hebrew University of Jerusalem, 2000), 1–2. It was discussed shortly afterward and at greater length by Frank Moore Cross, "A Fragment of a Monumental Inscription from the City of David," *IEJ* 51 (2001): 44–47. It is also included in the handbooks of Aḥituv, *Echoes*, 25–26; Dobbs-Allsopp et al., *Hebrew Inscriptions*, 227–29; and Renz and Röllig, *Handbuch*, I/190–91. The first preserved line contains a form of the root √šbr and the second and third preserved lines probably involve numbers—{šbʿ ʿšr} and {[...]rbʿy}—but little more can be said. The second fragment was published by Ronny Reich and Eli

While little can therefore be said from their content, their media allows some important conclusions. In the first place, those responsible for deciding what stone to use for Israelian and Judahite monumental inscriptions appear to have taken the path of least resistance in lithic terms. This could have been a conscious or unconscious response to economic or social factors, or in more precise terms, having less money or manpower than was generally necessary for quarrying, transporting, and incising basalt. Secondly, the more friable nature of limestone might help to explain the relative dearth of excavated monumental inscriptions in Israel and Judah. Put another way, the archaeological gap may proceed from a media divergence that was itself the result of considerations around material availability and incision expediency rather than a political or even theological choice.[24] Third, limestone has particular aesthetic qualities that might have made it a preferable epigraphic medium, namely its usually light color and smooth, sometimes almost reflective, surface. The limestone comparanda from Phoenician and Philistine sites should be enough, however, to caution against simplistically positioning this lithic use as an Israelian and/or Judahite expression of distinction.

The process of creating a stone monument, whether limestone or basalt, involved many steps.[25] First the rock needed to be quarried from a source and hewn into manageable blocks for transport and manufacture.[26] Iconographical and archaeological evidence from Anatolia, Syria, Mesopotamia, and Egypt suggests that basalt statuary was generally processed very near the quarry, in "sculptural workshops," rather than first transported and then chiseled.[27] Since no statuary recovered in Anatolian or Levantine quarries has ever been found to be already inscribed, it is possible that the inscriptional process, unlike the formative and decorative chiseling processes, took place after the monument was transferred to a more central location. Monumental inscriptions may have been drafted on papyrus or writing boards[28] and/or chalked or inked onto the stone before the chiseling

---

Shukron, "A Fragmentary Palaeo-Hebrew Inscription from the City of David, Jerusalem," *IEJ* 58 (2008): 48–50. It has no complete words on its two lines, which read {[…] q y h […] / […] k h . b […]}. The first of these lines plausibly contains a Yahwistic name ending in {yh}.

[24]Cf. Gary A. Rendsburg, "No Stelae, No Queens: Two Issues Concerning the Kings of Israel and Judah," in *The Archaeology of Difference: Gender, Ethnicity, Class and the "Other" in Antiquity. Studies in Honor of Eric M. Meyers*, ed. Douglas R. Edwards and C. Thomas McCullough, AASOR 60–61 (Boston: American Schools of Oriental Research, 2007), 95–107.

[25]There have been only a few attempts in Northwest Semitic scholarship to describe the monument from "birth" (quarrying) until "death" (destruction, whether inadvertent or purposeful), but see Athas, *Tel Dan*, 18–93. Several recent works on multimodality move in this direction, e.g., Mandell and Smoak, "Multimodality." B. H. McLean (*An Introduction to Greek Epigraphy of the Hellenistic and Roman Periods from Alexander the Great down to the Reign of Constantine* [Ann Arbor: University of Michigan Press, 2002], 4–21) does sketch such a monument biography on the basis of classical sources and artefactual data. This study has been referred to by some of those working on similar topics in Near Eastern studies (see below).

[26]Various aspects of quarrying are discussed in Koller, *Cutting Tools*, 129–61. Quarries and associated processes in Roman-period and Late Antique Israel are discussed by Zeev Safrai and Avi Sasson, *Quarrying and Quarries in the Land of Israel in the Period of the Mishnah and Talmud* (Elkanah: Eretz Heifetz, 2001 [Hebrew]). A comparably general volume on Egyptian quarries is Rosemarie Klemm, *Stones and Quarries in Ancient Egypt* (London: British Museum, 2008). Jean-Claude Bessac studies quarrying at Ugarit in Late Bronze Syrian context ("Les roches de construction d'Ougarit: production, façonnage, mise en ouevre," in *Études ougaritiques III*, ed. Valérie Matoian and Michael al-Maqdissi, RSO 21 [Leuven: Peeters, 2013], 111–41). For relevant publications of Anatolian quarries, see the following note.

[27]Quarrying and transport of colossi in Assyrian reliefs and texts are discussed in John Malcolm Russell, *Sennacherib's Palace without Rival at Nineveh* (Chicago: University of Chicago, 1991), 98–116. Anatolian sculpture quarries are a prime source for archaeological reconstruction; see, e.g., on Sikizlar, Stefania Mazzoni, "A Sculptures Quarry at Sikizlar," *AAAS* 26–27 (1986–87): 268–75; on Yesemek, Refik Duru, *Yesemek: The Largest Sculpture Workshop of the Ancient Near East* (Istanbul: Türsab, 2004); and on Karakız Karabası, Geoffrey D. Summers and Erol Özen, "The Hittite Stone and Sculpture Quarry at Karakız Karabası and Hapis Boğazı in the District of Sorgun, Yozgat, Central Anatolia," *AJA* 116 (2012): 507–19.

[28]Archaeological evidence for wax-covered writing boards is discussed in, e.g., Robert Payton, "The Ulu Burun Writing-Board Set," *AnSt* 41 (1991): 99–106. Lexical evidence for the practice in Mesopotamia and Syria is summarized in, e.g., John MacGinnis, "The Use of Writing Boards in the Neo-Babylonian Temple Administration at Sippar," *Iraq* 64 (2002): 217–36; and Dorit Symington, "Late Bronze Age Writing-Boards and Their Uses: Textual Evidence from Anatolia and Syria," *AnSt* 41 (1991): 111–23.

process commenced, but there remains no direct evidence for this.[29] This phase would likely have been the responsibility of a literate individual who was capable in general composition, including penmanship, orthography, lexical choice, formulae, and so on. After this individual had completed this phase, it is likely that a separate craftsperson, whose training was primarily in chiseling and other stoneworking, would take over and use a separate tool set to copy or "trace" the product of the first individual's work. This process of stone-working can be evaluated from lithic analysis of Northwest Semitic-language monuments, which show a restricted set of incision types. This suggests a restricted and stereotyped set of stoneworking instruments.[30]

Once the process of chiseling was complete, the now-inscribed monument could be transported and displayed. It is this display process that has received the most attention in recent studies of Levantine epigraphic materiality and monumentality.[31] In general, monuments were erected in locations of high public traffic and/or of sociopolitical prestige. When the display context of an inscription is known, archaeologists and other scholars can reconstruct how the inscription would have looked in its built environment and even the precise sight-paths by which and at what distance an inscription would have been visible.[32] It is now generally agreed that the vast majority of the viewing populace would not have been able to *read* a monumental inscription from start to finish; popular literacy was likely variable and restricted, even among communities that utilized alphabetic as opposed to logographic and/or syllabic scripts.[33] Even those who could make out only certain sentences, certain words, or certain letters would nevertheless have been impacted by the total sight of an inscribed monument. It was through this impact that organs capable of displaying inscribed monuments communicated their power and, at a glance, the entire manufactural process as just described.

## 2. THE LAND OF LOST PAPYRI

Although monuments were certainly important, scribal practices elsewhere in the Near East and in later periods of the southern Levant itself suggest that most literate energy in Iron Age Israel and Judah was directed towards the production of texts on papyrus.[34] Ostraca would mostly have served

---

[29] Scholars often assume this, but the closest proofs are comparative. For example, Zhakevich's ("Tools," 178) source for the chalking procedure is McLean's (*Greek Epigraphy*, 11–12) reconstruction of Greek stele production practice; McLean's own main datum for this point is the discovery of stelae with gaps "to be engraved later with the customary formulae." As he notes (ibid.), "An incomplete inscription of this kind would only have been possible if the engraver had first traced the text out in full graphic form," or at least, I would add, measured out space for the requisite graphemes. Like Zhakevich, Athas (*Tel Dan*, 26; see also ibid., 28, 42, 64, 66) consistently assumes that the Tel Dan inscription "must have been chalked or marked out before any chisel was put to stone," but he cites no direct or comparative evidence for this.

[30] This process is discussed in detail in Keimer, "Impact," 194–204.

[31] See, e.g., Mandell and Smoak, "Multimodality," 96–111; Smoak, "Inscribing"; Smoak and Mandell, "Texts in the City," 319.

[32] Formal approaches to visibility analysis include Kevin D. Fisher, "Investigating Monumental Social Space in Late Bronze Age Cyprus: An Integrative Approach," in *Spatial Analysis and Social Spaces*, ed. Eleftheria Paliou, Undine Lieberwirth, and Silvia Polla (Berlin: de Gruyter, 2014), 167–202; and James F. Osborne and Geoffrey D. Summers, "Visibility Graph Analysis and Monumentality in the Iron Age City at Kerkenes in Central Turkey," *Journal of Field Archaeology* 39 (2014): 292–309.

[33] The now-classic discussion of this in ancient Northwest Semitic context is Christopher A. Rollston, "Scribal Education in Ancient Israel: The Old Hebrew Epigraphic Evidence," *BASOR* 344 (2006): 47–74, here 48–49.

[34] The likely predominance of papyri and parchment in earlier periods is suggested by such later document caches as the Wadi ed-Daliyeh Aramaic papyri (450–332 BCE; Jan Dušek, *Les manuscrits araméens du Wadi Daliyeh et la Samarie vers 450–332 av. J.-C.*, CHANE 30 [Leiden: Brill, 2007]) and, of course, the Dead Sea Scrolls. Aramaic papyri from the Achaemenid period were best preserved in Egypt; see comprehensively Bezalel Porten and Ada Yardeni, *Textbook of Aramaic Documents from Ancient Egypt*, 4 vols. (Jerusalem: Hebrew University, 1986–99; hereafter *TAD*). The earliest papyri from Egypt are from the late seventh century BCE, i.e. roughly contemporary with both the minimal known papyrus/i from the southern Levant and with theoretical late Judahite monarchic papyrus production; see, e.g., the Saqqara Papyrus (*RÉS* 1791; *TAD*

as a secondary, disposable medium,[35] and it is only by accident that this material has survived to the present day long after papyri—the pride and joy of southern Levantine scribalism—have almost entirely disintegrated. Despite the prominence of parchment in later periods, there are no material or lexical pointers to its widespread use in the Iron Age Levant.[36]

The only Iron Age Hebrew papyrus that is likely authentic is a palimpsest purchased among mostly later inscriptions reportedly from caves in Wadi Murabbaʿat, eleven miles south of Qumran on the Dead Sea.[37] The lower, older inscription on this palimpsest appears to be a letter, and the upper, newer inscription is a list of names; both can be palaeographically dated to the seventh century BCE.[38] An additional, recently published papyrus whose script can be palaeographically dated to the same century mentions wine shipped to Jerusalem.[39] This papyrus was, however, seized from the antiquities market and is of debated authenticity.[40]

Evidence for the use of papyri and parchment in the Iron Age southern Levant therefore remains mostly indirect. Biblical texts, for example, occasionally describe writing on a מגלה, "scroll" (e.g. Jer 36; Zech 5). More telling, though, is the fact that bullae—or the rounded clay pieces into which seals were impressed—occasionally preserve imprints of papyrus fibers and/or the cords that were used to secure these papyri.[41] Because such bullae usually have flat rather than concave backs, it is

---

C3.1), the Göttingen Papyrus (*TAD* C3.2), and the Adon letter (*TAD* A1.1; *KAI* 266), sent to Egypt by one of Necho II's (r. 610/09–595/4 BCE) Levantine vassals. The oldest Egyptian-language papyri are of course much older than these Aramaic documents. A very general survey of manufacture, finds, etc. is Richard B. Parkinson and Stephen Quirke, *Papyrus* (Austin: University of Texas Press, 1995). The chronological horizon of Egyptian-inscribed papyri has recently been extended back to the fourth-dynasty reign of Khufu (ca. twenty-sixth century BCE) by finds at the Wadi al-Jarf harbor on the Red Sea; official publication has begun in Pierre Tallet, *Les papyrus de la mer Rouge. 1, Le "journal de Merer" (Papyrus Jar A et B)*, MIFAO 136 (Cairo: Institut français d'archéologie orientale, 2017).

[35] The three largest corpora of ostraca are: (1) the Samaria ostraca (eighth century BCE; George Andrew Reisner et al., *Harvard Excavations at Samaria, 1908–1910* [Cambridge, MA: Harvard University Press, 1924]), recording shipments of wine and oil; (2) the Arad ostraca (ninth–early sixth centuries BCE; Yohanan Aharoni, *Arad Inscriptions* [Jerusalem: Israel Exploration Society, 1981]), of varied content including letters and economic documents; and (3) the Lachish ostraca (early sixth century BCE; Harry Torczyner, *The Lachish Letters*, Lachish 1 [London: Oxford University Press, 1938]), mostly letters, many describing the military situation in late Iron Age Judah. André Lemaire, *Inscriptions hébraïques, Tome I. Les ostraca*, LAPO 9 (Paris: Cerf, 1977) collects the ostraca inscriptions known to that date; more recent finds are documented most comprehensively, as usual, by Renz and Röllig, *Handbuch*, esp. II/1 9–25. Most provenanced ostraca finds since that publication are mentioned in either André Lemaire, "Levantine Literacy ca. 1000–750 B.C.E.," in Schmidt, *Contextualizing*, 11–45, and/or Nadav Naʾaman, "Literacy in the Negev in the Late Monarchical Period," in Schmidt, *Contextualizing*, 47–70.

[36] This is stressed by Menahem Haran in a series of articles, esp. "Book-Scrolls in Israel in Pre-Exilic Times," *JSS* 33 (1982): 161–73; and "Book-Scrolls at the Beginning of the Second Temple Period: The Transition from Papyrus to Skins," *HUCA* 54 (1983): 111–22.

[37] The purchase from the famous antiquities dealer Kando on January 11, 1952 is described by Roland de Vaux, "Historique des découvertes," in *Les Grottes de Murabbaʿât*, DJD 2 (Oxford: Clarendon, 1961), 3–8, here 5. Both texts of the palimpsest are edited for the first time in that volume by J. T. Milik, "17. Palimpseste: Lettres, liste de personnes (VIII^e [sic] siècle avant J.-C.)," in *Murabbaʿât*, 93–100, pl. 28.

[38] This palaeographic dating is argued by Frank Moore Cross, "Epigraphic Notes on Hebrew Documents of the Eighth–Sixth Centuries B.C.: II. The Murabbaʿât Papyrus and the Letter Found Near Yabneh Yam," *BASOR* 165 (1962): 34–46, here 36–42 (reprint idem, *Leaves from an Epigrapher's Notebook: Collected Papers in Hebrew and West Semitic Palaeography and Epigraphy*, HSS 51 [Winona Lake: Eisenbrauns, 2003], 116–24).

[39] First edition: Shmuel Ahituv, Eithan Klein, and Amir Ganor, "The 'Jerusalem' Papyrus: A Seventh-Century BCE Shipping Certificate," *IEJ* 67 (2017): 168–82.

[40] Although the inscription has been discussed frequently in online forums, so far the only detailed published comments debating its authenticity are those of Christopher A. Rollston, "The Putative Authenticity of the New 'Jerusalem' Papyrus Inscription: Methodological Caution as a Desideratum," in *Rethinking Israel: Studies in the History and Archaeology of Ancient Israel in Honor of Israel Finkelstein* (Winona Lake: Eisenbrauns, 2017), 319–28.

[41] This fact is frequently discussed by scholars seeking to reconstruct ancient Judahite documentary and literary procedures, e.g., Nathan Mastnjak, "Jeremiah as Collection: Scrolls, Sheets, and the Problem of Textual Arrangement," *CBQ* 80 (2018): 25–44, here 34–37; Jessica Whisenant, "Let the Stones Speak! Document Production by Iron Age West Semitic Scribal Institutions and the Question of Biblical Sources," in Schmidt, *Contextualizing*, 133–60.

likely that papyri were folded or rolled flat rather than rolled cylindrically.[42] Hoards of bullae have been found at Lachish and Jerusalem. In the former case, seventeen intact bullae were found in a juglet of Stratum II (ca. 701–586 BCE); thirteen of the seventeen were inscribed and all show papyrus impressions.[43] They are plausibly the remains of a small archive, the papyri of which have disintegrated. The inscribed bullae found in Yigal Shiloh's City of David excavations were also discovered intact.[44] As in the case of the Lachish bullae, their intact nature suggests that they were being used to seal archived documents and survived even when fire destroyed those documents. A different situation obtains for uninscribed bullae found in the more recent City of David excavations directed by Ronny Reich and Eli Shukron; these are usually broken, probably because they once sealed incoming documents that were opened and read.[45]

For the same basic artifact, therefore, one can reconstruct two very different but equally important historical processes—archiving and circulation—even when the documents themselves have long since been destroyed. This fact, however, goes only a short way towards the very difficult task of reconstructing what sorts of texts would have been written on papyrus. The situation is parallel to that which plagues reconstruction of the lost Phoenician papyrus archives, which several classical authors suggest were extensive and ancient, but which have perished and taken with them most that could be known of Phoenician religious and literary writing.[46]

## 3. FROM EPIGRAPHY TO BIBLICAL TEXTS

Because Levantine written documents on papyri mostly do not survive from the Iron Age, one must turn largely to other media to find parallels for those products that were incorporated into the Hebrew Bible. One interesting fact is that the types of texts that were eventually collected and transmitted as important works of literature and/or history—and that thereafter became "canonical" and "biblical"—are known from multiple diverse media rather than just one stream of production. Hebrew and other Northwest Semitic monumental inscriptions provide close stylistic and syntactic parallels for historical and particularly military-focused texts in the Hebrew Bible, and some scholars have therefore suggested that such biblical texts were based on monuments—or vice versa.[47] But there are several other media that must be mentioned as preserving parallels to biblical texts and therefore perhaps revealing something about their documentary history.

---

[42]This observation is made by Nahman Avigad, *Hebrew Bullae from the Time of Jeremiah: Remnants of a Burnt Archive* (Jerusalem: Israel Exploration Society, 1986), 18. This volume publishes over 200 unprovenanced bullae from the late seventh or early sixth century BCE, some of which have papyri and cord marks.

[43]These bullae are published in Yohanan Aharoni, *Investigations at Lachish: The Sanctuary and Residency*, Lachish 5 (Tel Aviv: Institute of Archaeology, 1975), 19–22.

[44]The final publication of these bullae is Yair Shoham, "Hebrew Bullae," in *Excavations at the City of David 1978–1985 Directed by Yigal Shiloh*. Vol. 6, *Inscriptions*, ed. Donald T. Ariel, Qedem 41 (Jerusalem: Hebrew University of Jerusalem, 2000), 29–57. For the archaeological context of these bullae, see pp. 29–32.

[45]Ronny Reich, Eli Shukron, and Omri Lernau, "Recent Discoveries in the City of David, Jerusalem," *IEJ* 57 (2007): 153–69, here 156. Reich et al. count 170 bullae bearing complete or partial seal impression along with "several hundred" unimpressed bullae.

[46]Recent surveys of what little is known about putative Phoenician, especially Tyrian, archives are presented by Carolina López-Ruiz, "Phoenician and Carthaginian Literature," in *The Oxford Handbook of the Phoenician and Punic Mediterranean*, ed. Carolina López-Ruiz and Brian Doak (Oxford: Oxford University Press, 2019), 257–69; and Josephine Quinn, *In Search of the Phoenicians* (Princeton: Princeton University Press, 2018), esp. 60–61, 231.

[47]This view has been championed by Nadav Na'aman in the recent past (e.g. "Royal Inscriptions and the Histories of Joash and Ahaz, Kings of Judah," *VT* 48 [1998]: 333–49) but has predecessors. Simon B. Parker ("Did the Authors of the Books of Kings Make Use of Royal Inscriptions?" *VT* 50 [2000]: 357–78) cites many of these and argues that current evidence does not support such claims.

First, epigraphs similar to poetic and prophetic texts have been recovered at greatest, albeit fragmentary, length in ink-on-plaster display inscriptions.[48] An inscription from Deir 'Alla,[49] in northern Jordan, describes visions of the prophet Balaam, who is also a central character in Numbers 22–24. Both cohesive "combinations" of plaster fragments appear to contain oracles of doom, the former with extensive animal imagery and the latter with many mentions of death and its attendants. Parallels have been marshalled from all corners of biblical literature for both lexical understanding of the text and its reconstruction.[50] Conversely, the text reveals new possibilities for understanding how Northwest Semitic prophetic texts might have been objects for display and devotion,[51] even in communities with—as mentioned above—relatively low levels of literacy. Such communities might therefore have interacted primarily with the iconicity rather than the linguistic features of the text. Something similar might be said of the even more fragmentary but formally similar ink-on-plaster inscriptions found at the caravansary of Kuntillet 'Ajrud, in the western Negev desert.[52] Unlike the famous "Yahweh and His Asherah" ink-on-ceramic pithos votive texts from the site, these disjointed plaster texts have only recently been published.[53] Scholars are divided in their interpretations of them, with several having proposed extensive imaginative reconstructions.[54] Given, however, the extent to which these reconstructions are based on doing epigraphy from photographs and filling gaps based on biblical Hebrew texts, one should be very cautious of the circularity that might result from using these reconstructed texts to make claims about processes of biblical composition or

---

[48] The texts discussed in this paragraph have recently been studied together and with an eye towards what they tell us about the composition of biblical and other Northwest Semitic literary texts in Gareth Wearne, "The Plaster Texts from Kuntillet 'Ajrud and Deir 'Alla: An Inductive Approach to the Emergence of Northwest Semitic Literary Texts in the First Millennium B.C.E." (PhD diss., Macquarie University, 2015); see also Schniedewind, *Finger*, 23–48.

[49] First edition: Jean Hoftijzer and Gerrit van der Kooij, *Aramaic Texts from Deir 'Alla*, DMOA 19 (Leiden: Brill, 1976), with re-edition in Jo Ann Hackett, *The Balaam Text from Deir 'Allā*, HSM 31 (Chico: Scholars Press, 1984), and proceedings of a conference dedicated to the inscription in Jean Hoftijzer and Gerrit van der Kooij, eds., *The Balaam Text from Deir 'Alla Re-evaluated: Proceedings of the International Symposium Held at Leiden, 21–24 August 1989* (Leiden: Brill, 1991).

[50] In addition to sources cited in the preceding note, see recently Erhard Blum, "Die Kombination I der Wandinschrift vom Tell Deir 'Alla. Vorschläge zur Rekonstruktion mit historisch-kritischen Anmerkungen," in *Berührungspunkte: Studien zur Sozial- und Religionsgeschichte Israels und seiner Umwelt. Festschrift für Rainer Albertz zu seinem 65. Geburtstag*, ed. Ingo Kottsieper et al., AOAT 350 (Münster: Ugarit-Verlag, 2008), 573–601; idem, "'Versteht du dich nicht auf die Schreibkunst...?' Ein weisheitlicher Dialog über Vergänglichkeit und Verantwortung. Kombination II der Wandinschrift vom Tell Deir 'Alla," in *Was ist der Mensch, dass du seiner gedenkst? (Psalm 8,5): Aspekte einer theologischen Anthropologie. Festschrift für Bernd Janowski zum 65. Geburtstag*, ed. Michaela Bauks, Kathrin Liess, and Peter Riede (Neukirchen-Vluyn: Neukirchener Verlag, 2008), 33–53; and idem, "Die altaramäischen Wandinschriften vom Tell Deir 'Alla und ihr institutioneller Kontext," in *Materiale Textkulturen: Konzepte – Materialen – Praktiken*, ed. Thomas Meier, Michael R. Ott, and Rebecca Sauer (Berlin: de Gruyter, 2015), 21–52.

[51] Comparison of the Deir 'Alla plaster inscriptions with biblical prophetic texts has rarely gone beyond the observation that they may betray similar processes of prophetic composition and/or collection—e.g. David M. Carr, *The Formation of the Hebrew Bible* (Oxford: Oxford University Press, 2011), 336, 382—but see some exceptions in n. 56, below, and compare now the more extensive discussions in Schniedewind, *Finger*, 147–51; and Jordan Skornik, "Paradigms and Possibilities: On Literary Prophecy and the Hebrew Bible" (PhD diss., University of Chicago, 2018), 116–25.

[52] Hypotheses as to the function of Kuntillet 'Ajrud are recently surveyed in William M. Schniedewind, "Understanding Scribal Education in Ancient Israel: A View from Kuntillet 'Ajrud," *Maarav* 21 (2014 [2017]): 271–93, here 272–75; Israel Finkelstein, "Notes on the Historical Setting of Kuntillet 'Ajrud," *Maarav* 20 (2013 [2015]): 13–25; and Alice Mandell, "'I Bless You to YHWH and His Asherah'—Writing and Performativity at Kuntillet 'Ajrud," *Maarav* 19 (2012 [2015]): 131–62, here 131–38.

[53] The plaster texts from Kuntillet 'Ajrud are comprehensively edited by Shmuel Ahituv, Esther Eshel, and Ze'ev Meshel, "The Inscriptions," in *Kuntillet 'Ajrud (Ḥorvat Teman): An Iron Age II Religious Site on the Judah-Sinai Border*, ed. Ze'ev Meshel and Liora Freud (Jerusalem: Israel Exploration Society, 2012), 105–16.

[54] Examples of such reconstruction include Erhard Blum, "Die Wandinschriften 4.2 und 4.6 sowie die Pithos-Inschrift 3.9 aus Kuntillet 'Aǧrūd," *ZDPV* 129 (2013): 21–54; Nadav Na'aman, "The Inscriptions of Kuntillet 'Ajrud Through the Lens of Historical Research," *UF* 43 (2011): 300–24, here 307–12; idem, "A New Outlook at Kuntillet 'Ajrud and Its Inscriptions," *Maarav* 20 (2013 [2015]): 39–51, here 47–49.

tradition.[55] One is on more solid ground in paying attention to formal features of both these and the Deir 'Alla plaster texts, including their palaeography and materials, from which paths of scribal influence can be deduced.[56]

Although inscribed ostraca are abundant, as has been noted already above, only a singular ink-on-ceramic ostracon from Ḥorvat 'Uzza, an Iron Age fortress in the Negev, possibly contains a "literary" text. Most scholars have interpreted this ostracon as showing a poetic or wisdom text, but there is still substantial epigraphic, lexical, and syntactic debate regarding its precise contents.[57] This is not to say, of course, that other ostraca cannot be profitably compared with the biblical text and might be revealing of earlier phases of biblical compositions. Administrative lists, for example, are very common in the ostraca corpora, and similar genres might lie behind such biblical administrative lists as that of Solomon's officials in 1 Kings 4.[58]

Conversations about the "oldest biblical manuscripts" or the like often include mention of two silver amulets found in a burial cave at Ketef Hinnom, just west of the Old City of Jerusalem. These bear a text that is similar to that of the priestly blessing in Num 6:24–26.[59] The discovery shows that users were interred with and perhaps wore prayer amulets for beneficence and protection.[60] While these amulets are unique in many ways, they fit a broader pattern of epigraphic evidence discussed in this section; that is, early Hebrew epigraphic texts somewhat frequently show commonalities with biblical lexemes, syntax, and formulae, and these texts are often short, fragmentary, and—most importantly for present purposes—in numerous media. Moreover, the Ketef Hinnom amulets are just the only early Hebrew representative of a broader genre of inscribed metal amulets.[61] A focus on medium and praxis, rather than the relatively simplistic fact that the Ketef Hinnom inscriptions

---

[55] See similarly Joachim J. Krause, "Kuntillet 'Ajrud Inscription 4.3: A Note on the Alleged Exodus Tradition," *VT* 67 (2017): 485–90, expressing skepticism regarding Na'aman's proposed recovery of an Exodus tradition in the plaster inscription Kuntillet 'Ajrud 4.3.

[56] For example, Gareth Wearne ("'Guard it on your tongue!' The Second Rubric in the Deir 'Alla Plaster Texts as an Instruction for the Oral Performance of the Narrative," in *Registers and Modes of Communication in the Ancient Near East: Getting the Message Across*, ed. Kyle H. Keimer and Gillan Davis [London: Routledge, 2018], 125–42) suggests from close analysis of one of Deir 'Alla's red-letter rubrics and its excavation context the performative character of the text. Karel van der Toorn (*Scribal Culture and the Making of the Hebrew Bible* [Cambridge: Cambridge University Press, 2007], 175–76) observes that those red rubrics are reminiscent of similar Egyptian praxis and thus perhaps suggestive of Egyptian scribal influence. F. W. Dobbs-Allsopp (*On Biblical Poetry* [Oxford: Oxford University Press, 2015], 35) notes that although these texts are apparently columnar and linguistically reminiscent of biblical poetry, they do not use space to delineate poetic units. With a similar focus on inscriptional form rather than linguistic content, André Lemaire ("Remarques sur les inscriptions phéniciennes de Kuntillet 'Ajrud," *Semitica* 55 [2013]: 83–99) expands upon the palaeographic observations of the first edition to argue that several of the Kuntillet 'Ajrud plaster inscriptions show Phoenician script and might suggest the presence of Tyrians at the site.

[57] The *editio princeps* is Itzhak Beit-Arieh, "A Literary Ostracon from Ḥorvat 'Uza," *TA* 20 (1993): 55–63, with Frank Moore Cross, "A Suggested Reading of the Ḥorvat 'Uza Ostracon," *TA* 20 (1993): 64–65; the most recent thorough study is Nadav Na'aman, "A Sapiential Composition from Ḥorvat 'Uza," *HeBAI* 2 (2013): 221–33.

[58] Hebrew epigraphic lists have been studied in greatest detail by Anat Mendel-Geberovich, "Epigraphic Lists in Israel and Its Neighbors in the First Temple Period" (PhD diss., Hebrew University of Jerusalem, 2014 [Hebrew]). See pp. 40–43 of the aforementioned study for an in-depth discussion of biblical connections. A close analysis of one such epigraphic list is eadem, "Who Wrote the Aḥiqam Ostracon from Ḥorvat 'Uza?" *IEJ* 61 (2011): 54–67. A discussion of lists that attempts to extend these observations to address biblical composition is Schniedewind, *Finger*, 70–94.

[59] Revised edition: Gabriel Barkay et al., "The Amulets from Ketef Hinnom: A New Edition and Evaluation," *BASOR* 334 (2004): 41–71; and compare, e.g., Aḥituv, *Echoes*, 49–55.

[60] For the social contexts of the inscriptions, see Jeremy D. Smoak, *The Priestly Blessing in Inscription and Scripture: The Early History of Numbers 6:24–26* (New York: Oxford University Press, 2016); and now idem, "Wearing Divine Words: In Life and Death," *Material Religion* 15 (2019): 433–55.

[61] Phoenician and Punic metal amulets and bands are discussed most comprehensively in Carolina López-Ruiz, "Near Eastern Precedents of the 'Orphic' Gold Tablets: The Phoenician Missing Link," *JANER* 15 (2015): 52–91; and functionally (though not materially) comparable Punic papyrus amulets in Philip C. Schmitz, "The Phoenician Papyrus from Tal Virtù, Malta," in *"What Mean These Stones?" (Joshua 4:6, 21): Essays on Texts, Philology, and Archaeology in Honour of Anthony J. Frendo*, ed. Dennis Mizzi, Nicholas C. Vella, and Martin R. Zammit, ANESSup 50 (Leuven: Peeters, 2017), 61–71.

approximate biblical texts, can embed the amulets in a broader socio-religious history and foreground the apotropaic and iconic import of these inscribed artifacts.[62]

This embedding in broader history is also a general goal of a media-focused epigraphy. The privileging of epigraphic linguistic content tends to produce conclusions that might have been made from any textual source. The three direct studies above, however, show ways in which focus on materiality can be particularly illuminating for historical and other questions. Because inscriptions stand as close as modern scholars are likely to get to compositional processes, they reveal not only words and phrases but also concrete processes of textual meaning-making on the most immediate level. A media focus rounds out the field of Northwest Semitic epigraphy by looking at inscriptions at many different points in their lifetimes and from many points of view. These points of view are, importantly, distinct from that of the linguistically minded modern scholar, and they draw out textual production and reception in ways likely closer to the experiences of most individuals who interacted with inscriptions in ancient historical periods.

---

[62] These aspects are discussed in, e.g., Smoak, *Priestly Blessing*, 43–60; Schmidt, *Materiality of Power*, 132–44.

# Scribes and Scribalism in Archaic Crete*

ANSELM C. HAGEDORN

## INTRODUCTION

In both, anthropological and exegetical discourse the exploration of the role of writing has gained prominence,[1] leading to a new awareness of textual mediated worlds as well as of elite processes at work in the production of literature.[2] As far as the Hebrew Bible is concerned, scholars have detected a "scriptural turn," argued for a "theology of writing" and demonstrated that the biblical text transforms Moses into the first scribe.[3] A plethora of studies confirms that the societies of Eastern Levant and the ancient Near East were indeed scribal cultures and that the respective societies placed a high degree of value and prestige on written documents and monuments.[4] We generally remember the importance of writing in ancient Near Eastern Cultures such as Assyria and also in Egypt, where we encounter specialized deities such as Nabû and Toth who serve as the patrons of writing.[5] Greece, however, is often neglected in the discussion about Eastern Mediterranean scribalism.[6] This essay hopes to offer some comparable evidence for the existence of scribes and scribalism from a western perspective, namely archaic Crete and other Greek poleis. We will investigate how and why Greek city states during the sixth century BCE began to use writing and to enlist the services of specialists who were able to record laws and stipulations of the individual poleis. I have argued elsewhere that archaic Crete provides the best comparative evidence

---

*The following abbreviations of Greek epigraphic material are used: *IC* = M. Guarducci, ed., *Inscriptiones Creticae*, vols. 1–4 (Rome, 1935–50); *ICS* = O. Masson, *Inscriptions Chypriotes Syllabique*, Études Chypriotes 1, 2nd ed. (Paris, 1983); *IE* = H. Engelmann and R. Merkelbach, eds., *Die Inschriften von Erythrai und Klazomenai Teil 1 (Nr 1–200)*, Inschriften griechischer Städte aus Kleinasien 1 (Bonn, 1972); *IG* = *Inscriptiones Graece* (Berlin, 1897–); *IvO* = K. Dittenberger and W. Purgold, *Die Inschriften von Olympia* (Berlin, 1896); ML = R. Meiggs and D. Lewis, *A Selection of Greek Historical Inscriptions to the End of the Fifth Century BC*, rev. ed. (Oxford, 1999); *LSCG* = F. Sokolowski, *Lois sacrées des cités greque*, 2nd ed. (Paris, 1969); *Nomima* I–II = H. van Effenterre and F. Ruzé, eds., *Nomima. Recueil d'inscriptions politiques et juridiques de l'archaïsme grec I–II*, Collection de l'École française de Rome 188 (Rome, 1994/1995); SEG = Supplementum Epigraphicum Graecum.

[1] See the formulation of the classic and highly influential thesis in Goody (1986) and for the Hebrew Bible, Carr (2005) and van der Toorn (2007).
[2] See, e.g., Lauinger 2015 for an investigation how Assyrian Vassal Treaties were produced.
[3] Schaper 2004; 2009; 2016; Otto 2005, and especially Sonnet 1997; Heckl 2013.
[4] As far as the biblical world is concerned one must also mention the extensive phenomenon of rewriting—a process that signifies the remarkable importance of written interpretative processes; see, e.g., Crawford 2008; Kratz 2013; Teeter 2014; Zahn 2016.
[5] See Pomponio and Seidl 1998–2001.
[6] Carr (2005: 91–109) takes ancient Greece into account but focuses too much on the literature (and literacy) of ancient Athens. He, too, maintains that "text-supported education in Greece was not oriented toward producing identifiable 'scribes,' nor was it apparently required to assume specific roles in a palace or temple administration" (108). It seems that Havelock's prominent statements also influence Carr's view (see, e.g., Havelock 1976). We will see below that Carr's statement does not comply with the epigraphic record.

to several aspects of the Hebrew Bible.[7] In contrast to ancient Athens, for example, writing down the law in Crete did not lead to the development of a democratic society so that Crete represents an alternative to the legal culture of Athens.[8] For this enterprise, however, the individual laws will only serve as the backdrop for our investigation in the significance of scribes, their status and the act of writing.

The purpose of this essay is twofold. On the one hand it hopes to situate the scribes of archaic Crete firmly within the context of ancient Near Eastern and ancient Mediterranean scribalism. On the other hand, this essay will provide some comparative material about the status of the scribe in ancient society. Though the office of the scribe is well known in the ancient Near East, in the biblical context, scribes known by name are sparse.[9] Also, the portrait of Ezra as priest *and* scribe (Ezra 7:12, 21 etc.) shows that biblical tradition conflates two offices creating an exemplary person who transmits Torah.[10] The stipulations from the Greek poleis will provide us with a window into the social world of the scribe, his powers and privileges.

## 1. BEFORE THE SCRIBES—WRITING IN HOMER AND THE COMING OF THE ALPHABET

Writing is largely absent from the Homeric epics. Only in two passages from the Iliad (*Il.* 6.166–170 and 7.175–189) do we have some allusions to the problem of writing.[11] In the narration of the myth of Proitos and Bellerophon we read:

> ὣς φάτο· τὸν δὲ ἄνακτα χόλος λάβεν οἷον ἄκουσε.
> κτεῖναι μέν ῥ' ἀλέεινε, σεβάσσατο γὰρ τό γε θυμῷ,
> πέμπε δέ μιν Λυκίηνδέ, πόρεν δ' ὅ γε σήματα λυγρὰ
> γράψας ἐν πίνακι πτυκτῷ θυμοφθόρα πολλά,
> 170 δεῖξαι δ' ἠνώγει ᾧ πενθερῷ ὄφρ' ἀπόλοιτο.

> All of it false
> but the king seethed when he heard a tale like that.
> He balked at killing the man—he'd some respect at least—
> but he quickly sent him off to Lycia, gave him tokens,
> murderous signs, scratched in a folded tablet,
> and many of them too, enough to kill a man.
> He told him to show them to Antea's father:
> that would mean his death.[12]

The description seems to refer to tablets, possibly made from wax or wood that were joined.[13] "The single reference to this type of tablet in the early preserved literature suggests that such tablets were rare although they must have been recognizable to the audience at the time they were originally incorporated into the epic tradition."[14] In the context of the passage it appears to be a letter sent by

---

[7] Hagedorn 2004.
[8] See the overview of the characteristics of the Cretan legal material in Gagarin 2012 and Kristensen 2014.
[9] See, e.g., Baruch ben Neriah (Jer 36:32), Shimshai, the scribe, in Ezra 4:8, 9, 17, 23, Zadok (Neh 13:13), *mʾš*, son of Manoaḥ in Herr 110 (text in Gogel 1998: 479) and Yeremay, the scribe on Aramaic bullae collected in Avigad 1976: 7–8.
[10] See Kratz 2008.
[11] See the discussion in Jeffery 1968 and the extensive treatment of the problem in Heubeck 1979.
[12] Homer, *Il.* 6.166–170; English translation according to Fagels 1990: 201.
[13] The other occurrences of πίναξ in the Homeric epics suggest that it may have been wood (*Od.* 1.141; 4.57; 12.67).
[14] Shear 1998: 187.

Proitos, though Homer veils the reference to writing by using σῆμα instead of the more common γράμμα.¹⁵ This has already occupied the scholia on the passage when there is a debate about the character of the σήματα λυγρά with some scholars arguing for proper letters, i.e. γράμματα, while others seem to favour pictograms (εἴδωλα).¹⁶

The wording of the passage makes it quite clear that Homer does not understand the reference to writing. Writing, the process that ensures that his works are preserved and transmitted for posterity is unknown to him. A further passage proves this point: in the description of the procedure to determine who will fight Hector each of the Achaeans marks his lot (οἳ δὲ κλῆρον ἐσημήναντο ἕκαστος).¹⁷ When the lot of Ajax flies from the helmet none of the other heroes recognize the markings because the sign is unique to Ajax himself and not part of a writing system.¹⁸ This is confirmed by the further use of γραφεῖν in the Iliad, which seems to have the meaning "to scratch."¹⁹ "It is a test of Hellenic provincialism during the Iron Age that their epic poets, at its conclusion, have never heard of writing."²⁰

The Greeks themselves never regarded the art of writing as a new invention.²¹ Rather, they were distinctly aware that it was a technique taken over from the Phoenicians. "[T]he names and shapes of the letters…, as well as the retrograde orientation of the script of the first alphabetic inscriptions, leave no doubt that the Greek alphabet is closely linked to the northern Semitic scripts of the end of the second and the beginning of the first millennium BC which we (following the ancients) usually refer to by the general term *Phoenician script.*"²²

Herodotus, for example, acknowledges the well-known fact that the Phoenicians brought the alphabet to Greece:

> οἱ δὲ Φοίνικες οὗτοι οἱ σὺν Κάδμῳ ἀπικόμενοι, τῶν ἦσαν οἱ Γεφυραῖοι, ἄλλα τεπολλὰ οἰκήσαντες ταύτην τὴν χώρην ἐσήγαγον διδασκάλια ἐς τοὺς Ἕλληνας καὶ δὴ καὶ γράμματα, οὐκ ἐόντα πρὶν Ἕλλησι ὡς ἐμοὶ δοκέειν, πρῶτα μὲν τοῖσι καὶ ἅπαντες χρέωνται Φοίνικες· μετὰ δὲ χρόνου προβαίνοντος ἅμα τῇ φωνῇ μετέβαλλον καὶ τὸν ῥυθμὸν τῶν γραμμάτων. περιοίκεον δὲ σφέας τὰ πολλὰ τῶν χώρων τοῦτον τὸν χρόνον Ἑλλήνων Ἴωνες, οἳ παραλαβόντες διδαχῇ παρὰ τῶν Φοινίκων τὰ γράμματα, μεταρρυθμίσαντες σφέων ὀλίγα ἐχρέωντο, χρεώμενοι δὲ ἐφάτισαν, ὥσπερ καὶ τὸ δίκαιον ἔφερε, ἐσαγαγόντων Φοινίκων ἐς τὴν Ἑλλάδα, Φοινικήια κεκλῆσθαι.

These Phoenicians who came with Cadmus (of whom the Gephyraeans were a part) at their settlement in this country, among many other kinds of learning, brought into Hellas

---

¹⁵One of the earliest literary attestations of γράμματα seems to be found in Aischylos, *fr.* 705 (οἱ γὰρ πρεσβύτεροι πόρρω τὰ γράμματα τῶν ὀμμάτων ἀπάγοντες ἀναγινώσκουσιν, ἐγγύθεν δ' οὐ δύνανται) and *Septem* 646 (Δίκη δ' ἄρ' εἶναί φησιν, ὡς τὰ γράμματα).660 (εἴ νιν κατάξει χρυσότευκτα γράμματα); von Wilamowitz-Moellendorf (1920: 304–5 n. 2) remarks on the ambiguity of the passage: "Die σήματα λυγρά in einem zusammengefalteten Täfelchen sind ein Brief. Aber ob die Schrift aus Buchstaben oder aus Ideogrammen bestand, sagt der Dichter nicht. 'Schlage den Überbringer tot!' ließ sich ohne Buchstaben dem Empfänger deutlich machen…"
¹⁶Texts in Erbse 1971: 160–61.
¹⁷Homer, *Il.* 7.175–189.
¹⁸Already in 1795 F. A. Wolf observed that "the two passages in Homer where writing occurs are no more to be taken as about writing than is the famous one in Cicero to be taken as about modern printing" (Wolf 1985: 97). Wolf, then, uses the absence of writing in Homer to argue that Homer's world was illiterate.
¹⁹See Homer, *Il.* 4.139 (ἀκρότατον δ' ἄρ' ὀϊστὸς ἐπέγραψε χρόα φωτός); 11.388 (νῦν δέ μ' ἐπιγράψας ταρσὸν ποδὸς εὔχεαι αὔτως); 13.552–554 (... οὐδὲ δύναντο | εἴσω ἐπιγράψαι τέρενα χρόα νηλέϊ χαλκῷ | Ἀντιλόχου); 17.598–600 (βλῆτο γὰρ ὦμον δουρὶ πρόσω τετραμμένος αἰεὶ | ἄκρον ἐπιλίγδην· γράψεν δέ οἱ ὀστέον ἄχρις | αἰχμὴ Πουλυδάμαντος); see also *Od.* 22.279–280 (Κτήσιππος δ' Εὔμαιον ὑπὲρ σάκος ἔγχεϊ μακρῷ | ὦμον ἐπέγραψεν· τὸ δ' ὑπέρπτατο, πῖπτε δ' ἔραζε) and *Od.* 24.229 (γραπτῦς ἀλεείνων).
²⁰Powell 2002: 10.
²¹The literature on the advent of literacy and writing is legion. See, e.g., Baurain 1997: 444–53; Powell 2002; Thomas 1992; 2009; Wilson 2013; Wirbelauer 2005; Woodard 2010.
²²Voutrias 2007: 266.

the alphabet, which had hitherto been unknown as I think, to the Greeks; and presently as time went on the sound and the form of the letters were changed. At this time the Greeks that dwelt round them for the most part were Ionians; who having been taught the letters by the Phoenicians, used them with a few changes of form, and in so doing, they gave to these characters (as indeed was but just, seeing that the Phoenicians had brought them into Hellas) the name of Phoenician.[23]

It appears that the "Greeks of the archaic and classical periods retained the memory that their ancestors had received the alphabet from the Phoenicians."[24] The evidence from Herodotus is backed by the epigraphic record. Here the earliest examples of Greek writing come from places where there has been Greek–Phoenician contact.[25] The most famous one is the so-called Cup of Nestor found at the western Greek colony in Pithekoussai where there has certainly been Greek–Phoenician contact:[26]

Νέστορος: ε[2-3]ι: εὔποτ[ον]: ποτέριο[ν:]   ←
hὸς δ' ἀ‹ν› τόδε π[ίε]σι: ποτερί[ο]: αὐτίκα κῆνον   ←
hίμερ[ος]: hαιρ]έσει: καλλιστε[φά]νο: Ἀφροδίτες   ←

I am the cup of Nestor, good to drink from. Whoever drinks from this cup, may desire of fair-crowned Aphrodite seize him.[27]

Herodotus' view that the alphabet was taken over from the Phoenicians finds further support in a fragment from the elegiac poetry of Critias (ca. 460–403 BCE) who attributes the invention of the letters to the Phoenicians and regards them as "preserving discourse":

Φοίνικες δ' ηὗρον γράμματ' ἀλεξίλογα.[28]

Much of the interpretation of the passage from Critias depends on the translation of the *hapax legomenon* ἀλεξίλογα. The fragment lists several technological advances. While the Thessalian chair, for example, "is the most comfortable seat for the limbs" (Θεσσαλικὸς δὲ θρόνος γυίων τρυφερωτάτη ἕδρα. | εὐναίου δὲ λέχους †κάλλος† ἔχει), the line about the art of writing is the only one that qualifies the invention.[29] If we interpret ἀλεξίλογα in the light of the other evidence from the fifth century it may be possible to argue that we have another instance here that links writing to the preserving of memory as is the case in those episodes claiming that writing was an invention of the Greeks.

There is, nevertheless, also a different tradition found in Greek literature that attributes the invention of writing to a Greek hero or divinity.[30] The beginning is made by Aeschylus' drama *Prometheus Bound*. Here the Titan claims that he introduced humankind to a variety of cultural tools—amongst them the ability to combine letters (γραμμάτων τε συνθέσεις), i.e. to write:

---

[23]Herodotus, *Hist*. 5.58; translation according to Goodley 1922: 63, 65. See also the similar view echoed in Aristotle, *fr.* 501 (Rose).
[24]Voutrias 2007: 266.
[25]See Jeffery 1990: 347 (inscription from Rhodes [ϙοραϙο ημι ϙυλιχς]) and Wirbelauer 2005: 194–96 for further evidence of early Greek writing on pottery.
[26]See Ridgway 1994, and on the polis itself Fischer-Hansen, Nielsen, and Ampolo 2004.
[27]Greek text according to ML 1; English translation according to Osborne 1996: 117.
[28]Critias, *fr*. B2.9 (West) = *fr*. B2.10 (DK). The translation of ἀλεξίλογα follows Gerber 1999: 463; *LSJ*, 63 gives "prompting discourse"; Montanari 2015: 84 provides "one who wards off words"; Diels and Kranz 1952: 377 translate "Buchstaben als Helfer der Gedanken."
[29]Ceccarelli 2013: 65.
[30]See the extensive discussion in Ceccarelli 2013: 66–71.

> ἦν δ' οὐδὲν αὐτοῖς οὔτε χείματος τέκμαρ
> 455 οὔτ' ἀνθεμώδους ἦρος οὔτε καρπίμου
> θέρους βέβαιον, ἀλλ' ἄτερ γνώμης τὸ πᾶν
> ἔπρασσον, ἔστε δή σφιν ἀντολὰς ἐγὼ
> ἄστρων ἔδειξα τάς τε δυσκρίτους δύσεις.
> καὶ μὴν ἀριθμόν, ἔξοχον σοφισμάτων,
> 460 ἐξηῦρον αὐτοῖς, γραμμάτων τε συνθέσεις,
> μνήμην ἁπάντων, μουσομήτορ' ἐργάνην.

They had no sign either of winter or of flowery spring or of fruitful summer, on which they could depend but managed everything without judgment, until I taught them to discern the risings of the stars and their settings, which are difficult to distinguish. Aye, and numbers, too, chiefest of sciences, I invented for them, and the combining of letters, creative mother of the Muses' arts, with which to hold all things in memory.[31]

Though the persons who invent writing can be interchangeable, the message seems to be clear: "Writing, intended as the ability to assemble letters, is defined by its potential for memory."[32] With such a focus we enter a cultural-historical dimension, i.e. the preservation of Greekness for later generations.

In the following we will look at several poleis that succumbed to the "temptation of the scribes" towards the end of the archaic period.[33] We will focus on Crete—the island, where some Greek historians have even argued that the art of writing was invented.[34]

## 2. THE CONTRACT WITH SPENSITHIOS, THE SCRIBE

The clearest evidence for the existence of scribes in archaic Crete comes from the polis of Datala in northern Crete.[35] It is an inscription on a bronze plate now in the British Museum, London (BM inv. 1969.4-2.1) resembling a "mitra" (abdominal guard).[36] "The provenance of this inscribed bronze mitra or mitra-like object is not known. The alphabet, particularly the use of two concentric circles for *omega*...suggests that it comes from somewhere in the vicinity of Lyktos and possibly Aphrati."[37] It is quite small (25.2 × ca. 13cm) for a mitra proper and was hammered flat for reuse, i.e. the engraving of the inscription.[38] The bronze plate is inscribed on both sides. Despite some debate about the character of the inscription it appears that both sides are part of the same inscription.[39]

---

[31]Aeschylus, *Prometheus Bound* 454–461; English translation according to Smyth 1922: 257.
[32]Ceccarelli 2013: 66.
[33]The term is taken from Detienne 1992: 64 ("la tentation du scribe"); see also Jaillard 2013.
[34]See Dosiadas (von Kydonia) who deviates from the more standard view that writing was handed down from Phoenicians; Δοσιάδης δὲ ἐν Κρήτῃ φησὶν εὑρεθῆναι αὐτά· (FrGrHist III 458, *fr.* 6) and also FrGrHist III 468 *fr.* 1.74 (ταῖς δὲ Μούσαις δοθῆναι παρὰ τοῦ πατρὸς τὴν τῶν γραμμάτων εὕρεσιν καὶ τὴν τῶν ἐπῶν σύνθεσιν τὴν προσαγορευομένην ποιητικήν), where we can infer that the alphabet was invented by the Muses in Crete before the Phoenicians exported it.
[35]On the polis see Perlman 2004: 1155–57. The exact location is uncertain and archaeologists generally situate the polis in north central Crete between Knossos and Lato; see the proposal in Viviers 1994.
[36]See the detailed description in Jeffery and Morpurgo-Davies 1970: 119–20.
[37]Gagarin and Perlman 2016: 182, following Jeffery and Morpurgo-Davies 1970: 122–23; van Effenterre and Ruzé are certain that the plate comes from the sanctuary at Aphrati ("...provenant sans doute d'un sanctuaire d'Afrati...qui a fourni d'autres objets au marché des Antiquités").
[38]For photograph and drawing see Bile 1988: 39 [drawing] and plate II.
[39]Gagarin and Perlman 2016: 182; contrast van Effenterre 1973: 45 ("ce ne sont plus des privilèges accordés par a cité qui sont énoncés dans le contrat de travail") and more cautious Koerner 1981, who proposes that side B 11–17 is in fact an addendum ("Es ist sicher richtig, daß hier ein neues Thema beginnt..., das aber durchaus noch zum Arbeitsvertrag gehört..." [188]).

Though there is a possibility that one line of text is lost at the bottom of side A, the *vacat* after [πρειγ]ίστωι on side B seems to indicate that the end of the inscription is preserved here. The text, written in boustrophedon, reads as follows:

A

    Θιοί· ἔϝαδε Δαταλεῦσι καὶ ἐσπένσαμες πόλις     ←
    Σπενσιθίωι ἀπὸ πυλᾶν πέντε ἀπ' ἑκάστας θροπά-     →
    ν τε καὶ ἀτέλειαν πάντων αὐτῶι τε καὶ γενιᾶι ὤ-
    ς κα πόλι τὰ δαμόσια τά τε θιήια καὶ τἀνθρώπινα
5     ποινικάζεν τε καὶ μναμονεῦϝην. ποινικάζεν δὲ
    [π]όλι καὶ μναμονεῦϝεν τὰ δαμόσια μήτε τὰ θιήι-
    α μήτε τἀνθρώπινα μηδέν' ἄλον αἰ μὴ Σπενσίθ[ι]-
    [ο]ν αὐτόν τε καὶ γενιὰν τõνυ, αἰ μὴ ἐπαίροι τ-
    ε καὶ κέλοιτο ἢ αὐτὸς Σπενσίθιος ἢ γενιὰ
10     [τ]õνυ ὅσοι δρομῆς εἶεν τῶν [υἱ]ῶν οἱ πλίες.
    μισθὸν δὲ δόμεν τõ ἐνιαυτõ τῶι ποινι[κ]-
    [α]στᾶι πεντήϝοντά τε προϝόος κλεύκιο-
    ς κηνδυ[ . ]ε[ . . ]ς ἱκατιδαρκμίος ἢ καλ[ϝ]-
    ός· δόμεν δὲ τὸ κλεῦϝος ἐς τõ μόρο ὄ-
15     πω κα λῆι ἐλέσθαι. αἰ δὲ μὴ δοίη τὸ κλε[ῦϝ]-
    [ο]ς αιδε . . . σ[c.3-4]ᾳ[ . ]εσδ . . . ς ϝόσμ-
    ος ἐπεσταϝὼς ἀ[c. 4]ι[c. 4]λε[ . ]εκ[ . ]
    [1?]σαι ἀπλοπίᾳ[ι . ]ᾳ[ . ] αἰ μὴ αὐτοισ-
    ι . . . πολ[ . . ]αϝεσημεν τῶι ϝόσ-
    [μωι c.7]ε[ . ] τεμένια πε[ . ] . ϝ-
    [c.2] τὸ ϝῖσον λακὲν ϝό[σμωι ?] ασ[c.4]
    [ . . . . . . . . c.17 . . . . . . . . ]ᾳ[ . . . c.6 . . .]

B

    τὸ ϝῖσον λακὲν τὸν ποινικαστάν· καὶ παρῆμε-     ←
    ν καὶ συνῆμεν ἐπί τε θιηίων καὶ ἐπ' ἀνθρωπί-     →
    νων πάντε ὄπε καὶ ὁ ϝόσμος εἴη καὶ τὸν ποινι-
    καστάν, καὶ ὅτιμί κα θιῶι ἰαρεὺς μῆι δίαλο-
5     [ς] θύεν τε τὰ δαμόσια θύματα τὸ‹ν› ποινικαστὰ-
    ν καὶ τὰ τεμένια ἔκεν. μήδ' ἐπάγραν ἦμ[ε-]
    [ν] μήδε ῥύτιον αἰλẽν τὸν ποινικαστάν. δ-
    ίκα δέ, ὄτερόν κα .ώληται ὁ ποινικασ[τ]-
    [ὰ]ς αἷπερ οἱ ἄλοι χρήσεται, ἢν ϝόσ[[π]]-
10     μοι ἁ δίκα ϝοι τέλεται, ἄλε δὲ οὐδὲ
    ἕν. δίκαια ἐς ἀνδρήιον δώσει δ-
    έκα πέλεϝυς κρέων αἴ κα ϝōι ἄλο[ι]
    [ἀπ?]άρϝωνται, καὶ τὸ ἐπενιαύτιον· τὸ
    δὲ λάκσιον συνϝαλεῖ. ἄλο δὲ μ[ηδ]-
15     [ὲ]ν ἐπάνανϝον ἦμεν αἴ κα μὴ λῆι
    δόμεν. ἦμεν δὲ τὰ θιήια τ[ῶι]
    [ c. 4]ίστωι. *vacat*

*Translation*:

A

1-5   Gods. The Dataleis decided and we the polis promise Spensithios, from the tribes five from each, rations and full tax exemption to himself and his offspring so that they both write and remember for the polis public matters both sacred and secular

5-10   No one other than Spensithios himself and his offspring is to write and remember for the polis public matters, neither sacred nor secular, unless chosen or bidden by either Spensithios himself or his offspring, the majority of his sons who are adults.

11-15   As an annual stipend (the polis?) is to give the *poinikastas* fifty *prokooi* of must, [ — ] worth twenty drachmas (?), or bronze; it is to provide the must from whatever portion he should wish to take (the must).

15-16   If he (?) should not give the must [ — ]

16-17   [ — ] the *kosmos* who is in charge [ — ]

18-19   [ — ] without fault [ — ] not to them [ — ]

19-21   [ — ] to the *kos*[*mos* — ] revenue from sacred precinct [ — ]

21   [ — ] is to obtain the equal to the *ko*[*smos*? — ]

B

1-6   The *ponikastas* is to obtain the equal; wheresoever the *kosmos* should be, so too the *poinikastas* is to be present and attend at both sacred and secular (activities), and for whatever god there should be no clear (?) priest, the *poinikastas* is to perform the public sacrifices and to have revenue from the sanctuary (?).

6-11   There is to be no seizure of the person nor of the property of the *poinikastas*. As for trial, whichever the *poinikastas* wishes, he is to use, just as the others, or his trial will be before a *kosmos*, but not in any other way.

11-16   (As) *dikaia* to the *andreion* he shall give ten axes of meat when the others offer the first fruits (?) and the yearly obligation (?); but he will collect (?) the *laksion*. Nothing other is to be required unless he should wish to give.

16-17   The sacred matters are to be for the [ — ].[40]

After an invocation of the gods, known from other Cretan inscriptions,[41] the text stipulates the duties of a certain Spensithios and his descendants (αὐτῶι τε καὶ γενιᾶι) which they are to perform for the polis of Datala. The name is not elsewhere attested in the Greek world.[42] He is hired to write and remember (ποινικάζεν τε καὶ μναμονεῦϝην) the public matters of the polis, both sacred and secular (τά τε θιήια καὶ τἀνθρώπινα).[43] It is clear from the inscription that writing and remembering are two distinct procedures and not simply the description of the process of one function, i.e. first

---

[40]Greek text and English translation according to Gagarin and Perlman (2016), DA1 = *Nomima* I.22 = SEG 27.631.
[41]In the following inscriptions from Gortyn the same invocation [Θιοί] is found: *IC* IV 43 Ba.Bb; *IC* IV 51; *IC* IV 64; *IC* IV 65; *IC* IV 72 I.1; *IC* IV 78 and *IC* IV 80. For other occurrences in Crete see *IC* I xvi 26; *IC* I xvi 32. This invocation is not limited to Crete; see, e.g., *IG* VII 2789, 2809, 2811-2818, 2820, 3083 (Lebadeia/Boetia); *LSCG* 49 (Piraeus), *LSCG* 96 (Mykonos), *LSCG* 92 (Eretria), *LSCG* 102 (Amorgos); on the problem see Pounder 1984, who argues for an apotropaic function of the invocation and traces it back to Near Eastern origin.
[42]See Fraser and Matthews 1987: 410. Gagarin and Perlman 2016: 190 propose—on the basis of the name—that Spensithios' ancestors may have been priests.
[43]See the almost identical phrase in *IC* IV 72 X.42–43 (τὰ θῖνα καὶ | τὰ ἀντρόπινα).

remembering and then writing it down from memory.⁴⁴ That they are listed together may be an indication that "the duties of scribes had probably grown out of those held by individuals responsible for remembering and announcing public business to the early Greek community before the employment of writing."⁴⁵ At the same time it points to the continuing existence of aspects or preliterate culture even after the advent of writing. As compensation for his duties, Spensithios will be exempt from taxes and receive an allowance (θροπά-|ν τε καὶ ἀτέλειαν). The privileges granted are extended to his descendants, provided that they also serve as scribes to the city. This shows that the office was understood as hereditary;⁴⁶ "the absence of a term limit, and the apparent inability of the polis to modify or rescind the agreement are extraordinary and differ markedly from the (probable) one-year tenure of the *kosmos*."⁴⁷ That one office should remain in a certain family is reminiscent of a note in Herodotus where he states that at Sparta flute players, heralds and butchers inherit their trade from their fathers (ἐκδέκονται τὰς πατρωίας τέχνας) and that nobody dares to usurp their places.⁴⁸ If we look at the description of his duties it becomes clear that his civil status must have been very high.⁴⁹ We do not know how and where Spensithios acquired his writing skills but since it is decreed that his descendants will continue the office it may be safe to assume that he himself taught (or will teach) his sons the ability to write. Who wrote the contract with Spensithios and the polis we also do not know, but it seems likely that it was Spensithios himself—unlike in cuneiform and Aramaic documents the inscription does not list the name of the scribe.⁵⁰ The size of the bronze plate also suggests that it was the private copy of Spensithios, probably copied from a larger inscription originally written in stone.⁵¹ Maybe Spensithios realised that he was in a way excluded from the political arena and somehow suspected there would be a possibility that he was seen as a threat because he mastered a technique "that eluded the ordinary citizens."⁵² To avoid conflict, then, he would keep his own copy of the contract to be able to refer to it when needed. The detail of the stipulation suggests that this is the earliest record of the office for the very first ποινικάστας of the polis of Datala.⁵³ The civic status of Spensithios has been the subject of debate, but since he is a member of the *andreion*⁵⁴ (δίκαια ἐς ἀνδρήιον δώσει δ-|έκα πέλερυς κρέων, αἴ κα φώι ἄλο[ι] | [ἀπ ?] ἄρρωνται) and can act as priest (καὶ ὅτιμί κα θιῶι ἱαρεὺς μὴ ἰδιαλο-|[ς] θύεν τε τὰ δαμόσια θύματα τὸ⟨ν⟩ ποινικαστὰ-|ν καὶ τὰ τεμένια ἔκεν) we can assume that he was a citizen.⁵⁵

A Gortynian decree honouring a certain Dionysios (*IC* IV 64 = *Nomima* I.8) is often compared to the Spensithios decree.⁵⁶ Here, the polis of Gortyn and those living in Aulon (Γόρτυνς ἐπίπανσα | ϙ' οἱ ἐν Ἀϝλōνι ϝοικίοντες) grant Dionysios exemption from taxes (ἀτελεία) as a reward for his good

---

⁴⁴Following Gagarin 2008: 120.
⁴⁵Hawke 2011: 124; see also Ruzé 1992: 83–84 who argues for a continuity between the scribes and the Homeric *demiourgoi*.
⁴⁶Koerner 1981: 184.
⁴⁷Gagarin and Perlman 2016: 192.
⁴⁸Herodotus, *Hist.* 6.60: συμφέρονται δὲ καὶ τάδε Αἰγυπτίοισι Λακεδαιμόνιοι· οἱ κήρυκες αὐτῶν καὶ αὐληταὶ καὶ μάγειροι ἐκδέκονται τὰς πατρωίας τέχνας, καὶ αὐλητής τε αὐλητέωγίνεται καὶ μάγειρος μαγείρου καὶ κῆρυξ κήρυκος· οὐ κατὰ λαμπροφωνίην ἐπιτιθέμενοι ἄλλοι σφέας παρακληίουσι, ἀλλὰ κατὰ τὰ πάτρια ἐπιτελέουσι.
⁴⁹See the discussion in Gorlin 1988.
⁵⁰See, e.g., TAD B2.4 line 16 (כתב עתרשורי בר נבוראבן ספרא זנה); TAD B3.1 line 20 (כתב נתן בר ענני ספרא זנה).
⁵¹Gagarin and Perlman 2016: 182.
⁵²Ismard 2017: 28 quoting Ruzé 1992.
⁵³Jeffery and Morpurgo-Davies (1970: 148–49) followed by Gagarin and Perlman (2016: 189). Beattie (1975: 22) assumes the Spensithios' "father and grandfather may have held the office to which he is now appointed." If that is the case one wonders why the extensive stipulations are necessary to be listed again.
⁵⁴See Seelentag (2015: 374–443) on the institution and social role of the *andreion*.
⁵⁵Thus already Jeffery and Morpurgo-Davies (1970: 149, followed by Gagarin and Perlman (2016: 189) and Seelentag (2015: 312–19), who ponders the idea that Spensithios became a citizen when being appointed as scribe. A different view is presented by van Effenterre (1973: 37–39 and 1979) who regards Spensithios as a foreigner while Ismard (2017: 28) speculates that his expertise "would most often have been occupied in the classical period by public slaves."
⁵⁶See Kristensen 2012: 33–35.

service in the past.⁵⁷ Since the decree specifically stipulates that he shall receive "a citizen's justice and a house in Aulon inside of Pyrgos and a plot other than (agricultural?) lands"⁵⁸ (ϝα]στίαν δίκαν καὶ ϝοικίαν ἐν Ἀϝλôνι ἐ-|νδὸς Πύργο καὶ ϝοικόπεδον ἐϰσοι γᾶν), we can probably assume that Dionysios is not a citizen of Gortyn.⁵⁹ In contrast to the Spensithios decree, *IC* IV 64 only honours past services rendered and is not concerned about the future actions or duties of Dionysios.

As mentioned above, Spensithios' duties are twofold: he is to serve as "scribe" and "rememberer."⁶⁰ The word for "scribe" (ποινικαστάς) is only attested in the Spensithios' decree.⁶¹ An inscription from Eltynia also mentions πονικήια,⁶² i.e. "writings," which resembles the otherwise common τὰ ἐγράμμενα used elsewhere in Cretan inscription to denote law. The inscription sheds little light on the office of the scribe but πονικήια, like ποινικαστάς, seems to be related to φοῖνιξ referring either to the colour "purple" or to Phoenicia.⁶³ That letters (or writing) is the context can be gleaned from a fifth-century inscription from the Ionian city of Teos where sanctions are listed against a person who defaces the stelai:

```
35                      ὃς ἂν ταστήλ-
        ας : ἐν ἧισιν ἡπαρὴ : γέγρ-
        απται : ἢ κατάξει : ἢ φοιν-
        ικήια : ἐκκόψε[ι :] ἢ ἀφανέ-
        ας ποιήσει : κênον ἀπόλ-
40      λυσθαι : καὶ αὐτὸν : καὶ γ-
        ένος [τὸ κένο.]
```

Whoever (takes) the stelai on which the curse is written and breaks them or cuts the letters out or makes them illegible, he shall die, both himself and [his] family.⁶⁴

Related to ποινικαστάς is the word φοινικόγραφος attested in two inscriptions from Hellenistic Lesbos and again at Teos.⁶⁵ All these words draw attention to the foreign, i.e. Phoenician origin of the skill of writing. That they first occur in Crete may not be surprising as we know of at least one Phoenician inscription at Knossos and of large volumes of Cypro-Phoenician-type lekythoi at several major settlements such as Gortyn and Eleutherna.⁶⁶ This points to some form of influence and exchange.⁶⁷ It is not possible to argue for Crete as the place of the first introduction of the

---

⁵⁷"All of Gortyn," which only occurs here, has to be distinguished from the Gortynians, a term that only seems to refer to the free citizens. Maybe it is used here—like πόλι πάνσαι in *IC* IV 13 e2 = *Nomima* I.1—to state that the decree was accepted unanimously.
⁵⁸Gagarin and Perlman 2016: 330.
⁵⁹Kristensen (2012: 34) rightly states "he was naturalised in the polis of Gortyn, as were his descendants."
⁶⁰See the detailed study of the "office" in Seelentag 2015: 194–203.
⁶¹Beattie (1975: 28–31) departs from the scholarly consensus and traces ποινικάζεν back to ποινή. This is hardly convincing and has been rightly refuted by Edwards and Edwards (1977).
⁶²[ — τὰ] πονικήια | τάδε | ἄ κ. [—]. Text according to Gagarin and Perlman 2016: 261; first edition in Kritzas 2010: 3–23.
⁶³See the discussion in Edwards and Edwards 1974. Later scholia infer from the relation to φοῖνιξ that it was Phoenix, the teacher of Achilles (see Homer, *Il.* 9.485–622), who invented the skill of writing (texts in Ceccarelli 2013: 357–59).
⁶⁴*Nomima* I.104 = ML 30; English translation according to Fornara 1983: 63. For a detailed treatment of the *Dirae Teiae* see Hagedorn 2005.
⁶⁵*IG* XII/2.96 (φοινικόγραφος Ἰ[α.........ἀλ]κειος | [γρα]μμ[ά]τευς M — — — — — — — ) and *IG* XII/2.97 ([— — — στεφανώθεντες] ὑπὸ τᾶς πόλιος | [καὶ — — — — ὁ φ]οινικόγραφος Ἕρμαι. | [ὁ δεῖνα — — — ]εἴδαος); *Nomima* I.105 D19–21 (ἢ [φ]-|οινικογρα-|φέων).
⁶⁶See Peckham 2014: 157 and Wallace 2010: 210–12.
⁶⁷Wirbelauer (2005: 189) observes that every place where there was Greek–Phoenician contact could serve as a possible place for such exchange; see also Woodard (2010: 39–42), who remarks that all that was required for the adaptation of the Phoenician alphabet by the Greeks was "a bit of Greek ingenuity situated within the context of a Phoenician social and commercial presence" (41).

(adapted) Phoenician alphabet but the epigraphic evidence allows for the conclusion that in Crete the memory of the foreign origin was maintained.

What exactly Spensithios is to write, the decree does not say and it has been observed that we do not have any other written public texts in archaic Crete than laws.[68] This would allow for the conclusion that he wrote down the decisions and stipulations the city of Datala wanted to display publicly as law.[69] If this assumption is correct, Spensithios would play a crucial role in the formation of the legal culture of the polis while at the same time he was responsible for remembering the proceedings in court. Furthermore, a law from the polis of Eleutherna allows for additional evidence what a scribe was to record:

> [ — . αἴ τι]ς πέρανδε πλέοι ἢ θιαρὸς ἢ . [ — — ]
> [ — — ]ος διαλαιη ἐκσενιοϝτιτό[ς — — ]
> [ — — ]οπιος. αἴ τις τõινυ ποινικα[κσίε ?[70] — ]
> [ — — τ]õινυ μὴ δικάζοντας τὸς ζ[ — — ]
> 5  [ — — ] ἀπάτος ἤμεν. αἰ δὲ καρπόσαιτο [ — — ]
>
> — . If someone sails abroad, either a *thiaros* or —
> — should be away (?) in the sixth year (?) —
> — . If someone serves as writer for him —
> — those who do not decide the case for him, the —
> — are to be immune. But if he should harvest —[71]

The law seems to address questions of the legal status of citizens who have been abroad. The absentee is described as being a *thiaros*, i.e. "a sacred envoy sent either to consult an oracle or to represent Eleutherna at a distant festival."[72] The context appears to be issues regarding the property of the person who is abroad. If that is the case, the phrase αἴ τις τõινυ ποινικα[κσίε could refer to "the use of writing in judicial procedure"[73] or that the absent citizen was able to enlist the service of the scribe to be a representative for his claims.[74] If the latter is the case, the memory of the scribe would have been important to the solution of the conflict.

The verb μναμονεῦϝην used in the Spensithios decree is not otherwise attested in Cretan epigraphic material.[75] Several laws from Gortyn, however, mention the office of the *mnamon*. The office is not restricted to the island of Crete as we encounter them, for example, in a law from Halikarnassos and later as archivists at Athens.[76] At Gortyn the *mnamon* accompanies other

---

[68] Gagarin 2008: 120–21.
[69] Gagarin 2003: 66–67.
[70] Restoration following Gagarin and Perlman (2016: 233), who think of a verb here. *Nomima* I.14 restores ποινικά[ζοντας to achieve symmetry with μὴ δικάζοντας in line 4.
[71] *IC* II. xii.11 = *Nomima* I.14; English translation according to Gagarin and Perlman 2016: 233.
[72] Gagarin and Perlman 2016: 234. For the extensive contacts of Eleutherna to the rest of Greek and Cretan world, see Erickson 2004.
[73] Gagarin and Perlman 2016: 235.
[74] Seelentag 2015: 202.
[75] Raubitschek (1970: 155) wants to interpret μναμονεῦϝην as indicating that the scribe's duty "consisted not only in recording the public decisions but also in reading aloud the texts of the documents which had been recorded in the past." As reading aloud—as known from Athens—is not mentioned in the decree or any other Cretan passages referring to the *mnamon*, this is unlikely.
[76] See ML 32 and Aristotle, *Pol.* 1321b (ἑτέρα δ' ἀρχὴ πρὸς ἣν ἀναγράφεσθαι δεῖ τά τε ἴδια συμβόλαια [35] καὶ τὰς κρίσεις τὰς ἐκ τῶν δικαστηρίων· παρὰ δὲ τοῖς αὐτοῖς τούτοις καὶ τὰς γραφὰς τῶν δικῶν γίνεσθαι δεῖ καὶ τὰς εἰσαγωγάς. ἐνιαχοῦ μὲν οὖν μερίζουσι καὶ ταύτην εἰς πλείους, ἔστι δ' οὗ μία κυρία τούτων πάντων· καλοῦνται δὲ ἱερομνήμονες καὶ ἐπιστάται καὶ μνήμονες καὶ τούτοις ἄλλα [40] ὀνόματα σύνεγγυς); see the discussion in Carawan 2008.

officials,⁷⁷ just like Spensithios who accompanies the *kosmos* when conducting public business (πάντε ὄπε καὶ ὁ ϙόσμος εἴη καὶ τὸν ποινι-|κασταν). He seems to be a specialist with detailed knowledge of laws and legal procedure and was able to repeat older laws and decisions of the polis from memory.⁷⁸ Whether there was only one *mnamon* for each polis is a matter of debate. Since at Gortyn we know, for example, of the "rememberer of the *esprattai*" ([μνάμ]ονος τō τōν ἐσπραττᾶν)⁷⁹ and the Great Code, when regulating adoption, speaks of a "rememberer for the foreigners' official" (ὁ δὲ μνάμον ὁ τō κσεν-|ίο ἀποδότο τōι ἀπορρεθέντι),⁸⁰ we may assume that—at least at Gortyn—there were more than one *mnamon* working for the polis.⁸¹ Though Spensithios is never called a *mnamon*, "it seems likely that as an assistant to the *kosmos*, he would be fulfilling the same function as the *mnamon* at Gortyn, though he would also have the additional duty of writing."⁸² Maybe the reason for not calling Spensithios a *mnamon* is that the polis of Datala regarded the act of writing his most important task.⁸³

The *mnamon* seems to be related to the office of the *gnomon* only known from one sixth-century inscription from Gortyn:⁸⁴

— — ] λέβητας κα[τ]αστᾶσαι ϝέκαστον. | τρι[ō]ν ϝετίον τὸν ἀϝτὸν μὴ ϙοσμε͂ν, | δέκα μὲν γνόμονας, | πέντε [δὲ κσ]ενίος | *vac.*⁸⁵

—each is to pay—cauldrons. The same person is not to serve as *kosmos* again for three years, as *gnomones* for ten years, and as the foreigners' official for five years *vac.*⁸⁶

The context is a law prohibiting the iteration of office. Such laws are well known from Crete as, for example, one of the oldest Cretan inscriptions, found at Dreros forbids the repeated tenure of the office of *kosmos*.⁸⁷ Apart from the fact that the office of gnomon is mentioned in connection with two further offices one can only speculate what he was.⁸⁸ A scribe seems unlikely and so are the duties known to us from Athens, "where the *gnomones* were inspectors of the sacred olive trees."⁸⁹ Aristotle mentions that the members of the council in Crete made their decisions not on the basis of written law but αὐτογνώμονας.⁹⁰ This would imply that they were some sort of decision makers, who may serve as judges and who use what they know while in office.⁹¹

---

⁷⁷See *IC* IV 42B (τὸν δικαστ-| ὰν καὶ τὸμ μνάμονα); *IC* IV 72 IX.32 (ὁ δικαστὰς κō μνάμον), XI.16 (ὁ δὲ μνάμον ὁ τō κσεν- | ίο ἀποδότο τōι ἀπορρεθέντι), XI.52–55 ([τ]ōι | μνάμονι προτέταρτον ἀντὶ μ-|αί̣τυρος πεντεκαιδεκαδρόμο | ἒ πρείγονος.) and possibly *IC* IV 87 (παριόντον τōν ἐσπραττ[ᾶν καὶ τō] | [μνάμ]ονος τō τōν ἐσπραττᾶν).
⁷⁸Koerner (1981: 184) who calls him "ein lebendes Archiv."
⁷⁹See *IC* IV 87.8 = *Nomima* I.97.
⁸⁰See *IC* IV 72 XI.10-17 = *Nomima* II.40.
⁸¹Seelentag 2015: 196–97.
⁸²Gagarin and Perlman 2016: 75.
⁸³Gagarin 2008: 121.
⁸⁴See Seelentag 2015: 194.
⁸⁵*IC* IV.14 p-g₂ = *Nomima* I.82.
⁸⁶English translation according to Gagarin and Perlman 2016: 279.
⁸⁷*Nomima* I.81.
⁸⁸See Koerner 1987: 455–57.
⁸⁹Gagarin and Perlman 2016: 280.
⁹⁰Aristotle, *Pol.* 1272a (τὸ γὰρ ἀνυπεύθυνον καὶ τὸ διὰ βίου μεῖζόν ἐστι γέρας τῆς ἀξίας αὐτοῖς, καὶ τὸ μὴ κατὰ γράμματα ἄρχειν ἀλλ' αὐτογνώμονας ἐπισφαλές).
⁹¹Gagarin and Perlman (2016: 281) draw attention to *IC* I.x.2 = *Nomima* II.80 (Eltynia) where γ[ι]γνόσκεν is used meaning "to judge."

## 3. PROTECTION OF AND PROBLEMS WITH SCRIBES

Though the relevant passage of the inscription (B 6–11) is difficult to interpret,[92] it appears that the decree also protects Spensithios by providing him "a choice of legal procedures for adjudicating any dispute."[93] In probable contrast to other citizens, he was allowed to have a trial before the *kosmos*, the highest official of a Cretan polis.[94] This does not necessarily mean a more competent solution to a legal dispute but rather an increase in the prestige of one party.[95] The (possible) involvement of highest official, then, protects Spensithios and his descendants from legal action against them. Additionally, it is forbidden to seize person or property of the scribe (μήδ' ἐπάγραν ἦμε-|[ν] μήδε ῥύτιον αἰλῆν τὸν ποινικαστάν...). "The seizure could be intended as a means to collect an unpaid debt or fine."[96] This stipulation implies that seizure was probably allowed at Datala and that the scribe is exempted from it.

That scribes were offered special protection is further attested by a bronze tablet (πίναξ), now in the museum at Olympia (Inv. 771).[97] It preserves a decree of the Eleans (ἁ ϝράτρα τοῖς ϝαλείοις) and records protection and guarantees for a man called Patrias,[98] who is later identified as a scribe (Πατρίας ὁ γροφεύς):

> ἁ ϝράτρα τοῖς ϝαλείοις· Πατρίαν θαρρῆν καὶ γενεὰν καὶ ταὐτο͂·
> αἰ ζέ τις κατιαραύσειε, ϝάρρεν, ὀρ ϝαλείο· αἰ ζὲ μἐπιθεῖαν τὰ ζί-
> καια ὂρ μέγιστον τέλος ἔχοι καὶ τοὶ βασιλᾶες, ζέκα μναῖς κα
> 4   ἀποτίνοι ϝέκαστος τõν μὲ 'πιποεόντον κα(θ)θυταῖς τοῖ Ζὶ Ὀλυν-
> πίοι, ἐπένποι ζέ κ' ἐλλανοζίκας, καὶ τἆλλα ζίκαια ἐπενπ-
> έτο ἁ ζαμιοργία· αἰ ζὲ μὲ 'νποι, ζίφυιον ἀποτινέτο ἐν μαστρά-
> αι· αἰ ζέ τις τὸν αἰτιαθέντα ζικαιõν ἰμάσκοι, ἐν ταῖ ζεκαμναῖαι κ' ἐ-
> 8   νέχο[ιτ]ο, αἰ ϝειζὸς ἰμάσκοι. καὶ Πατρίας ὁ γροφεὺς ταὐτά κα πάσκοι,
> [αἴ τ]ιν' [ἀζ]ικέοι. ὁ π[ί]ναξ ἰαρὸς Ὀλυνπίαι *vacat*.[99]

Decree of the Eleans. Patrias and his descendants and his property shall be immune. If somebody curses (him), he shall be sent into exile as in the case of an Elean. If he who holds the highest office and the *baseileis* do not impose the fines, let each of those who fail to impose them pay a penalty of ten minas dedicated to Olympian Zeus (and) the Hellanodica shall enforce this (and) the body of the *damiourgoi* shall enforce the other fines. If it (he?) does not enforce this, let it (him?) pay double the penalty in his/its accounting. If anyone punishes somebody who is in the right, he shall pay a fine of ten minas if he does so wittingly. And Patrias the scribe will suffer the same penalty if he does somebody an injustice. This tablet is sacred at Olympia.

In many ways the inscription is close to the Spensithios decree. Though *Nomima* I.23 does not record the specific duties of Patrias we can, nevertheless, assume that they were similar to Spensithios' at Datala. Since both Patrias and his descendants are placed under protection one could

---
[92] See the discussion in Gschnitzer 1974: 271–74 and Koerner 1981: 188.
[93] Gagarin and Perlman 2016: 194. Seelentag (2015: 317) proposes that the decree contains a significant modification of Spensithios' legal status.
[94] On the role and status of the office of *kosmos* see Seelentag 2009.
[95] Seelentag 2015: 318. Van Effenterre (1973: 44–45) even proposes that the special status of Spensithios is equal to the one of the *kosmos*.
[96] Gagarin and Perlman 2016: 194.
[97] For photographs see Jeffery 1990: plate 43, No. 15.
[98] Πατρίαν is seen as a personal name here (cf. Koerner 1981: 191) and not as related to φρατρίαν, i.e. meaning "gens" (thus Buck 1955: 260).
[99] Text according to *Nomima* I.23 = SEG 29.402 = *IvO* 2.

argue that the family was probably not native to the Elis.[100] Whether Patrias' family also served as scribes is not stated—in the light of *Nomima* I.22 this can be a possibility. The phrase Πατρίας ὁ γροφεύς allows for the assumption that he was the only scribe employed at Elis.[101] This would have given him influence and status and the inscriptions seems to support that when it allows for the possibility that Patrias could do others injustice (ταὐτά κα πάσκοι, | [αἴ τ]ιν' [ἀζ]ικέοι). Since the last clause is not part of the protection of Patrias but seems to serve as protection against him it is likely that he is not exempt from punishment. This implies that—at least at Elis—even a scribe has to comply to the laws of the polis. The plate is deposited at the sanctuary at Olympia. Such procedure is common for enactments of various poleis[102] but only seldom the case with contracts between individuals and communities.[103]

In a recent contribution, P. Ismard—following an earlier proposal by H. van Effenterre—has argued that Patrias was originally a slave.[104] Much of his interpretation hinges on the semantic meaning of ἱμάσκοι. If it is indeed derived from ἱμάς meaning "whip" or related to Attic ἱμάσσω it could refer to flogging, a punishment "constitutive of the stigma of being a slave."[105] However, the problem with this interpretation is that the inscription does not yield sufficient evidence for a change of status, i.e. it is never mentioned that Patrias became δημόσιος. Maybe the phrase ϝάρρεν, ὂρ ϝαλείο suggests that Patrias was originally a foreigner who was now granted rights similar to a citizen.

A further scribe that is known to us by name is mentioned in Herodotus.[106] The tyrant of Samos, Polycrates, sent his scribe Maeandrius (ὅς οἱ ἦν γραμματιστής) to negotiate with Oroetes. The only other information Herodotus provides about Maeandrius is a short note about his future wealth when he states that the scribe dedicated all the adornments of the men's apartment to the Heraion (ὃς χρόνῳ οὐ πολλῷ ὕστερον τούτων τὸν κόσμον τὸν ἐκ τοῦ ἀνδρεῶνος τοῦ Πολυκράτεος ἐόντα ἀξιοθέητον ἀνέθηκε πάντα ἐς τὸ Ἥραιον). We can only assume that Maeandrius amassed the wealth because of the importance of his office.[107]

There is also evidence that individual poleis started to limit the power of scribes. Two inscriptions from Erythrai in Asia Minor restrict the tenure of the office of scribe:[108]

> Ἀπελλίας εἶπεν· ὅσοι ἤδη ἐγρα-
> μμάτευσαν ἀπὸ Χαλκίδεω ἔκαθ-
> εν, τούτων μὴ ἐξεῖναι γραμματ-
> εῦσαι ἔτι μηδενὶ μηδεμιῆι ἀρ-
> 5   χῆι, μηδὲ τὸ λοιπὸν γραμματεύ-
> εν ἐξεῖναι μηδενὶ πλέον ἢ ἅπα-
> ξ τῆι αὐτῆι ἀρχῆι, μηδὲ ταμίηι

---

[100] Koerner 1981: 191.
[101] Koerner 1981: 194.
[102] Hölkeskamp 2000.
[103] A similar case is found in *Nomima* I.31 = *ICS* 217, a fifth-century bronze tablet from Idalion on Cyprus (see Maier 2004), written in syllabic script. It is a contract between the king and the polis, mentioning the special services of a family of physicians that provided healthcare while Idalion was under siege from the Persians (ὅτε τὰ(ν) πτόλιν Ἐδάλιον κατέϝοργον Μᾶδοι κὰς Κετιῆϝες). The decree grants property to Onalisos and his brothers. King and polis place the tablet in the temple of Athena at Idalion: ἰδὲ τὰ(ν) δάλτον τὰ(ν)δε, τὰ ϝέπιμα τάδε ἰναλαλισμένα(ν), | βασιλεὺς κὰς πτόλις κατέθιγαν ἰ(ν) τὰ(ν) θιὸν τὰν Ἀθάναν τὰν περ' Ἐ[δάλιον, σὺν ὅρκοις μὴ λῦσαι τὰς ϝρήτας τάσδε ὐϝαις ζα(?)ν. | Ὅπι (?) σίς κε τὰς ϝρήτας τάσδε λύση, ἄνοσιγα ϝοι γένοιτυ.
[104] Ismard 2017: 28–29 following van Effenterre 1979: 284 n. 35.
[105] Ismard 2017: 29.
[106] Herodotus, *Hist.* 3.123.
[107] Hawke 2011: 123.
[108] *IE* I.1 (fourth/fifth century BCE) and *IE* I.17.

```
           πλέον ἢ ἑνί μηδὲ δύο τιμαῖς τὸ-
           ν αὐτόν· ὃς δ'' ἂγ γραμματεύσηι
      10   ἢ ἀνέληται ἢ εἴπηι ἢ ἐπιψηφίσ-
           ηι, κατάρητόν τε αὐτὸν εἶναι κ-
           αὶ ἄτιμον καὶ ὀφείλεν αὐτὸν ἑ-
           κατὸν στατῆρας· ἐκπρηξάσθων
           δὲ οἱ ἐξετασταὶ ἢ αὐτοὶ ὀφειλ-
      15   όντων· ἄρχεν δὲ τούτοις μῆνα Ἀ-
           ρτεμισιῶνα ἐπ' ἱροποιο͂ Πόσεο-
           ος·

           [gap of two lines]

           ἔδοξεν τῆι βου[λῆι· ὃς ἄν ποιή]-
           σηται γραμμα[τέα παρὰ τὴν στ]-
      20   ήλην, ὀφε[ιλέτω — στατῆρας]
```

Apellias has proposed: People who were secretaries from the year when Chalkides was archon and onwards, no one of them is allowed to be secretary or to hold any other office. No one is allowed in the future to become a secretary more than once for the same office or treasurer more than once or to be elected in two offices simultaneously. Anyone who becomes a secretary or is elected or proposes or votes for such a proposal, he shall be damned and disenfranchised (*atimos*) and he shall owe a hundred staters. The *exetastai* shall exact the money, otherwise they will owe the same amount of money themselves. This law shall take effect from the month Artemision when Posis was *hieropoios*. The council has decided: anyone who selects a secretary in conflict to the provisions on the stele shall owe {...} staters.[109]

This is one of four instances from Erythrai where an individual takes the initiative to propose a law/statue.[110] The normal procedure seems to have been that the council puts forth such things as is the case in *IE* I.8 (ἔδοξεν τῆι βουλ[ῆι, στρατηγῶν] | γνώμη). Here, the council simply amends the existing stipulation, when "a clause penalising breach of the decree turns into an entrenchment clause against repeal of it."[111] The decree stipulates that no person can serve more than once as a scribe for the polis and that the persons who have already been scribes before Chalkides took office are excluded from the office of scribe. One gets the impression that the polis was quite suspicious of previous scribes. Since Erythrai changed the office of the scribe from a permanent appointment to a changing one we can infer two things. Firstly, the polis had negative experiences with a longer appointment; most likely because the scribes used the acquired knowledge to their advantage. Secondly, there must have been several members of the polis who were able to fulfil the duties of the office of γραμματεύς so that we can assume that literacy had increased in Erythrai. The various prohibitions against the iteration of the office of scribe show what status the γραμματεύς must have had within the political and societal organisation of the polis.[112]

---

[109] English translation according to Arnaoutoglou 1998: 92.
[110] See *IE* I.10, 24, 27.
[111] Rhodes and Lewis 1997: 370.
[112] Ruzé 1992: 90.

## CONCLUSION

The evidence from archaic Crete and other Greek polis clearly shows that from the middle of the sixth century BCE onwards communities began to enlist the services of individuals to record (and remember) their public and legal affairs. The terminology used to describe the skill required reflects the foreign origin of the technology. The complex enactment phrase at the beginning of the contract with Spensithios points to the importance of the appointment and—possibly—to an attempt to control the scribe. The appointment does not imply an abandonment of oral legal procedure in favour of written law. Rather it shows that Spensithios exemplifies the duality of both aspects in early Cretan law.[113]

Since the polis of Datala also granted Spensithios the right to serve as priest (καὶ ὅτιμί κα θιῶι ἱαρεὺς μῆι δίαλο-|[ς] θύεν τε τὰ δαμόσια θύματα τὸ‹ν› ποινικαστὰ-|ν καὶ τὰ τεμένια ἔκεν) this is a further indication of the high status and the competence attached to the office. We know from other Cretan poleis that priests received a share of the sacrificial meat, this would contribute to the more than generous provisions of the scribe.[114] He is, of course, not the only priest of Datala but most likely responsible for those cults, which—like the office of scribe—were newly established.[115]

The manifold privileges granted to Spensithios and his descendants are reminiscent of the scribal classes in the ancient Near East whose members almost jealously guard their skills.[116] It may be no coincidence "that, in a social and cultural sense, Archaic Cretan writing retained many of the features that we associate with the function of writing in Near Eastern societies and lacked those features common in other parts of Archaic Greece."[117] That the scribal family of Datala was able to guard its privileges was the result of the desire of the polis to preserve the memory of certain legal procedures beyond the lifespan of one individual. Though the pooling of such an important office in one single family may result in the creation of a powerful group that equals the college of *kosmoi*, it is also an important measure to guarantee the peace under the law.

What do we learn from the Cretan evidence for our understanding of scribes in the biblical world? Of course, such consideration can be only of a speculative nature. Maybe it is not as far fetched that scribes enjoyed similar social privileges as recorded in the Greek inscriptions. What we learn from the contemporary extra-biblical material is that scribes seem to have had similar administrative duties—this is expected as "the vast majority of inscriptions consists of economic and administrative documents."[118] However, when the nature of the writing changed from simply recording affairs of the state to rewriting, reworking and inventing the biblical tradition, maybe also the status of the scribe changed. The carriers of the biblical tradition probably came "from scribal schools and other such institutions within the two provinces, only to distance themselves later, at the very least internally."[119] If that is the case, the technique of writing would become a tool for theological innovation, which, of course, will have to be guarded. The peace under the law, ensured by scribes and magistrates in Crete will become the observance of the Law in Judaism that guarantees social peace.

---

[113] Gagarin 2003: 67.
[114] Seelentag 2015: 317.
[115] Willetts (1972: 96) thinks of "certain cults not already managed by existing hereditary priesthoods."
[116] Gagarin (2008: 71) remains skeptical whether the term "scribe" is an adequate title for the "writers" (or "masons") as they lack many of the ancient Near Eastern features.
[117] Whitley 1997: 659.
[118] Kratz 2015: 66.
[119] Kratz 2015: 185.

# BIBLIOGRAPHY

Arnaoutoglou, I. 1998. *Ancient Greek Laws: A Sourcebook*. London: Routledge.

Avigad, N. 1976. *Bullae and Seals from a Post-Exilic Judean Archive*. Qedem 4. Jerusalem: Institute of Archaeology, Hebrew University.

Baurain, C. 1997. *Les Grecs et la Méditerranée orientalie: Des siècles obscurs à la fin de l'époque archaïque*. Nouvelle Clio. Paris: Presses Universitaires de France.

Beattie, A. J. 1975. "Some Notes on the Spensithios Decree." *Kadmos* 15: 8–47.

Bile, M. 1988. *Le dialecte Crétois ancien. Étude de la langue des inscriptios receuil des inscriptions postérieures aux IC*. École française d'Athènes. Études Crétoises 27. Paris: Paul Geuthner.

Buck, C. D. 1955. *The Greek Dialects: Grammar, Selected Inscriptions, Glossary*. Chicago: University of Chicago Press.

Carawan, E. 2008. "What the *mnemones* Know." Pages 163–84 in *Orality, Literacy, Memory in the Ancient Greek and Roman World*. Edited by A. Mackay. Mn.S 278. Leiden: Brill.

Carr, D. M. 2005. *Writing on the Tablet of the Heart: Origins of Scripture and Literature*. Oxford: Oxford University Press.

Ceccarelli, P. 2013. *Ancient Greek Letter Writing: A Cultural History* (600 BC–150 BC). Oxford: Oxford University Press.

Crawford, S. W. 2008. *Rewriting Scripture in Second Temple Times*. Studies in the Dead Sea Scrolls and Related Literature. Grand Rapids: Eerdmans.

Detienne, M. 1992. "L'espace de la publicité, ses opérateurs intellectuels dans la cite." Pages 29–81 in *Les savoirs de l'écriture en Grèce ancienne*. Edited by M. Detienne. Cahiers de Philologique 14. Lille: Presses universitaires du Septentrion.

Diels, H., and W. Kranz. 1952. *Die Fragmente der Vorsokratiker II*. 6th ed. Berlin: Weidemann.

Edwards, G. P., and R. B. Edwards. 1974. "Red Letters and Phoenician Writing." *Kadmos* 13: 48–57.

———. 1977. "The Meaning and Etymology of *poinikastas*." *Kadmos* 16: 131–40.

Effenterre, H. van. 1973. "Le contrat de travail du scribe Spensitios." *BCH* 97: 31–46.

———. 1979. "Le statut compare des travailleurs étrangers en Chyphre, Crète et autres lieux à la fin de l'archaisme." Pages 279–93 in *Acts of the International Archaeological Symposium: The Relations between Cyprus and Crete, ca. 2000–500 B.C.* Nikosia: Department of Antiquities.

Erbse, H. 1971. *Scholia Graeca in Homeri Iliadem (scholia vetera)* II. Berlin: de Gruyter.

Erickson, B. 2004. "Eleutherna and the Greek World, ca. 600–400 B.C." Pages 199–212 in *Crete Beyond the Palaces: Proceedings of the Crete 2000 Conference*. Edited by L. P. Day, M. S. Mook and J. D. Muhly. Prehistory Monographs 10. Philadelphia: INSTAP Academic Press.

Fagels, R. 1990. *The Iliad*. London: Penguin.

Fischer-Hansen, T., T. H. Nielsen, and C. Ampolo. 2004. "Pithekoussai." Pages 285–87 in *An Inventory of Archaic and Classical Poleis: An Investigation Conducted by The Copenhagen Polis Centre for the Danish National Research Foundation*. Edited by M. H. Hansen and T. H. Nielsen. Oxford: Oxford University Press.

Fornara, C. W. 1983. *Translated Documents of Greece and Rome*. Vol. 1, *Archaic Times to the End for the Peloponnesian War*. 2nd ed. Cambridge: Cambridge University Press.

Fraser, P. M., and E. Matthews. 1987. *A Lexicon of Greek Personal Names*. Vol. 1, *The Aegean Islands, Cyprus, Cyrenaica*. Oxford: Clarendon.

Gagarin, M. 2003. "Letters of the Law: Written Texts in Archaic Greek Law." Pages 59–77 in *Written Texts and the Rise of Literate Culture in Ancient Greece*. Edited by H. Yunis. Cambridge: Cambridge University Press.

———. 2008. *Writing Greek Law*. Cambridge: Cambridge University Press.

———. 2012. "The Laws of Crete." Pages 17–29 in *Transferts culturels et droits dans le monde grec et héllenistique. Actes du colloque international (Reims, 14–17 mai 2008)*. Edited by B. Legras. Histoire ancienne et médiévale 110. Paris: Publications de la Sorbonne.

Gagarin, M., and P. Perlman. 2016. *The Laws of Ancient Crete c. 650–400 BCE*. Oxford: Oxford University Press.

Gerber, D. E. 1999. *Greek Elegiac Poetry: From the Seventh to the Fifth Centuries BC*. LCL 258. Cambridge, MA: Harvard University Press.

Gogel, S. L. 1998. *A Grammar of Epigraphic Hebrew*. SBL Resources for Biblical Study 23. Atlanta: Scholars Press.

Goodley, A. D. 1922. *Herodotus Books V–VII*. LCL 119. Cambridge, MA: Harvard University Press.

Goody, J. 1986. *The Logic of Writing and the Organization of Society*. Studies in Literacy, Family, Culture and the State. Cambridge: Cambridge University Press.

Gorlin, C. E. 1988. "The Spensithios Decree and Archaic Cretan Civil Status." *ZPE* 74: 159–65.

Gschnitzer, F. 1974, "Bemerkungen zum Arbeitsvertrag des Schreibers Spensithios." *ZPE* 13: 265–75.

Hagedorn, A. C. 2004. *Between Moses and Plato. Individual and Society in Deuteronomy and Ancient Greek Law*. FRLANT 204. Göttingen: Vandenhoeck & Ruprecht.

———. 2005. "Wie flucht man im östlichen Mittelmeer? Kulturanthropologische Perspektiven in die *Dirae Teiae* und das Deuteronomium." Pages 117–50 in *Kodifizierung und Legitimierung des Rechts in der Antike und im alten Orient*. Edited by M. Witte and M. T. Fögen. BZAR 5. Wiesbaden: Harrassowitz.

Havelock, E. A. 1976. *Origins of Western Literacy*. The Ontario Institute for Studies in Education Monograph Series 14. Toronto: Ontario Institute for Studies in Education.

Hawke, J. 2011. *Writing Authority: Elite Competition and Written Law in Early Greece*. DeKalb: Northern Illinois University Press.

Heckl, R. 2013. "Mose als Schreiber. Am Ursprung der jüdischen Hermeneutik des Pentateuchs." *ZAR* 19: 179–234.

Heubeck, A. 1979. "Homer und die Schrift." *Archaeologica Homerica* III/10: 126–84.

Hölkeskamp, K.-J. 2000. "(In-)Schrift und Monument. Zum Begriff des Gesetzes im Archaischen und Klassischen Griechenland." *ZPE* 132: 73–96.

Ismard, P. 2017. *Democracy's Slaves. A Political History of Ancient Greece*. Cambridge, MA: Harvard University Press.

Jaillard, D. 2013. "Memory, Writing, Authority: The Place of the Scribe in Greek Polytheistic Practice (Sixth to Fourth Centuries BCE)." Pages 23–34 in *Writing the Bible: Scribes, Scribalism and Script*. Edited by P. R. Davies and Th. Römer. BibleWorld. Durham: Acumen.

Jeffery, L. H. 1968. "Das Schreiben und die Gedichte Homers." Pages 262–68 in *Das Alphabet. Entstehung und Entwicklung der griechischen Schrift*. Edited by G. Pfohl. Wege der Forschung 88. Darmstadt: Wissenschaftliche Buchgesellschaft.

———. 1990. *The Local Scripts of Archaic Greece: A Study of the Origin of the Greek Alphabet and Its Development from the Eighth to the Fifth Centuries B.C.* Oxford Monographs on Classical Archaeology. 2nd ed. Oxford: Oxford University Press.

Jeffery, L. H., and A. Morpurgo-Davies. 1970. "ΠΟΙΝΙΚΑΣΤΑΣ and ΠΟΙΝΙΚΑΖΕΝ: BM 1969.4-2.1: A New Archaic Inscription from Crete." *Kadmos* 9: 118–54.

Koerner, R. 1981. "Vier frühe Verträge zwischen Gemeinwesen und Privatleuten auf griechischen Inschriften." *Klio* 63: 179–206.

———. 1987. "Beamtenvergehen und deren Bestrafungen nach frühen griechischen Inschriften." *Klio* 69: 450–98.

Kratz, R. G. 2008. "Ezra—Priest and Scribe." Pages 163–88 in *Scribes, Sages, and Seers: The Sage in the Eastern Mediterranean World*. Edited by L. G. Perdue. FRLANT 219. Göttingen: Vandenhoeck & Ruprecht.

———. 2013. "Rewriting Torah in the Hebrew Bible and the Dead Sea Scrolls." Pages 273–92 in *Wisdom and Torah: The Reception of "Torah" in the Wisdom Literature of the Second Temple Period*. Edited by B. U. Schipper and D. A. Teeter. JSJSup 163. Leiden: Brill.

———. 2015. *Historical and Biblical Israel: The History, Tradition, and Archives of Israel and Judah*. Oxford: Oxford University Press.

Kristensen, K. R. 2012. "Defining 'Legal Place' in Archaic and Early Classical Crete." Pages 31–46 in *Transferts culturels et droits dans le monde grec et héllenistique. Actes du colloque international (Reims, 14–17 mai 2008)*. Edited by B. Legras. Histoire ancienne et médiévale 110. Paris: Publications de la Sorbonne.

———. 2014. "Archaic Laws and the Development of Civic Identity in Crete, ca. 650–450 BCE." Pages 141–57 in *Cultural Practices and Material Culture in Archaic and Classical Crete: Proceedings of the International Conference, Mainz, May 20–21, 2011*. Edited by O. Pilz and G. Seelentag. Berlin: de Gruyter.

Kritzas, Ch. 2010. "Φοινικήια γράμματα. Νέα Αρχαϊκή Επιγραφή απο τον Ἐλτυνα." Pages 1–26 in Το γεομετρικό Νεκροταφείο Ελτύνας. Edited by G. Rhetheomiotakis and M. M. Englezou. Heraklion.

Kuhrt, D. 1986. Art. Thot (*Ḏḥwtj*). Pages 497–523 in vol. 6 of *Lexikon der Ägyptologie*. Wiesbaden: Harrassowitz.

Lauinger, J. 2015. "Neo-Assyrian Scribes, 'Esarhaddon's Succession Treaty,' and the Dynamics of Textual Mass Production." Pages 285–314 in *Texts and Context: The Circulation and Transmission of Cuneiform Texts in Social Space*. Edited by P. Delnero and J. Lauinger. Studies in Ancient Near Eastern Records 9. Berlin: de Gruyter.

Maier, F. G. 2004. "Idalion." Pages 1225–26 in *An Inventory of Archaic and Classical Poleis: An Investigation Conducted by The Copenhagen Polis Centre for the Danish National Research Foundation*. Edited by M. H. Hansen and T. H. Nielsen. Oxford: Oxford University Press.

Montanari, F. 2015. *The Brill Dictionary of Ancient Greek*. Leiden: Brill.

Osborne, R. 1996. *Greece in the Making 1200–479 BCE*. Routledge History of the Ancient World. London: Routledge.

Otto, E. 2005. "Mose der erste Schriftgelehrte: Deuteronomium 1,5 in der Fabel des Pentateuch." Pages 273–84 in *L'Ecrit er l'Esprit. Etudes d'histoire du texte et de théologie biblique en hommage à Adrian Schenker*. Edited by D. Böhler, I. Himbaza, and P. Hugo. OBO 214. Göttingen: Vandenhoeck & Ruprecht.

Peckham, J. B. 2014. *Phoenicia: Episodes from the Ancient Mediterranean*. Winona Lake: Eisenbrauns.

Perlman, P. 2004. "Crete." Pages 1144–95 in *An Inventory of Archaic and Classical Poleis: An Investigation Conducted by The Copenhagen Polis Centre for the Danish National Research Foundation*. Edited by M. H. Hansen and T. H. Nielsen. Oxford: Oxford University Press.

Pomponio, F., and U. Seidl. 1998–2001. "Art. Nabû A–B." Pages 16–29 in vol. 9 of *Reallexikon der Assyriologie und Vorderasiatischen Archäologie*. Berlin: de Gruyter.

Pounder, R. L. 1984. "The Origin of θιοί as Inscription-Heading." Pages 243–50 in *Studies Presented to Sterling Dow on His Eightieth Birthday*. Edited by K. J. Rigsby. Greek Roman and Byzantine Monographs 10. Durham: Duke University Press.

Powell, B. B. 2002. *Writing and the Origins of Greek Literature*. Cambridge: Cambridge University Press.

Raubitschek, A. E. 1970. "The Cretan Inscription BM 1969.4–2.1: A Supplementary Note." *Kadmos* 9: 155–56.

Rhodes, P. J., and D. M. Lewis. 1997. *The Decrees of the Greek States*. Oxford: Clarendon.

Ridgway, D. 1994. "Phoenicians and Greeks in the West: A View from Pithekoussai." Pages 35–46 in *The Archaeology of Greek Colonisation: Essays Dedicated to Sir John Boardman*. Edited by G. R. Tsetskhladze and F. De Angelis. Oxford: Oxford University Committee for Archaeology.

Ruzé, F. 1992. "Au début de l'écriture politique: Le pouvoir de l'écrit dans la cite." Pages 82–94 in *Les savoirs de l'écriture en Grèce ancienne*. Edited by M. Detienne. Cahiers de Philologique 14. Lille: Presses Universitaire du Septentrion.

Schaper, Joachim. 2004. "A Theology of Writing: The Oral and the Written, God as Scribe, and the Book of Deuteronomy." Pages 97–119 in *Anthropology and Biblical Studies: Avenues of Approach*. Edited by L. J. Lawrence and M. I. Aguilar. Leiden: Deo Publishing.

———. 2009. "'Scriptural Turn' und Monotheismus: Anmerkungen zu einer (nicht ganz neuen) These." Pages 275–91 in *Die Textualisierung der Religion*. Edited by J. Schaper. FAT 62. Tübingen: Mohr Siebeck.

———. 2016. "Anthropologie des Schreibens als Theologie des Schreibens. Ein medienarchäologischer Gang durch das Buch Exodus." Pages 281–96 in *Metatexte. Erzählungen von schrifttragenden Artefakten in der alttestamentlichen und mittelalterlichen Literatur*. Edited by F. E. Focken and M. R. Ott. Materiale Textkulturen 15. Berlin: de Gruyter.

Shear, I. M. 1998. "Bellerophon Tablets from the Mycenaean World? A Tale of Seven Bronze Hinges." *Journal of Hellenic Studies* 118: 187–89.

Seelentag, G. 2009. "Regeln für den Kosmos. Prominenzrollen und Institutionen im archaischen Kreta." *Chiron* 39: 65–99.

———. 2015. *Das archaische Kreta: Institutionalisierung im frühen Griechenland*. Klio Beihefte 24. Berlin: de Gruyter,

Smyth, H. W. 1922. *Aeschylus I*. LCL 145. Cambridge, MA: Harvard University Press.

Sonnet, J.-P. 1997. *The Book Within the Book: Writing in Deuteronomy*. BibInt 14. Leiden: Brill.

Teeter, D. A. 2014. *Scribal Laws: Exegetical Variation in the Textual Transmission of Biblical Law in the Late Second Temple Period*. FAT 92. Tübingen: Mohr Siebeck.

Thomas, R. 1992. *Literacy and Orality in Ancient Greece*. Key Themes in Ancient History. Cambridge: Cambridge University Press.

———. 2009. "Writing, Reading, Public and Private Literacies: Functional Literacy and Democratic Literacy in Greece." Pages 13–45 in *Ancient Literacies: The Culture of Reading in Greece and Rome*. Edited by W. A. Johnson and H. N. Parker. Oxford: Oxford University Press.

Toorn, K. van der. 2007. *Scribal Culture and the Making of the Hebrew Bible*. Cambridge, MA: Harvard University Press

Viviers, D. 1994. "La cité de Datalla et l'expansion territorial de Lyktos en Crète centrale." *BCH* 118: 229–59.

Voutrias, E. 2007. "The Introduction of the Alphabet." Pages 266–76 in *A History of Ancient Greek: From the Beginning to Late Antiquity*. Edited by A.-F. Christidis. Cambridge: Cambridge University Press.

Wallace, S. 2010. *Ancient Crete: From Successful Collapse to Democracy's Alternatives, Twelfth to Fifth Centuries BC*. Cambridge: Cambridge University Press.

Whitley, J. 1997. "Cretan Laws and Cretan Literacy." *AJA* 101: 635–61.

Wilamowitz-Moellendorff, U. von. 1920. *Die Ilias und Homer*. 2nd ed. Berlin: Weidemann.

Willetts, R. F. 1972. "The Cretan Inscription BM 1969.4–2.1: Further Provisional Comments." *Kadmos* 11: 96–98.

Wilson, J.-P. 2013. "Literacy." Pages 542–63 in *A Companion to Archaic Greece*. Edited by K. A. Raaflaub and H. van Wees. Blackwell Companions to the Ancient World. Malden: Wiley-Blackwell.

Wirbelauer, E. 2005. "Eine Frage der Telekommunikation? Die Griechen und ihre Schrift im 9.–7. Jahrhundert v. Chr." Pages 187–206 in *Griechische Archaik: Interne Entwicklungen—Externe Impulse*. Edited by R. Rollinger and C. Ulf. Berlin: Akademie.

Wolf, F. A. 1985. *Prolegomena to Homer (1795): Translated with Introduction and Notes by Anthony Grafton, Glenn W. Most, and James E. G. Zetzel.* Princeton: Princeton University Press.

Woodard, R. D. 2010. "*Phoinikēia Grammata*: An Alphabet for the Greek Language." Pages 25–46 in *A Companion to the Ancient Greek Language.* Edited by E. J. Bakker. Blackwell Companions to the Ancient World. Malden: Blackwell.

Zahn, M. M. 2016. "Innerbiblical Exegesis—The View from Beyond the Bible." Pages 107–20 in *The Formation of the Pentateuch: Bridging the Academic Cultures of Europe Israel, and North America.* Edited by J. C. Gertz, B. M. Levinson, D. Rom-Shiloni, and K. Schmid. FAT 111. Tübingen: Mohr Siebeck.

PART TWO

# Power and Status

# Scribes, Schools and Ideological Conflict in Ancient Israel and Judah

BRIAN RAINEY

Various modern scholarly reconstructions of scribal education in antiquity depict it as a more or less standardized curriculum that was designed to enculturate and socialize elite men (and occasionally women) into the ideology of the ruling class. It is common to talk about the Egyptian and Mesopotamian curricula as "standardized" or a part of one scholarly "tradition." If that is the case, how did ideological differences within biblical texts develop? The portrait of ancient Israel and Judah that we receive from various biblical texts is that of a society in which there were deep ideological divisions and disagreements that found their way into the different strands and "sources" of the Hebrew Bible. There are, of course, the divergent strands that went into the composition of the Torah (JE, D, P, H), but some prophetic traditions also set themselves up explicitly in opposition to other ideological viewpoints. Jeremiah 8:8 famously fumes against the false pen of the scribes, showing animosity toward whatever scribal tradition is the target of the invective, and Isa 10:1 also condemns writers (*měkattěbîm*) who "write oppression." A number of modern interpreters employ the word "school" to describe these different ideological perspectives. Some refer to various "sources" of the Pentateuch as "schools,"[1] and others argue that prophetic schools existed in ancient Israel and Judah. André Lemaire suggests that there were royal schools, priestly schools and possibly prophetic schools in ancient Israel.[2] Part of the confusion stems from the definition of the word "school" and what is meant by that expression. The question that arises from the repeated use of the word "school" is, did ideological divisions manifest themselves at the level of scribal training, or at the level of "formal standardized education?"[3] Were scribal curricula specialized around particular ideological viewpoints? Did scribal training take place in the home or in institutions such as the royal palace and Temple? Or did scribal training take place in all three places, and more? And if training did take place in those various locales, did locale determine the viewpoint of the scribes trained there? For example, if scribes were trained in the Temple, would these supposed "temple scribes" have taken a more "priestly" viewpoint? The theory that there were conflicting schools and strands of thought in ancient Israel diverges significantly from the scholarly reconstruction of scribal

---

[1] See, e.g., Moshe Weinfeld, *Deuteronomy and the Deuteronomic School* (Winona Lake: Eisenbrauns, 1992); Israel Knohl, *The Sanctuary of Silence: The Priestly Torah and the Holiness School* (Minneapolis: Fortress Augsburg, 1995); Raymond F. Person, *The Deuteronomic School: History, Social Setting and Literature*, Studies in Biblical Literature 2 (Atlanta: Society of Biblical Literature, 2002); Menahem Haran, "Ezekiel, P, and the Priestly School," *VT* 58 (2008): 211–18.
[2] André Lemaire, *Les écoles et la formation de la Bible dans l'ancien Israël* (Göttingen: Vandenhoeck & Ruprecht, 1981), 49.
[3] Christopher A. Rollston's term for scribal training which avoids the problematic term "school" ("Scribal Education in Ancient Israel: The Old Hebrew Epigraphic Evidence," *BASOR* 344 [2006]: 50).

culture in Egypt and Mesopotamia, which stresses uniformity and ideological conformity among the elite.[4]

To explore the relationship between "schools," scribes and ideological change I will revisit two well-known examples in the Hebrew Bible that depict ideological change or conflict within Judah: 2 Kings 22 and Jeremiah 36. I will argue that the portrait of scribes in these two examples suggests that whatever scribal training looked like in ancient Israel, the "household" or **é-dub-ba**/*bīt ṭuppi* model of scribal training attested in Mesopotamia may be the closest approximation to the details presented in these stories. I further argue that these episodes indicate that leaders of major ideological change were often elites who may not have been literate or elites who achieved a level of literacy lower than that of a professional scribe. Rather, scribes—or scribal families—could align themselves with individual ideologues, or political and theological currents in society.[5] Consequently, *scribal* "schools" in which people were trained in the arts of reading and writing should be separated from *ideological* "schools" of thought, or "schools" that consist of disciples who might follow a particular figure (such as disciples of a prophet). Additionally, it appears as though not all education in ancient Israel is necessarily specialized scribal education. A prophet or tutor could pass on cultural knowledge to elite students of the ruling class by mouth, but I maintain here that reading and especially writing are technical skills that require advanced specialization that many elites did not achieve—and may not have even found desirable or necessary for their social roles.[6]

A scribe or scribal family might support a particular ideological current. It does not automatically follow that a scribal "school," complete with a specialized curriculum, developed around that particular ideological current. Rather, the scribe or scribal family offered their skills both as experts in the technical skill of writing and as advanced developers of original content in their own right, collaborating with the leaders of the ideological charge. Scribes, then, are like other powerful, influential figures in ancient Israel and Judah. They could take sides in major divisions and use their technical powers to support one group or the other. Some Egyptian texts show that ancient scribes could be quite aware of the awesome power they possessed;[7] in ancient Israel and Judah there is no reason to think that scribes did not have a similar kind of self-awareness.

In my reading of these biblical texts, scribes are presented as a specialized, largely hereditary class (though note the figurative use of "son" with respect to Mesopotamian scribal training described below). Additionally, the description of Jeremiah's relationship with scribes suggests that scribes can be quite divided amongst themselves ideologically. On the one hand, the book of Jeremiah portrays scribes as a source of falsehoods (Jer 8:8). On the other hand, Jeremiah works intimately with one family of scribes (the Neriah family) and has allies among another family of scribes (the Shaphan

---

[4] David M. Carr writes, "Where Mesopotamian and Egyptian traditions often manifest a single redaction of a given tradition, the Pentateuch and other key traditions appear to have gone through multiple stages of revision" and he explains these stages as a result of massive socio-political changes that affected the systems of "textuality-enculturation" in ancient Israel and Judah. He further contends, reasonably that, "In Israel we have the remnants of an educational-enculturational corpus of a land often dominated by more powerful neighbors. The resulting long duration literature has fractures and crosscurrents that mark the impact of successive dislocations and Israelite reactions to them" (*Writing on the Tablet of the Heart* [New York: Oxford University Press, 2005], 162).

[5] Karel van der Toorn, *Scribal Culture and the Making of the Hebrew Bible* (Cambridge, MA: Harvard University Press, 2007), 184–86.

[6] This possibility must be considered. As M. C. A. MacDonald puts it, for traditional and tribal societies, "even when literacy is available, individuals and communities can often make the positive choice to remain non-literate" (51). As a primary example, MacDonald uses the Bedouin in Jordan for which there are advantages to remaining non-literate. Many of his other cross-cultural studies show that there can be different levels of literacy within a society, including those who can read and write, but choose to "operate socially as non-literates" (50). See "Literacy in an Oral Environment," in *Writing and Ancient Near Eastern Society: Papers in Honour of Alan R. Millard*, ed. Piotr Bienkowski, Christopher Mee and Elizabeth Slater, LHBOTS 426 (New York: T&T Clark, 2005), 49–118.

[7] Ronald J. Williams, "Scribal Training in Ancient Egypt," *JAOS* 92 (1972): 214–21 (217–18).

family). We need not posit that the book of Jeremiah offers historically verifiable details about the prophet's life in order to appreciate the possible historical value of its depiction of scribal activity.

It has been convincingly argued that text production in the ancient world was the result of an interplay between oral tradition and writing.[8] Here, I admittedly make a somewhat artificial, but hopefully useful, distinction between the production of ideas and the physical process of writing. There is a complex relationship between these two processes in the ancient world, and ultimately they cannot be separated when a modern exegete of the Hebrew Bible considers "authorship" and "source." Additionally, it is not my intention to argue that ancient scribes were mere xerox machines for those who produced ideas; ancient scribes are indeed experts in oral traditions and creative producers of original content. I do not propose a dichotomization between the oral and the written, but seek to isolate and observe some of the moving parts that might have gone into the complex process of textual production in ancient Israel and Judah. I surmise that in ancient Israel and Judah, scribes and non-literate elites shared training in the oral traditions of their society, but that specialized scribes—probably members of a class that consisted of several scribal families—were an indispensable part of putting ideological material to paper (or to papyrus or to animal skin). All members of the elite could probably memorize, absorb (audially) and recite key oral traditions, thus participating intimately in the process of producing literature. But for figures who were not professional scribes to both read and write complex textual media seems logistically less feasible. In antiquity, one could participate in a society's oral tradition without possessing the ability to read and write—after all, oral traditions got along just fine without writing for hundreds of years before writing became dominant. But the reverse was not true; written texts necessarily had a relationship with orality.

Prophets, and their "schools" (more on that below), in particular, but also other elites, such as those interested in leading cultic reform projects (2 Kgs 22–23), may have recited and composed much *oral* "literature," but they collaborated with supportive members of the scribal class, whose expertise was necessary to put these ideas into complex written form. The importance of scribes for the preservation and transformation of prophetic material has already been noted by many modern exegetes.[9] Here, I support these scholarly insights in the following ways: (1) I emphasize the possible collaboration between scribes and non-literate elites in writing. That is, I argue for the possibility that in ancient Israel and Judah, non-literate elites routinely worked closely with literate scribes to produce textual material of ideological value. (2) I clearly separate "schools" of thought, or schools that might organize around a prophetic figure, which would pass on knowledge orally, from "schools" that trained people in advanced scribal skills. (3) I argue for the possibility that professional ancient Israelite and Judahite scribes were primarily organized by and trained by members of a scribal family, and that they were not parochialized in institutions like the Temple or palace. According to this theory, which reorients focus on the scribal clan, temples and palaces would not primarily train scribes—a scribal family would. It is conceivable that a scribal family might also be a priestly family or an elite family whose members are royal bureaucrats. But generally, priests, prophets and other elites who needed their ideas written down for posterity would collaborate with professional scribes who were typically trained in some kind of familial apprenticeship setting.

I suspect that close collaboration between non-literate elites and scribes was the more common model for literary text production in ancient Israel and Judah because I remain skeptical that people other than professional scribes could compose complex literary texts in these societies. While

---

[8]Van der Toorn, *Scribal Culture*; Carr, *Tablet of the Heart*; Susan Niditch, *Oral World and Written Word* (Louisville: Westminster John Knox, 1996).
[9]Van der Toorn, *Scribal Culture*, 188–204; Mark Leuchter, "Jehoiakim and the Scribes: A Note on Jer 36, 23," *ZAW* 127 (2015): 320–25.

parallels with Egypt and Mesopotamia are useful for imagining how scribal training in ancient Israel and Judah might have looked, for a variety of reasons, ancient Israel and Judah might not have been able to support the same kinds of persistent, sophisticated institutional edifices for scholarly education. Nevertheless, I concede that this speculative collaborative model could have co-existed with other models of text production. After all, biblical texts are not necessarily a realistic projection of facts on the ground. 2 Kings 22 and Jeremiah 36 at least raise the strong possibility that elite, non-literate ideologues worked frequently with members of a professional, family-educated scribal class together to develop texts.

## THE HOUSEHOLD MODEL

Scribal training in the Old Babylonian Period was done in the **é-dub-ba** or *bīt ṭuppi*, a model that seems to have fallen out of use in Babylonia around 1500 BCE.[10] Students were bilingually trained, and in a variety of genres. The beginning lessons involved syllabaries and copying vocabulary lists of Sumerian and Akkadian vocabulary.[11] They also learned formulae for stela, as well as dialogues, legal and contract terminology. Examination Text A[12] suggests that students studied terminology for a variety of fields, including different kinds of priests, tradespeople, shepherds and merchants. Perhaps, even musical training was a part of the training of scribes in the **é-dub-ba**. Poetic depictions of scribal training from hymns suggest that students learned accounting, surveying, construction and mathematics.[13] Original texts seem to have been composed in the **é-dub-ba** as well.[14]

All indicators suggest that education in the **é-dub-ba** was a small operation.[15] The training took place in the home of the tutor (**ummia**) and probably involved a small group of students, "sons" and more advanced students who assumed a leadership role ("elder brothers," **šeš-gal**). As has been noted repeatedly, in some instances, these "sons" may not have been literal sons, but in many instances the tutor would have taken in, or adopted, students not related to him as pupils.[16] The curriculum of these scribal schools seems broad, but it also appears to have changed over time.[17] Some have argued that there was a kind of "tracking" in Babylonian scribal training,[18] in which there was a basic education in writing and the ideologies of the ruling classes, but that more advanced students who would go on to be scholars or official scribes would learn more technical, specialized texts relating to omens, divination, and spells.[19] This second phase of scholarship seems to have attracted a small sliver of those who entered scribal education.[20] Similarly, Egyptologists argue that in ancient Egypt, there might have been a more basic scribal education and a more advanced scribal education via apprenticeship with a learned tutor.[21]

---

[10] Ake W. Sjöberg, "The Old Babylonian Edubba," in *Sumerological Studies in Honor of Thorkild Jacobsen*, ed. Stephen J. Lieberman, University of Chicago Assyriological Studies 20 (Chicago: University of Chicago Press), 159–60; van der Toorn, *Scribal Culture*, 55–56.
[11] Sjöberg, "Edubba," 162–63.
[12] On the date and use of Examination Text A, see ibid., 160. The earliest extant manuscript dates from 900 BCE, after the Old Babylonian period, but parallels with other Old Babylonian texts.
[13] Ibid., 173–74.
[14] Ibid., 171.
[15] Steve Tinney, "Texts, Tablets and Teaching: Scribal Education at Nippur and Ur," *Expedition* 40 (1998): 49.
[16] Carr, *Tablet of the Heart*, 20–21.
[17] H. L. J. Vanstiphout, "On the Old Babylonian Eduba Curriculum," in *Centers of Learning: Learning and Location in Pre-Modern Europe and the Near East*, ed. Jan Willem Drijvers and Alasdair A. MacDonald, Brill's Studies in Intellectual History 61 (Leiden: Brill, 1995), 12.
[18] Carr, *Tablet of the Heart*, 26–27; van der Toorn, *Scribal Culture*, 57–60.
[19] Carr, *Tablet of the Heart*, 76–77; van der Toorn, *Scribal Culture*, 57.
[20] Van der Toorn, *Scribal Culture*, 58.
[21] Williams, "Scribal Training," 216.

## THE INSTITUTIONAL MODEL

Lemaire argues that the early Israelite monarchy necessitated specialists skilled in writing, and he looks to the Egyptian model of scribal education as a possibility.[22] During the New Kingdom period (1570–1069 BCE), at least, there were formalized scribal schools and scriptoria found in temples and palaces.[23] There was the famous "House of Life," a place under royal sponsorship and attached to the temple where texts were copied and preserved, and there are clear examples of literate priests.[24] It is certainly possible that ancient Israel adopted aspects of Egyptian scribal education. Egyptian influence on Israelite writing can be seen in the use of Egyptian hieratic numbers.[25] The fact that papyrus might have been imported from Egypt[26] and the reference to the *qeset*, an Egyptian loanword for the case in which scribal utensils were carried, also hint at Egyptian influence on Israelite scribal practice. Furthermore, the impact of Egyptian "wisdom texts" such as the Instruction of Amenemopet on passages like Prov 22:17–24:33 is well known. During the Kassite period of Babylonia (1595–1155 BCE), and afterwards, institutional training was also common. In Mesopotamia, scribes were often associated with temple workshops, or *bīt mummu*.[27]

## THE COMPLEXITY OF LITERACY

Menachem Haran maintains that "literacy is not a concept determinable by well-defined borders, as it is susceptible to variation in extent and in level."[28] He notes, as others do,[29] that reading and writing are two different skill sets. The archaeological record, which has yielded letters and inscriptions, such as Lachish Letter 3 and the Siloam Inscription, as well as ostraca, seal inscriptions and abecedaries from the pre-exilic period (mainly eighth and seventh centuries BCE)[30] indicates that there were possibly different kinds literacy in ancient Judah, and that some officials who were not professional *sōpěrîm* could read and write to some extent. However, a few modern scholars have probably overstated the extent of literacy and have asserted that ancient Israel was a "literate society…where writing was familiar to and employed by laymen of all walks of life."[31] Ian M. Young rightly details some problems that come with assuming that inscriptions and graffiti demonstrate literacy outside of a scribal class.[32] Christopher A. Rollston notes that the simplicity of writing Hebrew has probably been exaggerated, and that learning to write even in an alphabetic script takes a considerable amount of time and education.[33] He notes that the examples of short writing found

---

[22]Lemaire, *Les écoles*, 47; Carr, *Tablet of the Heart*, 163.
[23]John Baines, *Visual and Written Culture in Ancient Egypt* (New York: Oxford University Press, 2007), 43–45.
[24]Baines, *Visual and Written Culture*, 45; Carr, *Tablet of the Heart*, 79; Alan H. Gardiner, "The House of Life," *Journal of Egyptian Archaeology* 24 (1938): 157–79.
[25]William M. Schniedewind, *How the Bible Became a Book* (New York: Cambridge University Press, 2004), 100; Rollston, "Scribal Education," 66–67.
[26]Aaron Demsky, "Writing in Ancient Israel and Ancient Judaism, Part One: The Biblical Period," in *Mikra: Text, Translation, Reading and Interpretation of the Hebrew Bible in Ancient Judaism and Early Christianity* (Minneapolis: Fortress, 1990), 13.
[27]A variety of cultic activity, including the activation of cult statues would take place in the *bīt mummu*. See Van der Toorn, *Scribal Culture*, 56–57; Alexander Heidel, "The Meaning of *mummu* in Akkadian Literature," *JNES* 7 (1948): 103–4.
[28]Menahem Haran, "On the Diffusion of Literacy and Schools in Ancient Israel," *Congress Volume: Jerusalem, 1986* (Leiden: Brill, 1988), 83.
[29]MacDonald, "Oral Environment," 52.
[30]For an overview of the archaeological data, see Demsky, "Writing," 11–16; Niditch, *Oral World*, 45–53; Carr, *Tablet of the Heart*, 164–66; Gabriel Barkay, "Iron Age II–III," in *Archaeology of Ancient Israel*, ed. Ammon Ben-Tor (Raanana: Open University of Jerusalem, 1992), 349–51.
[31]Demsky, "Writing," 15.
[32]Ian M. Young, "Israelite Literacy: Interpreting the Evidence, Part One," *VT* 48 (1998): 240.
[33]Rollston, "Scribal Education," 48–49.

from ancient Israel and Judah, especially on ostraca, demonstrate that the writers were formally educated. As a result, to argue that literacy in some way extended to those outside of professional scribes is to say that these hypothetical, functionally literate people would still be members of a small subset of the population, i.e., the elite.

One example used to support widespread literacy in ancient Israel and Judah is the late eighth-century BCE Siloam Inscription, which was written on the wall of a water tunnel, most likely commissioned by Hezekiah (2 Kgs 20:20). The tunnel brought water from the Gihon spring to the Siloam Pool and an inscription was made to commemorate the completion of the project, when the two teams of diggers, who started in opposite directions, met. Gabriel Barkay argues that the inscription does not demonstrate highly professional training because the writing is much smaller than the space prepared for it, even though the letters show "fine execution."[34] Nevertheless, if the chief engineers or chief builders of the project wrote the inscription, as is commonly assumed,[35] the inscription does indicate that some form of literary education could have extended to those who were not professional scribes.

Lachish Letter 3, a letter dating from the sixth century BCE, was written by a soldier who responds to an accusation that he cannot read, by forcefully asserting that he can indeed read letters:

> And now please, explain to your servant the meaning of the letter which you sent to your servant yesterday evening because the heart of your servant has been sick since your sending to your servant and because my lord said, "you do not know (how) to read a letter." As Yahweh lives, never has any man had to read a letter to me. And also every letter that comes to me, surely I can read it, and moreover, I can repeat it completely![36]

Susan Niditch draws attention to the part of the letter that stresses the soldier's ability to repeat letters, presumably from memory, which, she rightly contends, reflects the importance of orality even in military correspondence.[37] Additionally, Schniedewind notes that orthographic and grammatical details in Lachish Letter 3 suggest that someone who was not a professional scribe composed the letter, which means that a kind of basic and functional literacy could have expanded beyond professional scribes into other elite classes.[38]

The lower level of literacy demonstrated by these archaeological finds raises the possibility that there were levels or "tracks" of scribal training for the elite within Israel, much like the different levels of scribal education in ancient Egypt and Mesopotamia briefly discussed above. Some officials and members of the elite would receive a kind of functional scribal training, but those who aspired to be professional scribes, and those capable of composing complex material, would move on to more advanced studies. Orthographic and grammatical analyses of the epigraphic data seem consonant with the idea that there was a lower tier of scribal education in ancient Israel, that non-specialists like military officials would have achieved. However, even with a lower level of literacy, an ideologically invested member of the elite could have an appreciation for the power of writing, and a basic training in reading and writing could have formed a strong foundation for close collaboration with professional scribes.

Based on the information from scribal practices in other ancient Near Eastern societies, when I discuss the role of professional scribes, I assume that Israelite and Judahite *sōpĕrîm* are advanced professionals who master a variety of scribal arts, especially the composition of complex literature,

---

[34] Barkay, "Iron Age II–III," 350.
[35] Ibid.
[36] Schniedewind's rendition in "Sociolinguistic Reflections on the Letter of a 'Literate' Soldier (Lachish 3)," *Zeitschrift für Althebraistik* 13 (2000): 158–59.
[37] Niditch, *Oral World*, 53.
[38] Schniedewind, *How the Bible Became a Book*, 163.

in a variety of genres (e.g., prophecy, legal material, sapiental texts, songs and psalms). I also assume that an Israelite or Judahite professional scribe would have a broad education like his (and occasionally her) counterparts in Egypt, Ugarit and Mesopotamia, and achieved the highest level of training in the craft. If there were functionally literate people in ancient Israel and Judah, I assume these elites did not produce major literary texts but may have achieved a lower level of literacy.

There may indeed have been other officials who were literate in some sense. Haran argues that the šōṭēr may have served some kind of writing function, based on the Akkadian and Aramaic cognates, šatāru ("to write"), šĕtar ("document") (Deut 1:15; 16:18; 20:5; Josh 3:2; 8:33; 23:2; Exod 5:6, 10, 15; Num 11:16).[39] In biblical examples, writing is not the sole function of the šōṭēr, but writing or record keeping could be a part of his profession. If the position of šōṭēr did involve writing, it seems that their tasks were closely associated with legal or bureaucratic matters. The šōṭĕrîm are paired with the judges to be appointed in all of the cities of Israel (Deut 16:18), and are closely involved with the oversight of corvée labor in another example (Exod 5:6, etc.). If a šōṭēr could write, this official's association with (forced) labor projects in Exodus 5 may have some resonance with the writing ability of the engineers of the Siloam Inscription, who also might have been overseers of a (voluntary?) labor project. And the presence of šōṭĕrîm in the war camp (Josh 3:2) is reminiscent of the lower level of literacy that the solider of Lachish Letter 3 seems to have achieved. There are other potential references to a lower level of writing for the purposes of record keeping. For instance, in Judg 8:13–17, a servant (na'ar) writes down the names of the princes and elders.[40] By contrast, the sōpēr is often associated with the transmission of ideological knowledge, for better (2 Kgs 22; Jer 36) or worse (Jer 8:8).

With respect to the production of ideologically rich literary texts the division of labor seems pronounced. In the two major depictions of literary production in the Hebrew Bible I discuss, the scribes have distinctive roles from those who are leading the ideological charge. There are, on the one hand, those who promote an ideological project, such as Hilkiah, Huldah, Josiah, and especially Jeremiah. On the other hand, there are scribes who play a significant role in the transmission and preservation of the ideological material, such as the Shaphan and Neriah families. But the major producers of ideas are not necessarily "literate" in the sense that they write literary texts—i.e., they do not actually put "pen to paper." They are, however, probably very well-versed in the oral traditions of ancient Israel and Judah. Jeremiah 8:8, the transmission of the Jeremiah tradition, and parallels in Mesopotamia and Egypt also strongly suggest that scribes had a major hand in the transformation and reshaping of ideological content.[41] The narrative content from the Hebrew Bible about scribes, then, supplements the comparative evidence that scribes reworked ideational content.[42]

## 2 KINGS 22

The story of the discovery of the law book during the reign of Josiah (640–609 BCE) is very telling. As numerous interpreters have pointed out, it is not unusual for important texts to be "found" hidden in temples. In Egypt, for example, writings were given prestige by asserting that they were discovered in temples.[43] In this well-known story in 2 Kgs 22:8–13, Hilkiah, Josiah's high priest, reportedly finds a law book in the temple:

---

[39] Haran, "Literacy and Schools," 85.
[40] Compare Isa 10:19, where another na'ar writes, this time clearly to sarcastically convey a lower level of writing.
[41] With respect to the Jeremiah tradition, see van der Toorn, *Scribal Culture*, 182–204; Leuchter, "Jehoiakim," 322.
[42] Schniedewind, *How the Bible Became a Book*, 122–28.

Hilkiah the High Priest said to Shaphan the *sōpēr*, "I have found the Book of the Torah in the temple of Yahweh." So Hilkiah gave the book to Shaphan and he read it (*qr'*). Then Shaphan the *sōpēr* came to the king and he recounted the affair to the king…Shaphan the *sōpēr* told the king, "Hilkiah the priest gave me a book." And Shaphan read (*qr'*) it in front of the king. As soon as the king heard the words of the book, he rent his garments. Then the king commanded Hilkiah the priest, Ahiqam, Shaphan's son, and Akhbor, son of Micaiah, as well as Shaphan the *sōpēr* and Asaiah the king's servant: "Go, inquire of Yahweh on my behalf, on behalf of the people and on behalf of all Judah concerning the words of this discovered book. For the wrath of Yahweh, which has kindled against us, is immense because our ancestors did not obey the words of this book to act according to what was written concerning us."

Various actors in this episode seem dependent on Shaphan's literary skills. Hilkiah the high priest *finds* the book, but he does not read it himself. Instead, he gives the book to Shaphan who reads it. When Shaphan tells the king that the high priest has found the Book of the Torah, the king does not read the scroll; rather, Shaphan reads it to him. Finally, when it comes to divination to confirm the legitimacy of the book, literate professionals are involved in the process—both Shaphan the *sōpēr* and his son, who presumably is trained in the same craft as his father, are a part of the entourage sent to Huldah the prophetess. Interestingly, in v. 16, Huldah says that the king has "read" (*qr'*) the book, but it was the professional scribe Shaphan who did the actual reading (22:10).[44] Huldah's comment confirms what some have pointed out,[45] which is that biblical references to "reading" (*qr'*) by non-professionals should not necessarily be understood as references to their ability to read textual media fluently, much less write complex literary texts. To be sure, just because someone from the ancient world has a text read to them, which was a common practice in antiquity, does not mean that they are illiterate.[46] But the literacy of high ranking officials in this pericope is at best unclear, while the presence and literary activity of professional scribes is conspicuous. Consequently, it may be useful to take a close look at the main actors in the story in order to discuss their possible relationship to literacy.

*Priests*

Hilkiah may find the book, but since he does not read the law book himself, it raises the question of whether priests were necessarily literate (or literate at the level of professional scribes) in ancient Israel and Judah. Numbers 5:23 is often marshaled as evidence that some level of writing is necessary for the priesthood. But, again, considering that there could have been different levels of literacy in ancient Israel, writing incantations is not the same as proficiency in writing complex literary texts. Literate cultic officials are certainly attested in Mesopotamia and Egypt and scribal training in some periods of Mesopotamian and Egyptian history seems to have taken place in temples and palaces, as noted above. There is at least one instance of a probably literate priest (*khn*) from Ugarit as well.[47] Some argue that Ezekiel's consumption of a divine scroll (Ezek 2:8–3:3) supports the idea that Ezekiel received a literary education due to the importance of writing.[48] Notably, however,

---

[44] Young, "Israelite Literacy," 248
[45] Ibid., 248–49.
[46] Though MacDonald makes a useful distinction between illiteracy and non-literacy ("Oral Environment," 50 n. 1).
[47] Attenu the *rb khnm* in the colophon of the Baal Cycle (KTU/CAT 1.6 VI) seems to be depicted as both a priest (*khn*) and cult official (*t'y*). Ilimalku, the "scribe" (*spr*), the putative writer of the Baal Cycle is Attenu's "student" (*lmd*). See the discussion in van der Toorn, *Scribal Culture*, 86 and in Mark S. Smith and Wayne T. Pitard, *The Ugaritic Baal Cycle*, Vol. 2, VTSup 114 (Leiden: Brill, 2009), 725–29. There are late texts (third to second century BCE) from Mesopotamia that might show that some priests were simultaneously writers; see Wilfred G. Lambert, "Ancestors, Authors, and Canonicity," *JCS* 11 (1957): 4–5.
[48] Carr, *Tablet of the Heart*, 149.

Ezekiel does not read the scroll, but eats it and *speaks* its words. This passage can be understood as evidence that Ezekiel, the priest, could read and write and received an education in literacy; or, alternatively, it could be interpreted as an expression of the collaboration between those who were capable of reciting a tradition orally and those who wrote the tradition. Even though someone else—presumably Yahweh—actually wrote the scroll (2:10), Ezekiel can absorb its contents (in an explicit and graphic portrayal of receiving something by mouth) and recite it. Most of the writing that Ezekiel actually does seems consonant with a lower level of literacy (Ezek 4:1[?]; 24:2; 37:16, 20).

Biblical references imply that some kind of scribal activity took place in Israelite and Judahite temples. The fact that Egyptian and Mesopotamian societies, in certain periods, trained their scribes in temples has led a number of number Hebrew Bible specialists to suggest that transmission of texts was connected with the Temple, but it remains unclear that Israelite and Judahite institutionalized "schools" for training in scribal arts were located there. Some biblical texts reveal that temples were probably a repository for textual media, even if not exclusively. 1 Samuel 10:25 claims that Samuel wrote a document about the regulations for kingship and deposited (*wayyanaḥ*) it "before Yahweh," presumably in a cultic locale.[49] Jeremiah 36:10 says that Gemariah, one of Shaphan the *sōpēr*'s sons, has an "office" (*liškâ*) in the Temple in which Baruch the *sōpēr* read Jeremiah's prophecies from a scroll. These "offices," when associated with *sōpĕrîm*, are places where texts are read before an audience and stored (Jer 36:12, 20), though the explicit reference to storing texts in an "office" takes place in the palace, not the temple.

That texts could be deposited in temples does not necessarily mean that priests in the pre-exilic period were, as a rule, as literate as professional scribes, nor does it mean that there were parochial "schools" of scribal training in Israelite and Judahite temples for religious specialists. It is certainly possible that Gemariah tutored scribes in some fashion out of his Temple office. But even if we understand Gemariah's office in the Temple as a scriptorium or the locus of a school, neither Gemariah, nor any other member of the Shaphan family, is identified as a priest. I will discuss the relevance of Jeremiah 36 to literacy more below, but the presence of a Shaphanite in the Temple makes me wonder whether priests who may not have achieved the same level of literacy as a professional scribe, might have made use of non-priestly scribes when they needed ideological content developed in writing.[50] Schniedewind argues that Hilkiah's discovery of the book suggests that the social control of writing shifted from the palace to the Temple.[51] Similarly, van der Toorn contends that Hilkiah's discovery shows that this "Torah was written by Temple scribes."[52] Yet the details of 2 Kings 22 suggest that Shaphan family scribes, in this story associated with the palace, not the Temple, were deeply involved in the transmission of this discovered book. This story indeed suggests that there was probably a "connection between the temple and the palace,"[53] but if there was this kind of interchange between Temple and palace, positing parochial "temple scribes" or priest-scribes seems incongruous with this kind of exchange between the two institutions. As we will see below with regard to Jeremiah 36, the likely ideological interchange between palace and Temple can also be explained by rooting scribal training in clans or families that specialize in scribal training.

---

[49]The verb *nûaḥ* is used in a cultic sense elsewhere; see, e.g., Exod 16:33–34; Lev 16:23; Num 17:4, 7; Deut 26:4; 1 Chr 28:2; 2 Chr 4:8, and in reference to the depositing of a sacred text 1 Kgs 8:9.

[50]Van der Toorn notes that though most scribes were affiliated with temples in first millennium Mesopotamia, they were not *priests* and "in spite of their academic expertise, the scholars were subordinate to the real priests of the temple—such as the *aḫu rabû*, or high priest—who were responsible for the daily care and feeding of the gods. Scribal skills and scholarship did not have the same prestige as a position as steward to the gods" (*Scribal Culture*, 59).

[51]Schniedewind, *How the Bible Became a Book*, 112.

[52]Van der Toorn, *Scribal Culture*, 87.

[53]Ibid., 86.

In addition, we cannot rule out that the *ideological* content of the book of the law was composed by priests, but that they were dependent on the specialization of professional scribes for the physical writing. It is also possible that some Israelite and Judahite priests were literate, but others were not, both in a diachronic and synchronic sense. If Hilkiah was not literate at the level of a professional scribe, other High Priests before or succeeding him could have been, and there could have been other priests highly trained in the scribal arts at the same time. Yet, our detailed descriptions of scribal practices in the Hebrew Bible make no mention of them. In this story, the only clearly literate person is Shaphan.

*Prophets*

Huldah, the prophetess, is also a notable source of ideological support for the Josianic changes to the cult because she, through her role as a prophetic figure, confirms the divine origin of the discovered book of the Law. The text does not suggest that anyone reads the book to Huldah, but she does seem to be familiar with its contents. Biblical passages from the Persian period explicitly present quite a few prophets (or "seers") as literate,[54] but the general literacy of prophets in the pre-exilic period is very unclear. Young suggests reasonably that some were probably literate and some were not, but that prophets "as a whole cannot at present be treated as a literate class."[55] There are some other biblical references to prophets writing. As noted, Samuel writes a document about the regulations for kingship (1 Sam 10:25). I have also recounted commands Ezekiel receives to write certain, small formulaic statements. In Isa 1:8, Yahweh commands Isaiah to write (*ktb*) "belonging to Maher-shalal-hash-baz" with a "common writing implement" (*ḥereṭ ʾĕnôš*). Another oracle from First Isaiah commands, "Go write it on a tablet, inscribe it in a book that it might be for future times a witness forever" (Isa 30:8).

None of these biblical passages unequivocally demonstrate widespread advanced literacy among prophets. Samuel's ability to write a document in 1 Sam 10:25 may be an expression of the multiple roles that Samuel plays in the traditions about him. Samuel performs priestly (1 Sam 7:9–10), judicial (1 Sam 7:6, 16), military/political (1 Sam 8:4) and prophetic functions (1 Sam 3:20). As a "jack of all trades," acting as a professional scribe who can produce a document would be one more task to add to the list of Samuel's reputed social roles. Also, notably, prophets can have other careers outside of their prophetic role. Amos is a stockbreeder (*nōqēd*, Amos 7:14), and Ezekiel is a priest (Ezek 1:3). It is conceivable that someone with a professional scribal career could also be a prophet, but it still may not have been common for prophets to pursue professional scribal education. Adding to the lack of clarity about prophetic literacy is the fact that commands to *write* oracular pronouncements do not necessarily mean that the prophet actually wrote the oracles. As some have observed, Yahweh directly commands Jeremiah to "take a scroll and *write* on it all the matters that I have spoken to you" (Jer 36:2). Yet, immediately following this command, Jeremiah calls on Baruch, son of Neriah to actually write the scroll (36:4). Similarly, Jer 51:60 says that *Jeremiah* "wrote in a scroll all the woe that would come to Babylon in one book" (*wayyiktōb yirmĕyāhu ʾēt kol-hārāʿâ ʾăšer tābôʾ ʾel-bābel ʾel-sēper ʾaḥad*). Yet, 51:59 clearly says that Seraiah, Baruch's brother, actually writes the document. As a result, when, for example, Yahweh commands Habakkuk to write the divine vision he sees (Hab 2:2), or when other prophets are commanded to

---

[54] In 2 Chr 21:12, Elijah the prophet sends a correspondence (*miktāb*), and other post-exilic texts claim that prophets (or "seers") write records (1 Chr 29:29; 2 Chr 9:29; 12:15; 13:22; 20:34; 26:22; 32:32; 33:19).
[55] Young, "Israelite Literacy," 252.

write, we cannot assume that the prophet himself actually commits the oracular vision to textual media.[56]

Also, interestingly, with respect to the prophet Isaiah, son of Amoz, like 2 Kgs 22:14–20, when Hezekiah consults Isaiah he is sure to send Shebna the *sōpēr* with the delegation (2 Kgs 19:1). It is very possible that 2 Kgs 19:1 and 22:14–20 present a particularly ideological, Deuteronomistic view of text transmission with the purpose of domesticating the prophetic tradition to a scribal class. Yet, the references to scribes in 2 Kings as well as Jeremiah are the only detailed portrait of text transmission from ancient Israel and Judah, and one could argue that all presentations of scribal culture from the ancient Near East are ideological products.

There is clearer support for the existence of prophetic "schools" in the sense of disciples who are affiliated with a particular prophetic figure. Some passages indicate that prophets gained committed followers and supporters (1 Kgs 19:19–21; 2 Kgs 2:1–18). Elisha's "servants" (2 Kgs 6:3) build a compound so that they could live with him in a community of *běnê-něbî'îm* (2 Kgs 6:1–7). There were also evidently pronounced ideological differences between some prophetic traditions and others (Isa 28:7–13[57]). Isaiah 8:16 mentions "disciples" (*limmûdîm*) of Yahweh for whom Isaiah will "bind up the testimony" and "seal the teaching" (compare exilic 50:4–5; 54:13). As Lemaire suggests, Isa 8:16 raises the prospect of prophetic schools in ancient Israel,[58] but he also notes that how, exactly, the words of the prophet were transmitted to disciples remains unclear. Carr, while acknowledging that the passage does not make any clear reference to writing, argues that because of the relationship between the oral and the written in the ancient world, the educational process described in Isa 8:16–22 was "both written and oral."[59] That writing was involved in the transmission of tradition is certainly possible, but according to the collaboration model that I have proposed, were writing involved in the transmission of these traditions, this prophetic "school" would have needed to collaborate with literate specialists for the written transmission of their ideas. Consequently, the "school" of thought that might have organized around the figure of Isaiah (or any other prophet) and its *limmûdîm* should be differentiated from *scribal* schools for training in advanced literacy.

## Kings

In the story of the discovery of the book of the law in 2 Kings 22, Josiah does not actually read the book initially, but 2 Kgs 23:2 claims that Josiah "read" the book in public. The king's public reading of the book forces us to ask whether kings were literate in ancient Israel and Judah. A handful of kings from other societies of the ancient Near East were said to be literate, such as Assurbanipal, Shulgi, Lipit Ishtar,[60] and pharaohs Sneferu and Izezi (Old Kingdom).[61] But it seems that literacy among monarchs was not very common. The relief accompanying one of the Aramaic Bar-Rakib

---

[56] Interestingly, the person commanded to write the text (presumably Habakkuk) does not appear to be the same as the "reader" (*qōrē*) who runs with it.
[57] Isaiah 28:9–10 is often taken as evidence that training in literacy began from youth: "To whom should one teach knowledge? To whom should one explicate the message? Those who are weaned from milk? Those separated from the breast? *Ṣaw lāṣāw, ṣaw lāṣāw, qaw lāqāw, qaw lāqāw.* Here a little, there a little." Some argue that *ṣaw lāṣāw, qaw lāqāw* are references to letters of the alphabet (William W. Hallo, "Isaiah 28:9–13 and the Ugaritic Abecedaries," *JBL* 77 [1958]: 337–38). Ultimately, because the meaning of *ṣaw* and *qaw* are unclear and due to the sarcastic nature of this verse, Isa 28:9–10 cannot be marshaled to support the existence of education in literacy from a young age. See A. van Selms, "Isaiah 28:9–13: An Attempt to Give a New Interpretation," *ZAW* 85 (1973): 332–39, and James L. Crenshaw, "Education in Ancient Israel," *JBL* 104 (1985): 602.
[58] Lemaire, *Les écoles*, 37–38.
[59] Carr, *Tablet of the Heart*, 144.
[60] Crenshaw, "Education in Ancient Israel," 608.
[61] Williams, "Scribal Training," 215. For more information on royal literacy in Egypt, see Baines, *Visual and Written*, 78–80.

inscriptions (ca. 730 BCE), which pictorially represents the king and his scribe, visually conveys the close connection a king in the Levantine region could have with his scribe.[62] Like the prophetic examples above, perhaps the scribe acted as the eyes and pen of the king so that when the scribe reads *to* the king and writes *for* the king, according to the idioms for reading and writing in ancient Israel and Judah, the king has effectively "read" and "written" the text.

As a result, that Josiah "reads (*qr'*) the words (*dĕbārîm*) of the book of the covenant into the ears of the people" does not necessarily mean that he reads printed words from a scroll in real time. The flexibility of the words *qr'* and *dābār* and the evidence for functional literacy leave the king's educational background in literacy obscure. Does the king recite the words of the scroll from memory? Did the king only achieve a lower level of literacy? Could the king only read and write as well as the soldier who composed Lachish Letter 3? In my opinion, from the perspective of modern literacy, in 2 Kgs 23:2 the king is probably reciting the words of the book of the covenant from memory, not reading the book in real time.

There are other references to kings "writing" in the Hebrew Bible, such as 2 Sam 11:1, 2 Kgs 10:1, and Isa 38:8. The latter passage records a reputed poetic "writing (*miktāb*) of Hezekiah." Post-exilic 2 Chr 35:4 has David and Solomon composing texts (*miktāb*) as well. Deuteronomy 17:18–19 says that the king should "write" (*ktb*) a copy of the Torah for himself and "read" (*qr'*) it all the days of his life. Considering the fact that *qr'* and *ktb* do not necessarily mean "read" and "write" from the perspective of modern literacy, Deut 17:18–19 probably does not literally command the king to read and write. Rather, the king should have someone write the copy of the law for him and have someone read the law to him, which he will then memorize and recite. According to the same passage, this copy of the Torah comes from (*millipnê*) the Levitical priests, but this also does not mean that Levitical priests, as a rule, were literate, or had their own scribal schools. Rather, the Levitical priests are identified as the producers of ideas, which may have been largely oral. Professional scribes—who might operate between the Temple and palace—could have been recruited so that the ideology of the Levitical priests could be committed to a *sēper*.

If we drew conclusions about Israelite and Judahite scribal practices from 2 Kings 22, then the process of reading and writing—that is, committing literary ideas and speech to physical textual media and comprehending written texts fluently—involves professional scribes who perform the specialized skills of reading and writing with dexterity. Nevertheless because they are sources of ideational content, prophets, priests and the monarchy are deeply involved in the process of "writing." And so if written texts cannot be separated from their oral component, non-literate elites who developed ideological content orally are an inextricable part of the writing process, when it comes to the literary texts of the Hebrew Bible. Several actors are involved in the ideological project portrayed in 2 Kings 22: the High Priest, the king (and his officials), a prophetess, and scribes. Yet, scribes are present throughout the entire process in 2 Kings 22, from start to finish, suggesting that scribes are also an intrinsic part of ideological change.

## JEREMIAH 36

I have already referred to some of the elements of Jeremiah 36, in relation to the question of literacy. One narrative detail I referenced was that when Yahweh commands Jeremiah to write his

---

[62] For a good, clear picture of this relief, see Carr, *Tablet of the Heart*, 114. For information about the inscription, see Scott C. Layton and Dennis Pardee, "Literary Sources for the History of Palestine and Syria: Old Aramaic Inscriptions," *Biblical Archaeologist* 51 (1983): 183.

oracles on a scroll, Jeremiah commissions Baruch the *sōpēr* to actually commit the words to textual media:

> This word came to Jeremiah from Yahweh: Take a scroll and write on it all the words that I have spoken to you against Israel and Judah and all the nations, from the day I spoke to you, from the days of Josiah until today. Perhaps the house of Judah will hear of all the disasters that I am planning to do to them, so that every one may turn from their evil ways, and I may forgive their iniquity and their sin. Then Jeremiah called Baruch son of Neriah, and Baruch wrote on a scroll, from the mouth of Jeremiah, the words of Yahweh that he had spoken to him. (36:1b–4)

The book of Jeremiah does not provide many details about Baruch, except that he is a *sōpēr*, that he is the son of Neriah, that his grandfather is named Mahseiah (Jer 32:12) and that he has a brother named Seraiah, whom Jeremiah also commissions to write a scroll (Jer 51:59). We also do not know anything about Baruch's institutional affiliation.[63] His brother, Seraiah, is the quartermaster, which connects him with the palace, but there is nothing explicitly connecting Baruch to either the palace or the temple.

Adding to the haziness of Baruch's institutional affiliation, just because one family member finds a career in an institution does not mean that other members of the family are affiliated with the same institution. This strongly suggests that scribal training in the late monarchy was rooted primarily in the family, rather than in institutions like the palace or Temple. These professional scribes, who are affiliated primarily with their family, could then be recruited by institutions that required their expertise. If we use the Shaphan family as a guide, one family could operate as literate specialists in multiple institutional spaces. Gemariah, one of the Shaphanites, has an office where texts are read in the Temple,[64] but his father Shaphan was associated with the palace as royal *sōpēr*. Gemariah's brother Elasah also seems to be connected with the palace in some way because he was sent to Babylon by Zedekiah, but Elasah also helps deliver Jeremiah's letter to people in exile, which points to Elasah's literacy. If the Jaazaniah son of Shaphan mentioned in Ezek 8:11 is related to the Shaphan family, there is no indication of what his profession might be. It is interesting that he is the only person mentioned by name in the passage, which might mean that he stands out (as a literate specialist for the elders?) in some way. Additionally, though Gemariah has an office in the Temple, he himself can operate in different institutional spaces. He is part of the audience in the palace office of Elishama the *sōpēr* to whom Baruch reads his scroll again (Jer 36:11). The institutional affiliation of Micaiah, Gemariah's son (and Shaphan's grandson) is also unclear. He too seems to be able to operate between the palace and the Temple, listening to the reading of Jeremiah's scroll in an office of the Temple and reporting it to royal officials in the palace. The ability of these Shaphanites to move between Temple and palace militates against the notion of parochialized temple scribes, priest-scribes or palace scribes, and forces us to consider that scribes constituted an independent class, based around families, that could operate in a variety of social milieus.

It should be especially noted here that Micaiah does not actually read Baruch's scroll. He "*heard* all the words of Yahweh from the scroll" (Jer 36:11) and *told* (*ngd*) the audience in Elishama the *sōpēr*'s room "all the words he had heard when Baruch read from the scroll in the ears of the people"

---

[63] Van der Toorn, *Scribal Culture*, 84.
[64] There are no explicit references to Gemariah's literacy, but the fact that texts are read in his office just as they are in Elishama the *sōpēr*'s office and the fact that Jer 36:10 reminds the reader that his father Shaphan, was the royal *sōpēr* strongly associate Gemariah with literacy. For possible *liškôt* in the archaeological record, see J. Andrew Dearman, "My Servants the Scribes: Composition and Context in Jeremiah 36," *JBL* 109 (1990): 415–17.

(Jer 36:13). According to the portrayal here, this is an entirely oral transmission of the scroll's contents, reaffirming the relationship between orality and the written word. Additionally, Micaiah's ability to recall the words of the scroll from memory is one way of looking at Josiah's ability to "read" the book of the covenant in 2 Kgs 23:1–2. Perhaps Josiah was recalling the words of the book in front of the people, just as Micaiah was recounting the words of Jeremiah's scroll before the audience in the king's palace.

Since Baruch's institutional affiliation is unclear, could he be a kind of freelance scribe who acted as Jeremiah's personal secretary? After all, Baruch does not simply write oracles for Jeremiah, he is involved in Jeremiah's financial transactions as well (Jer 32:12–13, 16). There is not a great deal of information to draw such a conclusion, so it remains a mere possibility. What is significant about Baruch is that he is capable of composing complex literary texts and he has a family member who is also highly literate, supporting the possibility that literacy was a family affair.

After Baruch reads the scroll in the office of Elishama, and the audience resolves to report its contents to the king, they ask him, "How did you write all these words from [Jeremiah's] mouth?" And Baruch responds, "He called out all these words to me *while* I was writing them with ink on the scroll" (Jer 36:17–18). Unlike other verses in which the passage of time is unclear, making whether the person actually read the material in real time or recited it from oral memory unclear (e.g., Josiah in 2 Kgs 23:2 above), the syntax of v. 18 intimates that Baruch is writing at the same time that Jeremiah is speaking. While I am not ready to assert that 36:18 conveys dictation or transcription as a modern literate person would understand it, the verse does communicate a close, intimate relationship between the words of Jeremiah and the writing of Baruch. Indeed, the idea that Baruch wrote the words of the scroll from Jeremiah's mouth is repeated throughout the chapter to emphasize this intimacy in the production of the textual medium (36:4, 17–18, 27, 32).

Next, Yehudi, an apparently literate official of unknown title, takes Baruch's scroll from the palace office of Elishama and reads it in front of King Jehoiakim and some of his officials in the king's winter palace (36:16–22). As Yehudi reads three or four columns of text, Jehoiakim cuts that section of the scroll off and throws it into the fire until the entire scroll is destroyed. After Jeremiah and Baruch come out from hiding, Yahweh commands Jeremiah to "write (*ktb*) all of the former words" on another scroll (36:27–28), which he then dictates again to Baruch, "and many similar words were added to them" (Jer 36:32). This last reference is practically an admission that texts are often expanded.

## CONCLUSION

The portrait offered by 2 Kings 22 and Jeremiah 36 is one in which powerful, ideologically interested figures of questionable literary skills work closely with professional scribes (*sōpĕrîm*). In 2 Kgs 22:8, Shaphan reads the scroll to Hilkiah, suggesting—while not necessarily proving—that the High Priest is not literate. Shaphan then reads the scroll to Josiah (2 Kgs 22:10), which also suggests that the king is not literate. Josiah sends Shaphan and his son to consult the prophetess Huldah, making scribes involved in the oracular legitimation of the book (2 Kgs 22:12; compare 2 Kgs 19:1). In Jeremiah 36, the prophet Jeremiah is commanded to write (*ktb*) a scroll of oracles twice (36:2, 28), a task actually performed by Baruch the *sōpēr* (36:4, 32; compare 51:59–60). The question of literacy is complicated by the possibility that there were different levels of scribal education and training within ancient Israel and Judah. The assumption here is that the only people capable of producing complex literary texts with dexterity were professional *sōpĕrîm*. Even if officials such as priests, retainers and kings achieved different levels of literacy, their lower level of proficiency in reading and writing required them to employ the skills of a professional scribe when they wanted to produce ideologically rich texts. If any information about literacy in ancient Israel and Judah can be gleaned from 2 Kings 22 and Jeremiah 36 (admittedly, a big, "if"), these stories add a new layer of complexity to the relationship between orality and writing and the assessment of literacy in ancient Israel and Judah.

The examples found in these chapters suggest that "authorship" of a "text" is a result of a great deal of input from people who perhaps cannot—or *do* not—read and write, but who collaborate with those who can. Based on this model, ideological change can be spearheaded by non-literate or functionally literate elites, but scribes would still be necessary for the preservation of their ideas. One advantage of a collaboration model of text production in ancient Israel and Judah is that it gives more agency to non-literate social actors in the process of ideological change. Ultimately, scribes are custodians of these traditions and have the power to alter and refashion them. But scribes are not entirely autonomous and their decisions are contestable, even by non-literate people (Jer 8:8). Consequently, scribes, as embedded members of their society must still contend with influential social forces and figures outside of their scribal circles. All of the important, seminal scholarship about scribal culture in the ancient Near East rightly emphasizes the role of the scribe in the transmission of ideas. We would do well to remember that there were other actors, well-versed in the oral tradition, that could work in collaboration and in conflict with scribes, as well. Additionally, this collaboration model takes into account the possibility that people in a society in which literacy is available might choose not to become literate.

In 2 Kings 22 and Jeremiah 36, the professional scribe's familial connections are conspicuous, suggesting a strong family component to scribal training. The Shaphanites are involved with the reporting of the Josianic law code and two members of the Neriah family (Baruch and Seraiah) are involved with the transmission of Jeremiah's oracles. Furthermore the Shaphanites, Gemariah and Micaiah are also involved with the communication of Jeremiah's scroll or oracles. While it is conceivable that Gemariah or Elishama (another scribal ally of Jeremiah, not related to the Shaphanites) could have trained scribes inside their respective offices, that model of scribal education still seems different from Egyptian temple and palace "schools" and the Mesopotamian *bīt mummu*. If scribal training took place in these offices, the offices are possessed by one literary specialist, which seems closer to the **é-dub-ba** model which were small family operations in which a tutor trained a few pupils, identified as the tutor's "sons." Furthermore, that different members of the same family can take different positions in different institutions points away from the idea that the Temple (i.e., priests) or the palace are the main agents of scribal training. Rather, the picture presented here suggests the purview of scribal training was inside the family, whose members then worked within the various institutions of Israelite and Judahite society. An ideological current led by the priests, the king or an influential prophet could certainly attract, recruit or, in the case of the palace, conscript scribes to commit its ideational material to writing. But priests, prophets and most royal officials need not be literate themselves to have a profound impact on writing and written materials.

This portrayal has implications for depictions of reading and writing outside of the Deuteronomistic History and the book of Jeremiah. The semantic range of *qr'* and *ktb* makes the literary skills of prophets commanded to "write" uncertain (e.g., Hab 2:2). Additionally, it seems likely that there were, in fact, disciples who clustered around a prophetic figure (e.g., Isa 8:16–22; cf. 2 Kgs 6:1–7). But there is no clear indication that these students were trained in advanced scribal skills, and the instruction could have been entirely audial and haptic. The same goes for the "instruction" portrayed in wisdom texts, such as Proverbs (e.g., Prov 5:13).

Finally, let us assume, for the sake of argument, that the portrait of collaboration in 2 Kings 22 and Jeremiah 36 is a scribal projection, informed by the ideological interests of later scribes who wish to ground their texts in the authority of prophetic figures and other prominent people from ancient Israel's history, such as Josiah, Huldah, Hilkiah and Jeremiah. Perhaps the scribes who were custodians of the Deuteronomistic tradition and the Jeremiah tradition could have invented stories that depict close collaboration between prophets, kings, priests and scribes to legitimate their own literary texts. However, it bears repeating, that while almost all of the information from the ancient Near East about scribal education and practice comes from ideologically interested scribal portrayals of literacy, modern scholars assume there is some information to be gleaned from them. Second, even if these portrayals of collaboration are ideological scribal concoctions, with little historic value, they are interesting in their own right. For example, we can compare ways of legitimating texts in Mesopotamia with ways of legitimating texts in ancient Israel and Judah. Whereas in Mesopotamia, scribes might give their texts legitimacy by rooting them in the sages of old, the scribal traditions that composed and compiled Deuteronomistic and Jeremiah texts develop rather complex stories showing that their texts are a result of close collaboration and interaction between scribal families and historic figures. Consequently, if these stories of collaboration are scribal creations, we would have an Israelite twist on the general ancient Near Eastern practice of legitimating literary texts by appealing to the sages of old. The picture of collaboration found in 2 Kings 22 and Jeremiah 36 is also distinct from post-exilic texts that routinely portray kings and prophets as being literate themselves.

# Ecclesiastes and the Problem of Transmission in Biblical Literature

JACQUELINE VAYNTRUB

## *NEFESH* AS EMBODIED VOICE: AN ANCIENT PROBLEM OF TRANSMISSION

How did the biblical authors conceptualize transmission and the role of transgenerational relationships in this process? Genesis 27 narrates the transmission of blessing and responsibility in the context of the patriarch's impending death. Isaac summons his eldest son, Esau, to receive the blessing of his *nefesh*—a term whose conventional translation as "soul" will require unpacking in the discussion that follows.[1] For now, however, I leave the term untranslated. Isaac, blind in his advanced age, calls to Esau to hunt some game for him, and to prepare a dish from the meat, so that Isaac can bestow upon him this blessing of the *nefesh*. The Hebrew reads in v. 4: בעבור תברכך נפשי בטרם אמות, "so that my *nefesh* may bless you before I die." Rebecca, Esau and Jacob's mother, has other designs. She strategizes to have the younger son, Jacob, take advantage of Isaac's poor sight, and prepares a dish for Jacob to bring before his father Isaac before Esau returns, so that he might receive the blessing of Isaac's *nefesh* instead of Esau. Rebecca drapes Jacob with animal skins—the very skins of the domesticated animals slaughtered for Isaac's requested meal of wild meat. Going before Isaac, Jacob announces a deception to his father in v. 19,

אנכי עשו בכרך עשיתי כאשר דברת אלי קום־נא שבה ואכלה מצידי בעבור תברכני נפשך

> It is I, Esau, your first-born. I did as you instructed me. Please now sit up and eat of my game so that you might bless me with your *nefesh*.

But Isaac senses there is something wrong. Feeling Jacob wrapped in the hairy animal skins, Isaac exclaims (v. 22): "The voice is the voice of Jacob, yet the hands are the hands of Esau." Recognizing Jacob's mis-embodied voice—in what Isaac believes to be the body of Esau, and claiming to be Esau—Isaac still blesses Jacob. Isaac relies on his sense of touch and smell, dismissing the suspicions raised by his auditory sense: the voice, belonging to Jacob, claims to be Esau, and this claim is sufficiently compelling for Isaac.[2] There is much artistry and intrigue to this story that the scope of the present essay cannot allow. Here I will only deal with the problem of the blessing. What does it mean for Isaac's *nefesh* to give a blessing? What is the nature of this blessing?

---

[1] Here I build upon my previously published work on Genesis 27, Jacqueline Vayntrub, "Like Father, Like Son: Theorizing Transmission in Biblical Literature," *Hebrew Bible and Ancient Israel* 7, no. 4 (2018): 500–526
[2] For discussion on the important role sight plays in the particular narrative history to which this episode belongs, and especially in this episode, see Joel Baden, *Promise to the Patriarchs* (New York: Oxford University Press, 2013), 114.

A hint is provided in the story itself. After Isaac blesses Jacob posing to be Esau, the real Esau returns looking for his rightful blessing. But the first blessing cannot be undone: Isaac says to Esau in v. 33, "I blessed him"—that is, Jacob—"and he will remain blessed." Esau reacts to these words with sobbing and demands a blessing, for which Isaac gives him a consolation. He will "enjoy the fat of the earth and the dew of heaven above" (v. 39). Yet, Esau will serve his younger brother Jacob, who has tricked him in this episode out of the deathbed blessing reserved for the first born, the blessing of the *nefesh*. What is the blessing of the *nefesh*? In this story, the blessing is one of abundance, fertility, and *patria potestas*, that is, authority over the family as exercised through the embodied voice of the patriarch. The blessing constitutes no less than the ritual transfer of the authority of the patriarch as embodied in the living voice of Isaac to exercise authority over the family, to his son. Earlier scholarship tended to characterize blessings, along with curses, as stable entities whose materiality transcends the ephemeral nature of words spoken in a single, transient moment.[3] Recent scholarship on blessing and cursing has argued that the view that the biblical authors viewed speech and language as *inherently* powerful to entail problematic theological assumptions.[4] Wherever the biblical authors understood the power of the blessing of the *nefesh* to reside—whether in the words themselves or in the conventions of their use—the fact remains that this blessing was understood by the authors to irrevocably endow its recipient with particular qualities, rights, and responsibilities. The fact that this particular blessing is a deathbed blessing makes it all the more interesting for a study of ancient Israelite conceptions of individual death, the self, and father-to-son transmission.[5]

Semantically speaking, the *nefesh* is not Isaac's "soul" as our own culturally configured lens might have us believe. A fuller understanding of this term considers the physiological dimensions of the Hebrew. Whatever non corporeal elements the term might indicate, it also designates the physical locus of speech and breathing.[6] Moreover, the *nefesh* is *the* life supporting organ, through which life-sustaining nutrients pass.[7] In Northwest Semitic, the term *nefesh* functions

---

[3] Johannes Pedersen in his encompassing work, *Israel: Its Life and Culture*, vols. 1 and 2 (London: Oxford University Press, 1926, 1940), had already articulated a similar understanding of the porous nature of the ancient Israelite self as exemplified in the relationship between the spoken words of blessing/instruction (particularly as the moment of death approaches) and the "soul": "The soul is a whole saturated with power. It is the same power which acts in the centre and far out in the periphery, as far as the soul extends…this vital power, without which no living being can exist, is called by the Israelites [ברכה], blessing. The Israelite does not distinguish between the power, as it acts in the soul, and as it manifests itself outwardly. For him the capacity and the result is the same…blessing is the inner strength of the soul and the happiness it creates" (p. 182).

[4] James K. Aitken points out that while performative speech acts like blessing and cursing *attribute* power to speech, one should not assume that the biblical authors believed in a numinous power of words. Aitken's work builds on the work of Anthony Thiselton ("The Supposed Power of Words in the Biblical Writings," *JTS* 25, no. 2 [1974]: 283–99). Aitken further explains that the notion that the biblical authors believed blessings or curses to have inherent power emerges from projected theological assumptions. Instead, Aitken points to the "conventions of their use." See *The Semantics of Blessing and Cursing in Ancient Hebrew* (Dudley: Peeters, 2007), 21. See also the discussion in my *Beyond Orality: Biblical Poetry on Its Own Terms* (Abingdon: Routledge, 2019), 143 n. 70.

[5] See Claus Westermann on this point, that the *nefesh qua* blessing "is vitality that is passed on by the one who is departing from life to the one who is continuing in life… [N]o distinction is made between the corporal and the spiritual…because the blessing is concerned with vitality as a whole, the blessing cannot return or be subsequently altered" (*Genesis 12–36: A Commentary*, trans. John J. Scullion [Minneapolis: Augsburg Publishing, 1984], 436). Somewhat differently, Tzvi Abusch speaks of the "death soul, the soul of the individual after death…that gradually loses individuality until it becomes part of the collectivity of the ancestors," and in a note adds that Akkadian *napištu* and Hebrew *nefesh*, as well as Akkadian *zaqīqu* / Sumerian LÍL, are conceptually related to this phenomenon of a post mortem survival of the individual. See "Ghost and God: Some Observations on a Babylonian Understanding of Human Nature," in *Studies in the History of Religions*, ed. H. G. Kippenberg and E. T. Lawson (Leiden: Brill, 1998), 363–83 at 372.

[6] See Richard C. Steiner, *Disembodied Souls: The Nefesh in Israel and Kindred Spirits in the Ancient Near East, With an Appendix on the Katumuwa Inscription*, ANEM 11 (Atlanta: SBL, 2015).

[7] See, e.g., the sense of the term in Hab 2:5, that the defiant man "who has made his *nefesh* as wide as Sheol, is insatiable like death." That is, he has made his gullet wide to gobble up people as does the grave. See also Eccl 6:7, where the term is parallel with "mouth," cited below.

as a metonym for the self.[8] Eventually, the term undergoes grammaticalization, functioning as a reflexive pronoun where then Hebrew נפשי or Arabic *nafsi* means "myself." This is, in fact, largely how *nefesh* is used in Ecclesiastes,[9] though the term is also attested as the life-supporting organ as well.[10] But before *nefesh* becomes the separable "soul" in the Western imagination, *nefesh* in the Semitic speaking ancient world is the embodied self. Matthew Suriano importantly distinguishes between the metaphysical sense of the English "soul"—which is "released [from the body] at death," a concept which has been shaped by Plato's *psychē* to a certain extent—and the concept bound up in Northwest Semitic *napš/nabš*.[11] Suriano explains that while the translation of *nefesh* as soul problematically and anachronistically imposes a Western mind–body dualism onto the West Semitic situation, the monism of a *nefesh* inseparable from the body is also not quite correct.[12] Suriano avoids these problematic solutions by examining the term itself as it appears in the texts, and produces a description of *nefesh* outside of a dualistic or monistic framework but as an entity which experiences different types of embodiments.[13] Jean Bottéro, in his own discussion of Mesopotamian conceptions of death, points to a letter from Mari which references an ox slaughtered "by making him blow out his last breath," indicating that "like the ancient Hebrews, the Mesopotamians of the past considered death as the final return of the 'breath,' which had been given *ad tempus* by the gods."[14] When Isaac's *nefesh* gives its blessing to Jacob, then, this blessing is seemingly the last words voiced by the passing breath, immediately before it transitions out of its present embodied state.

In this study, I am not particularly concerned with describing how the *nefesh* functions in conceptions of death and the afterlife. Here I utilize insights articulated by Bottéro and Suriano—in particular, the description of an "embodied afterlife"—to demonstrate how imagination of the embodiment and reembodiment of the *nefesh* is inherently connected to the discourse surrounding the production and transmission of speech and texts. The concept of the embodied and potentially reembodied breath and voice-passage—and self, through synecdoche—is central to how ancient authors understood the transmission of speech, power, and texts. Whether this transmission is patrilineal or teacher-to-student succession, transmission across generations affords a form of existence beyond individual death. Through the lens of horizontal, transgenerational passage as the embodied and reembodied voice, one observes an ancient debate that has been obscured by modernity's focus on the stability of written text. This ancient debate concerns the authority and authenticity of speech when such speech is detached from the living speaker's voice.

---

[8]Here I am referring to the semantic shift in which the term *nefesh* moves from being used to describe the specific life-supporting organ (throat, gullet) or bodily function (the passage of breath and nutrients) to the whole human. Steiner engages the recent studies of the Kutamuwa inscription by David Schloen and Amir Fink ("New Excavations at Zincirli Höyük in Turkey [Ancient Sam'al] and the Discovery of an Inscribed Mortuary Stele," *BASOR* 356 [2009]: 1–13) and importantly the work of Dennis Pardee which suggests the possibility of the reembodiment of "free-moving ghosts" or "entities" into funerary monuments ("A New Aramaic Inscription from Zincirli," *BASOR* 356 [2009]: 51–71, at 63 n. 18). Steiner thus contends that "the semantic development by which Aramaic and Hebrew נבש/נפש came to refer to the funerary monument can now be explained as a case of synecdoche (*pars pro toto*) or metonymy rooted in the belief that the soul resides in its funerary monument" (*Disembodied Souls*, 15).
[9]Eccl 2:24; 4:8; 6:2, 3; 7:28.
[10]Eccl 6:7: כל־עמל האדם לפיהו וגם־הנפש לא תמלא, "All a person's toil is for their mouth, and yet his gullet is not filled."
[11]See Matthew Suriano, *A History of Death in the Hebrew Bible* (Oxford: Oxford University Press, 2018), 153, 277. The Septuagint is rather consistent in its translation of Hebrew נפש as *psychē* with a few exceptions. For example, in Gen 14:21 LXX translates *tous andras*, and MT has הנפש which in the context means "the person," but there are a number of other places in which MT has נפש with the valence of "person" or "self" and LXX gives *psychē*.
[12]Ibid.
[13]Ibid.
[14]Jean Bottéro, *Mesopotamia: Writing, Reasoning, and the Gods*, trans. Zainab Bahrani and Marc Van De Mieroop (Chicago, IL: University of Chicago Press, 1992) 271.

The episode in Genesis 27 depicts a stable, transmittable voice. This transmittable voice bears the patriarchal promise of God to Israel.[15] But the book of Ecclesiastes offers a coherent and radically different position on the stability of instruction transmission, and relatedly, a radically different position on the meaning of individual death. I argue that the intertwined concepts of transgenerational responsibility, transmission, and individual personhood in life and death manifest differently in ancient compositions. When these concepts of transgenerational responsibility and transmission do surface in the texts, they do so as specific positions on a debate of whether or not words retain truth when separated from the speaker's voice. Taken as a unified composition consisting of two voices, a frame speaker and the voice of Qohelet, the book of Ecclesiastes advances a position on this debate that is radically distinct from the understanding of stable transmission presented in Pentateuchal narrative.[16]

In a 1977 essay, Michael Fox examined the juxtaposition between Ecclesiastes's frame speaker and the voice of Qohelet. I aim to build upon Fox's insight, which brought the incoherence of these two voices—Qohelet and the frame speaker—to the surface of the evaluation of the work as an instruction.[17] Here, I go beyond Fox's recognition of the rhetorical role of the epilogue in Ecclesiastes to draw out the text's conceptual moves in its structure.[18] In the analysis that follows, I reread the frame of Ecclesiastes with the express purpose of bringing together three seemingly disparate areas of concern alluded to in the essay's introduction: instruction transmission, transgenerational reward and punishment, and mortal anxiety. This complex of ideas is brought together to demonstrate how Ecclesiastes engages a set of concerns regarding the epistemological status of words when they are detached from the living voice of their speaker.[19] Thus the ancient debate surrounding the question "Are these words reliable?" is entangled with concerns of the individuality of the speaker's voice, the speaker's connection to or detachment from a line of dead ancestors, and the meaning of individual death.

## MORTAL OBLIVION AND INSTRUCTION TRANSMISSION

Ecclesiastes, like a number of other biblical and parabiblical texts, situates instruction in the context of the approaching death of the speaker.[20] In Ecclesiastes, however, the deathbed context has a

---

[15]From a Neo-documentarian perspective, one observes the consistency of this idea in the J narrative history, where the promise as blessing comes in the form of these staged performances of deathbed testament *qua* instruction (Gen 49; Deut 33) and instruction/blessing *qua* prophecy (Num 23–24). For a fuller description of this argument through an analysis of Num 23–24, see my *Beyond Orality*, 103–32, which follows broadly the outline of the promise in this narrative history, as discussed in Joel S. Baden, *The Promise to the Patriarchs* (Oxford: Oxford University Press, 2013).
[16]Fox describes the literary work of the frame speaker in Ecclesiastes as "not the creator of Qohelet's words but as their transmitter." See Michael Fox, "Frame-Narrative and Composition in the Book of Qohelet," *HUCA* 48 (1977): 83–106, at 91.
[17]Ibid., 83–106.
[18]On the connection between the concluding frame of Ecclesiastes to the didactic function of first-person autobiography, Tremper Longman, III, *Fictional Akkadian Autobiography: A Generic and Comparative Study* (Winona Lake: Eisenbrauns, 1991), 120–23. Matthew Suriano, citing Longman's work, emphasizes the significance of this point: the persona of Qohelet as "a king…in the first-person" draws upon the wisdom which would be culturally associated with such a voice; see Suriano, "Kingship and *Carpe Diem*, Between Gilgamesh and Qoheleth," *VT* 67 (2017): 285–306, at 290.
[19]Such a debate would be necessarily connected to the concern of prophetic speech, but since this kind of speech involves the embodiment of the divine voice in the prophet, and not the horizontal, transgenerational dimension, this aspect of the transmission debate is to be left for a later study. Significant advances have been already made in this area, particularly with respect to masculinity, in the recent work of Rhiannon Graybill, *Are We Not Men: Unstable Masculinity in the Prophets* (Oxford: Oxford University Press, 2016).
[20]Fox makes note of Deuteronomy and Tobit as framed texts to compare to Ecclesiastes, but does not make the connection to deathbed testaments; see Fox, "Frame-Narrative," 93–4. An increasing number of studies are paying attention to the central role death plays in Ecclesiastes. In addition to the recent work by Suriano, "Kingship and *Carpe Diem*," discussed below, see Shannon Burkes, *Death in Qoheleth and Egyptian Biographies of the Late Period* (Atlanta: Society of Biblical Literature, 1999),

somewhat more subtle and complex presentation than it does in other biblical texts.[21] We might think of Jacob's deathbed speech in Genesis 49, or Moses's last words in Deuteronomy 33, which are most clearly and explicitly "deathbed instructions," where the anxiety of impending loss of voice is resolved through its transmission to the next generation. Further, we might expand our definition of "instruction" to include "blessing," or to see the two as related speech acts, and incorporate Isaac's final blessings to Jacob and Esau in Genesis 27 to our list of deathbed instructions.[22] As James Kugel points out, these types of blessings were understood in their broader literary culture to participate in a temporal blending of past events and future predictions.[23] One might further posit that the transmission of the deeds, words, and authority of the individual to the next generation demands the suspension of linear time to allow for the incorporation of the dying individual's personhood into the recipient. Similarly, we might see the entire frame of Deuteronomy as a final instruction, where Moses has a successor in Joshua, but the real successor is the text itself.[24]

Annette Reed, in her study of parabiblical testaments, "Textuality between Death and Memory: The Prehistory and Formation of the Parabiblical Testament," articulates how this genre seizes upon the "persuasive power" of the moment immediately preceding death, where the anxiety of mortality and the loss of voice is resolved through instruction transmission. The texts themselves, according to Reed,

> embody one particular solution to the problem of ensuring survival of knowledge in the cases that succession fails, or family lines are broken, or death extinguishes memory.[25]

That these texts are so rhetorically successful in their literary culture is not merely the result of an intertextual relationship with biblical deathbed instruction like Jacob's blessing in Genesis 49 or participation in the genre of final testament. As Reed points out, these works emerge from a cultural landscape in which the transmission of voice resolves anxiety surrounding impending death.[26] The medium of text itself poses a second-order resolution to this problem, in that written text can stand in for the voice.[27]

This is one way we might read ancient Levantine memorial inscriptions, a category to which the stele of Hammurabi belongs. These texts are inscribed on stone monuments, often with visual

---

and Matthew Rindge, who observes that the theme of death in Ecclesiastes is in fact bound up in the problem of material wealth and their loss upon individual death; see Rindge, "Mortality and Enjoyment: The Interplay of Death and Possessions in Qoheleth," *CBQ* 73 (2011): 265–80, at 268.

[21] Suriano connects the messages of *carpe diem* in Gilgamesh and Ecclesiastes for their shared autobiographical royal frame, and, significantly, Northwest Semitic memorial inscriptions. Perhaps even more significant—and certainly within the orbit of Suriano's work generally—is not only that these texts are staged in the royal voice but also that they are framed in the context of impending death and the threat of oblivion. See Suriano, "Kingship and *Carpe Diem*," 302–3.

[22] In his discussion of Gen 27, Gunkel identified deathbed testament as "a favorite legend motif" appearing elsewhere with Abraham (Gen 24:1–9), Jacob (Gen 48:10–49:33), Joseph (Gen 50:24–25), Moses (Deut 33), Joshua (Josh 23), David (2 Sam 23:1–7 and 1 Kgs 2:1–9), Elisha (2 Kgs 13:14–19), as well as in 1 Macc 2:49–69 and Tob 14:3–11. Gunkel connects these final speech performances with prophetic vision that accompanies the final moments before death. Gunkel traces this idea back to a moment in which the dying father "determin[ed] his heir." See Hermann Gunkel, *Genesis*, trans. M. E. Biddle (Macon, GA: Mercer University Press, 1997), 292, 302.

[23] James L. Kugel writes that, "however much the blessings make reference to the past, they are essentially predictions of the future—the future of both the individual sons and of the tribes that will spring from them…the blessings contained *predictions*, prophecies." *Traditions of the Bible: A Guide to the Bible as It Was at the Start of the Common Era* (Harvard, MA: Harvard University Press, 1999), 468–89.

[24] Eva Mroczek, *Literary Imagination in Jewish Antiquity* (Oxford: Oxford University Press, 2016), 185–86. See also Fox, "Frame-Narrative," 93.

[25] Annette Y. Reed, "Textuality Between Death and Memory: The Prehistory and Formation of the Parabiblical Testament," *JQR* 104, no. 3 (2014): 381–412, at 383.

[26] Ibid., 400.

[27] I advanced a similar argument about the voicelessness of Solomon in the anthological shaping and framing of Proverbs in my "The Book of Proverbs and the Idea of Ancient Israelite Education," *ZAW* 128 (2016): 107–109.

representations of the speaker's image.[28] Their messages are framed in the first-person voice, that is, in the voice of the memorialized speaker.[29] These inscriptions indexically preserve the voice of the speaker in its first-person voicing. Take the prologue to the Code of Hammurabi, for example: "At that time, the gods Anu and Enlil…named me by my name, Hammurabi," and "I am Hammurabi, king of justice, to whom the god Shamash has granted (insight into) the truth."[30] Memorial inscriptions also pragmatically preserve the speaker's voice in their threat to curse any future reader who would erase the name of the speaker in the text.[31] For example, in the epilogue to the Code of Hammurabi, the speaker lists a long series of curses for anyone who would not only fail to heed the pronouncements inscribed in the stele, but anyone who would alter the engraved image of Hammurabi, erase his name, or inscribe their own name, presumably in the place of Hammurabi's name. The name stands in metonymically, symbolically, and substantially for the person: its continuation is treated as the perpetuation of the individual beyond death, and relatedly, the name's erasure is treated as an erasure of the person and their memory.[32] Likewise, the voice functions metonymically for the person, and its textual preservation in first-person discourse can be understood as a perpetuation of that person. This first-person voice, therefore, engages the problem of individual death and the transmission of voice, authority, and personhood across generational lines.

The language of these inscriptions in their material context suggests a kind of embodiment of the speaker's persona in the stones themselves. One such inscription, the recently discovered Sam'alian inscription memorializing Katumuwa, an eighth-century BCE royal official in southeastern Anatolia, unequivocally speaks to the reembodiment of the speaker's persona in the stone monument itself:[33]

> [1]I am Katumuwa, servant of Panamuwa, who commissioned for myself (this) stele while [2]still living. I placed it in my eternal chamber (?) and established a feast (at) [3]this chamber (?)
> …
> [5]a ram for Kubaba, and a ram for my "soul" {*nbšy*} that (will be) in this stele.

We see then in memorial inscriptions a similar type of resolution of the threat of mortal oblivion. Instead of the narrative framing of the transgenerational transmission of the voice through instruction or blessing—which are themselves situated in the medium of text—here in the memorial

---

[28]The stelae of Kulamuwa (*KAI* 24), Zakkur (*KAI* 202), Barrakib (*KAI* 216), the bilingual Aramaic–Akkadian statue inscription from Tell Fakhariyah, and the newly discovered Kutamuwa mortuary stele from Zincirli all integrate the written text (announcement of the speaker's lifetime accomplishments) in images of the speaker's face and/or body. See the detailed description of the iconography of the Kutamuwa stele, which features the image of the named speaker and subject of the inscription in profile, in Eudora Struble and Virginia Hermann, "An Eternal Feast at Sam'al: The New Iron Age Mortuary Stele from Zincirli in Context," *BASOR* 356 (2009): 15–49, at 21–22.
[29]Douglas J. Green, *"I Undertook Great Works": The Ideology of Domestic Achievements in West Semitic Royal Inscriptions* (Tübingen: Mohr Siebeck, 2010).
[30]Laws of Hammurabi, i. 27–49; xlviii 95–xlix 17 (Marta T. Roth, *Law Collections from Mesopotamia and Asia Minor*, SBLWAW 6 [Atlanta: Scholars Press, 1997], 76, 135).
[31]Take, for example, the following curse of the Phoenician Kulamuwa stele, "Whoever of my sons who will sit in my place and damages this inscription…and whoever strikes out this inscription, may [multiple deities listed] strike his head," and the Azatiwada stele, "If a king…prince…man of renown…shall erase the name of Azatiwada from this gate and shall place (his) name (on it)…then may [multiple deities listed] erase that kingdom, and that king, and that man who is of renown. Only may the name of Azatiwada be forever like the name of the sun and the moon." "The Kulamuwa Inscription," trans. K. Lawson Younger, Jr. (*COS* 2.30:147–48); "The Azatiwada Inscription," trans. K. Lawson Younger, Jr. (*COS* 2.31:148–49).
[32]See the classic study by Herbert Chanan Brichto, "Kin, Cult, Land and Afterlife—A Biblical Complex," *HUCA* 44 (1973): 1–54, at 23, and see especially 21–25, where he discusses the transgenerational dimension of the שם, that this term "and its synonym זכר stand for '(line of) descendant(s)' and not merely for 'name' or 'memory'."
[33]Translation of this inscription has been excerpted from Pardee, "A New Aramaic Inscription," 53–54. See also Seth L. Sanders, "The Appetites of the Dead: West Semitic Linguistic and Ritual Aspects of the Katumuwa Stele," *BASOR* 369 (2013): 35–55; Matthew J. Suriano, "Breaking Bread with the Dead: Katumuwa's Stele, Hosea 9:4, and the Early History of the Soul," *JAOS* 134, no. 3 (2014): 385–405.

inscriptions we witness the unframed situating and reembodiment of the voice in the text of the stone monuments. This rhetorical reembodiment of the voice is accompanied with various visual representations of the memorialized speaker as well as the long-lasting medium (stone) and its upright and tall form, not unlike the form taken by a standing man. One observes marked differences in the presentation and framing of instruction transmission narratives, deathbed testaments, and Northwest Semitic memorial stelae. Unifying these different types of texts, however, is an underlying, unstated position on the stability of voice beyond the life of its speaker.

Instruction and blessing, along with the accomplishments of the individual (the father), are conceptualized in these texts as experiences which are bound to the speaker's personhood. When these experiences, as speech, are transmitted to the next generation, the new individual (the son) assumes the personhood, the voice of the father and, in this fiction, is authorized to then transmit to future generations. Thus a single family line staves off mortal oblivion. This transgenerational immortality, available to mortals provided they configure their lives within the larger context of a family over time, is a discourse that is connected to transgenerational reward and punishment.

Ecclesiastes takes up the problems inherent to the discourses of transmission across generational lines and tests the metaphysical limitations of reconceptualizing instruction and death in the context of individual personhood. As Matthew Rindge observes, "Qoheleth perceives death as a destroyer of memory, since the memory of a dead person vanishes among the living."[34] Horizontal transmission—the discourse surrounding the passage of objects, instruction, and responsibility from one generation to the next—functions, conceptually, to alleviate the anxiety generated by the imminent threat of mortal oblivion.[35]

## DEATH AND ECCLESIASTES'S TRANSMISSION PROBLEM

Ecclesiastes, in contradistinction to deathbed testaments, does not narratively situate itself in the context of immediate impending death. That is, death moves from the abstract inevitability (all humans die) to the specific experience (the aging process) only at the end of Qohelet's speech. Within the *inclusio* of his motto, "Utter futility," in 1:2 and 12:8, the speaker reflects upon his own lived experiences in a highly abstract way, without reference to specific individuals or situations. It is in this same highly abstract way that the speaker comes to the conclusion of a reflection upon his experiences with a description of the process of aging, a process which inevitably ends in silence—death. In this highly metaphorical description, Qohelet makes no reference to his own personal experiences, and as a result, the death recounted in Qohelet's final speech cannot be related to the speaker's *own* death. In a certain sense, Qohelet resists imparting his embodied experience in this instruction. The speaker had long ago abandoned his first-person discourse—a voice typical of kings memorializing themselves in Levantine monumental inscriptions—and now speaks in generalizations. Qohelet has abandoned the mantle of kingship, since even the extraordinary experience of kingship cannot provide lasting wisdom. Such an idea is reflected in Qohelet's movement away from personal experience and the first-person voice.

As a work, Ecclesiastes stakes out a radically new position on the debate of the transgenerational stability of speech, and does so in a coherent way which requires the text to be read as a single-authored work. Ecclesiastes does not explicitly take the form of a deathbed testament. That is, the

---

[34] Rindge, "Mortality and Enjoyment," 269.
[35] Concerns about the problems of the materiality of text are expressed in Ecclesiastes—particularly in the so-called epilogue (12:9–14), in the discussion of the written recording of instruction (12:10) and in the warning against the "making of many books" (12:12). These concerns, however, should be considered in the context of the more central problem of the stability of speech, action, and their effects (including punishment) beyond the limits of the individual, embodied, and living voice.

work does not clearly situate Qohelet's words at the end of his own life since the work is framed as instruction more broadly. One observes, for example, the structural similarity between the ascription in Ecclesiastes and Proverbs:

Prov 1:1
משלי שלמה בן־דוד מלך ישראל
The proverbs of Solomon son of David, king of Israel.

Eccl 1:1
דברי קהלת בן־דוד מלך בירושלים
The words of Qohelet son of David, king in Jerusalem.

Beyond the structural similarities, one notes that no other son of David, other than Solomon, is listed in the title of biblical books. Solomon in 1 Kgs 5:12 is described as having composed legion משל, "proverbs," and שיר, "song," corresponding nicely to the Solomonic titles in Prov 1:1 (also Prov 10:1 and 25:1) and in Song 1:1.[36] The identification of Qohelet with Solomon is more fraught—indeed, according to the recent work of Thomas Bolin, this identification, the "riddle" of Ecclesiastes's authorship, is precisely the point of the work.[37]

One might consider the ascription in Eccl 1:1 in light of 1 Kgs 11:41, which alludes to a lost chronicle of Solomon's acts—not only his accomplishments, as typical for such annals, but also his words of wisdom in particular:

ויתר דברי שלמה וכל־אשר עשה וחכמתו הלוא־הם כתבים על־ספר דברי שלמה

The rest of the acts of Solomon and all his accomplishments and his wisdom, are they not recorded in the book of the Acts of Solomon?

Ecclesiastes is entitled דברי קהלת, whose title dangles multiple interpretive possibilities before the reader. The דברי element of the title could refer to the *Acts* of Solomon, as the title recalled in 1 Kgs 11:41, to a no-longer extant (or perhaps invented) work. Or, the title could indicate a generic designation of wisdom and prophetic texts, דברי חכמים, "The *Words* of the Wise," and דברי עמוס, "The *Words* of Amos." Perhaps the simple element of the title embeds in itself the very paradox which is central to Ecclesiastes: that even its very formulaic and straightforward title is not as simple as it appears—it too is fraught with ambiguity and resists stable interpretation.

The traditional association of the figure of Qohelet is with Solomon: he is identified by the frame speaker as a son of David and is said, both by the frame speaker and by the autobiographical voice himself, to have been king in Jerusalem. In fact, the one and only time the autobiographical voice identifies himself by name as Qohelet is to assert that he was king in Jerusalem over Israel (Eccl 1:12). This, and the many other allusions to traditions of Solomon, his wisdom, and his accomplishments as given by the account in 1 Kings, may be seen as deliberate engagement with a literary tradition of Solomon as performer of wise speech.[38] Likewise, the use of an otherwise unattested name or title for a son of David, king in Jerusalem, Qohelet, may be seen as a deliberate attempt to influence the immediate reception of the text. For Proverbs and Ecclesiastes—as for many of the other ancient Near Eastern didactic works—attribution is a central aspect of how the work is shaped literarily. Others have discussed how attribution to a legendary figure of the distant past can lend an

---

[36] See Jacqueline Vayntrub, "Before Authorship: Solomon and Prov. 1:1," *BibInt* 26, no. 2 (2018): 182–206.
[37] Thomas M. Bolin, *Ecclesiastes and the Riddle of Authorship* (London: Routledge, 2017).
[38] Much of the ensuing discussion appeared in Jacqueline Vayntrub, "Proverbs and the Limits of Poetry" (PhD diss., University of Chicago, 2015), 333–36. I have developed the discussion herein in relation to the tenor of this essay.

air of authority to a work.[39] But the practice of attribution can do much more than establish a text's authority; it can contribute to meaning in the text, as it shapes and even gives rise to the prominence of the named figure.

The name of the speaking voice in Ecclesiastes—Qohelet—can be seen as part of the author's deliberate construction of a persona. That is, despite the many allusions in Qohelet's character to the biblical presentation of Solomon, the name itself has only the imprimatur of traditions of Solomon.[40] The name of Qohelet is deliberately *not* Solomon. The name is, rather, part of the persona which the author constructs for the purposes of the literary work. Qohelet is "The Gatherer," whose title implies the assembly of an attentive audience.[41] A similar argument has been made for Hesiod, who, like Qohelet, assumes an autobiographical voice. As I have discussed elsewhere, in the opening to the *Theogony*, Hesiod says that it was the muses who "breathed a divine voice [*audēn*] into me."[42] Four times Hesiod describes the Muses as "sending forth their voice," *ossan hieisai*.[43] Some have suggested that Hesiod's name could be understood as "He who emits the voice [*audē*]" or "He who emits song [*aoidē*]."[44]

But there is more to Qohelet's name than meets the eye. On a basic level, the title "The Gatherer" indicates the resistance of the frame speaker (and the speaker himself, in Eccl 1:12) to memorialize the works of this king. This is, in itself, an outright challenge to the ideological work done by the so-called royal autobiographical genre: the king who wishes to memorialize himself by reembodying his name in the text along with his accomplishments explicitly threatens the future reader who might attempt to erase his name and therefore his memory and very personhood. But in the case of Ecclesiastes, this erasure has already taken place, because the reader cannot definitively say that this son of David, king in Jerusalem *was* in fact Solomon. Further, the title "The Gatherer" undermines the purpose of the royal autobiographical genre, in that the semantic content of the title, as one who gathers an audience (of disciples), is not a king forever memorializing his accomplishments to be engraved in stone or the permanence of text, but rather passing on, through speech, the wisdom

---

[39] Michael V. Fox, *Proverbs 1–9: A New Translation with Introduction and Commentary*, AB 18A (New York: Doubleday, 2000), 57–58; J. L. Perdue, *Proverbs* (Louisville: John Knox, 2000), 64–65.

[40] The name itself is a by-form of the G fem. sing. active participle of QHL. Summaries of the various proposals for the meaning of the term can be found in C. L. Seow, *Ecclesiastes: A New Translation with Introduction and Commentary*, AB 18C (New York: Doubleday, 1997), 95–97, and a more introductory overview is given in J. L. Crenshaw, *Ecclesiastes: A Commentary* (Philadelphia: Westminster, 1987), 32–34. One of the persistent suggestions is that of Frank Zimmerman, who argued that Biblical Hebrew *qohelet* is a mistranslation of an Aramaic G masc. sing. active participle in the emphatic state which would look identical to a G fem. sing. active participle in the absolute state. He suggests the Aramaic would be *kānšāh*, whose numerical value (= 375) would be exactly that of the consonants of Solomon's name, *šlmh*. The suggestion is interesting but difficult to verify, and relies upon many assumptions, foremost that for the numerology to work properly in its association with Solomon, the Hebrew name *qohelet* depends upon an original Aramaic of a *different* root when QHL is productive in Aramaic for the same meaning as the Hebrew. For Zimmerman's argument, see his "The Aramaic Provenance of Qohelet," *JQR* 36 (1945–46): 17–45. This note appears in Vayntrub, "Proverbs and the Limits of Poetry," 334 n. 140.

[41] QHL means "to assemble," usually individuals, not texts. See D. J. A. Clines, *Dictionary of Classical Hebrew* (Sheffield: Sheffield Academic, 2010), 7:205. See also Eliezer Ben Yehuda, *A Complete Dictionary of Ancient and Modern Hebrew*, vol. 12 (Jerusalem: Hemda and Ehud Ben Yehuda; Tel Aviv: La'am, 1951), 5806. Seow (*Ecclesiastes*, 97) offers a similar translation of Qohelet's name. The following note appears in Vayntrub, "Proverbs and the Limits of Poetry," 334 n. 141.

[42] See the discussion in Vayntrub, *Beyond Orality*, 209 n. 26. See Hesiod, *Theogony* 31.

[43] Hesiod, *Theogony* 10, 43, 65, 67, where the epithet is *ossan hieisai*; *ossan* is synonymous with *audē*, which describes the voice of the Muses in 39, 97.

[44] See the discussion in Vayntrub, "Before Authorship," 198 n. 40, and that article's adaption (with permission) in *Beyond Orality*, 190–91, and 209 n. 26. The quoted suggestion comes from Gregory Nagy, "Hesiod and the Ancient Biographical Traditions," in *The Brill Companion to Hesiod*, ed. F. Montanari, C. Tsagalis, and A. Rengakos (Leiden: Brill, 2009), 286. See also Glenn W. Most, *Hesiod: Theogony, Works and Days, Testimonia*, LCL 57 (Harvard, MA: Harvard University Press, 2006), xv. Michael Fox in his commentary understands the anonymous frame speaker presenting Qohelet "as a personage of the past, whose teachings are admired but viewed with a certain hesitation" (*Ecclesiastes* [Philadelphia: Jewish Publication Society, 2004], 82–83).

that led to his success to be appropriated and internalized by the future generation, thus erasing his own individuality so that a chain of tradition can continue.[45]

While the identification of Qohelet as Solomon tantalizes and challenges the modern reader, it is not the title of the work that poses the greatest problems but its paradoxical conclusion. I read in Ecclesiastes such an intentionally disrupted transmission of knowledge in the epilogue. The frame speaker receives Qohelet's teachings and presents a summary of these teachings in his conclusion in a way that undermines Qohelet's own arguments.

Whereas the shaping of a tradition of Solomon and his capacity to speak in Proverbs—or rather, the negation of Solomon as performer—comes solely from short titles and various other organizational elements of the book, the author of Ecclesiastes gives his frame speaker much more latitude.[46] In the final verses of the book the anonymous frame speaker offers his own reception of Qohelet's words. These concluding words of the frame speaker, unlike the concluding words of Job, do not conclude a narrative of Qohelet's life or offer a happy ending. Ecclesiastes 12:9–14, instead, presents a different perspective from the autobiographical voice of Qohelet. The voice of Qohelet can be described as the ramblings of a self-proclaimed former king who resists the pithy and prosodic judgments *expected of kings*.[47] By contrast, the voice of the frame speaker does not resist such summaries, and presents a number of them, with specific reference to the figure of Qohelet himself.

It appears that Ecclesiastes has a transmission problem. In some ways this transmission problem finds itself within a particular tradition in the broader instruction genre. In the New Kingdom Egyptian instruction text attributed to Any, we find at the end a dialogue between the father, Any, and his son, the recipient of the instructions, Khonshotep, who pushes against the instructions of his father in the conclusion of the text.[48] Another, more pronounced example of disrupted transmission can be found in Ahiqar, an instruction collection whose elaborate frame narrative has to a certain extent eclipsed the instructions themselves. Ahiqar's frame narrative presents the instructions contained within the frame of the text as the wise words of Ahiqar, who attempts to transmit his wisdom to his nephew and adopted successor Nadin. Unfortunately for Ahiqar, Nadin, and the fate of the wise words, Nadin does not live to succeed Ahiqar and thus cannot reliably take his place or continue the chain of transmission.[49] One wonders how the transmission narrative maintains its authenticity as "Ahiqar's Wise Words" to the reader without demanding the preservation of his speech in the medium of text.

---

[45] For the point that Ecclesiastes in its frame is more explicitly wisdom than royal autobiography, see Suriano, "Kingship and *Carpe Diem*," 290.

[46] See Vayntrub, "Before Authorship," 204–6, and idem, "The Book of Proverbs and the Idea of Ancient Israelite Education," 107–109.

[47] Not only Solomon's many *mashal*, but also David's in 1 Sam 24:14. Saul's character never speaks *mashal*; instead, he becomes the subject of one (1 Sam 10:12). Similarly, Balaam is hired by King Balak to curse Israel, but instead directs his instruction towards the king, in the form of a *mashal*. The speech in Isa 14 is directed against the king of Babylon. The relationship between the root MŠL, "rule over," and MŠL, "discourse of classification and categorization," need not be etymological, but simply a function of homophony and the association of *mashal* with kings. A similar situation could be imagined for MLK in Hebrew if we had evidence of the use of the root as "counsel," as it regularly functions in Akkadian. Unfortunately, MLK in Hebrew seems to refer exclusively to "rulership" and MLK in Akkadian seems to refer only to "advice," with MLK in Akkadian as "rulership" only as a West Semitic loan. See the verb *malāku* (entry A) in *CAD*, "to give, to ponder, deliberate, to come to a decision" (vol. 10. M. Part 1 [1977]: 154–58). See also the substantive *milku*, "advice, instruction, order (of a deity)" and "intellectual capacity, mood, spirit," as well as "conscious intent, consent." See especially the *milku* of one's father in the sense of "instruction" as instructions elsewhere in the Ancient Near East (vol. 10. M. Part 2 [1977]: 66–69). See also *malku* (entry C) in *CAD*, "advice, counsel," as in Lamashtu's "improper counsel" in BIN 4 126:9: *malkiša parru'im*; also "decision," as in "I will make my decision" in CCT 2 45a:12: *anāku malkī laṣbat* (vol. 10. M. Part 1 [1977]: 169). The data are suggestive, yet incomplete to establish any definitive relationship between MŠL, "to rule," and MŠL, "to perform (discourse specific to the term)." This note appears in Vayntrub, "Proverbs and the Limits of Poetry," 335 n. 154

[48] "The Instruction of Any" (Miriam Lichtheim, *Ancient Egyptian Literature* [Berkeley: University of California Press, 1976], 2:135–46).

[49] See my previous discussion in Vayntrub, "The Book of Proverbs and the Idea of Ancient Israelite Education," 107–109.

The way in which Qohelet's transmission is interrupted, while within a literary tradition already attested for instruction, is uniquely fitting to the message communicated by the work as a whole: transmission is inherently unstable, because the wisdom meritocracy is inherently flawed. In this way, Qohelet's message of *carpe diem* is mangled by its recipient in the form of the frame speaker at the end, who again reverts to a message of following God's commandments and racking up the rewards such "good" behavior brings.

Through his meditations, which are encased within the received frame of the recipient (i.e., the frame speaker, the text itself, or both), Qohelet communicates a message of the ultimate instability of meaning and the impossibility of lasting change in the world. New phenomena, for Qohelet, are not actually new, and there are no lasting impacts of occurrences. For Qohelet, this is true for man's actions in nature, for his own experience seeking skill and success, in mastering nature, in acquiring possessions, and even in transmitting that success to future generations. The transmission problem exposes an inherent instability in the wisdom theology. If goodness bears reward in this life, in the form of softened mortality (longer days, greater wealth, and sons to "replace" one's experience and mastery over the world after death), then how does one make sense of transmission? The passage of such reward from one generation to another assumes that the subsequent generation will be just as deserving, a seemingly impossible premise. Even more radically, rigorously preserving the passage of reward across generational lines within the wisdom theology will inevitably demand that there be no individuals: there can only be generation after generation of the same actor in the form of a new recipient.[50] And if there are no individuals, only generations of the same, then Qohelet's point is correct: there is nothing new under the sun, individual actions bear no lasting meaning.[51]

Eccl 2:18–19, 21

ושנאתי אני את־כל־עמלי שאני עמל תחת השמש שאניחנו לאדם שיהיה אחרי

ומי יודע החכם יהיה או סכל וישלט בכל־עמלי שעמלתי ושחכמתי תחת השמש גם־זה הבל

כי־יש אדם שעמלו בחכמה ובדעת ובכשרון ולאדם שלא עמל־בו יתננו חלקו גם־זה הבל ורעה רבה

I hated all the rewards I reaped under the sun. For I will bequeath it to the man who will succeed me,

and who knows whether he will be a fool—and control all the rewards I reaped under the sun—or he will be wise, and this too is futility.

...

For sometimes a person whose rewards were reaped with wisdom, knowledge, and skill must give that to be the inheritance of someone who did not deserve it. That is also futility and a great evil.

---

[50] I have elsewhere examined this idea of transmission, that the stable passage of knowledge, responsibility, and speech from one generation to the next require the fiction that sons wholly replace their fathers. See my study of the transmission and performance of the "Filial Duties" in Aqhat, in "Transmission and Mortal Anxiety in the Tale of Aqhat," in *Like 'Ilu Are You Wise: Studies in Northwest Semitic Languages and Literature in Honor of Dennis G. Pardee*, ed. Humphrey H. Hardy II, Joseph Lam, and Eric Reymond (Chicago: Oriental Institute Publications, forthcoming). There is a gendered dimension to the discourse surrounding transmission, where identical transmission (son becomes the father) is especially male, and other types of transmissions are gendered differently. See, e.g., Rhiannon Graybill, *Are We Not Men: Unstable Masculinity in the Prophets* (Oxford: Oxford University Press, 2016), where the prophetic male body is opened by the deity, for example, in Ezek 2, the prophet is inhabited by a רוח, and he is told to open his mouth and physically consume an inscribed scroll; through Graybill's reading of such texts, this process destabilizes the prophet's masculinity. See also Ingrid E. Lilly, "*Rûaḥ* Embodied—Job's Internal Disease from the Perspective of Mesopotamian Medicine," in *Borders: Terminologies, Ideologies, and Performances*, ed. Annette Weissenrieder (Tübingen: Mohr Siebeck, 2016), 323–36, and idem, *Winds in the Body: A Medical Anthropology of Spirit in the Ancient Near East, Hebrew Bible, and Second Temple Jewish Literature* (Cambridge: Cambridge University Press, forthcoming).

[51] See Brichto for this notion of the de-individuating transmission chain, "Kin, Cult, Land and Afterlife," 24. I discuss the operation of this idea in the unfolding of the tale of Aqhat in Vayntrub, "Transmission and Mortal Anxiety."

Qohelet's assertion of the incoherence of the reward-punishment system leads him to a recommendation of a *carpe diem* attitude at the end of the second chapter, offering an important twist on the traditional wisdom theology. Good behavior that is pleasing to God does not result in material reward, but rather in the skill to enjoy life:

Eccl 2:26a

כי לאדם שטוב לפניו נתן חכמה ודעת ושמחה

The person who is pleasing to [God], He gives him wisdom, knowledge, and joy.

By contrast, bad behavior does not result in punishment—meaning, shortened life, illness, and loss of material possessions—but rather in the impulse to collect and amass.

Eccl 2:26b

ולחוטא נתן ענין לאסף ולכנוס

To the sinner, He gives the impulse to collect and amass.

One might confine the activity of collecting and amassing to that of material possessions, as the context of the discussion of transmission seems to imply. But again and again, in Proverbs and in other, nonbiblical instruction texts, the transmission of words, of advice, of strategy and blessing, seems to function as a material object, and even takes the place of the transmission of material objects in that wisdom and blessing perpetually generate material (and nonmaterial) rewards. And so, it seems especially bizarre when our frame speaker enters after Qohelet offers his seemingly final words, "Utter futility," to sum up Qohelet's activities as such:

Eccl 12:9–10

ויתר שהיה קהלת חכם עוד למד־דעת את־העם ואזן וחקר תקן משלים הרבה
בקש קהלת למצא דברי־חפץ וכתוב ישר דברי אמת

> Not only was Qohelet wise, he instructed the people in knowledge, he evaluated and examined, he arranged many proverbs,
> Qohelet deduced fitting words,[52] and faithfully wrote[53] true words.

This summary of Qohelet's work by the frame speaker draws heavily on the image of the wise king transmitting instruction.[54] Qohelet is described as having certain qualities for producing and exhibiting knowledge: he is described as חכם, "wise," ואזן וחקר, capable of "evaluating and examining," and בקש למצא...דברי־חפץ, "deducing fitting words." Qohelet "instructed the people in knowledge," a sentiment parallel to the second half of the next phrase, where he is said to have

---

[52] In Eccl 12:10, חפץ means "words (pertaining to) a matter," that is, "fitting words." Therefore we see a variety of translations possible: KJV gives "acceptable words" and JPS has "useful sayings," although some translations go with "delight" (so LXX, *logous thelēmatos*, "words of desire," and NRSV, "pleasing words"). A version of this note appears in Vayntrub, "Proverbs and the Limits of Poetry," 337 n. 147.
[53] I read the consonants of the MT כתוב as indicating an infinitive (absolute) of KTB, parallel to the infinitive construct in the first half of the verse, למצא, in sequence with the verb בקש gapped from the first half of the verse, so "(Qohelet sought to) write." Some Masoretic manuscripts attest וכתב, thus allowing for the reading of the verb as a 3 masc. sing. G SC, i.e., "he wrote," parallel with the other 3 masc. sing. SC verbs of the sequence (ואזן וחקר תקן...בקש). Early translations (Syriac, Vulgate) rendering a past tense "he wrote" may reflect this, but, as Seow (*Ecclesiastes*, 383) points out, that versions like the Syriac and Vulgate which render "he wrote" may either reflect this or an infinitive absolute that would conform to the attested consonantal form כתוב. A version of this note appears in Vayntrub, "Proverbs and the Limits of Poetry," 337 n. 148.
[54] This discussion appears in Vayntrub, "Proverbs and the Limits of Poetry," 337–40.

"arranged many proverbs," and also parallel to the final half of the third phrase, that he "faithfully wrote true words." Qohelet, at least according to the frame speaker, exceeds even the Solomon of 1 Kings 5 because here the capacity for erudition is transformed into the capacity for imparting these qualities beyond his lifetime—teaching others, collecting knowledge, and ultimately, inscribing them for posterity.

The vocabulary of this passage recalls the initial poetic units of the third and final collection of the proverbs attributed to Solomon in Proverbs 25–29:[55]

| | | |
|---|---|---|
| | הסתר דבר | כבוד אלהים |
| | חקר דבר | וכבוד מלכים |
| The glory of God | is to hide a matter, | |
| and the glory of kings | is to examine a matter. | |

This follows the title in Prov 25:1, "These too are the proverbs of Solomon which the men of Hezekiah, king of Judah, transcribed." The proximity of these two statements suggests a relationship between the inherent participation of kings in knowledge production, and specifically, the participation of Solomon and Hezekiah in the transmission of *these* wise words. The activities of the wise, "evaluating and examining," are the same terms Elihu uses in Job 32:11 to describe his previous participation as audience—אזין עד־תבונתיכם, "giving ear to your theories"—and the discourse of Job's three friends—עד־תחקרון מלין, "as you examined the matters." In the fictional world of Job and his interlocutors, knowledge production is an activity of oral performance. It is not that writing does not exist in the world created by the author. In fact, Job's character twice despairs that his spoken words are not written down.[56] And so, in Ecclesiastes, the words used by the frame speaker in this passage in 12:9–10 speak *especially* to the transmission activities demanded by wisdom production. By drawing upon this traditional language, the frame speaker revokes Qohelet's systematic argument for the instability of transmission. Paradoxically, and here is the great brilliance I see in Ecclesiastes's structure as a work, the frame speaker is unable to maintain Qohelet's radical argument. He reintroduces the traditional view of stability across generational lines, precisely proving Qohelet's point: even Qohelet's own new argument cannot remain stable, and what has always been will continue to always be.

## UNLINKING THE MODERN DEBATE OF "WRITTEN VS. ORAL" FROM ANCIENT THEORIES OF TRANSMISSION

Whether by its disconnection from an explicitly Solomonic chain of tradition or the undermining final advice of the frame speaker to "keep God's commandments," Qohelet's radical message crumbles under the weight of scholarly fidelity to a "wisdom canon." This imagined canon sees Proverbs as the aesthetic and conceptual paradigm to which all other "wisdom" texts are evaluated. Ecclesiastes "speaks" the wisdom language and so its radical upending of the basic concept at the heart of the wisdom thesis—the idea that transmission is stable from one generation to the next—is missed. Indeed, as his frame speaker informs us, Qohelet does evaluate, examine, and arrange many proverbs—but the meaning in what Qohelet does lies in the *how*. Qohelet's transmission,

---

[55]Prov 25:2.
[56]Job 19:21–24; 31:35.

rearrangement, and deployment of prosodic instructions, as in 7:1, טוב שם משמן טוב, "A name (reputation) is better than the finest oil," serves to undermine their very purpose. When Qohelet says, "One's name is better than the finest oil," a saying the likes of which would fit easily in any biblical or ancient Near Eastern instruction collection, he follows immediately: ויום המות מיום הולדו, "and the day of one's death (is better) than the day of one's birth." How deftly Qohelet has pushed the logic of a saying which vaunts postmortem reputation over limited material gain to its absurd end![57] In Qohelet's reformulation, if one seeks only reputation in this way, then one prizes death and the climax of reward over the limitless potential of experience afforded at birth.

But Ecclesiastes is not the lone work on the problem of the credibility of transmitted texts; the question of transgenerational stability of words, deeds, and their consequences was not probed by biblical authors alone. In *How the Bible Became a Book*, William Schniedewind comments, "Writing is not necessarily considered a universal good," citing Plato's *Phaedrus*, where Socrates takes on Thoth, the Egyptian god of writing, for having invented a poor substitute for instruction. For Schniedewind, who seeks to challenge a scholarly narrative of an uncomplicated ancient welcoming of the technology of writing, Socrates's words on the inherent instability of *written* text proves to be a brilliant rebuttal. Schniedewind teases out what he sees as a debate baked into the rise of the technology of writing, observing that on the one hand, "The text allows one to read 'without instruction' and can also displace the traditional teacher," but on the other hand, "one can argue, as Plato does, that it is instruction from the living teacher rather than the text itself that makes one wise."[58] But what if in identifying an ancient debate between "text and tradition, the written and the oral," we have missed the point?[59] What if what Plato's Socrates was getting at was *not* the medium or the technology of writing when he says that "written words go on telling you the same thing forever," but rather, that such a position on writing reveals an ongoing debate on the truth value of quoted speech?

While at first blush the discussion about writing in Plato's *Phaedrus* could refer to the stability of *written* text, one might look elsewhere in the dialogues where Plato has Socrates criticizing an interlocutor for using the words of someone else and not their own words. Take, as an example, Socrates' reaction to how Protagoras uses the words of Simonides:

> A gathering like this of ours…requires no extraneous voices, not even of the poets, whom one cannot question on the sense of what they say; when they are adduced in discussion we are generally told by some that the poet thought so and so, and by others something different, and they go on arguing about a matter which they are powerless to determine…; putting the poets aside, let us hold our discussion together *in our own persons*, making trial of truth and of ourselves.[60]

We start to see that the written is merely a single medium that poses the problems of disembodied words.

---

[57] Michael Fox (*A Time to Tear Down and a Time to Build Up: A Rereading of Ecclesiastes* [Grand Rapids: Eerdmans, 1999], 251) makes the explicit connection between the "name" and the "memory," that is, one's reputation after one's death or at the time of one's death, explaining that the connection the speaker makes between the two is one of "ratio," that is, "just as a reputation is preferable to good oil, so is the day of death preferable to the day of birth…one's reputation is not secure until he dies and can no longer damage it," following Ibn Ezra. For this point with specific reference to poetics, see also James Kugel, *The Idea of Biblical Poetry: Parallelism and Its History* (New Haven: Yale University Press, 1981), 10.
[58] William Schniedewind, *How the Bible Became a Book* (Harvard, MA: Cambridge University Press, 2004), 14.
[59] Ibid.
[60] Plato, *Protagoras* 347e–348a; also earlier in 341a-e. Translation by W. R. M. Lamb, *Laches, Protagoras, Meno, Euthydemus*, LCL (London: Heinemann, 1924).

## CONCLUSION

This essay has not attempted to address the material problem of the text, that is, the modern scholarly challenge of stabilizing a text received from antiquity. Rather, we have focused on the discourse surrounding ancient text production and transmission specifically in Ecclesiastes. How did authors producing texts in and around the biblical world understand the nature of their work? How did they conceptualize their own position as text producers, and more generally, as actors in a line of transmission? What types of framing and rhetorical strategies authorize a given text as "true" or "authentically transmitted"? In approaching these questions, we should, as much as possible, separate modern concerns—such as the distinction between modernity and antiquity, and the correlated concerns of media, the written versus the oral—from concerns that present themselves in these texts. The question, "Are words true when detached from the speaker's voice?" inevitably countenances the problem of the material written text. I do not intend to deny that the written text becomes a concern of this question. Rather, my intention has been to show how the question of the authenticity of the written versus the oral can be seen as a secondary concern to a now-obscured primary debate surrounding the fate of words when their speaker no longer speaks them.

Discourses surrounding the transmission of instruction, responsibility across generational lines, and the meaning of individual death are connected to ancient understandings of the voice and its embodied nature. This set of concerns appears to transcend the purely horizontal concern of transgenerational passage to the vertical dimension of prophetic transmission. How does one ensure the passage of a message from one speaker to another, even when both are confined to the same living moment? Future studies should consider the problem of transmission within the broader project of recovering ancient conceptions of personhood and the self, as such conceptions are expressed in the textual and iconographic corpus.

# Textualization and the Transformation of Biblical Prophecy

HEATH D. DEWRELL

Ancient Near Eastern prophecy was originally an oral phenomenon. Prophets spoke, not wrote, on behalf of one or more deities, and their audiences heard, not read, the oracles. In a letter from Mar-Issar to Esarhaddon, king of Assyria, the former reports, "I have heard" ([a]*sseme*) what the "prophetess" (*raggintu*)[1] "has said" (*taqti*[*bi*]).[2] Similarly, the verb typically used in the Mari letters to describe the means by which a prophetic message was delivered is *qabû*, "to speak."[3] Even in an exceptional case in which a prophet chooses to deliver an oracle in writing, the prophet requests a scribe to record the spoken oracle, which would have been subsequently delivered to its intended recipient orally.[4] Likewise in the Hebrew Bible, prophets[5] "speak" (דבר)[6] and "say" (אמר);[7] only occasionally do they "write" (כתב).[8] Even in these exceptional cases, though, the thing that the prophet "writes" is not the prophetic oracle itself, but a sort of sign act[9] or a record to preserve an (originally oral) oracle for future generations.[10] As in the case of Mesopotamian prophecy, in those uncommon cases in which an oracle was written down in order to be disseminated, the prophet often employs a scribe rather than writing it out himself.[11] As Nissinen correctly observes, "not a single source from the entire [extra-biblical] Near Eastern documentation even remotely alludes to

---

[1] The Neo-Assyrian term *raggimu/raggintu*, "prophet/ess," from *ragāmu* "to call, to call out" (*CAD* R 62–66), itself points to the fundamentally oral nature of prophecy.
[2] SAA 10 352 (= WAW 12 109): 22–25. For a discussion of this text see Martti Nissinen, *References to Prophecy in Neo-Assyrian Sources*, SAAS 7 (Helsinki: University of Helsinki Press, 1998), 68–77.
[3] See, e.g., WAW 12 1:3, 29, 42, 47, 61; 2:4, 17; 3:9; 4:20; 7:9, 20; 9:43; 16:17, 25, 33; 18:14; 19:7; 20:10; 21:9; 24:7; 25:17; 30:24; 31:20; 32:21; 34:8'; 38:8.
[4] WAW 12 48:29–42.
[5] Here I use the word "prophet" in its loosest and most ambiguous sense, although it is not at all clear that the various characters to whom the Hebrew Bible refers by the term נביא would have been so designated during the preexilic period. As Diana Edelman perceptively observes concerning the various forms of Hebrew prophecy: "They may have been different sub-specialities in which visions were induced by different technical means. The different types of specialists may even have functioned in different contexts" ("From Prophets to Prophetic Books: The Fixing of the Divine Word," in *The Production of Prophecy: Constructing Prophecy and Prophets in Yehud*, ed. Diana V. Edelman and Ehud Ben Zvi [London: Equinox, 2009], 32]).
[6] E.g., Deut 18:18; 2 Kgs 1:16; Isa 39:8; Jer 7:27; 9:21; 20:8; 23:16; 25:2, 3; 26:2, 7, 8; 26:16; 27:12, 16; 34:6; 38:1, 4; 43:1; 44:16; 45:1; Ezek 2:7; 3:1; 11:25; 14:4; 20:3, 27; 24:18; 29:3; 33:2; 37:19, 21; Zech 13:3.
[7] E.g., 2 Sam 12:1; 1 Kgs 17:1; 22:19; Jer 11:3; 13:12; 14:17; 16:11; 18:11; 19:3, 11, 14; 21:3, 8; 22:2; 25:27, 28, 30; 26:4; 28:11, 13; 29:24; 32:6; 34:2; 35:13, 18; 38:17; 39:16; 43:10; 44:20, 24; Ezek 2:4; 3:11, 27; 6:3; 11:16, 17; 12:10, 11, 19, 23, 28; 13:18; 14:4, 6; 17:3, 9, 12; 19:2; 20:3, 5, 27, 30; 21:3, 8, 14, 33; 22:3; 24:3, 21; 25:3; 27:3; 28:2, 12, 22; 29:3; 30:2; 31:2; 32:2; 33:2, 10, 11, 12, 25, 27; 34:2; 35:3; 36:1, 3, 6, 22; 37:4; 38:3, 24; 39:1, 17; 44:6; Amos 7:8; Jon 3:4; Hag 1:13; 2:2, 21; Zech 1:3; 6:12; 7:5.
[8] Isa 8:1; 30:8; Jer 30:2; 36:2, 28; 51:60; Ezek 24:2; 37:16; 43:11; Hab 2:2.
[9] Isa 8:1; Ezek 24:2; 37:16; 43:11.
[10] Isa 30:8; Hab 2:2.
[11] So Jer 36:4–6, 17–18, 32; 45:1.

a prophet writing a text her- or himself."[12] Yet it is only through written sources that we have access to the oracles of ancient Israelite prophets, and the relationship between what may have been the underlying orally delivered oracles and the written prophecies contained in the Hebrew Bible is not necessarily straightforward.[13]

Nonetheless, thanks to comparative evidence from Assyria, one may map the general path that prophecy took during its transformation from an oral to a written phenomenon. Two sorts of tablets containing prophetic oracles have been unearthed at Nineveh dating to the reigns of Neo-Assyrian kings Esarhaddon and Assurbanipal.[14] The first are the *u'iltu* tablets (SAA 9 5–8 [= WAW 12 90–93]), which are arranged horizontally and contain only a single oracle. The purpose of these tablets appears to have been to convey the oracle from the place in which it was uttered to the concerned party—in the case of the extant oracles always the Assyrian king or the queen mother. In this regard, they closely resemble the prophecies contained in the Mari correspondence dating to a millennium earlier, which also served to convey oracles from their place of delivery to their interested parties.[15] In this case, the textualization of prophecy served the practical function of getting the oracle from one place to another.

On the other hand, a second type of Assyrian prophetic literature is represented by oracles recorded on larger, vertically oriented *ṭuppu* tablets, each of which contains multiple oracles (SAA 9 1–3 [= WAW 12 68–88]).[16] Unlike *u'iltu* tablets, *ṭuppu* tablets were typically employed to record

---

[12] Martti Nissinen, "Since When Do Prophets Write?," in *In the Footsteps of Sherlock Holmes: Studies in the Biblical Text in Honour of Anneli Aejmelaeus*, ed. Kristin De Troyer, T. Michael Law, and Marketta Liljeström, CBET 72 (Leuven: Peeters, 2014), 592.

[13] Scholarly work on the relationship among orality, literacy, and scribalism in ancient Israel has been extensive over the past few decades. Important studies on the role of orality and literacy in the making of the Hebrew Bible include Susan Niditch, *Oral World and Written Word: Orality and Literacy in Ancient Israel*, LAI (London: SPCK, 1997); William M. Schniedewind, *How the Bible Became a Book: The Textualization of Ancient Israel* (Cambridge: Cambridge University Press, 2004); David M. Carr, *Writing on the Tablet of the Heart: Origins of Scripture and Literature* (Oxford: Oxford University Press, 2005); idem, *The Formation of the Hebrew Bible: A New Reconstruction* (New York: Oxford University Press, 2011); Karel van der Toorn, *Scribal Culture and the Making of the Hebrew Bible* (Cambridge, MA: Harvard University Press, 2007); Stuart Weeks, "Literacy, Orality, and Literature in Israel," in *On Stone and Scroll: Essays in Honour of Graham Ivor Davies*, ed. James K. Aitken, Katharine J. Dell, and Brian A. Mastin, BZAW 420 (Berlin: de Gruyter, 2011), 465–78; and the various essays in Brian B. Schmidt, ed., *Contextualizing Israel's Sacred Writings: Ancient Literacy, Orality, and Literary Production*, AIL 22 (Atlanta: Society of Biblical literature, 2015). The interface between orality and textuality specifically vis-à-vis Israelite and other ancient Near Eastern prophecy has been explored in the various essays in Ehud Ben Zvi and Michael H. Floyd, eds., *Writings and Speech in Israelite and Ancient Near Eastern Prophecy*, SymS 10 (Atlanta: Society of Biblical Literature, 2000); as well as Aaron Schart, "Combining Prophetic Oracles in Mari Letters and Jeremiah 36," *JANES* 23 (1995): 75–93; Karel van der Toorn, "From the Mouth of the Prophet: The Literary Fixation of Jeremiah's Prophecies in the Context of the Ancient Near East," in *Inspired Speech: Prophecy in the Ancient Near East: Essays in Honour of Herbert B. Huffmon*, ed. John Kaltner and Louis Stulman, JSOTSup 378 (London: T&T Clark, 2004), 191–202; Edelman, "From Prophets to Prophetic Books"; Martti Nissinen, "How Prophecy Became Literature," *SJOT* 19 (2005): 153–72; idem, "Since When Do Prophets Write?"; Konrad Schmid, "Hintere Propheten (Nebiim)," in *Grundinformation Altes Testament*, ed. Jan Christian Gertz (Göttingen: Vandenhoeck & Ruprecht, 2006), 303–401, esp. 307–14; and Jean-Daniel Macchi and Thomas Römer, "La formation des livres prophétiques: enjeux et débats," in *Les recueils prophétiques de la Bible: Origines, milieux, et contexte proche-oriental*, ed. Jean-Daniel Macchi, Christophe Nihan, and Thomas Römer, MdB 64 (Geneva: Labor et Fides, 2012), 9–27.

[14] For previous discussions of the Assyrian oracles and their intended use, see especially Simo Parpola, *Assyrian Prophecies*, SAA 9 (Helsinki: Helsinki University Press, 1997), liii–lv; Manfred Weippert, "Assyrische Prophetien der Zeit Asarhaddons und Assurbanipals," in *Assyrian Royal Inscriptions: New Horizons in Literary, Ideological, and Historical Analysis: Papers of a Symposium Held in Cetona (Siena) June 26–28, 1980*, ed. F. M. Fales, OAC 17 (Rome: Istituto per l'Oriente, 1981), 71–115; idem, "'König, fürchte dich nicht!' Assyrische Prophetie im 7. Jahrhundert v. Chr.," *Or* 71 (2002): 1–54; Martti Nissinen, *Prophets and Prophecy in the Ancient Near East*, WAW 12 (Atlanta: Society of Biblical Literature, 2003), 97–98; and van der Toorn, "From the Mouth of the Prophet," 191–94.

[15] Mari letters containing prophetic oracles are conveniently collected in WAW 12 1–50.

[16] In addition to these, there is also one other fragment of a *ṭuppu* tablet containing a prophecy (SAA 9 4 = WAW 12 89), but only a handful of lines, none fully preserved, remain. There is some debate about whether SAA 9 3 [= WAW 12 84–88] should be classified as the same sort of oracle collection as SAA 1 and 2 [= WAW 12 68–83]. Mathijs J. de Jong considers SAA 9 3 to be not "a straightforward prophetic oracle, but is rather to be qualified as a derivative of prophecy"; it represents "reworking of oracles" rather that direct oracle reports (*Isaiah among the Ancient Near Eastern Prophets: A Comparative Study of the Earliest*

important information such as treaties, census reports, inventories, and so on for future reference.¹⁷ Thus one can infer that the purpose of these tablets was to archive the prophecies and to preserve them for later use. Here, like with the *u'iltu* tablets, the textualization of prophecy also serves as a means of transmission, but transmission of a different sort. As van der Toorn elegantly expresses it, "The literary fixation served the purpose of either transmission in space or transmission in time. The two types of transmission command their own forms: the letter or letter report in the first case, the memorandum or oracle collection in the second."¹⁸ This raises the question of why anyone would care to refer to prophecies after the original circumstances that had given rise to them had passed, since prophecies typically addressed concrete circumstances relating to the prophet's own time. Further, why would anyone be interested in transmitting prophetic oracles to a future audience? The move to put prophecies into writing may seem obvious to those of us who are well acquainted with written prophetic oracles in the form of the Latter Prophets in the Hebrew Bible. The fact that there are only a handful of Mesopotamian texts from a relatively brief window of time that exhibit any interest in preserving prophetic oracles for posterity, however, indicates that the act of preserving prophecy in writing for future readers was not as obvious of an act to the ancients as it may be to us today.

While there are no explicit statements in Assyrian texts concerning why prophecy came to be archived and for what use they were intended, the obvious reason for textualizing, collecting, and preserving information of any sort is in order to consult and/or cite it at a later date, and there is clear evidence that the Assyrians were indeed citing old prophecies. For instance, a letter from a certain Bel-ušezib to Esarhaddon concerning a campaign against the Manneans (SAA 10 111 [= WAW 106])¹⁹ opens by citing two astronomical omens, both of which appear to be propitious for Esarhaddon (e.g., "If a star flashes like a torch at the rising of the sun and sets in the setting of the sun, then the host of the enemy will fall in its main body"). Bel-ušezib then concludes his letter by citing a prophecy, "Bel has said, 'May Esarhaddon sit on his throne like Marduk-šapik-zeri. I will deliver all lands into your hands.'" Thus Bel-ušezib's letter frames its report with two sorts of supernaturally revealed messages, applying them both to the present situation. Significantly, neither the omen nor the prophecy mentions the Manneans or Cimmerians, the two groups immediately at issue, indicating that neither the omen nor the oracle was originally composed in reference to Esarhaddon's Mannean campaign. While there is no extant oracle from the Assyrian archives that declares that Esarhaddon will "sit on his throne like Marduk-šapik-zeri," the fact that the astronomical omens that open the letter do have a good parallel in an astronomical report from the archives (see SAA 8 552²⁰) suggests the archives as the probable source for the prophecy as well.²¹

In another case (SAA 16 59 [= WAW 12 115]), one Nabu-rehtu-uṣur reports to Esarhaddon that a slave girl in the suburbs of Harran has become ecstatic (*sarḥat*²²) and declared, "This is the

---

*Stages of the Isaiah Tradition and the Neo-Assyrian Prophecies*, VTSup 117 [Leiden: Brill, 2007], 174, 411–12). So also Jonathan Stökl, *Prophecy in the Ancient Near East: A Philological and Sociological Comparison*, CHANE 56 (Leiden: Brill, 2012), 106–7.
¹⁷Parpola, *Assyrian Prophecies*, liii.
¹⁸Van der Toorn, "From the Mouth of the Prophet," 192. But cf. Stökl, who is more skeptical that one can discern a difference in function based on differences in the shape and orientation of the two sorts of tablets (*Prophecy in the Ancient Near East*, 129–31).
¹⁹For a discussion of this letter, especially with regard to the prophetic oracle contained therein, see Nissinen, *References to Prophecy*, 96–101.
²⁰The close correspondence is observed by ibid., 97 n. 400.
²¹So also Nissinen, who suggests that Bel-ušezib's quotation of prophecy indicates that prophecies had become "part of the scholarly lore" (ibid., 101).
²²This word is difficult; *saraḥu* appears to mean something like "to ruin, destroy" (*CAD* S 171–72; *AHw* 1028), but such a meaning ill suits the context. Simo Parpola suggests that the term here is an Aramaism cognate to Syriac *šrḥ*, "to range," and, in the Ethpaal, "to be immoderate, run riot, etc." (*apud* Nissinen, *References to Prophecy*, 111 n. 430; followed by Nissinen, *Prophets and Prophecy*, 171–72).

word of Nusku: 'The kingship is for Sasî. I will destroy the name and seed of Sennacherib.'" Nabu-rehtu-uṣur appends to this news—almost certainly not received positively by Esarhaddon, current king of Assyria and "name and seed of Sennacherib"—a reminder concerning "the words of [the goddess] Nikkal." Unfortunately, the content of this prophecy of Nikkal is difficult to reconstruct due to the tablet's poor state of preservation at this point, but it appears to refer to the destruction of Esarhaddon's enemies and to divine protection for his household.[23] The citation of this earlier prophecy serves to contradict the more recent prophecy of the slave girl, and thus to establish the latter as "pseudo-prophecy."[24] In yet another case, in a letter regarding Sasî's attempted coup d'état, Nabu-rehtu-uṣur alleges that Sasî has rejected the decrees of Bel, Nabû, and Ištar (SAA 16 60 [= WAW 12 116]:10'–11'), apparently another allusion to earlier prophecies. Here the cited prophecy of Bel, Nabû, and Ištar may actually be preserved as SAA 9 1.4 (= WAW 12 71), which contains oracles from all three deities to Esarhaddon.[25] Thus, although not every quoted prophecy has been preserved, there are several examples of old Assyrian prophecies being cited in later contexts.[26]

Collecting and preserving prophecies in order to allow them to be reused in new contexts provided an obvious benefit for the reigning king, since he or his functionaries had the privilege of deciding which prophecies would be archived and which would not, and thus which became authoritative and which did not. Oracles that promised prosperity and protection could be archived and then later used to counter those—like that of the slave girl at Harran—that opposed the king's interests. Oracles given early in a king's reign promising success in one endeavor could be reapplied in a later context, ensuring success in that endeavor as well, even without a new prophecy promising success, or even in the face of one predicting failure! Oracles hostile to the king's interests, on the other hand, could be discarded. Selectively textualizing and archiving prophecies thus provided those with the authority to do so with the power of determining what constituted true and false prophecy and thereby even a degree of control over prophecy itself.[27]

---

[23] So also Nissinen: "The complete wording and syntactic structure of the following text is difficult to reconstruct, but the message is clear enough: the adversaries of the king will die, but the king (together with the royal family) will save his life and his kingdom will be guarded by divine powers" (*References to Prophecy*, 119).

[24] Ibid., 121.

[25] Ibid.

[26] Concerning the ability of prophecy, especially written prophecy, to transcend its original context, Schart observes, "because the oracles were words of the gods, their meaning transcends the one specific situation in which they were originally spoken" ("Combining Prophetic Oracles in Mari Letters and Jeremiah 36," 92). Similarly, Nissinen observes, "The very act of collecting individual oracles enables them to transcend specific historical situations and gives them a generally applicable meaning" ("Spoken, Written, Quoted, and Invented: Orality and Writtenness in Ancient Near Eastern Prophecy," in Ben Zvi and Floyd, eds., *Writings and Speech*, 254); and van der Toorn, "Prophecies are no longer ad hoc utterances, meaningful once but irrelevant ever after, but on the contrary are valid over a longer period of time. Prophecy is the word of God, and the word of God transcends the situation to which it originally applied" ("Mesopotamian Prophecy between Immanence and Transcendence," in *Prophecy in Its Near Eastern Context: Mesopotamian, Biblical, and Arabian Perspectives*, ed. Martti Nissinen, SymS 13 [Atlanta: Society of Biblical Literature, 2000], 77). See also de Jong, *Isaiah among the Ancient Near Eastern Prophets*, 400; and Stökl, *Prophecy in the Ancient Near East*, 132–34.

[27] Of course, this is not the only possible use for textualized and archived prophecy. As Nissinen points out, in at least one instance archived prophecies were used as source material for royal inscriptions. Esarhaddon's Nin. A inscription has close parallels with sections of SAA 9 1–3 (= WAW 12 68–88), which may suggest that the prophetic corpora served as source material for royal inscriptions (*References to Prophecy*, 14–34, esp. 31). There is also evidence that prophets themselves cited old prophecies in delivering new oracles. For example, SAA 9 7 (= WAW 12 92), which contains an oracle of reassurance for King Assurbanipal in the context of his Cimmerian and Egyptian campaigns, opens with a reference to previous oracles of reassurance delivered during his time as crown prince. The fulfillment of past oracles is presented as evidence for future support. Likewise, in SAA 9 3.3 (= WAW 12 86) recounts an oracle of the god Aššur early in the reign of Esarhaddon, promising deliverance from his enemies along with a report concerning the fulfillment of that oracle. The reader is then invited to praise Aššur in response. On this sort of "self-citation" in both Assyrian prophetic texts and in the Hebrew Bible, see Manfred Weippert, "'Das Frühere, siehe, ist eingetroffen...': über Selbstzitate im altorientalischen Prophetenspruch," in *Oracles et prophéties dans l'Antique: Acts du Colloque de Strasbourg 15–17 juin 1995*, ed. Jean-Georges Heintz, Travaux du centre de recherche sur le Proche-Orient et la Grèce antiques 15 (Paris: de Boccard, 1997), 147–69.

This control over prophecy by means of selective preservation represents something akin to the situation described in Jeremiah 36. There Jeremiah, forbidden from entering the temple himself, has his scribe Baruch write down the words of Jeremiah's oracle and read them aloud in the people's hearing. In this way, Jeremiah employs textualization for "transmission in space," as in the case of the prophecies from the Mari correspondence and the *u'iltu* tablets from Assyria. When King Jehoiakim hears of the prophecy, which was unfavorable to the king and his court, he has the document read aloud before him, cutting off and burning each section after its being read. In this case, a king attempts to counteract a prophecy via destruction, an attempt ultimately thwarted by the creation of a second expanded edition of the scroll (Jer 36:28–32).[28] While Jehoiakim attempts to counteract prophecy by destroying it, the Neo-Assyrian kings demonstrate that one could achieve the same end of exerting royal control over prophecy just as well via selective preservation.

The Assyrian tradition of archiving prophetic oracles was relatively short lived; the extant Assyrian prophetic texts all date to the reigns of Esarhaddon and his successor Assurbanipal (ca. 681–627 BCE). Since the Assyrian Empire itself did not long outlast the death of the latter, the Assyrian tradition of archiving prophecies ended a bit over half a century after it began. As Nissinen observes, in Assyria "the process was too short to bear fruit comparable to the blossoming of the prophetic literature in the Hebrew Bible."[29] Thus one major difference between the Assyrian and biblical prophetic traditions is the longevity of the latter in comparison with the former, and one may therefore expect a degree of change and development in the biblical prophetic tradition not attested in Assyria.

Regarding the initial impetus for textualizing Hebrew prophecy, there are hints that at least one motivation for the phenomenon was the same as in Assyria: to preserve oracles in order to allow for their reinterpretation and reapplication in later circumstances. It is difficult, however, to trace the reuse of old prophecies in a new context based solely on oracle collections themselves, which is the primary way in which biblical prophecy has been preserved. Unless the rereaders[30] of prophetic texts textualize their own rereadings in the way that the Assyrians did in their correspondence or in the way that the Qumran scribes did in their *pesharim* (i.e., unless the rereaders write their reinterpretations into the text that they are reinterpreting as they copy it), modern readers are left without any direct access to the way in which ancient audiences reappropriated prophetic texts as they reread them. What then can we say about the way in which Israelite prophecy was reread based on our extant evidence? While the data in this regard is less robust in the case of biblical prophecy than for Assyrian prophecy, there is some suggestive evidence nonetheless.

Perhaps the clearest case of reapplying an old oracle to a new context in the Hebrew Bible is found in Isa 16:13–14. These verses conclude a collection of oracles concerning Moab (Isa 15–16). The oracles describe the desolation of Moab, expressing sympathy for the plight of the Moabite people. In the face of Moab's destruction, the oracles declare, "My heart cries out for Moab" (15:5), and exhort the reader/listener, "Let the fugitives of Moab sojourn among you" (16:4). They paint a dismal picture of Moab's circumstances in the present and immediate future, but they do not appear

---

[28] On the interaction among orality, textuality, performance, preservation, and authority as exhibited in Jer 36, see especially Robert R. Wilson, "Orality and Writing in the Creation of Exilic Prophetic Literature," in *Worship, Women, and War: Essays in Honor of Susan Niditch*, ed. John J. Collins, T. M. Lemos, and Saul M. Olyan, BJS 357 (Providence: Brown University, 2015), esp. 93–96; Nathaniel B. Levtow, "Text Production and Destruction in Ancient Israel: Ritual and Political Dimensions," in *Social Theory and the Study of Israelite Religion*, ed. Saul Olyan, RBS 71 (Atlanta: Society of Biblical Literature, 2012), esp. 120–25; Joachim Schaper, "On Writing and Reciting in Jeremiah 36," in *Prophecy in the Book of Jeremiah*, ed. Hans M. Barstad and Reinhard G. Kratz, BZAW 388 (Berlin: de Gruyter, 2009), 137–47; van der Toorn, *Scribal Culture and the Making of the Hebrew Bible*, 184–88; and Niditch, *Oral World and Written Word*, 1046.

[29] Nissinen, "Spoken, Written, Quoted, and Invented," 254.

[30] By "rereaders" and "rereading," I indicate those who took a text composed and originally read in the context of one occasion and intentionally applied it to a new situation, especially their own.

to take any particular joy in Moab's misfortune. In 16:13–14, however, both the content and tone shift: "This was the word which Yahweh spoke in the past (מאז). But now (ועתה) Yahweh speaks: 'In three years, like the years of a laborer, the glory of Moab, with all its great crowd, will be dishonored—a small, trifling, and powerless remnant.'" The fact that these concluding verses explicitly refer to the preceding material as having been delivered "in the past," in contrast to the "now" in which the conclusion is set, has led the majority of scholars to conclude that they represent a later addition to the oracle collection.[31] The situation assumed by 16:13–14 is starkly different from that described in 15:1–16:12. In the latter, Moab is ruined, the people are mourning in sackcloth, and their only possible source of deliverance is to flee their homeland and live as refugees in Judah. In 16:13–14, on the other hand, Moab is presented as a "great crowd," but despite present prosperity, destruction awaits a mere three years in the future. A picture of Moab's present prosperity with a promise of impending calamity stands in direct opposition to the depiction of Moab's current state of distress in the preceding oracles. Thus, the oracles describing Moab's destruction during an earlier period have been reappropriated for use in a later period to predict impending judgment. The oracle that once *described* Moab's suffering in the present now serves to *predict* it in the future, similar to the way in which Bel-ušezib reappropriated oracles promising success from early in Esarhaddon's reign in reference to his later Mannean campaign.

Another possible case in which an old prophecy has been reapplied to a new context is found in Ezekiel 12, although unlike in the case of Isaiah 15–16 this instance requires reconstructing the textual history of the oracle rather than simply reading it as it currently stands. Here we have a declaration of impending exile, especially concerning the "the chief" (הנשיא) in Jerusalem, that is, King Zedekiah of Judah.[32] While previous scholars had detected layers of redaction and reworking in this oracle,[33] Moshe Greenberg focuses specifically on 12:12b. The MT reads פניו יכסה יען אשר לא יראה לעין הוא את הארץ, "He shall cover his face since he will not see with(?) the eye himself the land." The awkwardness of the English translation here reflects the awkwardness of the Hebrew syntax. There have been a variety of proposed emendations,[34] but Greenberg's solution provides the most satisfying explanation. In his view, the text originally read פניו יכסה יען אשר לא יראה לעין, "He shall cover his face since he will not *be seen* to the eye" (emphasis mine).[35] That is, originally יראה represented a Niphal form, a conclusion supported by OG ὁραθῇ.[36] Thus the prediction was that Zedekiah will flee from the land, and thus not "be seen." Later, after Zedekiah's capture and blinding (2 Kgs 25:7), the consonantal text of the prophecy was reinterpreted as a Qal form, "he shall not see." The awkward הוא את הארץ represents a later addition appended to provide an object for what the prince "shall not see" once the verb had been (mis)understood as an active form.[37] That

---

[31] See, e.g., George Buchanan Gray, *A Critical and Exegetical Commentary on the Book of Isaiah I–XXXIX*, ICC (Edinburgh: T. & T. Clark, 1912), 1:295; Otto Kaiser, *Isaiah 13–39: A Commentary*, trans. R. A. Wilson, OTL (Philadelphia: Westminster, 1974), 74; Hans Wildberger, *Isaiah 13–27*, trans. Thomas H. Trapp, CC (Minneapolis: Fortress, 1997), 117; Joseph Blenkinsopp, *Isaiah 1–39: A New Translation with Introduction and Commentary*, AB 19 (New York: Doubleday, 2000), 300; and Brevard S. Childs, *Isaiah*, OTL (Louisville: Westminster John Knox, 2001), 132. It should be observed, however, that there is much less agreement on the composition history of the various oracles concerning Moab in Isa 15–16 that precede these concluding verses.
[32] So, e.g., G. A. Cooke, *A Critical and Exegetical Commentary on the Book of Ezekiel*, ICC (Edinburgh: T. & T. Clark, 1936), 131; Walther Eichrodt, *Ezekiel: A Commentary*, trans. Cosslett Quin, OTL (Philadelphia: Westminster, 1970), 152–53; Walther Zimmerli, *Ezekiel 1: A Commentary on the Book of the Prophet Ezekiel, Chapters 1–24*, ed. Frank Moore Cross and Klaus Baltzer, trans. Ronald E. Clements, Hermeneia (Philadelphia: Fortress, 1979), 272–73; and Daniel I. Block, *The Book of Ezekiel: Chapters 1–24*, NICOT (Grand Rapids: Eerdmans, 1997), 373–74.
[33] So Eichrodt, *Ezekiel*, 146–55; and Zimmerli, *Ezekiel 1*, 265–75.
[34] For a convenient overview of previous suggestions, see Block, *Ezekiel 1–24*, 363–64.
[35] Moshe Greenberg, *Ezekiel 1–20: A New Translation with Introduction and Commentary*, AB 22 (Garden City, NY: Doubleday, 1983), 213–15.
[36] So also Cooke, *Ezekiel*, 132; and Zimmerli, *Ezekiel 1*, 267.
[37] Greenberg also points to the absence of this final phrase in the important textual witness p967 (*Ezekiel*, 213).

is, while originally the oracle declared that Zedekiah would depart without *being seen*, the oracle was reread after the fact as referring to the fact that Zedekiah left the land blind, without *seeing*. Admittedly, this example is less straightforward than the one in Isaiah 15–16 presented above, but it remains suggestive nonetheless.[38] If Greenberg is correct, then an oracle originally given prior to the fall of Jerusalem that depicted Zedekiah's flight before the Babylonians was reread some time later as describing his capture, blinding, and exile.

As observed above, unlike the short-lived case of written Neo-Assyrian prophecy, the phenomenon of the textualization of Israelite prophecy continued to develop over the course of several centuries. One should not be surprised then to find that biblical prophecy did not retain a static shape during this time. While one could explore the evolution of any number of themes and features that developed in biblical prophecy over the course of time, here I would like to call attention to the way in which the textualization of prophecy served to transform the content of prophecy.[39] Specifically, the textualization of prophecy creates future secondary audiences that will encounter the written prophetic oracles, in addition to the original listening audience who were the prophet's contemporaries. In the wake of the revolution that the textualization of prophecy represented, both prophet and scribe would have become increasingly aware of this new secondary audience. They would have themselves witnessed oracles of previous generations read in light of new circumstances, and it would be difficult for them not to envision the later readers who would serve as future audiences for their own oracles. One would naturally expect, then, that prophets and scribes would begin to orient their oracles toward these later audiences to one degree or another.

It is one thing for an oracle originally addressed to a particular historical situation to be reused in a new context, as in the cases outlined above, but once this reappropriation of prophecy became standard practice, then there would be an impetus to compose prophetic texts in such a way that they are more amenable to reinterpretation and reapplication. Thus, for example, one would expect to see a move away from specificity and toward ambiguity, since an oracle that explicitly identifies its referents is more difficult to map onto new referents than one that speaks in more ambiguous terms. A lack of specificity facilitates reuse by later readers and allows them to read themselves and their own historical circumstances into the text more easily. To employ terminology coined by Roland Barthes, one may expect to observe a general move toward more "writerly" (*scriptible*) and less "readerly" (*lisible*) prophecies. Barthes distinguishes between the readerly text, in which the author produces and the reader passively consumes, and the writerly text, in which the reader plays an active role in the production of the text. Of course, a purely writerly text, in which the writer plays *no* role in the meaning of the text, is more of an ideal than an actual possibility; it "is not a

---

[38] Michael Fishbane holds up both of these examples, along with Ezekiel's oracles concerning the imminent destruction of Tyre (26:7–14) that went unfulfilled and were later reapplied to Egypt (29:17–21), as examples of prophecies that went unfulfilled but were then reinterpreted (*Biblical Interpretation in Ancient Israel* [Oxford: Clarendon, 1985], 476–77). It is unclear that either Isa 15–16 or Ezek 12 would have been perceived as having been "unfulfilled" though. Whatever the historical circumstances underlying Isa 15–16, the oracles appear to assume that Moab was currently undergoing distress. Indeed, very little is "predicted" there at all. Likewise, even without the inclusion of an allusion to Zedekiah's blinding, Ezek 12 does accurately predict his leaving the land, even without its later expansions. Neither of these requires the sort of revision that Ezekiel's unfulfilled oracle against Tyre did, so one cannot attribute the motivation for their reinterpretation to a need to correct an erroneous prediction as in that example.

[39] In her seminal *Swallowing the Scroll: Textuality and the Dynamics of Discourse in Ezekiel's Prophecy*, JSOTSup 78 (Sheffield: Almond, 1989), Ellen F. Davis in many respects anticipates the observations here concerning the fundamental ways in which the form and content of prophetic oracles change when oral prophecy is transformed into text. Davis's argument that the book of Ezekiel represents a turning point in the corpus of biblical prophetic literature, in that its oracles appear to have been written from the start, and that the literary origins of the book have clearly observable effects on the shape of its contents, remain cogent. In many ways, the arguments here represent an extension of Davis's work, suggesting that even a generation after Hebrew prophecy was first committed to writing, the effects of the textualization of prophecy on the content of the oracles already began to manifest themselves, albeit typically in more subtle ways than in Ezekiel.

thing, we would have a hard time finding it in a bookstore." Rather, readerly and writerly are two ends of a spectrum that consists of "texts whose plural is more or less parsimonious."[40] Texts that are more amenable to a multiplicity of meanings are thus more "writerly" in Barthes's terminology. Of course, the sort of activity that Barthes has in mind is the reading of (primarily modern Western) literature, quite a different genre of text than prophetic texts of the first millennium BCE, and the sort of plurality and multivalence that Barthes has in mind is rather different from the kind of ambiguity under discussion here. Nonetheless, the terms "readerly" and "writerly" can be employed with some advantage with regard to the various collections of prophetic literature in the Hebrew Bible.

In this regard, one may compare the oracles against the nations preserved in the relatively early prophetic book of Amos (ca. eighth century[41]) and those contained in the later book of Zephaniah (seventh century or later[42]). Amos's oracles exhibit a high degree of specificity and fall on the more "readerly" end of the prophetic spectrum. For instance, its oracle against Damascus refers to Hazael and Ben-Hadad by name, excoriating them for having "threshed Gilead with sledges of iron" (1:3); Gaza "exiled an entire community, delivering them to Edom" (1:6); and Moab is condemned for having "burned the bones of the king of Edom to lime" (2:1). While our ignorance of the finer points of eighth-century international policy in the Levant leaves us unable to identify the particular events and actions being described, it is clear that the oracles do refer to specific historical events. Amos's specificity in language would have made his message quite clear to his contemporaries, as there would have been little room for interpretation concerning which particular actions Amos had in view. The audience may either accept or reject Amos's message, but there is little room for the reader to write meaning into the text. Of course, the advantage that specificity provides vis-à-vis a contemporary audience also becomes a disadvantage for later rereaders, since it is more difficult (albeit obviously not impossible) for a future audience to reapply oracles with such specific referents to later situations.

---

[40]Roland Barthes, *S/Z: An Essay*, trans. Richard Miller (New York: Hill & Wang, 1974), 3–6.

[41]A full examination of the compositional history of Amos's oracles against the nations is out of place here. For a discussion of the issue, see Tchavdar S. Hadjiev, *The Composition and Redaction of the Book of Amos*, BZAW 393 (Berlin: de Gruyter, 2009), 41–59; Dirk U. Rottzoll, *Studien zur Redaktion und Komposition des Amosbuchs*, BZAW 243 (Berlin: de Gruyter, 1996), 22–80 ; Jörg Jeremias, *The Book of Amos: A Commentary*, trans. Douglas W. Stott, OTL (Louisville: Westminster John Knox, 1999), 17–25; Shalom M. Paul, *Amos: A Commentary on the Book of Amos*, ed. Frank Moore Cross, Hermeneia (Minneapolis: Fortress, 1991), 16–27; Francis I. Andersen and David Noel Freedman, *Amos: A New Translation with Introduction and Commentary*, AB 24A (New York: Doubleday, 1989), 26–38; Hans Walter Wolff, *Joel and Amos: A Commentary on the Books of the Prophets Joel and Amos*, ed. S. Dean McBride Jr., trans. Waldemar Janzen, S. Dean McBride Jr., and Charles Muenchow, Hermeneia (Philadelphia: Fortress, 1977), 148–52; and James Luther Mays, *Amos: A Commentary*, OTL (Philadelphia: Westminster, 1969), 12–14. Both here and in the discussion of the dates of various biblical material below I speak of necessity in generalities. I do not pretend that the entirety of the book of Amos, or even of the oracles against the nations contained therein, date to any particular period. There has almost certainly been a degree of scribal glossing, redaction, and expansion during the history of the transmission of each of the collections of prophetic material contained in the Hebrew Bible, but there is no room here to wade into the many debates concerning the redactional histories of each prophetic book. When I refer to the date of a prophetic book, I refer to the initial date of composition of the bulk of its material as reconstructed by modern historical-critical scholarship.

[42]Although traditionally scholars have followed the lead of the book's superscription (1:1) and dated at least the core of the book of Zephaniah to Josiah's reign (so, e.g., J. J. M. Roberts, *Nahum, Habakkuk, and Zephaniah: A Commentary*, OTL [Louisville: Westminster John Knox, 1991], 163–64; and Marvin A. Sweeney, *Zephaniah: A Commentary*, ed. Paul D. Hanson, Hermeneia [Minneapolis: Fortress, 2003], 14–18), others date the book somewhat later (e.g., J. Philip Hyatt, "The Date and Background of Zephaniah," *JNES* 7 [1948]: 25–29; and Donald L. Williams, "The Date of Zephaniah," *JBL* 82 [1963]: 77–88). In a notable departure from the views of most previous scholars, Ehud Ben Zvi, while allowing for some pre-compositional material, reads the book as a postexilic composition (*A Historical-Critical Study of the Book of Zephaniah*, BZAW 198 [Berlin: de Gruyter, 1991]). Adele Berlin provides a convenient survey of previous suggestions concerning the date of the book, but does not come down firmly on the issue (*Zephaniah: A New Translation with Introduction and Commentary*, AB 25A [New York: Doubleday, 1994], 33–47). Tchavdar S. Hadjiev detects four distinct layers, ranging in date from the preexilic to the exilic periods ("Survival, Conversion and Restoration: Reflections on the Redaction History of the Book of Zephaniah," *VT* 61 [2011]: 570–81); and Walter Dietrich detects stages of composition spanning from the late seventh century to the postexilic period (*Nahum Habakkuk Zephaniah*, trans. Peter Altmann, IECOT [Stuttgart: Kohlhammer, 2016], 188–92).

The contrast between Amos's specificity and Zephaniah's ambiguity is striking. Zephaniah's oracles against the nations declare, "Gaza will be forsaken; Ashkelon will become a desolation; they will drive out Ashdod at noon; Ekron will be uprooted" (Zeph 2:4). Likewise, concerning Moab and the Ammonites we read, "I have heard that taunt of Moab, the revilings of the Ammonites, with which they taunted my people, and they increased their territory. Therefore, as I live—an oracle of Yahweh the God of Israel—Moab will be like Sodom and the Ammonites like Gomorrah" (2:8). In Zephaniah's judgment against Cush one finds the vague condemnation, "Also you, Cushites, are corpses for my sword" (2:12). The remainder of Zephaniah's oracles exhibit a similar lack of specificity compared to those of Amos. Destruction is declared, but the specific misdeeds that warrant this punishment are left ambiguous. These oracles could be applied to nearly any action taken by any of these nations at any period. The lack of specificity here would have made it more difficult for a contemporary audience to hear Zephaniah's message as intended by the prophet/scribe than would have been the case if the oracles were more specific in their referents. The listeners/readers of these oracles would have had to provide more information themselves, which would seem to represent a disadvantage if the goal was to communicate a specific message to a contemporary audience. On the other hand, one may also observe that a move toward ambiguity also has the effect of producing more "writerly" oracles, which allow for a larger variety of meanings and which thus allow later audiences to fit the oracles to their own contexts more easily.

One might also compare the oracle against Assyria in Isa 10:5–10, in which Calno, Carchemish, Hamath, Arpad, Samaria, and Damascus are all listed as territories conquered or soon to be conquered by Assyria during campaigns in the latter part of the eighth century, with the oracles against Assyria in the book of Nahum dating to a generation or two later.[43] Despite its superscript, which identifies the book as "an oracle concerning Nineveh" (Nah 1:1), the city of Nineveh and nation of Assyria are each mentioned only once in the book's oracles (3:7 and 3:18 respectively). Instead, Nahum declares Yahweh's judgment against "adversaries" (צר√, 1:2, 9), "enemies" (איב√, 1:2, 8), the "worthless one" (בליעל, 2:1 [Eng. 1:15]), and the "city of blood" (עיר דמים, 3:1). Even the instrument of Yahweh's judgment, Babylonia, is referred to not by name but as the "shatterer" (מפיץ, 2:2 [Eng. 2:1]). It is not difficult to imagine how a later audience might easily read their own adversaries into the text, even after the Assyrians had long ceased to present a threat and new enemies had arisen in their place. Likewise, one might observe that Habakkuk[44] contains only a single mention of the Chaldeans (1:6), the primary target of the book's oracles, or that Joel identifies its agents of destruction as several types of locusts (1:4) and "a great and powerful army" (2:2), not a specific group of people.[45] In contrast, during an earlier generation of Israelite prophecy, Hosea

---

[43] The reference to the fall of Thebes in 3:8 sets the book after 663, and that Nineveh's fall is still assumed to be in the future sets it before 612. For a convenient overview of attempts to narrow this range, including some who date the book in its present form to sometime later than the Neo-Assyrian period, see Duane L. Christensen, *Nahum: A New Translation with Introduction and Commentary*, AYB 24F (New Haven: Yale University Press, 2009), 52–56. Roberts argues for a date as precise as 640–630 (*Nahum, Habakkuk, and Zephaniah*, 38–39), while Dietrich detects four different stages of composition ranging in date from the preexilic to the Hellenistic periods (*Nahum Habakkuk Zephaniah*, 29–34).

[44] Habakkuk's lack of explicit referents makes it notoriously difficult to date. Francis I. Andersen lays out the possibilities offered by previous scholars—ranging from the sixth to second centuries—and tentatively leans toward the earlier end of this spectrum (*Habakkuk: A New Translation with Introduction and Commentary*, AB 25 [New York: Doubleday, 2001], 24–27), as does Roberts (*Nahum, Habakkuk, and Zephaniah*, 82–84). Dietrich detects two major layers, one dating to the seventh century and another to the sixth, with the psalm in ch. 3 dating to sometime later still (*Nahum Habakkuk Zephaniah*, 98–103).

[45] There have been a variety of suggestions concerning the identity of Joel's locusts, ranging from literal locusts to a human army to an eschatological army of God. For an overview of the various positions, see John A. Thompson, "Joel's Locusts in the Light of Near Eastern Parallels," *JNES* 14 (1955): 52–55; Pablo R. Andiñach, "The Locusts in the Message of Joel," *VT* 42 (1992): 433–41; James L. Crenshaw, *Joel: A New Translation with Introduction and Commentary*, AB 24C (New York: Doubleday, 1995), 88–94; John Barton, *Joel and Obadiah: A Commentary*, OTL (Louisville: Westminster John Knox, 2001); and Elie Assis, *The Book of Joel: A Prophet between Calamity and Hope*, LHBOTS 581 (New York: Bloomsbury, 2013), 24–54.

referred to specific nations such as Israel, Ephraim, Jacob, Assyria, and Egypt multiple times per chapter. Again, one can trace a general trend toward ambiguity in biblical prophecy over the course of time.

While there are certainly other possible explanations for this apparent increase in ambiguity in the prophetic texts of the seventh and sixth centuries as compared with those of the eighth century, this particular shift is not especially surprising if one considers the original motivation for the textualization of prophetic oracles. In the first stage of this process, an oracle primarily directed at contemporary circumstances was written down in order to be reapplied to later circumstances. In a later generation, an increased awareness that oracles would be reapplied in later situations encouraged the use of more ambiguous referents whose multivalence makes them more susceptible to reinterpretation. One can easily identify nearly any hostile foreign power as "enemies" or "a great and powerful army," and one could interpret nearly anything unfortunate that befell Moab or Cush as the referent of oracles like those contained in Zephaniah. On the other hand, it would take a somewhat more creative hermeneutic to apply Amos's condemnation of Moab's "burning the bones of the king of Edom to lime" to the acts of a later foe. While one could of course reinterpret oracles like those of Hosea and Amos in the context of new circumstances,[46] their more "readerly" oracles are not constructed in such a way as to facilitate multivalent readings in the same way as the more "writerly" oracles of later periods.

Interestingly, one might observe that this process reversed itself to some degree in later periods. Ezekiel's oracles against the nations are quite specific, for instance, so much so that the book's unfulfilled oracle concerning Nebuchadnezzar's conquest of Tyre (26:7–14) had to be amended by an oracle (also unfulfilled) concerning Nebuchadnezzar's conquest of Egypt (29:17–21). Likewise, Haggai and Zechariah 1–8 focus on specific characters such as Joshua and Zerubbabel, referring to them by name, and thus also lack the sort of ambiguity that one finds in Nahum, Habakkuk, and Zephaniah.[47] This may demonstrate a return to focusing on a prophet's/scribe's contemporary audience rather than future audiences of rereaders and would indicate that despite the increased focus on later secondary audiences enabled by the textualization of prophecy, contemporary audiences were not entirely overshadowed. The evidence would indicate that prophecy in the form of text addressed both a primary contemporary audience and secondary audiences of later generations. Some texts focus more on one audience than the other, but the very ability to choose to focus on

---

The date of the book is likewise uncertain, with suggestions ranging from the middle of the sixth century (so Assis, *The Book of Joel*, 3–23) to the late sixth or fifth century (so Crenshaw, *Joel*, 21–29) to the middle of the fifth century (so Barton, *Joel and Obadiah*, 14–18) to the early fourth century (so Wolff, *Joel and Amos*, 4–6). In any case, the references to the exile in Joel 4:2 (Eng. 3:2) would point to sometime after 586 and thus well after the first generation of textualized Israelite prophecy.

[46]And of course the fact that they now exist as component parts of a larger "Book of the Twelve" indicates that readers of Amos and Hosea have long been doing precisely that since well before the turn of the era. The question of the unity of the Book of the Twelve and the degree to which the individual "books" contained therein have been edited, reworked, and expanded as they were incorporated into the larger collection remain topics of debate. The literature on such issues is extensive, but for a helpful collection of essays devoted to these topics, see Rainer Albertz, James D. Nogalski, and Jakob Wöhrle, eds., *Perspectives on the Formation of the Book of the Twelve: Methodological Foundations—Redactional Processes—Historical Insights*, BZAW 433 (Berlin: de Gruyter, 2012); as well as James D. Nogalski and Marvin A. Sweeney, eds., *Reading and Hearing the Book of the Twelve*, SymS12 (Atlanta: Society of Biblical Literature, 2000).

[47]While the impetus for the shift back toward specificity in referents in Ezekiel and Persian-period prophetic oracles is an issue that is beyond the scope of the present study, it may be that the historical circumstances and social realities that served as the contexts for those oracles discouraged the kind of ambiguity that one finds in the earlier oracles of Nahum, Habakkuk, and Zephaniah. For example, Dalit Rom-Shiloni has argued that Ezekiel and later Persian-period prophecy shows a special concern for identifying the exiles/repatriates as the "true Israel" over against those who remained in the land (*Exclusive Inclusivity: Identity Conflicts Between the Exiles and the People Who Remained [6th–5th Centuries BCE]*, LHBOTS 543 [New York: Bloomsbury, 2013]). While ambiguity may be advantageous when a prophet or scribe wishes to allow an oracle concerning one of Israel's enemies to be reinterpreted and applied to a later foe, such ambiguity would be more than a little counterproductive in a context in which a major matter of contention was the precise identity of "Israel" itself.

any audience other than one's contemporaries is only made possible in the first place by the textualization of prophecy.

One may observe another possible way that the textualization of prophecy influenced the content of prophetic oracles was to encourage a shift in temporal focus toward the eschaton. That is, once one is aware that one's oracles may be reread by future audiences, one's mind might naturally tend toward the ultimate future audience, the one that would see the culmination of all history. Is it a coincidence that in Zephaniah the establishment of divine justice follows upon the destruction of the world (Zeph 3:8–10) or that Habakkuk concludes with an old hymn recounting Yahweh's conquest of both the nations of the world and the cosmic waters of chaos (Hab 3)? The "Isaiah Apocalypse" (Isa 24–27)[48] begins with the destruction of the world, and the "Gog and Magog" oracle in Ezekiel 38–39[49] presents a great eschatological battle that will usher in the restored fortunes of Israel. Rather than focusing on the affairs of the present like the bulk of First Isaiah, Hosea, and Amos, an awareness that one's oracles would be read and reread by future generations may encourage a prophet and/or scribe to focus his oracles on the events of the future, including the ultimate future. Perhaps, then, the shift in focus to the end of days can also be ascribed at least in part to the textualization of prophecy.

Of course, it would be naive to point to any single factor as being responsible for a particular shift in the content and focus of prophetic oracles over the course of history, and I do not believe that the changes that biblical prophecy underwent during its history can be solely attributed to any single factor. I do believe, however, that an underappreciated phenomenon in the history of Israelite prophecy is the very fact of its textualization. While there is no doubt that historical events and cultural shifts left their mark on the form and content of prophetic oracles, the phenomenon of textualization itself was likely a significant factor. I have suggested above that the consciousness of later rereaders who would reappropriate prophetic texts in their own contexts may be at least in part responsible both for the move toward ambiguity in referents and for the increased focus on the eschaton in prophetic texts during the generations following the textualization of prophecy. Although these are almost certainly not the only features of biblical prophecy that one can attribute to its textualization, hopefully the examination above provides a starting point for exploring the way in which the shift from orality to textuality came to shape the content of Israelite prophecy.

---

[48] There is a general consensus that Isa 24–27 dates to a period later than the bulk of Isa 1–39, but there is little agreement concerning to which particular period this material belongs. Roberts dates it to the late seventh/early sixth century (*First Isaiah*, 306–7); Blenkinsopp prefers a date around 539, i.e., the fall of Babylon (*Isaiah 1–39*, 346–48); Wildberger dates it even later, to the postexilic period (*Isaiah 13–27*, 445–47); and Kaiser traces several strata in the material dating from the fourth to the second centuries (*Isaiah 13–39*). For present purposes, the precise date or even century is relatively unimportant so long as one acknowledges that it represents relatively late material. One may observe, though, that the lack of consensus regarding the date of this material is largely due to the lack of concrete historical referents and a tendency for the oracles to speak in generalities, a feature already observed in other relatively late prophetic material in the Hebrew Bible.

[49] The date of this material is likewise a matter of debate. Zimmerli holds that the earliest form of the oracle may date to a later period of Ezekiel's own career (*Ezekiel 2: A Commentary on the Book of the Prophet Ezekiel Chapters 25–48*, ed. Paul D. Hanson and Leonard Jay Greenspoon, trans. James D. Martin, Hermeneia [Minneapolis: Fortress, 1983], 296–304), while Eichrodt dates it to the postexilic period (*Ezekiel*, 519–21). Again, the difficulty in dating the text is largely due to its ambiguous referents.

# Reorientation in Responsibility of Levites Taking Care of the Ark

*The Levites' Role in Samuel–Kings in Relation to Deuteronomistic Expressions Concerning Interpretation of the Law*

ANTJE LABAHN

When considering the role of the Levites within the comprehensive writings Samuel–Kings[1] one will surprisingly find no more than three references: 1 Sam 6:15; 2 Sam 15:24 and 1 Kgs 8:4. These references are rather short on detail, and each of these remarks comes as a short notice within a larger context which seems to disregard the Levites. All of these references, however, share the same depiction of Levites insofar as they are introduced as people carrying the ark. In referring to this responsibility, it seems that Levites have been added to these texts with a particular intention, namely, to remind the reader of their special role.

This essay intends to shed light on these brief notices. First, it analyzes the three references to Levites in Samuel–Kings. When clarifying the function of the Levites it will become clear that the references belong to literary developments within these particular texts. Second, I will look for a potential background for the literary addition of the Levites notices, which will be interpreted as part of the Deuteronomistic History. Some references in Deuteronomy present the Levites in a comparable manner, characterizing the ark as a box for the tablets of the law (Deut 9:9–10; 10:2, 5; 31:26; 1 Kgs 8:9) and the "ark of the covenant" (Deut 10:8; 31:9, 25; 2 Sam 15:24). Finally, the Levites' role in connection with the ark will be linked to their role as interpreters of the divine Torah in late Deuteronomistic writings. Thereby, they share a role of the Levites' portrait in Chronicles and their representations in early Jewish writings of the Second Temple period.

## 1. THE LEVITES IN SAMUEL–KINGS

### 1.1. *1 Samuel 6:15*

In 1 Sam 6:15 the Levites (הלוים) operate as a group of people responsible for moving the ark. According to the narrative, they do so in a special moment, when the ark has come back to Judah after its odyssey in Philistine territory.[2] The Levites remove the ark from its cart and put it on a large rock:

---

[1] This essay goes back to a paper read at the joint session of "Deuteronomistic History" with "Levites and Priests in History and Tradition" at the Annual Meeting of the Society of Biblical Literature in San Diego in 2014. I am grateful to Jeremy Hutton and Mark Leuchter, the organizers of the session, for their invitation. I was happy to become involved in the session project "Levites in the Deuteronomistic History." The idea to look for Levites in Samuel–Kings goes back to that theme.
[2] On the story cf. W. Dietrich, "Die Überführung der Lade nach Jerusalem (2 Sam 6): Geschichten und Geschichte," in *Die Samuelbücher im deuteronomistischen Geschichtswerk. Studien zu den Geschichtsüberlieferungen des Alten Testaments II*, BWANT 201 (Stuttgart: Kohlhammer 2012), 191–206.

The cart came into the field of Joshua of Beth-Shemesh, and stopped there. A large stone was there; so they split up the wood of the cart and offered the cows as a burnt offering to the Lord. The Levites took down the ark of the Lord and the box that was beside it, in which were the gold objects, and set them upon the large stone. Then the people of Beth-Shemesh offered burnt offerings and presented sacrifices on that day to the Lord. (1 Sam 6:14–15, NRS)

It is remarkable that in the context of the story 1 Sam 4:1–7:1, the Levites are the sole group explicitly mentioned for moving (ירד, Hiphil) the ark. Although the ark took the long way from Shiloh (4:3) to Ebenezer (4:1, 5), to Ashdod (5:1), Gath (5:8), and Ekron (5:10) and finally to Beth-Shemesh (6:11), there is no other group of people mentioned responsible for transporting the ark, neither in the Judean homeland nor in the lands of the Philistines. We are only informed about a cart[3] of two cows which moves the ark back to Judah, on its stage from Ekron to Beth-Shemesh. The biblical record simply talks about "them," an impersonal plural statement of an anonymous group. Yet no specification is given about who this anonymous group may be. The reference in 6:15 fills this gap by introducing the Levites: they are the group taking the ark off the cart and putting in on a large rock.

According to the narrative flow of the story there was no ultimate need to ascribe the moving of the ark to a particular group, let alone a group of Levites. If anything, the priests would have been the more plausible group because they were the ones busy with offerings;[4] and also the Deuteronomistic tradition knows the group of priests as the ones carrying the ark (cf. 2 Sam 15; 1 Kgs 8 [on which see below]; see also Josh 3–6).[5] Consequently, the priests were the ideal group to offer the burnt offerings and the grain offerings, which are mentioned later on in the story, and also to move the ark to the rocky place of offering (6:15b).

The reference to the Levites is astonishing since it is nowhere anticipated within the narrative. The Levites play no part in the previous story. Furthermore, the question may be raised, what do they *do* on the field of Joshua of Beth-Shemesh? Are they present there because Beth-Shemesh was assumed to be a Levitical city like it is presupposed in Josh 21:16 and, dependent on that, in 1 Chr 6:44?[6] Doubts arise on this connection because there is neither a direct link nor an allusion to such a tradition.[7] Beside the Levites, only the "people of Beth-Shemesh" are mentioned while harvesting and offering by themselves (1 Sam 6:14, 15); that is, the inhabitants are imagined as common Judahites. In the narrative flow, the Levites appear in 1 Sam 6:15 from nowhere, and disappear from the scene as quickly as they came. Because this statement is so unique in the entire narrative there is good reason to assume that it originates from a later redaction on the Deuteronomistic History[8]

---

[3] Transportation of the ark on a cart is rarely mentioned in Deuteronomistic historiography alongside other references in the Old Testament/Hebrew Bible. It indicates the presence of the "invisible god" in war, as proposed by J. M. Sasson, "The Lord of Hosts, Seated over the Cherubs," in *Rethinking the Foundations: Historiography in the Ancient World and in the Bible: Essays in Honour of J. Van Seters*, in S. L. McKenzie and T. Römer in collab. with H. H. Schmid, BZAW 294 (Berlin: de Gruyter, 2000), 227–34, here 234.

[4] That priests are legitimate for the making of offerings holds true for the Priestly tradition in Leviticus and Numbers. Although the Deuteronomistic History only sparsely refers to this tradition explicitly (cf., e.g., 2 Sam 5:24), it maintains the core cultic duties of the priests.

[5] Later on reworked into "the priests from the tribe of Levi" in Josh 3:3; 8:33 (see below, §1.4).

[6] On Levitical cities see, e.g., E. Ben Zvi, "The List of Levitical Cities," *JSOT* 54 (1992): 77–106; G. Schmitt, "Levitenstädte," *ZDPV* 111 (1995): 28–48; H.-D. Neef, "Art. Levitenstädte," *Calwer Bibellexikon* 2 (2003): 828; for Chronicles see also M. Kartveit, *Motive und Schichten der Landtheologie in I Chronik 1–9*, CB.OT 28 (Stockholm: Almqvist & Wiksell, 1989), 162–63.

[7] See also the doubts mentioned by H. Samuel, *Von Priestern zum Patriarchen: Levi und die Leviten im Alten Testament*, BZAW 448 (Berlin: de Gruyter, 2014), 339, who considers Beth-Shemesh a priestly Aaronite city in Josh 21 rather than a Levitical one. If such an argument holds true it is a further hint against a traditional connection.

[8] Already W. Gesenius, *Hebräisches und Aramäisches Handwörterbuch über das Alte Testament*, ed. H. Zimmern et al. (Dordrecht: Springer, 1962 [reprint of the 1915 ed.]), 382, takes this reference as one of the "interpolierten Stellen"; for a later addition

that includes the Levites for such a duty at a later stage. The story itself does not provide a reason why it is the Levites who are integrated in the narrative for such a duty.

Including the Levites in 1 Sam 6:15 is not only a matter of redactional adjustments in function (i.e. inserting a group as carriers of the ark); more than that, the addition redefines their role. The Levite's role is defined by the item they move, that is, the ark and what it contains or what it represents. Such an expression favors the view that the Levites represent a group with special responsibility for the ark. Their responsibility does not only touch the more or less simple process of relocating the ark during the movement of bringing it back from Philistine region to Kiriath-Jearim (1 Sam 6:21; 7:1–2). More than that, the ark is also relevant for what it resembles. Accompanying the military parade in the story, the ark works as a kind of portable war palladium.[9] As such, it represents the divine presence throughout the procession.[10] Along with a redefinition of the Levites' role, the addition affirms the group as authorized personnel for taking care of the ark as an object manifesting YHWH's immanence. Such a redefinition provides an appreciation of the Levites in particular.

### 1.2. *2 Samuel 15:24*

The second occurrence of the Levites is to be found in 2 Sam 15:24, where they are also present as personnel carrying the ark. The context presents David's flight leaving the city of Jerusalem. At the edge of town, David stops to watch the people of power and the soldiers passing by (15:17–23). At the rear end of the parade, the ark follows, carried by the Levites and accompanied by the two leading priests, Abiathar and Zadok:

> Abiathar came up, and Zadok also, with all the Levites (כל־הלוים), carrying the ark of the covenant of God. They set down the ark of God until the people had all passed out of the city. (2 Sam 15:24, NRS)

The episode of the ark (15:24–30) forms a small unit that was later inserted into the narrative of David's flight story. The episode, which starts anew with a new beginning (והנה), is rather loosely linked to the context.[11] This holds true also for the occurrence of the ark, which does not reappear in the rest of the flight story—the narrative itself concentrates on David and disregards the ark.

Though the episode 15:24–30 is short, the role of the Levites therein is remarkable. The Levites are only mentioned in v. 24, whereas the two priests Abiathar and Zadok appear on the scene again when they bring the ark back into the city of Jerusalem (vv. 25, 29). But the Levites disappear afterwards and it remains dubious what "all the Levites" are doing henceforth in the middle of nowhere. Next to the difference in personnel, a variation in terminology is also present. When the Levites move the ark, the term "to carry" (נשא) is used in v. 24. Yet, when the ark makes its way back to Jerusalem, the verb "to return" (שוב) is used instead. In clear Deuteronomistic terminology,[12] the

---

see, e.g., H. W. Herzberg, *Die Samuelbücher übersetzt und erklärt*, ATD 10, 5. Aufl. (Göttingen: Vandenhoeck & Ruprecht, 1973), 42, 45; H. J. Stoebe, *Das erste Buch Samuelis*, KAT VIII.1 (Gütersloh: Gütersloher Verlagshaus 1973), 148; I. L. Seeligmann, "Anfänge der Midraschexegese in der Chronik," in *Gesammelte Studien zur Hebräischen Bibel*, FAT 41 (Tübingen: Mohr Siebeck 2004), 31–54, here 47–48; P. Porzig, *Die Lade Jahwes im Alten Testament und in den Texten vom Toten Meer*, BZAW 397 (Berlin: de Gruyter 2009), 149–52; Samuel, *Von Priestern zum Patriarchen*, 338–39.
[9] Cf. G. von Rad, "Zelt und Lade," in *Gesammelte Studien zum Alten Testament*, ThB 8 (Munich: Kaiser 1958), 109–29.
[10] Cf. Sasson, "The Lord of Hosts, Seated over the Cherubs," 234.
[11] Cf. T. A. Rudnig, *Davids Thron: Redaktionskritische Studien zur Geschichte von der Thronnachfolge Davids*, BZAW 358 (Berlin: de Gruyter 2006), 347–63; Samuel, *Von Priestern zum Patriarchen*, 341, who regards the story as a later addition, originating from a "Theodizee-Bearbeitung."
[12] Cf., e.g., the classical elaboration by O. H. Steck, *Israel und das gewaltsame Geschick der Propheten: Untersuchungen zur Überlieferung des deuteronomistischen Geschichtsbildes im Alten Testament, Spätjudentum und Urchristentum*, WMANT 23 (Neukirchen: Neukirchener Verlag, 1967), 62–63, 68–74.

return (שוב) of the ark to its previous destination belongs to the main body of the short episode around the ark.

Within this episode, the remark on Levites is to be reckoned as another later redactional addition.[13] The involvement of Levites here is related in brief terms; no details regarding their relationship with the priests are provided. The variation in terminology as well as in personnel in v. 24 thus points to a unique statement which makes an impression of readjusting previous procedures in moving the ark, since the verse emphasizes *the Levites* in their particular role of carrying the ark.

The only hint as to why the Levites are added may be found in the specific terminological characterization of the ark in v. 24. Here, a theological appraisal regards the ark as "the ark of the covenant of God" (ארון ברית האלהים), whereas in the context in v. 25 and v. 29 it is simply called "the ark of God" (ארון האלהים). The notion of the covenant (ברית)[14] brings a special qualification to the ark, in as much as it qualifies the relationship between YHWH and his people. In this particular case here regarding the ark, the term "covenant" recalls the Deuteronomistic characterization "tablets of the covenant" (explicitly mentioned in Deut 9:9, 11, 15: לוחת הברית) where the covenant is linked with the idea of the tablets which themselves contain the law resting in the ark according to Deuteronomistic theology (cf. Deut 9:10; 10:2, 5; see also the reminder in Deut 31:26; 1 Kgs 8:9). To take this one little step further, that means that the tablets of the covenant contain the word of God in an elementary form of the law.[15] Due to such a content, the ark is evaluated not just as a symbol of God's presence but rather as a special case: as a precious home for God's word, which is so close.[16]

If the ark and the tablets inside are characterized in this way, it raises the question if such a qualification required a specific group of personnel moving it. The short notice in v. 24 linking the ark with the covenant, law and *also* with the Levites in its late Deuteronomistic outlook seems to address this matter. A particular appreciation as well as a theological qualification of the ark may have produced a link with the Levites who were elsewhere known to be capable of such qualifications (we will turn to this aspect below). The association with covenant, law and the ark establishes the Levites as the personnel authorized to hold a unique and close relationship with YHWH.

### 1.3. *1 Kings 8:4*

The Levites appear a third time in Samuel–Kings as carriers of the ark. It is a short statement within the story of moving the ark into the newly built Jerusalem temple ultimately prior to Solomon's dedication:

---

[13] H. J. Stoebe, *Das zweite Buch Samuelis*, KAT VIII/2 (Gütersloh: Gütersloher Verlagshaus, 1994), 364–65, 370; Herzberg, *Samuelbücher*, 282, assume a later Deuteronomistic addition.

[14] The Deuteronomistic conception of covenant (cf., e.g., Deut 5:2) depicts the way in which YHWH and the people interact: there is a strong assignment built upon particular legal advices which people have to obey in order to fulfil God's will, to have success, and to enjoy life. On theology and typical phraseology cf. M. Weinfeld, *Deuteronomy and Deuteronomic School* (Oxford: Clarendon, 1972); L. Perlitt, *Bundestheologie im Alten Testament*, WMANT 36 (Neukirchen-Vluyn: Neukirchener Verlag, 1969); R. Feldmeier and H. Spieckermann, *Der Gott der Liebe. Eine biblische Gotteslehre*, Topoi Biblischer Theologie / Topics of Biblical Theology 1 (Tübingen: Mohr Siebeck 2011), 445–49.

[15] Cf. Deut 4:13 (עשרת הדברים ויכתבם על־שני לחות אבנים) with the order of obeying. According to such an interpretation, the Decalogue represents the law in an abbreviated form. I allude to the Decalogue in Deut 5:6–21 and its Deuteronomistic interpretation (respectively, paraenetic preaching in Deut 5:1; 6:1 etc.), and do not intend to recall the entire law-code in its characteristic Deuteronomistic phraseology, such as "decrees and statutes and ordinances" (אלה העדת והחקים והמשפטים) in Deut 4:45, interpreting "the Torah that Moses has given to the Israelites" (זאת התורה אשר־שם משה לפני בני ישראל) mentioned in the verse immediately preceding, 4:44. Similar idioms appear throughout the text, although they may not all represent the same stage within the multi-layered redactional process of development, they share the (predominantly late) Deuteronomistic phraseological legal patterns (especially DtrN). On law and obedience, see, e.g., the illustrative compendium of phraseology and idioms in H. D. Preuss, *Deuteronomium*, EdF 164 (Darmstadt: Wissenschaftliche Buchgesellschaft, 1982), 194–201.

[16] On YHWH's "close word" as a main part of late Deuteronomistic conception DtrN, cf. M. Köckert, "Das nahe Wort: Wandlungen des Gesetzesverständnisses in der deuteronomisch-deuteronomistischen Literatur," in *Leben in Gottes Gegenwart. Studien zum Verständnis des Gesetzes im Alten Testament*, FAT 43 (Tübingen: Mohr Siebeck, 2004), 47–72.

So they (i.e. *the priests*) brought up the ark of the Lord, the tent of meeting, and all the holy vessels that were in the tent; the priests and the Levites (הלוים) brought them up. (1 Kgs 8:4, NRS)

A second brief notice provides further thematic emphasis:

There was nothing in the ark except the two tablets of stone that Moses had placed there at Horeb, where the Lord made a covenant with the Israelites, when they came out of the land of Egypt. (1 Kgs 8:9, NRS)

The entire passage, 1 Kgs 8:1–13, presents itself as a mosaic built from various traditions, such as Deuteronomistic traditions (ark of the covenant, Moses at Horeb, tablets of stone, vv. 1, 9),[17] old Israelite traditions (elders, tent and ark, vv. 1–4a),[18] motifs of Zion tradition (Zion, cherubs and darkness of clouds, vv. 1b, 6b, 12–13)[19] and priestly references (cloud, community in terms of עדה and priests carrying the ark, vv. 3, 4a, 5, 6a, 7–8, 10–11).[20] Regardless of post-Deuteronomistic additions are to be determined therein to a greater or lesser extent, the basic mosaic constitutes a late Deuteronomistic amalgamation of various sources combined into a polyvalent picture of the ark having reached its final resting place in the temple.

For the purposes of the present study, the most significant feature here is the reference to the Levites in v. 4b. Since the rest of the chapter mentions the priests alone (cf. vv. 3, 4a, 6) as personnel carrying the ark, it is surprising that the Levites appear in v. 4b alongside the priests carrying the ark and here also carrying the tent of meeting and the temple vessels. The awkward phrase "the priests and the Levites brought them up" (v. 4b) gives the impression of a later addition,[21] as it is only loosely connected to the entire context terminologically and semantically. The phrase altered the previous notion of the "priests" of v. 4a into "priests and Levites" in v. 4b.[22] The last four Hebrew words in v. 4b repeat the bringing of the ark. The verb "to bring up" (עלה, Hiphil) is simply reused from its previous use in v. 4a. The object "them" includes all three items mentioned in v. 4a, such as the ark, the tent and the holy vessels. In any case, the statement is superfluous, except if it wants to point to something new that was not presented in the previous context, and such is indeed the case vis-à-vis the introduction of Levites into the scene. Yet the inclusion of the Levites introduces something new into the scene.

The reference to the Levites carrying the ark is as unique in this chapter as it was in the previous ones in Samuel (as with the previous examples, this new group comes and goes in the same verse; the remaining story continues without them), though shorter here. Due to its incongruity with the context it may best be understood as a somewhat later addition. It presents a reflection of who is responsible for taking care for the ark according to late Deuteronomistic conception. Such a notion may have been put in the scene to establish a literary connection to 1 Sam 6:15 and 2 Sam 15:24. If it is true that all three references share the same idea of integrating and interpreting the

---

[17] Cf. Deut 9:7–12; 10:1–5.
[18] Linked with the heads of the tribes.
[19] Cf. YHWH as sitting on cherubs, recalling motifs of Canaanite traditions on Baal as weather god. Jerusalemite temple traditions finally find their way into Samuel here.
[20] Cf. on vv. 7–8: Exod 25:20; on the cloud: Exod 40:34–38; on community in terms of עדה: Num 16:2. See also C. M. McCormick, "From Box to Throne: The Development of the Ark in DtrH and P," in *Saul in Story and Tradition*, ed. C. S. Ehrlich and M. C. White, FAT 47 (Tübingen: Mohr Siebeck, 2006), 175–86, 182, who qualified 1 Kgs 8:8, 10–11 as "supplementations" originating from "Priestly descriptions."
[21] Already in Septuagint, the words are missing. A later addition is also proposed by Samuel, *Von Priestern zum Patriarchen*, 342–44.
[22] Cf. E. Würthwein, *Das erste Buch der Könige: Kapitel 1–16 übersetzt und erklärt*, ATD 11/1 (Göttingen: Vandenhoeck & Ruprecht, 1977), 85–86. Already Gesenius, *Hebräisches und Aramäisches Handwörterbuch*, 382, regards this reference as one of the "interpolierten Stellen" next to 1 Sam 6:15 (see above).

group of Levites, then it consequently follows that their interpretation as specialists for the ark and tablets of the law resting in the ark (1 Kgs 8:9) may also be recognized in 1 Kgs 8:4b. The material in 1 Kgs 8:9 reinforces the argument because the Deuteronomistic interpretation of the ark as a box for the tablets is also present there. Adding the Levites as carriers of the ark broadens the collection of motifs in 1 Kgs 8:1–13 while including another stream of tradition, that is, the Levites as carriers of the ark that is also prominent in Chronicles (cf. 1 Chr 15, see below). It includes the Levites as responsible personnel for the ark and what it means to the people of Israel devote to YHWH.

### 1.4. Late Deuteronomistic Presentations of the Levites and the Ark

To sum up, the three references on Levites in 1 Sam 6:15; 2 Sam 15:24 and 1 Kgs 8:4 present the group as carriers of the ark. The ark is characterized by the Deuteronomistic idea of a box filled only with the tablets of the covenant, inscribed with the law written by Moses at Horeb.

A similar notion can furthermore be found in Josh 3:3 and 8:33, where the Levites are mentioned as "Levitical priests" (הכהנים הלוים).[23] Like in the other references on Levites in Samuel, the ark works as a portable palladium guaranteeing YHWH's presence accompanying the people of Israel on their way crossing the Jordan (Josh 3) and in the conquest of Ai (Josh 8). The Deuteronomistic shape of the stories again characterizes the ark as the "ark of the covenant." The notion of Levites in Josh 3:3 carrying the ark against notions of an anonymous group or the priests in the larger context of that narrative presents itself as a later interpolation,[24] whereas the passage Josh 8:30–35 is based on late Deuteronomist presentations and reminiscent of Deuteronomy 27 and Deuteronomy 31.[25] That the role of Levites is presented accordingly does not come as a surprise.

The references to Levites in other parts of the Deuteronomistic History do not add a different perspective to the sparse Levitical portrait discussed here. On the contrary, the absence of Levites in the majority of the Deuteronomistic writings brings up the question of where the link between the Levites and the ark and the law comes from.

The near-absence of the Levites in Deuteronomistic history concerning the monarchic period (in Samuel–Kings[26]) is even more surprising because in the later re-narration of history, in Chronicles, the Levites (הלוים) play a major role. This is significant because Chronicles builds upon the Deuteronomistic History to a great extent and shares a huge amount of parallels with Samuel–Kings, since Chronicles took the Deuteronomistic report as a source for its later historical interpretation.[27]

---

[23]Joshua 3:2–3: "At the end of three days the officers went through the camp and commanded the people: When you see the ark of the covenant of the Lord your God being carried by the Levitical priests, then you shall set out from your place. Follow it" (NRS); Josh 8:33: "All Israel, alien as well as citizen, with their elders and officers and their judges, stood on opposite sides of the ark in front of the Levitical priests who carried the ark of the covenant of the Lord, half of them in front of Mount Gerizim and half of them in front of Mount Ebal, as Moses the servant of the Lord had commanded at the first, that they should bless the people of Israel" (NRS).

[24]This is not the place to demonstrate the development of the pericope in detail; but see, e.g., R. D. Nelson, *Joshua: A Commentary* (Louisville: Westminster John Knox, 1997), 56; Porzig, *Die Lade Jahwes*, 59, 63–68.

[25]See Nelson, *Joshua*, 118–20; Porzig, *Die Lade Jahwes*, 91–95. On Deut 31 see below, §2.1.2.

[26]One further reference to "Levites" in Samuel–Kings is to be found in 1 Kgs 12:31, but there they are mentioned with a divergent terminology: "sons of Levi" (בני לוי). Additionally, they are presented in a somewhat more priestly role. Due to these differences, I disregard that reference in this essay. But see Samuel, *Von Priestern zum Patriarchen*, 344–47.

[27]On the parallels cf. the basic analysis of I. Kalimi, *Zur Geschichtsschreibung des Chronisten: Literar-historiographische Abweichungen der Chronik von ihren Paralleltexten in den Samuel- und Königsbüchern*, BZAW 226 (Berlin: de Gruyter, 1995); see also J. Kegler and M. Augustin, *Synopse zum Chronistischen Geschichtswerk*, 2nd ed., BEATAJ 1 (Frankfurt am Main: Peter Lang, 1991); J. Kegler and M. Augustin, *Deutsche Synopse zum Chronistischen Geschichtswerk*, BEATAJ 33 (Frankfurt am Main: Peter Lang, 1993).

In Chronicles, the Levites are presented as a multi-functional group;[28] among their duties they are found connected with the ark. Another point is surprising since "Levitical priests" (הכהנים הלוים) often appear in Deuteronomy.[29] Compared to such comprehensive writings, the small number of occurrences of Levites in the in Deuteronomistic History is quite astonishing.

One cannot ignore the "Levitical quietness" in Samuel–Kings.[30] But such a "quietness" does not mean total silence. This raises the question of where the integration of Levites comes from and what is the idea behind connecting them with the ark. In my view, an important hint is to be reckoned in the concept of "ark of the covenant" containing the "tablets of the covenant." The notion of the covenant builds a specific link with the concept of the law, and the link leads to the Levites as those concerned both with carrying the ark and interpreting the law.

## 2. RESPONSIBILITIES OF THE LEVITES FOR THE ARK AND THE LAW

When Samuel–Kings includes the Levites in a somewhat later stage, they share, as seen, just one particular role—despite the multiple duties they carry in other Old Testament writings (especially in Chronicles). That these other duties are disregarded suggests that there must be a specific ideology or interpretation promoted in the late Deuteronomistic theology. Reckoning with the Levites as carriers of the ark defines the group so that their responsibility for the ark includes a certain theological dimension. The authoritative function of the Levites is linked with the Deuteronomistic interpretation of the ark and also with an interpretation of the Levites as responsible personnel for the content of the ark such as the law and, by implication, the Torah.

Looking for an origin of such an idea, we find analogies in Deuteronomy as well as in Chronicles. I would propose that these comparable portraits, at least to a certain extent, may have been of influence on Samuel–Kings in this regard. These issues will be dealt with subsequently.

### 2.1. *Analogies in Deuteronomy*

If we broaden the focus of Deuteronomistic writings to Deuteronomy itself there are a few references that link the Levites with the ark. We briefly need to investigate these references and see if they provide analogies for Samuel–Kings, either in the mode that Samuel–Kings may have built on ideas developed in Deuteronomy or that all relevant references here share the same theological or ideological conception in favor of the Levites and their role.

2.1.1. *Deuteronomy 10:8*. Within Deuteronomy, the exceptional reference Deut 10:8 gives various extraordinary rights to the Levites as follows:

---

[28]See A. Labahn, *Levitischer Herrschaftsanspruch zwischen Ausübung und Konstruktion. Studien zum multi-funktionalen Levitenbild der Chronik und seiner Identitätsbildung in der Zeit des Zweiten Tempels*, WMANT 131 (Neukirchen-Vluyn: Neukirchener Verlag, 2012).
[29]Cf. Deut 17:9, 18; 18:1, 7; 21:5; 24:8; 27:9, 14; 31:25. The term represents a late Deuteronomistic conception that favors Levites and establishes them as an elected group with particular qualifications, such as serving in the temple close to YHWH, blessing in his name, reading and interpreting the law respectively the Torah. These qualifications make the Levites a brilliant example for trustworthily observing the law. Cf., e.g., M. Rose, *5. Mose 12–25 Einführung und Gesetze / 5. Mose 1–11 und 26–34 Rahmenstücke zum Gesetzeskorpus*, ZBK.AT 5/1–2 (Zurich: Züricher Verlagshaus, 1994), 559–60.
[30]Cf., e.g., Samuel, *Von Priestern zum Patriarchen*, 344: "Für die Geschichtsschreibung in den Samuelis- und Königebüchern bleibt es…bei einem ursprünglichen 'Levitenschweigen'."

At that time the Lord set apart the tribe of Levi to carry the ark of the covenant of the Lord, to stand before the Lord to minister to him, and to bless in his name, to this day. (NRS)

This late Deuteronomistic expansion in Deut 10:8 interrupts the story about Moses writing the tablets and putting them into the ark (10:1–4, 10–11),[31] as does the immediately preceding notice about the Israelites' journey (10:5–7).[32] Deuteronomy 10:8 introduces the Levites, addressed as the "tribe of Levi" (שבט הלוי), as a group and sorted out by YHWH for specific tasks closely related to God. Deuteronomy 10:9 supplements the statement with an explanation concerning Levi himself who is appreciated as the only one who is close to YHWH because Levi is regarded as "YHWHs inheritance" (יהוה הוא נחלתו). Among further duties connected with the temple service mentioned in 10:8,[33] the tribe of Levi is given the right to carry the ark. This is a unique expression because nowhere else in Deuteronomy is the tribe linked with the ark. The ark is qualified as the "ark of the covenant," which presents itself as a late Deuteronomistic idea related to covenantal reevaluations.[34] All in all, Deut 10:8 reflects a late Deuteronomistic conception in favor for the Levites and their extraordinary status and role among the temple personnel.[35]

Deuteronomy 10:8 shares the motif of Levites carrying the ark with the occurrences of Levites in Samuel–Kings. But the use of the term "tribe of Levi" instead of calling the group "the Levites" distinguishes the reading of Deut 10:8 from the historical writings. More common is the terminology of the "ark of the covenant." The involvement of Levites as carriers of the ark provides an interpretive comment on the tablets of law from Horeb. The tablets are put into the ark that now functions as a box for the tablets, thus containing YHWH's engraved ten commandments, that is, the law, his written word.[36] Similarities as well as differences between Deuteronomy and Samuel–Kings show that an idea of Levites in that role was present in Deuteronomy but had not been recalled adequately to its full extent in Samuel–Kings.

2.1.2. *Deuteronomy 31.* The idea of a Levitical group carrying the ark is again present in Deuteronomy in the somewhat late ch. 31.[37] Twice a group of Levites is assigned the role of carrying the

---

[31] Cf. Preuss, *Deuteronomium*, 50, 102; R. Seitz, *Redaktionsgeschichtliche Studien zum Deuteronomium*, BWANT 93 (Stuttgart: Kohlhammer, 1971), 51–69; T. Veijola, *Das 5. Buch Mose Deuteronomium: Kapitel 1,1–16,17*, ATD 8/1 (Göttingen: Vandenhoeck & Ruprecht, 2004), 224–25, 239; Porzig, *Die Lade Jahwes*, 44–45; U. Dahmen, *Leviten und Priester im Deuteronomium: Literarkritische und redaktionsgeschichtliche Studien*, BBB 110 (Bodenheim: Philo, 1996), 31–34. Already N. Lohfink, *Das Hauptgebot: Eine Untersuchung literarischer Einleitungsfragen zu Dtn 5–11*, AnBib 20 (Rome: Pontificio Istituto Biblico, 1963), 63–67, assumes a Levitical gloss. Such an idea recurs in a more elaborated way in Samuel, *Von Priestern zum Patriarchen* 24, 28–29: the pro-Levitical extension redefines the Levitical heritage against the previous and subsequent context in favor of Aaronide priesthood.

[32] Cf. Samuel, *Von Priestern zum Patriarchen*, 18–19, 24, 29, who regards these verses as even later, originating from a post-Deuteronomistic extension revising the previous pro-Levitical verses in the way that the extension focuses on the priestly line again. Slightly differently, Porzig, *Die Lade Jahwes*, 44, regards Deut 10:1–5 as the oldest part of the chapter with later additions in vv. 8–9 and subsequently in vv. 6–7.

[33] According to Deut 10:8 such duties of the Levites are to serve before the Lord and to bless people in the name of the Lord; it links the duties of cultic servants and priests while establishing those as an extraordinary Levitical duty.

[34] On covenant in Deuteronomistic theology see above n. 14.

[35] According to M. Geiger, *Gottesräume: Die literarische und theologische Konzeption von Raum im Deuteronomium*, BWANT 183 (Stuttgart: Kohlhammer, 2010), 213, the occurrence of Aaron in the context (Deut 10:6) set up the involvement of Levites since Aaron was regarded as son of Levi. Such an assumption does not seem plausible because in Deuteronomy there is no explicit link between Aaron and the Levites, nor to the tribe of Levi, regarding the Levitical genealogical structures.

[36] Cf., e.g., G. Braulik, *Deuteronomium Teil 1: 1–16,17*, NEB 15 (Würzburg: Echter, 1986), 98; I. Wilson, "Merely a Container? The Ark in Deuteronomy," in *Temple and Worship in Biblical Israel*, ed. J. Day, LHBOTS 422 (New York: T&T Clark, 2007), 212–49 (esp. 213, as the starting point of his thesis; on that see below n. 53). See also A. Millard, "The Tablets in the Ark," in *Reading the Law: Studies in Honour of Gordon J. Wenham*, ed. G. J. McConville and K. Möller, LHBOTS 461 (New York: T&T Clark, 2007), 254–66. Millard agrees to this thesis concerning Deuteronomy, although he focusses his analyses on Exod 24.

[37] Various models ascribe a late function and character to ch. 31; see the presentation of research by, e.g., E. Talstra, "Deuteronomy 31: Confusion or Conclusion? The Story of Moses' Threefold Succession," in *Deuteronomy and Deuteronomic Literature*,

ark. Deuteronomy 31:9 mentions a group of "Levitical priests" (כהנים בני לוי) established with the right to carry the ark. Deuteronomy 31:25 simply installs "Levites" (הלוים) who are guaranteed such a privileged duty of carrying the "ark of the covenant."

> Then Moses wrote down this law, and gave it to the priests, the sons of Levi, who carried the ark of the covenant of the Lord, and to all the elders of Israel. (Deut 31:9, NRS)

> When Moses had finished writing down in a book the words of this law to the very end, [25] Moses commanded the Levites who carried the ark of the covenant of the Lord, saying, [26] Take this book of the law and put it beside the ark of the covenant of the Lord your God. (Deut 31:24–26, NRS)

In its current shape, Deuteronomy 31 presents a long divine speech addressing Moses and Joshua ultimately before Moses's death; Joshua is going to take the lead in guiding the people of Israel into the Promised Land. The chapter is not clearly structured; it is interrupted by multiple redactional reworking.[38] Although this essay is not the place to propose a theory of growth, it is quite obvious that the above-cited verses talking about Moses, the Levites and the ark as well as about the law and its written character belong to a single late stratum sharing the same conception.[39] Therein, Moses is presented as the writer of the divine speech. At the end, he gives the complete[40] written testimony into the hands of the Levites (vv. 24–26), establishing them as responsible personnel for the written "law" (תורה respectively ספר תורה).[41] Due to such a conception, the scene of establishing of the Levites therein presents itself as a later addition,[42] as it is quite loosely connected to the context. Beside these verses, the Levites do not play any other part within the chapter. The subsequent v. 27 continues v. 22 since both share the address of "Israelites." In between these verses, 31:24–26 reestablishes which personnel are responsible for the ark and redefines the role of the Levites.

To a lesser extent, both notions of the Levites in ch. 31 distinguish themselves in terminology concerning the nomination of the Levitical group. Whereas the term "Levites" (הלוים) in 31:25 recalls a common expression well known elsewhere in the Old Testament/Hebrew Bible, 31:9 simply adds the phrase "sons of Levi" (בני לוי; rare in Deuteronomy)[43] behind "the priests," thus turning the priestly group into Levites by determining their genealogical origin. Anyhow, such a notion in 31:9 is close to Deut 10:8, where the Levites came into view as descendants of Levi himself.[44] The differences in terminology may not be so relevant because the group of Levites as responsible personnel is already stressed in the chapter, and the references to Levites in Deuteronomy 31 maintain the conception in favor for Levites in Deut 10:8. Both occurrences reflect the same late Deuteronomistic idea presenting the Levites as special personnel introduced as responsible for the ark.[45]

---

ed. M. Vervenne and J. Lust, Festschrift C. H. W. Brekelmans, BETL 133 (Leuven: Leuven University Press, 1997), 87–110, esp. 87–94.
[38]For details see the report of various redactional theses by Preuss, *Deuteronomium*, 162–63. In any case, commentators agree in the late Deuteronomistic character of ch. 31 and its incongruent shape; see further Perlitt, *Bundestheologie im Alten Testament*, 115–28. Cf. also B. Britt, "Deuteronomy 31–32 as a Textual Memorial," *BibInt* 8 (2000): 358–74.
[39]Cf. Porzig, *Die Lade Jahwes*, 50, 52–53, stressing that the main intention is "die Niederschrift des Gesetzbuches" (50) while following the theological conception "zwischen *tôrāh* und Bundestafeln in der Lade einen Ausgleich zu schaffen" (53).
[40]See the interpretation of כל by Köckert, "Das nahe Wort," 63: "vollständig" (complete, entire).
[41]Cf. Perlitt, *Bundestheologie im Alten Testament*, 128, pointing to the literary scribal character of the writing and Levitical authority therein.
[42]Cf. Preuss, *Deuteronomium*, 60–61, 162–63; Rose, *5. Mose*, 559–60.
[43]There is just one more example of it: Deut 21:5, another late addition; cf. Samuel, *Von Priestern zum Patriarchen*, 125–28.
[44]For details see above, §2.1.1.1.
[45]Only at a late stage, Deuteronomy introduces the ark and alongside the Levites as a group responsible for it; cf. Porzig, *Die Lade Jahwes*, 53–54, who points out that "von einer deuteronomischen Ladevorstellung eigentlich nicht geredet warden kann."

Furthermore, the references to the Levites share the description of the ark as "ark of the covenant" (ארון ברית־יהוה). The phrase again clearly shows late Deuteronomistic terminology and theology in characterizing the ark as essential for the covenant that YHWH has drawn with his people.[46] While the ark is linked to covenant theology, according to late Deuteronomistic theology it contains the "tablets of the covenant" (Deut 9:9, 11, 15: לוחת הברית) expressing the law.

When the Levites are included into such an interpretation of the ark of the covenant, they are exclusively declared responsible for the law, that is, the Torah (31:9: התורה; 31:24: דברי התורה־ הזאת על־ספר; 31:26: ספר התורה הזה), which was written down by Moses (31:9, 24) and handed over to the Levites for further use (vv. 9, 25–26). Recognizing the verbal meaning, such a duty includes the handling of the "book of the Torah," yet putting it next to the ark and preserving it there (v. 26). Beyond the obvious advice, the order of Moses in its Deuteronomistic shape includes a more comprehensive responsibility for the "book of the law" (ספר התורה, v. 26; cf. 31:24). The notion of a "book" (ספר) points to an elaborate version of the Torah that exceeds the Decalogue inscribed on the stone tablets (לוחות; cf. Deut 5; 10:1–5), regardless of which law code in particular was to be identified with the "book of the Torah." According to such a late interpretation, the law (or Torah) is connected to the ark in the way that "Gesetzestafeln und Gesetzesbuch wie Urschrift und Auslegung" correspond to each other.[47]

The process of taking care of the "book of the Torah" includes an active relation toward its content, that is, the laws written in the Torah. Such laws (in particular המצוה החקים והמשפטים; cf. Deut 6:1; see also, e.g., Deut 4:45; 5:1) regulate the relation between YHWH and his people for the current generation (Deut 5:3: היום כלנו חיים), a relation working in terms of covenant (Deut 5:3: כרת יהוה את־הברית הזאת). Responsibility for the Torah thus includes an active role in preserving, transmitting, and interpreting the Torah, according to the Mosaic advice given to the Levites. Such a transmission does not only include the current generation—addressed by Deuteronomy's "today"—but even goes beyond when "transmitting the Torah to future generations" in "teaching it to Israel…available as a book to be read."[48]

The late extension with its focus on the Levites, the ark and the written law presents a new evaluation of responsibility. The new conception establishes a re-interpretation in as much as it creates the Levites as transmitters and, hence, interpreters of the Torah. Therewith, the Levites are turned into the group that is established with authority regarding relevant interpretation of the law.[49]

The conception of installing the Levites as responsible for the ark as well as the terminology of the conception in Deuteronomy 31 are close to the involvement of Levites in Samuel–Kings. Both conceptions follow their interest in integrating the Levites as relevant personnel and providing them with a responsible role concerning the ark and the law (the Torah). These analogies offer strong arguments to reckon with an influence of Deuteronomy 31 on the Levitical references in Samuel–Kings.

2.1.3. *The Ark and the Torah in Deuteronomistic Theology.* According to the late Deuteronomistic interpretation, provided by certain references in Deuteronomy as well as in Samuel–Kings, the ark is regarded as a box[50] which only contains the "two stone tablets" (Deut 4:13; 9:9–11; 10:1–5; 31:26; 1 Kgs 8:9) produced by Moses (Deut 10:5), who is regarded as YHWH's scribe whereas YHWH is assumed the true author (Deut 9:10; 10:2). The tablets contain the commandments of

---

[46] On covenant in Deuteronomistic theology, see above n. 14.
[47] Cf. Porzig, *Die Lade Jahwes*, 55.
[48] Cf. Talstra, "Deuteronomy 31: Confusion or Conclusion?," 96–97.
[49] See also Samuel, *Von Priestern zum Patriarchen*, 58: "Es sind die Leviten, denen die Bewahrung mosaischer Autorität für die Zukunft zugesprochen wird."
[50] See also McCormick, "From Box to Throne," 183.

YHWH, which represent a short version of his law, yet also his will and his word according to such a Deuteronomistic interpretation.[51] The ark is regarded as the container for this word and law.[52] With this idea, a new theological interpretation is developed in the Deuteronomistic History.

Such an assessment represents a reinterpretation of the ark. According to the previous literary portrait[53] and still reflected in 1 Kings 8, the ark was assumed an empty box, imagined as the divine footstool and representing the place of God's dwelling (cf., esp., Zion theology).[54] Therefore, the ark resembles God's presence (cf. 1 Sam 4:7–8).[55]

Next to that, the Deuteronomistic conception provides another interpretation of the law when it evaluates the tablets as "tablets of the covenant" (Deut 9:9, 11, 15). The law written on the tablets is integrated into the covenant conception regulating the relationship between YHWH and his people. Deuteronomy 4:13 is even more explicit as far as it defines that the covenant is to be identified with the "ten words written on the tablets." The addressee of the law is God's people, whose life is intended to be shaped by the regulations contained in the law code in order to make the people obedient to YHWH and effect a successful life.

Furthermore, the covenantal phrase "tablets of the covenant" links the law with the ark, because it resembles the characteristic Deuteronomistic interpretation of the ark represented by the term ארון ברית in 1 Sam 4:3–5; 1 Kgs 3:15; 6:19; 8:1, 6. The new late Deuteronomistic interpretation links the ark with YHWH's word and also with his relationship toward his people. His presence is much more substantiated through the ark. The written law as expression of God's word is close to people who enter into the realm of the covenant,[56] and the ark as its box guarantees YHWH's will substantially. Whereas YHWH himself is located in heaven distant from people on earth, his word is accessible in the ark.

A similar conception goes along with YHWH's name in later Deuteronomistic interpretation.[57] His name is close to people because it is accessible in the sanctuary when people call YHWH (cf.

---

[51]Cf. Weinfeld, *Deuteronomy and Deuteronomic School*, 63, 208.
[52]Therefore, Porzig, *Die Lade Jahwes*, 279, assumes that due to such a characterization as "Inhalt der Lade an ein Bundesdokument bzw. Gesetz gedacht ist."
[53]I do not intend to say anything about any stage of the ark in historical reality, neither its early stage nor its origin. Instead, I want simply to point to that preceding stage within its literary tradition which was ultimately taken up and reinterpreted. On theories about possible content of the ark, see Porzig, *Die Lade Jahwes*, 278–86. T. N. D. Mettinger, *The Dethronement of Sabaoth: Studies in the Shem and Kabod Theologies*, CBOT 18 (Lund: C. W. K. Gleerup, 1982), 51, stresses that the Deuteronomistic conception, while missing the cherubs, provides a reinterpretation in a way of "conscious suppression of the notion of the God who sat enthroned in the Temple."
[54]This classical thesis is present in numerous works, cf., e.g., H. Gunkel, "Die Lade ein Thronsitz," *Zeitschrift für Missionskunde und Religionswissenschaften* 51 (1906): 1–20; W. Beyerlein, *Herkunft und Geschichte der ältesten Sinaitraditionen* (Tübingen: Mohr, 1961), 125; F. Dummermuth, "Zur deuteronomischen Kulttheologie und ihren Voraussetzungen," *ZAW* 70 (1958): 59–98, here 71–72; B. Janowski, "Keruben und Zion. Thesen zur Entstehung der Zionstradition," in *Ernten, was man sät*, ed. D. R. Daniels, U. Glessmer and M. Rösel, FS Klaus Koch (Neukirchen-Vluyn: Neukirchener Verlag, 1991), 231–64.
[55]Due to the lack of archaeological and historical evidence, the content of the ark is historically still unknown (cf. Porzig, *Die Lade Jahwes*, 286). Nevertheless, the ark retains its value of representing YHWH's presence and was reckoned as a symbol of divine presence throughout its various (literary) interpretations and theological conceptions. The same idea is also present in Wilson, "Merely a Container?," esp. 234–37, when he argues for YHWH's presence linked with the ark in its Deuteronomistic appearance, although Wilson does not agree with the redactional assumptions proposed in this essay. Wilson points to strong parallels between the Levites carrying the ark standing in YHWH's presence and the ark sharing the same function (214).
[56]According to Weinfeld, *Deuteronomy and Deuteronomic School*, 208, the ark serves "an educational function…to the people so that they may learn to fear the Lord."
[57]Cf. Weinfeld, *Deuteronomy and Deuteronomic School*, 191–209; M. Rose, *Der Ausschließlichkeitsanspruch Jahwes. Deuteronomistische Schultheologie und die Volksfrömmigkeit in der späten Königszeit*, BWANT 106 (Stuttgart: Kohlhammer, 1975), 82–94; L. Perlitt, "Die Verborgenheit Gottes," in *Allein mit dem Wort, Theologische Studien*, ed. H. Spieckermann (Göttingen: Vandenhoeck & Ruprecht, 1995), 11–25; see also S. L. Richter, *The Deuteronomistic History and the Name Theology: leshakken shemo sham in the Bible and the Ancient Near East*, BZAW 318 (Berlin: de Gruyter, 2002 [with discussion of literature; however, I do not agree with all of her theses]).

1 Kgs 8), whereas God himself is inaccessible in heaven. His name replaces YHWH himself and provides nearness to people while yet preserving God's transcendence.

The same idea is transferred to the ark in the later Deuteronomistic conceptions. Since YHWH is imagined distant in heaven, there is need for an object to provide access to him for his adherents. The ark as the box containing YHWH's word and law (Deut 31:26) works as such an object breaking down the distance between YHWH and the people. The reinterpretation of the ark turns it into a strong object providing ultimate access to YHWH.

## 2.2. Analogies in Chronicles

The references to the Levites in Samuel–Kings connect strongly to 1 Chronicles 15, where the Levites alone act as bearers of the ark (1 Chr 15:2, 12, 14, 15, 26, 27; see also 1 Chr 16:4; 2 Chr 5:4; 35:3).[58] 1 Chronicles 15 retells the story of 2 Sam 6:12–16 and thereby reinterprets the personnel carrying the ark to a great extent. Whereas in 2 Samuel 6 there was no one explicitly mentioned carrying the ark,[59] 1 Chronicles 15 fills the gap of the story and introduces the Levites into that office. Such an appropriation does not only happen in retelling 2 Sam 6:13 and its anonymous carriers (נשׂאי ארון־ יהוה), but it does so in the entire story in 1 Chronicles 15 and beyond in the Chronicles' history where the Levites are regarded as responsible personnel for carrying the ark. Chronicles also gives a reason for introducing this personnel: YHWH himself has chosen the Levites for such a duty of carrying the ark (cf. 1 Chr 15:2; 16:41; see also 15:12, 14),[60] that is, YHWH himself has commissioned and sanctified them especially therefore. With such an explanation, Chronicles does not only fill a gap but creates a conception of putting the Levites exclusively in favor for an extraordinary duty in close relation to YHWH.

The fact that the ark contains the covenant, hence that it is called the "ark of the covenant," is also prominent in Chronicles (cf. 1 Chr 15:25–29; 16:6, 37; 17:1; 22:19; 28:2, 18; 2 Chr 5:2, 7; 6:11). Chronicles also captures the idea that the ark only contains the tablets of the covenant (cf. 2 Chr 5:2). Furthermore, the interpretation of the ark containing YHWH's word and the conception of YHWH's name representing God are closely connected in Chronicles (cf. 1 Chr 22:19; 2 Chr 6:10–11). Chronicles resumes the Deuteronomistic interpretation of the ark, agreeing to the evaluation that the ark represents God's word and guarantees access to God's will therein.

Beyond these ideas, Chronicles even expands the conception of responsible personnel. The ark as the box of YHWH's word is linked with personnel responsible for God's word. As such, Chronicles lets the Levites step in. They are the group that Chronicles regards as specialists for God's word, with the ability and responsibility to interpret it (cf. 1 Chr 23:14; 25:1–7; 2 Chr 17:7–9; 20:14; 35:3, 15).[61] In Chronicles, the Levites appear as interpreters of the law, as responsible scribes actualizing the law of God for present situations and communicating YHWH's current will to the people in an authoritative and prudent manner. The close connection between the Levites as scribes and the word of God is typical for Chronicles.

---

[58] Cf. Labahn, *Levitischer Herrschaftsanspruch*, 98–115.

[59] On ark narrative in 2 Sam 6 and the lack of Levites cf. the analysis of W. Dietrich, "Die Überführung der Lade nach Jerusalem (2 Sam 6): Geschichten und Geschichte," in *Die Samuelbücher im deuteronomistischen Geschichtswerk: Studien zu den Geschichtsüberlieferungen des Alten Testaments II*, BWANT 201 (Stuttgart: Kohlhammer, 2012), 191–206.

[60] Cf. E. Ben Zvi, "A Sense of Proportion: An Aspect of the Theology of the Chronicler," in *History, Literature and Theology in the Book of Chronicles*, BibleWorld (London: Equinox, 2006), 160–73, esp. 164–65.

[61] Cf. Labahn, *Levitischer Herrschaftsanspruch*, 192–258, 306–9, 366–94; see also J. Blenkinsopp, "The Sage, the Scribe, and Scribalism in the Chronicler's Work," in *The Sage in Israel and the Ancient Near East*, ed. J. G. Gammie and L. G. Perdue (Winona Lake: Eisenbrauns, 1990), 307–15, here 310–12; P. R. Davies, *Scribes and Schools: The Canonizing of the Hebrew Scriptures*, Library of Ancient Israel (Louisville: John Knox, 1998), 132–33.

Such a characterization of the Levites goes along with their responsibility for the ark. Both aspects of the Levites complement each other because they focus on two offices within the multi-functional portrait of Levites in Chronicles,[62] yet concentrate on the interpretation of the word of God and its representation. From the comprehensive multi-functional Levitical portrait of Chronicles, these duties are taken and reused in such a way that it was adapted to its new concept from its earlier place within Deuteronomistic theology.

Compared to the mention of Levites in Chronicles, the references to the Levites carrying the ark in Samuel–Kings are rather short and lack any details regarding their particular involvement, or why this group is finally put into such a position. To be sure, there must be an intention in Deuteronomistic History for presenting the Levites as carriers of the ark in Samuel–Kings, as it is significant that the same role is ascribed to the Levites, in late references in Deuteronomy as well as in Chronicles. Both writings seem to share an idea of responsibility linked with the Levites. Even more, they agree on a new interpretation of the relationship between the ark and the law. The new responsibility ascribed to the Levites in Samuel–Kings shares this thematic emphasis, though its reflections are integrated in a rather limited number of references.

### 2.3. Reflections of Chronicles' Conception in Early Jewish Writings

The conception of Levites that Chronicles elaborated in a particular way did not remain within the realm of Chronistic theology; it radiated into other early Jewish contemporary ideas. It emerged into a tradition in Early Judaism of the Second Temple period regarding Levites as legitimate and authoritative interpreters of the law (cf. T. Levi 2:2, 10; 8:17; 9:6; 13:1–7; T. Reub. 6:8, 10; Jub. 31:15; 45:16; 4Q159 Frg. 5; 4Q175 14–18).[63] In detail, the early Jewish conceptions differ in minor ways, yet they share the basic idea of Levites being responsible for interpreting the divine law, that is, the Torah. These references give ample evidence to prove the idea that the conception of Levites interpreting the divine word was present in Second Temple Judaism's writings. Although it is not evident everywhere in Second Temple Judaism, there are remarkable examples to reckon with a well-known conception about Levitical involvement. The examples clearly indicate that such a conception, developed in Chronicles and passing into early Jewish writings, was present and possessed the potential for usage in the production of further writings.

### 2.4. Recalling the Chronistic Conception in Reorientation

The influence of Chronicles' conception, which was partly present in Second Temple period early Judaism, may also have entered into late Deuteronomistic writings, in particular late Deuteronomistic additions in Deuteronomy and in Samuel–Kings. The involvement of Levites in the aforementioned few references is part of such a development that left its brief traces in late

---

[62] On the multi-functional portrait of the Levites in Chronicles (singers/musicians, gatekeepers, administrators, officers, cultic personnel, teachers, prophets, scribes, priests, interpreters of the Torah, carriers of the ark, tax collectors, overseers, "caretakers of the cult" [the last term quoted from S. J. Schweitzer, *Reading Utopia in Chronicles*, LHBOTS 442 (New York: T&T Clark 2007), 157] etc.), see the discussion in my *Levitischer Herrschaftsanspruch*, where I argue that the Levites' genealogically constructed identity binds the group together and creates internal coherence when faced with divergent functions. See also B. A. Levine, "Levites," in *The Encyclopedia of Religion* (New York: Macmillan, 1987), 8:523–32, who designates the Levites in Chronicles as "mobile professionals" (524) "with differentiated functions" (526).

[63] See the detailed analyses in my monograph *Levitischer Herrschaftsanspruch*, 85–87, 109–25, 155–59; Davies, *Scribes and Schools*, 18–19; R. A. Kugler, "The Priesthood at Qumran: The Evidence of References to Levi and The Levites," in *The Provo International Conference on the Dead Sea Scrolls: Technological Innovations, New Texts, and Reformulated Issues*, ed. D. W. Parry and E. Ulrich, STDJ 30 (Leiden: Brill, 1999), 465–79; G. J. Brooke, "Levi and the Levites in the Dead Sea Scrolls and the New Testament," in *The Dead Sea Scrolls and the New Testament: Essays in Mutual Illumination* (London: Fortress, 2005), 115–39, here 115–19, 127–38.

Deuteronomistic additions. In such late reflections, the Levites were included in a particular role as responsible for the spatial status of the ark as well as for the promotion of its content, namely, the Torah. If the ark turns into the box of YHWH's Torah it needs special caretakers; consequently, the adjustment of new personnel best reestablishes a group of people who had already been related to YHWH's Torah in disparate earlier textual traditions. In essence, the reinterpretation of the ark demanded a reinterpretation of its carriers. The connection of the divine word with the Levites was therefore appropriate. The Levites as interpretative scribes now were also put into the position of carrying and tending to the ark.[64]

A reorientation in the Deuteronomistic History as well as in late Deuteronomy constitutes the end result of this reorientation. The Levites as representatives of God's word and Torah were presented as the ones moving the ark, even backdating it into early times in history prior to the assumed resting of the ark in the Jerusalem temple. Their legitimation is also backdated to Horeb/Sinai (Deut 10:8).[65] The reorientation was not elaborated in the Deuteronomistic writings to a large extent, just sparsely used in a small number of references. But the reorientation was included into relevant passages within the writings where theological interpretations of the ark as the box containing God's word were given. According to such a conception, the box containing YHWH's law must, of course, rest on the shoulders of the group responsible for interpreting God's law, that is, the Levites (1 Chr 15:15; cf. 1 Kgs 8:4, 7–8). In a late stratum of the Deuteronomistic History, the Levites are finally established as the group who take care for YHWH's word[66] and are, after all, responsible for the law respectively the Torah and its interpretation as well as for its containing vessel.[67]

The reorientation in responsibility for the divine word and the ark concerning the Levites evident in Chronicles was expanded and developed in later writings. By contrast, the reshaped conception of Deuteronomistic History was narrower in focus; it did not recall the entire multi-functional portrait of Levites established in Chronicles. Rather, it simply recalled two particular aspects regarding the ark and the divine word. With them, it linked ideas developed in the Deuteronomistic History to the conception of Chronicles regarding the involvement of Levites. With the new involvement of Levites in late Deuteronomistic references, a reorientation in responsibility for the ark and for the divine Torah happens. It follows the intention of ascribing a new role to the Levites in the Deuteronomistic History while putting that group in favor among cultic personnel. But this occurs at a very late stage in the Deuteronomistic History's development, showing signs of interaction with the idea as it developed in Chronicles and beyond, as seen in early Jewish writings of the Second Temple period.

---

[64] Cf. the thesis of Dummermuth, "Zur deuteronomischen Kulttheologie," 74, who assumes that teaching of the law and carrying the ark were linked through the Levites.

[65] A similar estimation concerning retrospective involvement of the ark and cultic Levitical personnel is also made by Peter Porzig (*Die Lade Jahwes*, 68): "Im Schwange dieser (Rück-?) Projektion spielte das kultische Moment eine immer größere Rolle, die Lade wird mehr und mehr zur Vermittlerin der göttlichen Wundertaten, die nur vermöge der exakten Einhaltung priesterlich-levitischer Vorschriften ihre Wirkung entfalten können. Diese Vorschriften finden sich im Gesetz, das als Zeuge des Bundes vom Sinai sprichwörtlich in der Lade enthalten ist."

[66] Cf. Veijola, *Deuteronomium*, 240: "Damit sind die Leviten…auch treue Bewahrer des ihrer Obhut anvertrauten Gesetzes…, des höchsten Gutes der spät-dtr Theologen."

[67] The thesis favored here may to some extent support the idea of a Levitizing of priestly personnel in Deuteronomy (see Deut 10:8–9; 12:12; 14:27; 18:1; 21:5), although the examples of the ark present the group of Levites quite sparsely. On the idea of Levitizing of priesthood in Deuteronomy cf., e.g., Veijola, *Deuteronomium*, 2–5, 239–41; U. Dahmen, *Leviten und Priester im Deuteronomium. Literarkritische und redaktionsgeschichtliche Studien*, BBB 110 (Bodenheim: Philo, 1996), 13, 382, 383, 398–401; E. Otto, "Die post-deuteronomistische Levitisierung des Deuteronomiums. Zu einem Buch von Ulrich Dahmen," *ZAR* 5 (1999): 277–84; R. Achenbach, "Levitische Priester und Leviten im Deuteronomium. Überlegungen zur sog. 'Levitisierung' des Priestertums," *ZAR* 5 (1999): 285–309. These scholars argue for a redactional development with the result of linking genealogical Levitical implications with priests as well as ascribing special qualifications to such "Levitical priests."

## 3. CONCLUSION

The late Deuteronomistic references on Levites in 1 Sam 6:15; 2 Sam 15:24; 1 Kgs 8:4; Josh 3:3; 8:33 as well as in Deut 10:8; 31:9, 24–26 recall the idea of the Levites as the responsible group for interpreting the law and for carrying the box containing it. It does so by integrating the recalled idea into its own conception. Therewith, it provides a new interpretation of the ark and of the Torah as expression of YHWH's covenant-based relationship with his people. Ascribing responsibility to the Levites in interpreting the divine Torah, in transmitting its purpose to the people, and in carrying the ark, provides a new interpretation of processes and personnel acting in close connection to YHWH. Therein, the conception reevaluates the Levites' responsibility for the word of God as expressed in the law, that is, the Torah and written on the legal tablets housed within the ark.

Such a conception highlights the Levites and amplifies their role as scribes as well as responsible mediators[68] between YHWH and people when providing them with authoritative interpretation of God's word and will expressed in sacred texts.

---

[68] Regarding Levites as mediators, cf. M. Leuchter, "From Levite to Maśkil in the Persian and Hellenistic Eras," in *Levites and Priests in Biblical History and Tradition*, ed. M. Leuchter and J. M. Hutton, SBLAIIL 9 (Atlanta: SBL, 2011), 215–32, here 216–17.

PART THREE

# Between Ideology and Authority

# Writing in Three Dimensions

## Scribal Activity and Spaces in Jewish Antiquity

LAURA CARLSON HASLER

[T]he fiction of knowledge is related to this lust to be a viewpoint and nothing more.[1]

In one of several extended preambles to Second Maccabees, the writer likens the work of the historian to that of a master-builder (ἀρχιτέκτονι). The historian, the epitomizer suggests, is one who constructs memory like a builder does a house:

> καθάπερ γὰρ τῆς καινῆς οἰκίας ἀρχιτέκτονι τῆς ὅλης καταβολῆς φροντιστέον τῷ δὲ ἐγκαίειν καὶ ζωγραφεῖν ἐπιχειροῦντι τὰ ἐπιτήδεια πρὸς διακόσμησιν ἐξεταστέον οὕτως δοκῶ καὶ ἐπὶ ἡμῶν. τὸ μὲν ἐμβατεύειν καὶ περίπατον ποιεῖσθαι λόγων καὶ πολυπραγμονεῖν ἐν τοῖς κατὰ μέρος τῷ τῆς ἱστορίας ἀρχηγέτῃ καθήκει τὸ δὲ σύντομον τῆς λέξεως μεταδιώκειν καὶ τὸ ἐξεργαστικὸν τῆς πραγματείας παραιτεῖσθαι τῷ τὴν μετάφρασιν ποιουμένῳ συγχωρητέον.

> For as the master builder of a new house must be concerned with the whole construction, while the one who undertakes its painting and decoration has to consider only what is suitable for its adornment, such in my judgment is the case with us. It is the duty of the original historian to occupy the ground, to discuss matters from every side, and to take trouble with details, but the one who recasts the narrative should be allowed to strive for brevity of expression and to forego exhaustive treatment. (2 Macc 2:29–31)[2]

In its context, this image is deployed for the purposes of self-effacing and even playful contrast. It is one of several metaphors the writer uses to differentiate his own epitomizing work from that of the architect-historian. Yet seeing writers as architects and builders, and their products as spaces is not, or not merely, a playful semantic exercise. It has significant implications for how we view both scribe and text.

The concept of *rebuilding* within and by means of texts is pervasive (if perhaps unconscious) in modern scholarly practice. When we attempt to describe social worlds in antiquity, it is difficult to move away from metaphors of building. Scholars are often in the self-proclaimed business of reconstructing ancient cultures such that they, and their readers, may re-enter these worlds and view them more clearly. My purposes in this essay will not be to avoid but to press into this language of construction in order to consider how ancient Jewish scribes may have also remade their built environment within texts. Reconstructing scribalism in social context invites us to consider simultaneously the spaces that choreographed the life of these scribes and the spaces that were in turn built by

---

[1] Michel de Certeau, *The Practice of Everyday Life*, trans. S. F. Randall (Berkeley: University of California Press, 1984), 92.
[2] J. Schaper, "2 Makkabees," in *A New English Translation of the Septuagint*, ed. A. Pietersma and B, Wright (Oxford: Oxford University Press, 2007), 506–7.

them. Drawing analogies between building and writing, in other words, prompts us to think anew about the purposes and aesthetics of scribal practice in Jewish antiquity.

I am not the first to propose that we think more deeply about the spaces that shaped and that were consequently replicated by literary practices in this period. Pernille Carstens, **Ingeborg Löwisch**, Eva Mroczek, and Jeremy Smoak are among those who have redirected our interpretive vision towards ancient Jewish spaces and their interpretive consequences.[3] My purposes in this essay will be to offer an example of how one such space may serve as a model for this approach to scribal activity. I will then discuss the considerable implications and opportunities opened by viewing ancient Jewish texts as spaces.

In his 2007 book about scribal practice and the production of the Hebrew Bible, Karel van der Toorn likens this text to an archive at several junctures. Arguing against the notion that "each book of the Bible should be considered a carefully crafted whole," van der Toorn contends that the Bible's component texts "should rather compare to archives."[4] He goes on to argue that

> a biblical book is often like a box containing heterogeneous materials brought together on the assumption of common authorship, subject matter, or chronology. Whatever literary unity these books possess was imposed by the editors and is, to some extent, artificial. The editors could rearrange, expand, or conflate the separate units at their disposal in such a way as to achieve the illusion of a single book with a single message.[5]

Van der Toorn expands on this idea later on in his book, but some of the interpretive implications of this comparison already surface in this short passage. Seeing biblical texts like archives, van der Toorn argues, normalizes the heterogeneity of these collected materials. Reading the Bible as an archive, he contends, also highlights the secondarily imposed (in his words, "artificial") nature of their compositional unity. Yet within this passage there is also a faint suggestion that unity ("a single book with a single message") is the ultimate goal or end of scribal practice in Jewish antiquity, at least in later periods of scribal production. In what follows, I will also suggest that many ancient Jewish texts—even in their so-called final form—might be productively likened to an archive. Yet this archival form importantly functions apart from binaries and optics of literary disorder, which plots text on an evolutionary path from disunity to unity. When we interpret scribal practice in terms of archiving, the acts and aesthetics of collection may become vital literary strategies in their own right.[6]

In order to compare texts to archives it is important to comment briefly on what we know about physical text collections in this period. The literary reputation and archaeological record together attest to the prevalence of these structures—some massive, monumental collections, others smaller private archives—across the landscape of the ancient Mediterranean in the Second Temple period (and well before it).[7] The majority of these collections appear to serve administrative purposes,

---

[3] Pernille Carstens, "The Torah as Canon of Masterpieces: Remembering in Archives," in *Cultural Memory in Biblical Exegesis*, ed. P. Carstens et al. (Piscataway: Gorgias, 2012), 309–23; **Ingeborg Löwisch, *Trauma Begets Genealogy: Gender and Memory in Chronicles*** (Sheffield: Sheffield Phoenix, 2015); Eva Mroczek, *The Literary Imagination in Jewish Antiquity* (Oxford: Oxford University Press, 2016); Jeremy D. Smoak, "From Temple to Text: Text as Ritual Space and the Composition of Numbers 6:24-26," *JHS* 17 (2017): 1–26.
[4] Karel van der Toorn, *Scribal Culture and the Making of the Hebrew Bible* (Cambridge, MA: Harvard University Press, 2007), 16, see also 22–23.
[5] Ibid., 16.
[6] I take issue with formulations that divorce processes of collecting from literary creativity (e.g. William Schniedewind, *How the Bible Became a Book: The Textualization of Ancient Israel* [Cambridge: Cambridge University Press, 2004], 179).
[7] An exhaustive survey of ancient Near Eastern institutional archives in the first millennium BCE is not possible within the confines of this essay. Detailed surveys of their definitions and specific functions can be found in: Ernst Posner, *Archive in the Ancient World* (Cambridge, MA: Harvard University Press, 1972); Olof Pedersén, *Archives and Libraries in the Ancient Near East: 1500–300 BC* (Bethesda: CDL, 1998); Martha Brosius, ed. *Ancient Archives and Archival Traditions* (Oxford: Oxford

containing everything from letters, ration lists, and tax records. These collections were also not neatly separable from temple and treasury spaces. The witness of Ezra–Nehemiah attests to the confluence of treasury and archive.[8] Texts were not easily divorced from other objects of value.

It has been argued that famous ancient collections, like Assurbanipal's seventh-century BCE Neo-Assyrian archive, are symbols of imperial might, emblemizing a regime's dominance not only over nations and peoples, but also over memory and knowledge itself.[9] However, the prevalence of more quotidian collections also bears witness to how vital these institutions were to the functioning of communities on a variety of scales.[10] While communal memory can be preserved in many ways, not least through oral tradition, a community with an archive is a particular means by which a group not only remembers but also *demonstrates* that it remembers. Archives, in other words, both preserve and represent memory. Both of these functions demonstrate the centrality of institutionalized archives to the representation of cultural vitality in the ancient Mediterranean. But what would it mean to read texts *as* archives? I would like to press into van der Toorn's comment and consider how thinking about texts archivally rewires our expectations for ancient Jewish texts and the scribes that produced them.

Ezra–Nehemiah, as I have argued elsewhere, serves as a ready-to-hand example of this sort of archiving scribal practice for several reasons.[11] The first is that archival spaces show up in the narrative of Ezra–Nehemiah overtly as vital cultural touchstones. In Ezra 1–6, the imperial collection is the site where the fate of the nascent Second Temple is weighed: its reconstruction is first stopped (Ezra 4:17–24) then restarted (Ezra 6:1–5) on the basis of the contents of the Persian archives. The second reason that Ezra–Nehemiah serves as an illuminating site to think archivally about Jewish scribal practice is because it is brimming with other, apparently distinct, documents. Cited documents make up over half of Ezra–Nehemiah, by verse count. These relentless citations have been the root of modern scholarly despair—and disparagement—of these texts. These frequent and, at times, bewildering assortment of citations has led to the charge of sloppy or incompetent historiography.[12] If, however, we view Ezra–Nehemiah as an archival site—that is, as a text as much occupied

---

University Press, 2003); Jacqueline S. Du Toit, *Textual Memory: Ancient Archives, Libraries, and the Hebrew Bible* (Sheffield: Sheffield Phoenix, 2011).
[8] In Ezra 6:1, we are told that search was indeed made of the "house of the scrolls (בת ספריא), where the treasures (גנזיא) were kept" in Babylon. In Ezra 5:17 and 6:2, we have a system imagined where records (דכרונה) are perhaps kept in a particular section of the royal treasury (בית גנזיא).
[9] Steven W. Holloway, *Aššur Is King! Aššur Is King! Religion in the Exercise of Power in the Neo-Assyrian Empire* (Leiden: Brill, 2002), 80; cf. 81–90. Edward Said, Thomas Richards, Ann Stoler, among many others, have since theorized about the conjoined nature of the colonial enterprise and the sociopolitical power of imperial archives (Edward W. Said, *Culture and Imperialism* [New York: Vintage Books, 1994]; Thomas Richards, *The Imperial Archive: Knowledge and the Fantasy of Empire* [London: Verso, 1993]; Ann Laura Stoler, *Along the Archival Grain: Epistemic Anxieties and Colonial Common Sense* [Princeton, NJ: Princeton University Press, 2010]).
[10] Collections as large as Assurbanipal's at Nineveh and the Neo-Babylonian Shamash temple at Sippar housed tens of thousands of tablets (Pedersén, *Archives and Libaries*, 193–94; John MacGinnis, *Letter Orders from Sippar and the Administration of the Ebabbara in the Late-Babylonian Period* (Poznań: Bonami, 1995). Large palace complexes often featured multi-room collections, their texts sorted into various rooms by topic, or in the case of Mari, and Ugarit, by relevant geographical region. In late fifth-century Athens, when the council moved into the larger "bouleterion" (βουλευτήριον) the old council chamber was converted into a city archive, the "Metroön" (μητρῷον) (James P. Sickenger, "Literacy, Documents, and Archives in the Ancient Athenian Democracy," *AA* 62 [2002]: 229–46). Other collections, like those uncovered at Elephantine and those unearthed in private homes, like the Murashu collection, held a much smaller number of texts, typically receipts, letters, and deeds to property (Arthur E. Cowley, *Aramaic Papyri of the Fifth Century B.C.* [Oxford: Clarendon, 1923]; Posner, *Archives in the Ancient World*, 125; Matthew Stolper, *Entrepreneurs and Empire: The Murašû Archive, the Murašû Firm, and Persian Rule in Babylonia* [Leiden: Nederlands Historisch-Archaeologisch Instituut te Istanbul, 1985]).
[11] Laura Carlson Hasler, *Archival Historiography in Jewish Antiquity* (New York: Oxford University Press, 2020). See especially Chapter 3 and the Epilogue for an expanded version of the arguments found here.
[12] Lester Grabbe, in his 1998 Ezra–Nehemiah commentary, reflects on the style of these books this way: "We know we are not dealing with history but with something else, whether you call it legend, literature, or theology" (Lester Grabbe, *Ezra–Nehemiah* [London: Routledge, 1998], 153). See also n. 13.

with textual accumulation and preservation as it is about telling a linear story—we can encounter it in a very different way.

Perhaps the best example of an archival moment can be found in Ezra 4. Ezra 4 is regarded by some scholars as hopelessly fragmented and ill-composed because of its multiple, accumulated citations.[13] This chapter contains two letters exchanged between the Persian emperor and the Judeans' purportedly antagonistic neighbors. For my purposes we will look briefly not at the letters, but at the citation notices introducing these letters:

> And in the reign of Ahasuerus, in the beginning of his reign, they wrote an accusation against the inhabitants of Judah and Jerusalem. In the days of Artaxerxes, Bishlam and Mithredath and Tabeel and the rest of their associates wrote to Artaxerxes king of Persia. The letter was written in Aramaic and translated. Rehum the commander and Shimshai the scribe wrote a letter against Jerusalem to Artaxerxes the king as follows: Rehum the commander, Shimshai the scribe, and the rest of their associates, the judges, the governors, the officials, the Persians, the men of Erech, the Babylonians, the men of Susa, that is, the Elamites, and the rest of the nations whom the great and noble Osnappar deported and settled in the cities of Samaria and in the rest of the province Beyond the River. This is a copy of the letter that they sent. "To Artaxerxes the king…" (Ezra 4:6–11a)

These letters appear to introduce at least three, possibly four, documents in this brief passage: first, the letter from the עם הארץ to Ahasuerus (that is, Xerxes), in the first year of his reign (4:6); second, the letter from Bishlam and his colleagues to Artaxerxes (4:7); third, the letter from Rehum, Shimshai, and the displaced Samarians to Artaxerxes (4:8–11a).[14] These source texts identify a variety of senders and addressees. Adding to this confusion is the oft-cited distance between the content of the ensuing letters and the framing story: the preceding and subsequent narratives (Ezra 4:1–5, 23–24) pertain to drama surrounding the Judean's temple rebuilding efforts. The cited letters warn instead against the reconstruction of the city's foundation and walls (Ezra 4:12, 16, 21). When interpreted with the expectation of a linear narrative, this chapter is a mess: a jumble of disparate citations whose narrative thread cannot be followed without considerable confusion.

When interpreted as an archive, however, Ezra 4's preponderance of disparate cited material gains an aesthetic logic. Instead of interpreting its fragmentation as evidence of literary deficiency, we may think of scribes creating Ezra–Nehemiah with archival purposes in mind: to accumulate, sort, and preserve documents for future retrieval. We may think, in other words, of citation and interruption as working towards alternative literary purposes: to build an archive out of texts.[15] Indeed, perhaps the most significant impact of thinking about texts *archivally* is that it lends aesthetic intelligibility

---

[13] C. C. Torrey is perhaps the first of many twentieth-century classicists and biblical scholars to disparage the form of Ezra–Nehemiah. Torrey, in his landmark *Ezra Studies*, referred to Ezra as a "mutilated recension" of foregoing traditions (C. C. Torrey, *Ezra Studies* [Chicago: University of Chicago Press, 1910], 115). Decades later, classicist Arnaldo Momigliano reiterated this sentiment by terming the Ezra Memoir "sadly mutilated" (Arnaldo Momigliano, *The Classical Foundations of Modern Historiography*, Sather Classical Lectures 54 [Berkeley: University of California Press, 1990], 14). References to Ezra–Nehemiah's "apparent[ly] erratic" and "not ideal" compositional form are prevalent throughout more recent decades of biblical scholarship (Sara Japhet, "Periodization between History and Ideology II: Chronology and Ideology in Ezra–Nehemiah," in *Judah and the Judeans in the Persian Period*, ed. O. Lipschits and M. Oeming [Winona Lake: Eisenbrauns, 2006], 491–508 at 491; Grabbe, *Ezra–Nehemiah*, 52).

[14] Ezra 4:11a constitutes a possible fourth document.

[15] My argument here may be differentiated from Richard Steiner, who also invokes the archive to explain the odd literary for of Ezra 4 (Richard C. Steiner, "Bishlam's Archival Search Report in Nehemiah's Archive: Multiple Introductions and Reverse Chronological Order as Clues to the Origin of the Aramaic Letters in Ezra 4–6," *JBL* 125 [2006]: 641–85). Steiner argues that the multiple introductions of documents within this episode should be understood as distinctive documentary "strata" that can be indexed to two different, *literal* archives. My argument, by contrast, pertains to the archival nature *represented* by these citations and does not make a case for the origins of these documents, archival or otherwise.

to literary fragmentation, thus undoing our readerly attachment to linear narrative. Simply put, when we think about scribes as archivists, rebuilding sites of collection by means of their literary practices, we read with a more capacious view of a text's representative possibilities.

Reading Second Temple Jewish texts as archives should not be limited to Ezra–Nehemiah. Ingeborg **Löwisch**, in her recent multidisciplinary study of the genealogies of 1 Chronicles 1–9, has argued that these lists may be best read as archives that artfully join memories of a traumatic past to a revived, re-written future.[16] These genealogies, moreover, overturn more typical patrilineal forms, repopulating this virtual archive with the names of women. Eva Mroczek has also argued archival attentiveness especially when viewing the Dead Sea Scrolls.[17] Mroczek argues that the heavenly collections described in *Jubilees* and the multiple, multiform collections of psalms found at Qumran invite us to liken the literary imagination in Jewish antiquity to an ever-expanding archive.[18] Both of **Löwisch's** and Mroczek's arguments invoke the archive to help scholars think beyond fixity and closure when interpreting ancient scribal practice. If, as I have argued elsewhere, scribes in this period practiced "archival historiography," it frees us to consider forms of representation untethered to the formal constraints of straightforward narrative.

It may possible, moreover, to think archivally about larger swaths of the ancient Jewish textual tradition as well. We may see archival logics behind the evident seams and repetitions of the Pentateuchal literature, especially as extended narratives give way to series of legal collections in Leviticus and Numbers, culminating in the (self-consciously written) reiteration of the divine law in Deuteronomy. Reading this way may not necessarily way in on the chronologies of compositional development, but it does shed significant light on its purposes and logics.[19] Reading archivally helps us to see these seams and other indicators of textual assembly neither as accidental nor incidental to the scribal strategies that produced this literature. If read as an archival structure as well as a narrative, the optics of textual accumulation become integral to the literary achievements of these texts.

Reading ancient texts in terms of space, even beyond archival spaces, not only invites us to reevaluate apparent disruptions, it also helps us rethink scribal strategies of representation more generally. It is perhaps intuitive to us to think about literary representation first and foremost in terms of narrative: texts represent events through telling stories. But considering scribal strategies in terms of spaces as well as events helps us think about how texts might replicate lived experience beyond narrative retelling. As I suggested above, the use of citation and other indicators of textual collection, may work not to tell *about* but to *render present* an archival space in textual form.[20] This space may then take on some of the purposes of the represented space (i.e. the preservation of knowledge) or some of its broader cultural signification (i.e. the possession of knowledge). Other spaces may be replicated by these alternative scribal strategies. Jeremy Smoak has argued that portions of Numbers map temple spaces.[21] This literary ordering does not describe this space in a linear fashion but arranges its prayers such that the reader or hearer might experience the inscriptions and ritual sequences of this space. Scribal strategies move well beyond linear retelling, allowing readers and hearers to experience the medium of text according to movement within space as well as time.

---

[16]Löwisch, *Trauma Begets Genealogy*, 32–34.
[17]Eva Mroczek, "Thinking Digitally about the Dead Sea Scrolls: Book History Before and Beyond the Book," *BH* 14 (2011): 241–69.
[18]Mroczek, "Thinking Digitally," 251. See also Mroczek, *Literary Imagination*, 115–21.
[19]For an example of different ways of approaching overtly composite Pentateuchal moments to determine their *chronological* development, see Schniedewind's analysis of Exod 34 (Schniedewind, *How the Bible Became a Book*, 122–23).
[20]Both Ryan Olson and John Durham Peters describe the central problem that discursive technologies (and letters, in particular) seek to overcome is the problem of absence (Ryan Olson, *Tragedy, Authority, and Trickery: The Poetics of Embedded Letters in Josephus* [Washington: Center for Hellenic Studies; Cambridge, MA: Harvard University Press, 2010], 100–102; John Durham Peters, *Marvelous Clouds: Toward a Philosophy of Elemental Media* [Chicago: University of Chicago Press, 2015], 265).
[21]Smoak, "Temple to Text," 9, 25–26.

Invoking space to reveal new strategies of representation also helps to erode the boundary between material and literary worlds in biblical and Jewish studies. The notion that texts wed physical space to literary expression acknowledges the way the built environment conditions our aesthetic impulses. Scribes in the ancient world were not immune from this conditioning. We can see that in the way they were indeed using writing not only to replicate spaces but also to adapt them to their needs. For texts, more often then not, are *not* spaces in the traditional sense (pop-up books might be among the more whimsical exceptions to this claim). Scribal attempts to replicate their purposes onto the page thus necessarily involve adaptation. Such adaptations may constitute a kind of technological "upgrade," in the sense that the changes create conditions for greater resilience.[22] When an archive becomes a text, this collection becomes both more mobile and more easily replicable, rendering it less vulnerable to destruction. Textualizing spaces is one way of enhancing these sites' capacity for survival.[23]

Ultimately, thinking spatially about ancient Jewish texts can also reform our vision of what is sometimes seen as the capstone of ancient scribal practice: the canon. The last decade of biblical scholarship has productively revised our understanding of canon in terms of authorship, era, and even *telos* and limitation. Considering the formation of the canon in light of the archive, as Mroczek has argued, mitigates the limitation and determinism so often attached to the term and process of canonization itself.[24] But thinking about the canon as a space of collection also helps us think beyond the two dimensions of this vexed category. The term canon, which signifies "catalogue," "list," or even "rule," reifies its flatness, gesturing towards its affiliation with time over space. Some well-rehearsed metaphors about canonical composition, like beads on a thread, obliquely confirm the linear nature of discursive forms.[25] Too often we think of narratives, as we think of the development of the canon, and most literature, for that matter, in two dimensions, on a kind of inexorable progression from prototypes to final form, and from fragment to story.[26]

What happens when concepts of canon itself are more intimately connected with space, perhaps the particular space of a "national library"?[27] If archives served as sites of the scribal work of textual interpretation and addition, it lends further credence to the idea that "canon" ought to include notions of replication and expansion.[28] This possibility leads to a word of caution: despite lengthy discussion over the status of a Jerusalem library in this period, seeing canon *as* collection does not assume that the canon—in any form—replicated any single, specific space.[29] Indeed, the materialization of spaces into text may well indicate the *absence* of a given space, like a central Jerusalem archive. As they replicate spaces, in other words, texts may well replace them. The point here is to

---

[22] Peters, *Clouds*, 32–33.
[23] Ibid. See also Peters' discussion of the comparison between the "monumental" Egyptian structures versus the portability of Israelite media in the Exodus narrative (287–88). Mroczek also invokes metaphors of "software" versus "hardware" in reference to the mental sites of data organization and valuation (Mroczek, "Thinking Digitally," 262).
[24] Mroczek, *Literary Imagination*, 184–90.
[25] E.g. "The separate literary units were strung together like beads on the single thread of genre, purpose, protagonist or presumed author" (van der Toorn, *Scribal Culture*, 16).
[26] Contrary to contemporary assumptions about the continuous, linear use of scrolls, Mroczek argues that these collections not only often consisted of textual fragments, but also lent themselves to selective, "fragmented" reading (Mroczek, "Thinking Digitally," 255–56). Hindy Najman addresses manifold significations of the fragment in biblical studies, including how literary fragmentation invites readerly investment and response (Hindy Najman, "Ethical Reading: The Transformation of the Text and the Self," *JTS* 68 [2017]: 507–29).
[27] Van der Toorn, *Scribal Culture*, 260.
[28] Cf. Mroczek, *Literary Imagination*, 156–83.
[29] See, e.g., Schniedewind's discussion of the temple library, which links the temple library and "Nehemiah's library" to the preservation of the Bible (Schniedewind, *How the Bible*, 182–83). See also, Victor Hurowitz, *I Have Built You an Exalted House: Temple Building in Light of Mesopotamian and Northwest Semitic Writings* (Sheffield: JSOT, 1992); Nadav Na'aman, "The Temple Library of Jerusalem and the Composition of the Book of Kings," in *Congress Volume: Leiden, 2004* (Leiden: Brill, 2006), 129–52.

read texts, including canon(s), within the view of a world where certain monumental spaces, like temple and archives, wielded strong symbolic significance. This symbolic presence, manifest variously in extant physical structures or in cultural ideation, shapes the way texts were written.

Thinking of canon as an archive dismantles our expectations for reading biblical texts exclusively in terms of story. When we think of canon as a collection rather than as a "rule" or as a kind of end or "conclusion," our interpretation shifts. As the preamble of Second Maccabees suggests, scribes were builders, creating spaces that a community inhabited and that structured its shared life. These structures sometimes had to be rebuilt or abandoned in the wake of hostile forces.[30] Far from being a semantic conceit, this image of scribe-as-builder has wide-ranging implications for how we think about the logics of scribal practice and literary composition. Insofar as we think about archives as symbols of cultural vitality, this image can also shed light on the construction of textual authority itself.

Texts, like spaces, shape how and where we look.[31] Texts, like spaces, pervade social consciousness and choreograph human behavior. It may be argued that the most iconic spaces, like so-called authoritative (or indeed "iconic") texts may simply be those that most effectively arrest our attention. The transcription of space into text (and vice-versa) raises broader questions about the relationship between the body and discourse, asking us to account for the multiple and fragmentary way that language inflects and modifies corporeal experience and how embodied life creates, shapes, and ultimately evades language.[32] Reading spatially locates authors and readers alike. It may finally inhibit our "lust" to be disembodied interpreters, reading apart from or, in Michel de Certeau's formulation, *above* the particular physical and discursive spaces we build and occupy.[33]

Merging consideration of space and text not only undermines the dominance of linear narrative and erodes the boundary between the material and the literary in the ancient world, it also invites us to ask fundamental questions about the spatial experience of reading, writing, and living with texts in Second Temple Judaism and beyond. Thinking of canon—and text, writ large—as space helps us think more holistically about how we look at and live with texts.

---

[30]Cf. Fernando Báez, *A Universal History of the Destruction of Books: From Ancient Sumer to Modern Iraq*, trans. A. MacAdam (New York: Atlas & Co., 2008).
[31]For another articulation of the idea of "Scripture as space," see Dale Martin, *Sex and the Single Savior: Gender and Sexuality in Biblical Interpretation* (Louisville: Westminster John Knox, 2006), 161–84. Martin likens reading the Bible to entering several spaces, including an art museum. As formative, "living" spaces, art museums, Martin argues, help us think about biblical interpretation beyond the authorities of history and authorial intention (Martin, *Single Savior*, 170–71). I am grateful to Matthew Croasmun who has also shared with me his own interpretation of the Bible as a space of collection.
[32]De Certeau, *Everyday Life*, 102.
[33]Ibid., 91–94.

# Rejecting "Patriarchy"

## Reflections on Feminism, Biblical Scholarship, and Social Perspective*

SHAWNA DOLANSKY

I was in the middle of conducting a close reading of Genesis 16 in my introductory Hebrew Bible class when I heard a loud whisper and the sound of a book slamming shut from somewhere near the back of the room. I looked up from my Bible and made eye contact with a slightly flustered and embarrassed student. I raised an eyebrow at her as heads turned and necks craned to see what the disruption was about. Red-faced, she sputtered "I'm sorry, I just never knew how *immoral* the Bible was!" I laughed reflexively and pointed out the irony of her statement, but then realized that a sober teaching moment had presented itself in Sarah's presentation of Hagar to Abraham as sexual partner and potential surrogate mother. I closed my Bible and started a class discussion about morality—what it was, and where it came from—and then guided them toward the concept of cultural relativism. We talked about polygamy, and the kinds of sexual values that might prevail in a culture that prized patrilineage for purposes of maintaining both birthrights and covenantal blessings. We talked about the worldview of the biblical texts that we had examined thus far, and juxtaposed it with the worldviews of the Bible's modern readerships. We also contrasted the oral nature of individual tales like Genesis 16, with the way in which we were reading the text in a physical book that was understood to be a sacred text about the origins of God's people. Although the term "patriarchy" was bandied about by students in the context of our discussion, we concluded that if we wanted to understand the values and mores of the society that produced the text, we would have to refrain from judging them based on twenty-first-century Western standards of behavior.

To arrive at this conclusion, we explored the concept of patriarchy in some depth; what it meant, and whether or not it was an appropriate term to use to describe the world portrayed in Genesis. Carol Meyers has been calling for biblical scholars to discontinue using the term "patriarchy" to describe biblical Israel for more than 30 years.[1] Meyers' argument has been accepted by some scholars, but ignored or vociferously rejected by others. Most vocal among those who refuse to reject the use of the term "patriarchy" for ancient Israel have been feminist biblical scholars.

---

*An earlier version of this essay was presented as "Rejecting Patriarchy: On Clarifying the Objectives of Feminist Biblical Scholarship" at the Society of Biblical Literature 2014 Annual Meeting in Biblical Hermeneutics and Women in the Biblical World joint session discussing Carol Meyers' call for the rejection of the term "patriarchy" in biblical scholarship. I am grateful to Susan Ackerman and Adele Reinhartz for commenting on pre-presentation drafts, and to the audience at the Annual Meeting for their feedback and encouragement. A separate version of this paper, "What is Gendered Historiography and How Do You Do It?," was immeasurably enriched by co-authorship with Sarah Shectman, whose insights have also been brought to bear on the present work (see further n. 8, below).

[1] The first well-known publication in which Meyers advances this argument is *Discovering Eve: Ancient Israelite Women in Context* (Oxford: Oxford University Press, 1988), but see earlier "Procreation, Production, and Protection: Male–Female Balance in Early Israel," *Journal of the American Academy of Religion* (1983): 489–514, and also "Gender Roles and Genesis 3:16 Revisited," in *The Word of the Lord Shall Go Forth: Essays in Honor of David Noel Freedman on his Sixtieth Birthday*, ed. C. Meyers and M. P. O'Connor (Winona Lake: Eisenbrauns, 1983), 118–41. Most recently, see Meyers' *Rediscovering Eve: Ancient Israelite Women in Context* (Oxford: Oxford University Press, 2012).

The following morning, I met my upper-level seminar entitled "Theory and Method in the Study of Religion." That day, our topic was feminist theory; a concept that, like the Bible (or the term "patriarchy" for that matter), tends to be one that everyone thinks they understand because they've seen it depicted often enough in popular culture. Much of our discussion ended up focusing on distinguishing between feminist activism and feminist causes, on the one hand, and feminist analysis and theories on the other. One of the students asked me if I considered myself a feminist biblical scholar. My answer, after a pause, was a qualified "yes"—qualified, because I disagree with fundamental positions held and advocated by most biblical scholars who label themselves feminist, who focus on literary criticism and/or seek theological meanings from the text to make a case for female empowerment.

As a historian, I understand that there is already a great divide between what I do and what many post-modern literary critical readings of biblical literature posit is possible. Literary criticism often asserts that authorial intention and even context cannot be adequately reconstructed, denying the ability of a modern reader to know what an author was thinking when that author wrote. Literary critical methods are often in fact explicitly a-historical. At the same time, however, literary criticism does not deny *history* or the possibility of history, or even the importance of historical context in at least looking at the authors' texts; the problem arises only in terms of reading *meaning*. For example, studies of Shakespeare can look at reconstructing who he was and what we can know of his context and/or they can look at the history of the ways in which Shakespearean plays have been read, acted, and appropriated in later contexts. These are acknowledged as related but distinct enterprises. Theoretically as well, the history of biblical interpretation is a separate undertaking in scholarship than reconstructing the origins of the Bible. Both are historical projects, and both seek to understand text in relation to context. But since the Bible is most often read in society as though it were speaking to us today, modern readings interested in "the meaning of the text" tend to collapse incredibly diverse layers of meaning built up over thousands of years into a single framework of interpretation that itself is a-historical—or as theologians might prefer, "timeless" and "eternal"—in its intended meaning. Unlike Shakespeare, reading the Bible for meaning has, in all places and times, been ultimately a reader-centred enterprise.

Feminist theology, another sub-discipline of feminist biblical scholarship, grapples with the problem of asserting equal rights for women in the context of a received Jewish and Christian biblical tradition that they perceive as irreparably sexist and patriarchal. This has meant that feminist theologians have had either to leave their traditions in search of entirely new spiritualities that are more empowering to them as women,[2] or to attempt to reform their traditions from within. This has often involved radical revision and reinterpretation of those traditions, starting with recovering what they see as the hidden power and agency of women in biblical texts.[3] Feminist literary critics, on the other hand, have often devoted enormous effort to exposing the inherent "patriarchy,"

---

[2] See, e.g.: Carol P. Christ and Judith Plaskow, eds., *Womanspirit Rising* (San Francisco: Harper & Row, 1979); Naomi R. Goldenberg, *Changing of the Gods* (Boston: Beacon, 1979); Mary Daly, *Beyond God the Father: Toward a Philosophy of Women's Liberation* (Boston: Beacon, 1973); and Gerda Lerner, *The Creation of Patriarchy* (Oxford: Oxford University Press, 1986); for a comprehensive overview see R. Radford Ruether, *Goddesses and the Divine Feminine: A Western Religious History* (Berkley: University of California Press, 2006). For a useful discussion of the origins of a split between "Reformers" and "Revolutionaries," see M. Weaver, "Who Is the Goddess and Where Does She Get Us?" *Journal of Feminist Studies* 5 (1989): 49–64.

[3] The 1970s saw a revolution in feminist biblical interpretation focused on reclaiming the biblical text for women, starting with Phyllis Trible's 1972 article "Eve and Adam: Genesis 2–3 Reread," *ANQ* 13 (1972): 251–58, and her 1973 follow-up, "Depatriarchalizing in Biblical Interpretation," *JAAR* 41 (1973): 30–48. Trible further developed her arguments in her 1978 book, *God and the Rhetoric of Sexuality* (Philadelphia: Fortress), which expanded on the idea of the equality of the sexes in the Bible as a reflection of a biblical portrait of God with both male and female qualities. Feminist theology continues to plumb the depths of potential meanings for women within both testaments in the works of Elisabeth Schüssler Fiorenza, Carole Fontaine, Athalya Brenner, and many others.

"androcentrism," and "misogyny" of the biblical authors' worldviews, arguing that the Hebrew Bible's enduring cultural and religious legacy in the modern West undermines feminist activist efforts toward social equality.[4]

Although their goals are different (rejection vs. redemption), both stem from the dual recognition of androcentric biases in the Bible on the one hand, and the predominance of biblical symbolism and meaning in their own present world, interpreted as "patriarchy," on the other. Also common to both perspectives is their underlying method: all of these approaches employ narrative criticism to seek out the Bible's message for and about women. Most interestingly, those feminists who seek to reject the Bible define themselves over and against confessional attempts to redeem the biblical text for use by women, seeing themselves rather as "biblical scholars." However, even as they reject feminist theology for its goals, they also reject the historical-critical methods of traditional non-theological biblical inquiry as the tools of "malestream" scholarship that is equally responsible for suppressing women-centered readings. Thus they have appropriated for themselves the title of feminist biblical scholars, simultaneously eschewing traditional biblical scholarship *and* feminist theology. These feminist literary critics demonstrate the ways in which the overall ideology of the text is patriarchally determined, and thus even when women are depicted as exercising power, this is only in support of a patriarchal agenda.[5]

In both confessional and non-confessional literary analyses, however, present ways of reading the text, and present frameworks for understand gender and power structures and constructions—such as the term "patriarchy"—are imposed on the Bible. Such presentist ideologies are attributed to the scribes who stood behind the Bible's production and transmission, portraying them as oppressors of women and thereby painting the original context of the Bible's authorship as a patriarchal one that simultaneously produces and mirrors our own worldview. But scribal androcentrism is not patriarchy, and the milieu of biblical production in Iron Age Israel does not socially, culturally, or politically resemble the West in the twenty-first century.

So, in my "Theory and Method" class, we also talked about cultural relativism, patriarchy, and biblical scholarship, and I came to the conclusion that feminist theorists, rather than thinking about the Bible as patriarchal, are in fact uniquely positioned to argue *with* Meyers that the term "patriarchy" has no place in historical-critical scholarship of the Hebrew Bible.

Before delving into the reasons why I think feminists *in particular* should take up Meyers' call to reject the use of the term "patriarchy" for ancient Israel, I want to offer some definitions. "Patriarchy" denotes the social-science concept of systemic male dominance. It assumes a strictly hierarchical dichotomy between male and female at every level of society, and the concomitant limitation on female power, autonomy, and agency. It was a term coined in a nineteenth-century post-industrialist capitalist economic and political system to describe a world run by men, in which women's social, political, and economic power are all severely circumscribed; a world in which men are considered autonomous agents, and women are not. "Androcentrism," on the other hand, is a

---

[4] There are many examples of this type of feminist criticism. Mieke Bal is explicitly concerned with a reader-centered approach to the text and what she terms the "cultural function" of the Hebrew Bible in its constructions of gender. Her work has been extremely influential on other feminist biblical critics, such as J. Cheryl Exum, Esther Fuchs, and Susanne Scholz. It is not within the purview of the present study to review the history of feminist biblical scholarship, including for example the more literarily and historically inclined contributions of Phyllis Bird, Susan Niditch, and others: for an excellent comprehensive overview of the history of feminist biblical scholarship, see chapter 1 of Sarah Shectman's *Women in the Pentateuch: A Feminist and Source-Critical Analysis* (Sheffield: Sheffield Academic, 2009), and Susan Ackerman's "Digging up Deborah: Recent Hebrew Bible Scholarship on Gender and the Contribution of Archaeology," *Near Eastern Archaeology* 66, no. 4 (2003): 172–84.

[5] See, e.g., Exum's "Second Thoughts about Secondary Characters: Women in Exodus 1.8–2.10," in *Feminist Companion to Exodus to Deuteronomy*, ed. Athalya Brenner (Sheffield: Sheffield Academic, 2000), 75–87.

term that indicates a perspective focused on men—male rights, male privilege, male discourse, and male interests.

I would propose that the portrait of ancient Israel in the biblical texts is of a society that is androcentric. This makes sense from a historical perspective if we think about who composed and preserved these texts. Recent studies of scribal culture acknowledge the oral pre-history of biblical texts, preserved as cultural, social, and ethnic memories by groups over time, but emphasize that the textuality of the Hebrew Bible derives from official, elite settings like Temple and palace.[6] In particular, priests tend to be credited with the writing down of traditions, as well as with their preservation and dissemination. In both pre- and post-exilic Israel, priests were male. Thus, an androcentric perspective pervading the biblical corpus is not unexpected.[7]

However, while "androcentric" is appropriate here, the radical differences between ancient and modern political, economic, and social systems precludes a legitimate application of the term "patriarchy" to biblical literature and the society that produced it. Further, it seems to me that continuing to use the term "patriarchy" in descriptions of ancient Israel undermines and obscures historical—*and* feminist—theory and method.

My argument draws on the social-scientific principles of historical analysis and investigation on the one hand, and on feminist theory and method on the other. I understand feminist theory and method to be rooted in reflexive inquiry, acknowledging a variety of answers and aimed at bringing out intersectionalities, nuances, and complexities of human history, sociology, religion, and culture. As a feminist historian,[8] when interpreting ancient texts and artifacts I prefer to raise possibilities and make arguments from the evidence at hand, building on knowledge and expanding scholarly lenses rather than providing answers or imposing conclusions based on my own presumed scholarly objectivity.

Susan Ackerman, one of the leading proponents of feminist *historical* inquiry, has suggested that the reason why most feminist biblical scholars continue to approach the text from a literary rather than a historical perspective is that it is much more difficult to pursue more historical approaches.[9] Ackerman defines historians as those scholars who want to understand more fully the nature of

---

[6]See, e.g., William M. Schniedewind, *How the Bible Became a Book* (Cambridge: Cambridge University Press, 2004); Karel van der Toorn, *Scribal Culture and the Making of the Hebrew Bible* (Cambridge, MA: Harvard University Press, 2007).
[7]Ronald Hendel ("Historical Context," in *The Book of Genesis: Composition, Reception, and Interpretation*, ed. Craig A. Evans, Joel N. Lohr, and David L. Petersen [Leiden: Brill, 2012], 51–83) notes that in Deut 32:8 we can catch a glimpse of the nature of the oral tradition that precedes and lives alongside the written: "Remember the days of old, consider the years of antiquity. Ask your father and he will tell you, your elders and they will recount to you." Hendel remarks that this passage "evokes the family and tribal setting of oral traditions of the collective past. These are narratives handed down through the generations, recounted by fathers and elders, which acculturate young Israelites by initiating them into the ancestral stories. The fathers and elders speak with the authority of tradition, since they are vested with power and are the patriarchal agents for the preservation and flourishing of the lineage. The collective memories of the past are part of the vital 'social motor' that sustains and renews the group's identity and practices. This generational motor ensures the present relevance of the events of the remembered past." Although not the point Hendel is making here, if we assume with him that Deut 32:8 reflects a reality of male transmission of history, the legacy of the pre-scribal oral tradition is also, unavoidably, an androcentric one.
[8]That is: an historian making use of feminist theories and methods to produce a more nuanced "gendered historiography" of ancient Israel. For the exciting possibilities offered by a gendered historiographic approach, see my co-authored article with Sarah Shectman, "What Is Gendered Historiography and How Do You Do It?" *JHS* 19, no. 4 (2019): 3–18. This is an introduction to a collection of articles we originally convened for a session on Gendered Historiography under the auspices of the Pentateuch Unit at the 2016 Annual Meeting of the Society for Biblical Literature. For an important discussion of gender and method in biblical studies, see further Jacqueline Lapsley's "Introduction: Gender and Method," in *HeBAI* 5, no. 2 (2016): 75–77, and, in the same issue, Cynthia Chapman, "Modern Terms and Their Ancient Non-Equivalents: Patrilineality and Gender in the Historical Study of the Bible," 79–93; as well as the excellent collection of essays that explore gender construction and masculinity in the ancient world in Ilona Zsolnay, ed., *Being a Man: Negotiating Ancient Constructs of Masculinity* (New York: Routledge, 2016).
[9]Susan Ackerman, "Digging up Deborah: Recent Hebrew Bible Scholarship on Gender and the Contribution of Archaeology," *Near Eastern Archaeology* 66, no. 4 (2003): 172–84.

women's lives in ancient Israel by studying the Hebrew Bible alongside archaeological, sociological, and ethnographic data; alongside comparative materials (especially comparative materials from elsewhere in the west Semitic world); and alongside other extrabiblical evidence. The difficulty is that none of the texts of our primary written source, the Hebrew Bible, can be said to have been authored by a woman, and neither do any of the extrabiblical texts that we have from ancient Israel show any indication of female authorship. We thus lack the direct witness such texts might provide regarding the nature of ancient Israelite women's lives and experiences.

As has been noted as a central concern of feminist literary critics, the witness of male-authored texts regarding women suffers from the tendency to view women only in terms of their meaning for and significance to men. In addition, the witness regarding women available from ancient Israel's male-authored texts is flawed because it, almost without exception, reports the perspective of only the elite of the Israelite commonwealth. Almost all of the authors of the Hebrew Bible were members of Israel's religious institutions (the priests and the prophets) or members of aristocratic scribal groups.[10] Extra-biblical inscriptions likewise are concerned with major public institutions of the monarchy and their diplomatic and military relations with neighboring states. As Carol Meyers points out, these written archives cannot be assumed to accurately represent the experiences of ancient Israelite commoners, including the experiences of women commoners, and this even though it was commoners who comprised the vast majority of the ancient Israelite population.[11]

Meyers' work seeks to address this problem by viewing the biblical text in the context of the social worlds of ancient Israel as reconstructed through the interpretation of archaeological evidence. When Meyers and Ackerman do this, they use feminist methods to challenge, enrich, and broaden our understanding of the ancients who produced the Bible and their world.

In other words: they are engaging in historical-critical study of the Bible using both the traditional tools of such inquiry (source-critical, text-critical, comparative, archaeological, anthropological, *and* literary analysis), and they are explicitly feminist in both their methodology and the subject of their studies.[12]

And yet, when a session at the Annual Meeting of the Society of Biblical Literature calls for papers dealing with feminist issues, there seems to be little question that the session will focus on literary issues in an a-historical way, whether in confessional or non/anti-confessional discourse. And in fact, although the literary-critical conclusions will tend to be radically opposed to theological readings of the Bible, their methods and theoretical approaches will likely have much more in common with theological hermeneutics than they will with traditional historical-critical biblical study. The term "feminist biblical scholarship" has largely become synonymous with postmodern literary criticism of the Bible. As a biblical historian who relies on feminist theory and methods, I have personally felt very out of place in such sessions, and very alienated from the literature that pours forth under this general category.

---

[10] It should be noted that such categories as "priest," "prophet," and "scribe" were not mutually exclusive. Rather, distinctions among them pertained more to which modality was guiding the function or behavior of a biblical character at a given time. Isaiah, for example, was understood in the texts as a prophet when he delivered oracles, a priest by lineage (and possibly function; cf. Isa 6), and a scribe (cf. 2 Chr 26:22 and perhaps suggested in Isa 37–38).

[11] Carol Meyers, "Material Remains and Social Relations: Women's Culture in Agrarian Households of the Iron Age," in *Symbiosis, Symbolism, and the Power of the Past: Canaan, Ancient Israel, and Their Neighbors from the Late Bronze Age through Roman Palaestina*, ed. W. G. Dever and S. Gitin (Winona Lake: Eisenbrauns, 2003), 426.

[12] For discussions of the compatibility of historical-critical and feminist methods of inquiry, see, e.g., Monika Fander, "Historical-Critical Methods," in *Searching the Scriptures: A Feminist Introduction*, ed. Elisabeth Schüssler Fiorenza, trans. L. M. Maloney, 2 vols. (New York: Crossroad, 1993), 205–24; also Hanna Stenstrom, "Historical-Critical Approaches and the Emancipation of Women: Unfulfilled Promises and Remaining Possibilities," in *Her Master's Tools? Feminist and Post-Colonial Engagements of Historical-Critical Discourse*, ed. C. Vander Stichele and T. Penner (Atlanta: SBL, 2005), 31–45.

The further consequence of this, and a greater concern than my own discomfort, is that mainstream biblical scholarship continues to resist incorporating the insights of feminist biblical scholarship. Whatever the reasons were in the past, historical criticism's failure as a whole to engage with feminism in the present is largely due to the perception that feminism is synonymous with an a-historical, reader-centered literary criticism which may appear to most historians to have more in common with theological methods and hermeneutics than it does with historical ones. Feminist inquiry has in fact marginalized itself from mainstream inquiry by its explicit rejection of historical criticism, which is seen as an androcentric discipline and its tools those of patriarchy. Scholz believes that historical criticism of the Bible remains separate from feminism because it supports the status quo, keeping the Bible isolated from modern realities and the proliferation of worldviews in contemporary society.[13] Elisabeth Schüssler Fiorenza has made similar observations about the apparent incompatibility between feminist and historical-critical methods, particularly because feminists tend to dismiss the positivism they see as endemic to historical criticism.[14]

On the other hand, Monika Fander has argued that historical-critical methods are not only suitable for feminist criticism, but may also be a corrective for some of the problems inherent in feminist analysis; for example, the lack of distinction between older traditions and later redactional elements in terms of understanding the historical development of ideas about women.[15] Fander notes, however, that there is still tension between historical-critical study of the Bible and feminism, most notably the suspicion with which proponents of one regard the other, which she asserts is the result of the assumptions that scholars bring to the interpretational endeavor—particularly their stance on the authority of the text. Adele Reinhartz has also noted the tensions between traditional historical-critical scholarship and feminist sensitivity to women's voices and women's experiences.[16] Alice Keefe, who likewise notes the gap between ideological and social-scientific feminist approaches to the Bible, seeks to bring the two critical approaches into closer dialogue by demonstrating the need to ground ideological criticism in an understanding of the historical context of ancient Israel.[17]

It seems to me that the way to enact what Reinhartz and Keefe advocate is to do what Ackerman and Meyers are already doing: feminist historical criticism that bases its literary analysis in the historical context of ancient Israel rather than in the political, social, or religious concerns of modern feminist hermeneutics.

I propose that a starting point for such dialogue and cooperation is to take up Meyers' suggestion of rejecting the term "patriarchy" in studies of biblical Israel, and specifically in our thinking about scribes as the mediators of the traditions about Israel preserved in the biblical record. All feminist scholars—historians, and literary analysts alike—agree that the Bible is the result of a society in which male-centered norms are reflected in the text. And yet feminist literary critics often focus narrowly on what they see as "patriarchy" in order to expose and vehemently condemn it—and overlook the fact that there is more than simple male–female hierarchy at work in the text. Scribes were not just males, but *elite* males, and as such, potentially shared more in common with elite females than with males of lower social statuses. There are larger ideologies and theologies, and much more complex power structures, as well as relational social identities inherent in the text's

---

[13] Susanne Scholz, "'Tandoori Reindeer' and the Limitations of Historical Criticism," in Vander Stichele and Penner, eds., *Her Master's Tools*, 47–69.

[14] Elisabeth Schüssler Fiorenza, "Remembering the Past in Creating the Future: Historical-Critical Scholarship and Feminist Biblical Interpretation," in *Feminist Perspectives on Biblical Scholarship*, ed. Adela Yarbro Collins (Atlanta: Scholars Press, 1985), 43–63.

[15] Monika Fander, "Historical-Critical Methods," in Fiorenza, ed., *Searching the Scriptures*, 205–21 (212).

[16] Adele Reinhartz, "Margins, Methods, and Metaphors: Reflections on *A Feminist Companion to the Hebrew Bible*," *Prooftexts* 20, nos. 1 and 2 (2000): 43–60.

[17] Alice Keefe, "Stepping In/Stepping Out: A Conversation between Ideological and Social Scientific Feminist Approaches to the Bible," *Journal of Religion and Society* 1 (1999): 1–14.

implicit worldview that go far beyond the strict gender dichotomy proposed (or imposed) by the term "patriarchy." Developing a fuller portrait of how those involve and relate to women would serve not only feminist literary critical ends, but historical ones as well. It would also acknowledge that the Bible, as a literary product, reflects certain ideologies that are essential to understanding the texts themselves, whether one accepts or rejects such ideologies in the present. In order to understand the scribal culture reflected in the text, one needs to be able to reconstruct the society within which the scribes operated when they were transmitting the text, and also be able to do so in terms more familiar to that ancient society than those connoted by the term "patriarchy."

Meyers points out that using the patriarchy paradigm implies a fixed set of relationships, when in reality social arrangements are rarely static and power relations can shift over time. The focus on the subordination of women overlooks the fact that inequalities are a function of class or age as much as, if not more than, of gender. We think of "patriarchy" as the oppression of women by men at all levels of society. But ancient Israel had different levels and intersections of identity than we do, including servants, slaves, and strangers, as well as hereditary institutions like the priesthood, which excluded most men as well as women from arenas of community religious power. This means that in addition to thinking about text production occurring in inherently androcentric institutions, we also need to think about specific classes of males as responsible for producing, transmitting, and maintaining the written traditions. The term "patriarchy" obscures the way individuals and groups were organized in complex and interlocking spheres of activity.[18] Meyers concludes that patriarchy denotes a hierarchical model that cannot be uniformly applied to ancient complex societies.[19]

One does not have to agree with all aspects of Meyers' reconstruction of ancient Israelite life in the pre-monarchic period in order to recognize that the term "patriarchy" is not only no longer useful for understanding ancient Israel, but in fact obscures and undermines any historical reconstruction of gendered life in Israelite society by imposing presentist stereotypes on ancient realities. It is important to note that Meyers claims neither that hierarchies didn't exist in ancient Israel, nor does she claim gender equality or the absence of male privilege. She doesn't even claim that female sexuality was not controlled by men, or that the small group of educated scribal elites responsible for creating or recording the Hebrew Bible were male, and that the text reflects androcentric interests.[20] She simply questions the usefulness of a term that cannot adequately capture the realities of a place and time very different from our own, and the concomitant ways of reading the text and appropriating it into our own time as though the hierarchies we perceive and fight against today were relevant *in the same way* in that ancient world.

It is unfortunate that reactions from many feminist biblical scholars have been scornful, criticizing Meyers for producing a feminist revisionist treatise that is a-political and idealistic, stating for example "In regard to feminist thinking, Meyers is clearly not interested in the discourse of oppression,"[21] and asking what, ultimately, might be the purpose of producing such work. Setting

---

[18]Meyers, *Rediscovering Eve*, 198.
[19]Ibid., 195.
[20]Ibid., 199. It is in fact all the more interesting to note that, although there were multiple scribal groups operating in ancient Israel from different linguistic, social, political, and theological perspectives, they all seem to have been exclusively male. The intersection of a literate scribal class with a male gender, resulting in a *diversity* of scribal factions which explicitly espouse different ideologies, presents a more complicated and nuanced picture of the scribal elites than that captured by the notion that the Bible is "patriarchal," as though there were only one set of male perspectives, one male political ideology, universal in its oppression of all women by all men. Further, as discussed in Hilary Lipka's "Shaved Beards and Bared Buttocks: Shame and the Undermining of Masculine Performance in Biblical Texts," in *Being a Man: Negotiating Ancient Constructs of Masculinity*, ed. Ilona Zsolnay, SHANE (London: Routledge, 2017), 176–97, performances of a male gender differed among the various Israelite classes, opening up the possibility of further exploring the construction specific to a male scribal elite and whether/how much it differed among scribal groups, and/or from other elites, such as priests and kings.
[21]Mieke Bal, review of *Discovering Eve: Ancient Israelite Women in Context* by Carol Meyers (Oxford University Press 1988), *Journal of the American Academy of Religion* (1990): 511–13.

aside the possibility that Meyers' conclusions may actually be understood as *explicitly* political—since finding evidence of more equality for women in the biblical world than modern users of the Bible generally understand there to have been can be perceived *precisely* as a political act on her part—I think the question "to what purpose?" is most important.

As with Shakespeare, a scholar reading the Bible can do so for a multiplicity of purposes (if not most simply, for the sheer pleasure of the literature itself). We can seek to reconstruct the world of the author. We can try to understand his values, his fears, his ideologies. We can try to psychoanalyze him. We can focus on the reception history of his work. Or we can read or watch Shakespeare's plays and see ourselves and our lives, our values and fears reflected and refracted in them, and marvel at the timelessness of the underlying issues that pervade literature from all places and times and speak to the essence of what it means to be human. When a scholar reads the Bible, in theory there is little difference; one can choose any or all of these approaches. But as with reading Shakespeare, to combine them all uncritically—to read the story of Romeo and Juliet and decry the patriarchy inherent in its construction of society and therefore invalidate its use in our own society—would not be considered a contribution to either a historical understanding of Shakespeare or an appreciation of his art.

Similarly, reading the Bible as patriarchal—or even for the purpose of understanding "the discourse of oppression"—does not contribute to our understanding of the biblical texts' historical contexts and origins, and arguably likewise produces nothing useful in terms of feminist politics for our own world (especially for non-confessional discourse). Fundamentally, by blaming the ancient world for patriarchy, it obscures an exposition of both the ways in which the Bible is used today to justify women's oppression, and the underlying history of interpretation that is far more responsible for oppression of women in our world.

That is not to say that value judgments and literary hermeneutics do not have a place in biblical scholarship, nor that they do not have something important to contribute to political conceptions of feminism and its applicability today. It is rather to point out that value judgments should be reserved for biblical interpretation and its history, as biblical texts became the ideological justification for the sexism and misogyny of those who have used the Bible as a religious text for the last two thousand years. Those patterns of interpretation grounded in and justified by biblical androcentrism are too often antithetical to current egalitarian values.[22] Meyers points out that her historical reconstruction in fact can be used to inform feminist hermeneutics and theology: the implication here is that interpretative traditions that anachronistically read the gender hierarchies in biblically based Judaism and Christianity back into Iron Age Israel can be challenged by a model that sees Iron Age Israel as something other than patriarchal. But in order to establish a model in the first place, feminist biblical scholarship needs to have some basis in historical-critical study.

As Meyers points out:

> After all, ancient Israel was first and foremost a community, a social entity. That its literary creation, the Hebrew Bible, was to become an authoritative *religious* document should not blind us to the fact that what we call *religion* was but one mode—albeit the most enduring and influential one—of ancient Israel's existence as a *society*. Social science appraisals of ancient Israel are based on the fundamental premise of its social existence. To understand the living community of ancient Israel means examining it in the context of its own multidimensional environment, including its social and political prehistory, its ecological environment, and its

---

[22]Meyers, *Rediscovering Eve*, 201–2.

agrarian-pastoral economic base. Using a variety of resources, scholars have made significant strides in reconstructing the social history of ancient Israel. Our knowledge of the people of the Book is thus no longer limited by the information contained in that Book.[23]

To be clear, in terms of the reception history of the Hebrew Bible and the ways in which it is used to justify ongoing oppression and subjugation of women today, feminist hermeneutics—confessional and non-confessional—are invaluable ways of reading against traditional androcentric patterns of interpretation. But feminist biblical scholarship that defines itself in this way without engaging in or even by eschewing historical-critical understanding of the ancient context in which the Bible emerged, limits its usefulness to modern interpretation and disables historical reconstruction potentially performed without the baggage of the concept of patriarchy.

The biblical text is not just an ancient artifact, but a scribal artifact. It was composed, produced, and transmitted by different groups over time. Although likely all male, literate, and elite, essentializing their perspective as "patriarchal" without historical-critical investigation into their methods, cultures, politics, and sociologies, flattens a diverse set of experiences and realities far beyond the corner of society that these scribes represent. Beyond obscuring the complexities of varied social realities, the categorical label "patriarchy" also assigns a totalizing agency to these scribes and what they produced, distorting and obscuring the process of production and ultimately reinforcing the politics of patriarchy in an ironic circularity.

Feminist literary criticism of the text that assumes a patriarchal model for ancient Israel starts from the premise that in ancient Israel, symbolic production was controlled by men and therefore female portrayals in the Bible are male constructs reflecting androcentric ideas and serving androcentric interests. For this reason, the feminist critic reads against the grain, adopting an extrinsic analysis in order to avoid complicity with the patriarchal ideology of the text and to enable the subversion of that ideology. In this way of thinking, biblical woman is always the Other, defining the boundaries of a patriarchal order at the same time as she threatens those boundaries. There is no question that the exercise of reading against the grain and demonstrating the subjugation and oppression of women in biblical texts is important both for overturning entrenched androcentric readings of the texts, and as a corrective to the enduring influence that biblical portraits of men and women have in contemporary consciousness. Such readings are crucial for a comprehensive understanding of biblical reception history. However, both theological hermeneutics and non-theological literary criticism that assume patriarchy for ancient Israel subject the biblical text to judgments based on the importation of modern notions of women's subjectivity into ancient contexts, and therefore are not conducive to a social-scientific re-construction of gender norms and behaviors in biblical Israel.

Because of this, rejecting the use of the term "patriarchy" is necessary as a point of social-scientific method. "Patriarchy" carries with it assumptions and associations generated by nineteenth-, twentieth-, and twenty-first-century experiences of post-industrial capitalistic Western societies, baggage which is simply not transferable to an ancient agrarian, kinship-based polity. We cannot assume for ancient Israel the connotation that the concept of patriarchy carries: namely, that ancient Israelite women possessed the kind of social and sexual autonomy which we in the modern world take as normative, where human value and meaning for us is predicated on individual autonomy and bodily self-possession. In ancient Israel, identity seems to have been relational, not autonomous or individual: the personal worth and dignity of women *and* men were defined in terms of each person's place within larger corporate structures of family and lineage, and by the way in which

---

[23]Ibid., 12.

each contributed to those structures. Applying terminology that only makes sense in the post-industrialist capitalist West in order to understand what those structures were in the past, is not only unhelpful, but distortive. Without the hierarchically based oppression of all women by all men connoted by the term "patriarchy" as one's premise, it is possible to read beyond a strict male vs. female, object vs. subject, empowered vs. submissive, dichotomy of gender relations and constructions in the ancient world. It is this nuanced, complex set of understandings of social relations in ancient Israel that Meyers and others who reject the term "patriarchy" are striving to re-construct.

Finally, use of the term "patriarchy" and the categories and constructions this term imposes on the ancient world not only undermines our ability to understand history, but in fact our ability to properly apply feminist theory itself to that history. We are unable to understand history because we are imposing our own gender-social-cultural-political frameworks on a distant place and time which we can't presume to have shared any of them. Feminist theory for the past 25 years has recognized these limitations of finding and defining women in other cultures by our own standards and according to our own concepts of patriarchal oppression, and the need for non-Western women and other groups that we classify as "oppressed" to speak in their own voices. Feminist theory has also recognized the *difficulty* of that.

In my "Theory and Method" class, we spent some time trying to understand Gayatri Spivak's post-colonialist concept of the subaltern. Spivak, in her classic 1988 essay "Can the Subaltern Speak?" discusses the race and power dynamics involved in the banning of *sati* by the British colonizers of India as a practice oppressive to women.[24] Subalterns are subjects rendered mute by the colonial discourse that speaks on their behalf about their experience, constructing it from the perspective of wise outsiders knowing and acting on what they consider to be the best interests of those who have been colonized; and doing so without feeling the need to understand an emic perspective on their practices, or hearing from the subalterns themselves. In fact, Spivak concludes that the subalterns *cannot* speak to the colonizers about their experience, because in the very act of learning the discourse that would allow them to do so, they of necessity adopt the frameworks of the colonizers and subvert their own to align them with the interests and authority of those in power. If Spivak doesn't think it's possible for subalterns to speak, even when they are alive and present, how much more is this the case in historical studies, when the subjects are dead and gone, remaining only as literary figments of an ancient male author's imagination and then re-construed in a modern Western post-industrialist capitalist world as exemplars of the patriarchy we are trying to subvert here and now?

Feminist theory provokes us to question our assumptions. If women in the ancient world were oppressed, as feminist biblical critics assert, we need to think about what we mean by the term "women" and by the term "oppressed" within the context of what these critics are insisting on calling "patriarchy." On the one hand, if we don't question those terms, or we take it as a premise that women in ancient Israel were oppressed, then these women can be understood as subalterns in Spivak's formulation of the term. But even if we don't accept *a priori* that women in the ancient world were oppressed—and I would argue that feminist theorists should never accept any such *a priori* assertions—there is a very real sense in which, in applying modern Western ways of thinking to the biblical text in order to read it and understand it, the people who give us the Bible are essentially subalterns within our dominant (and only) set of discourses. As biblical scholars we are of necessity giving voice to ancient communities that have left us only fragments of their own voices, out of space, out of time, out of context. Feminist literary critics who question neither their

---

[24]Gayatri Chakravorty Spivak, "Can the Subaltern Speak?," in *Marxism and the Interpretation of Culture*, ed. Cary Nelson and Lawrence Grossberg (Urbana: University of Illinois Press, 1988), 271–313.

assumptions nor their own authority in imposing the modern concept of patriarchy on ancient Israel, become akin to colonialists interpreting the experiences of others in terms of their own experiences of oppression without understanding the nuance of the culture under study.

In her work "Marginality as a Site of Resistance" (1990) bell hooks formulates the colonialist discourse of the oppressed in the following way:

[There is] no need to hear your voice, when I can talk about you better than you can speak about yourself. No need to hear your voice. Only tell me about your pain. I want to know your story. And then I will tell it back to you in a new way. Tell it back to you in such a way that it has become mine, my own. Re-writing you, I write myself anew. I am still author, authority. I am still [the] colonizer, the speaking subject, and you are now at the center of my talk.[25]

And so *post-colonialist feminist social scientists* conceive of their goal as listening to the subaltern subjects on their own terms, in their own contexts, without ascending to a position of dominance over the voice and thereby subjugating its words to the meanings we want to attribute to them within our own worldview. By subsuming the voices of subalterns into our own frameworks, we assume that our writings can serve as a transparent medium through which the voices of the oppressed can be represented, essentializing the subaltern and thus replicating the colonialist discourses we purport to critique. In other words, we "other" the subalterns even as we try to redeem them from having been "othered." Spivak reminds us that a person's or group's identity is relational, a function of its place in a system of differences. There is no true or pure "other"—instead, the "Other" always already exists in relation to the discourse that would name it as "other." By using the term "patriarchy," feminist biblical critics are naming "women" and "men" as whole categories in opposition to each other in ancient Israel; thus feminist readings of the biblical text are pre-determining a reality, imposing a framework from their own set of discourses and experiences, onto the ancient world. Perhaps, as Spivak suggests, the subalterns can never speak for themselves; but certainly through social-scientific methods that attempt to reconstruct the ancient frameworks rather than imposing our own, we have a better chance of hearing *their* voices and understanding *their* experiences.

It wasn't long before this ongoing conversation with my students (and in my head) found its way back into my Hebrew Bible class, in the context of "The Rape of Dinah." The ways in which feminist biblical scholars write about Genesis 34 illustrate this tendency to impose a modern voice on an ancient literary character for the purpose of decrying the patriarchy of the culture that produced the character.[26] In this story, Jacob's daughter Dinah has sexual intercourse with the prince of Shechem, who then asks Jacob for his daughter's hand in marriage. Dinah's brothers are angry that the intercourse took place without their knowledge and prior to negotiations around bride-price, depriving them of their ability to have a say in their familial marital alliances. Through deception, two of Dinah's brothers massacre the men of the town and capture the women and children.

Many modern biblical translations sub-title this story "The Rape of Dinah." And building on this assertion that Dinah was raped, feminist biblical scholars have produced a mountain of protest literature against the biblical text, the society that produced the text, and the culture that continues to use the text for spiritual guidance. A curious fact, however, is that there is no single word for "rape" in Biblical Hebrew, and there is no clear sense in the narrative that Dinah was coerced into

---

[25] bell hooks, "Marginality as a Site of Resistance," in *Out There: Marginalization and Contemporary Cultures*, ed. R. Ferguson et al. (Cambridge: MIT, 1990), 241–43.
[26] See, e.g., Susanne Scholz, *Rape Plots: A Feminist Cultural Study of Genesis 34* (New York: Peter Lang, 2000), and Caroline Blyth, "Terrible Silence, Eternal Silence: A Feminist Re-Reading of Dinah's Voicelessness in Genesis 34," *Biblical Interpretation: A Journal of Contemporary Approaches* 17, no. 5 (2009): 483–507.

sexual intercourse against her will. To be fair, there is no clear sense that she wasn't either. The scribes who constructed and transmitted this story are rather completely unconcerned with the question of Dinah's consent, and Dinah herself does not speak a single word in the story. And this is where the feminist social scientist ought to begin investigating: the issue of what we can learn about the society—and specifically the scribal agents responsible—that produced this text starts with the question of why Dinah's consent is not an issue to the authors, rather than with assumptions around bodily autonomy projected from our world onto theirs in order to castigate a society that would allow for Dinah's presumed bodily autonomy to be presumably attacked.

The biblical text tells us that Shechem saw Dinah, took her, lay with her, and then did something connoted by the Hebrew verb ענה (*'innah*). That final verb is a difficult one to translate, and is the one that many modern translators render in English with the word "rape."[27]

The modern concept of rape that many scholars read into this text is characterized by an aggressive act and lack of mutual consent. Rape does clearly occur in another instance in the Bible, and the word *'innah* is also found there: in 2 Samuel 13 Amnon rapes Tamar, with Tamar's lack of consent made clear by her protests. But there is a difference in the wording of both episodes as well. Genesis 34:2 states that the prince "took her and lay her down and *'innah*-ed her." In contrast, in 2 Sam 13:14, despite Tamar's protests, Amnon "overpowered [or "seized"—יחזק] her, he *'innah*-ed her, and he lay with [שכב] her."

The fact that the word *'innah* is found in both cases does not demonstrate that if Tamar is raped and this verb is used, then Dinah must have been raped as well. In fact, this same word *'innah* is used in Genesis 16 to describe what Sarah does to her handmaid Hagar, in her jealousy that Hagar was pregnant while Sarah was barren; this *'innah* action causes Hagar to flee from Sarah. There is no indication in the biblical text, in the history of interpretation, or in any translation in English (or any other language) that anyone thinks that Sarah rapes Hagar here. If this word doesn't mean "rape" here, then the word *'innah* cannot be translated as "rape" elsewhere: it must mean something else.[28]

Deuteronomy 22 develops laws about adultery, specifically construed in that text as sex with a virginal woman who is betrothed to another man, and posits two scenarios: one in which the woman is presumed to have consented, and the other in which she is presumed not to have consented. Deuteronomy 22:23 states that if a man sleeps with a betrothed virgin in the city the woman is

---

[27] I first developed this argument along with my colleague, Risa Levitt Kohn (in "Parshat Vayishlah," in *The Torah: A Women's Commentary*, ed. T. C. Eskenazi and A. L. Weiss [New York: Union of Reform Judaism Press, 2008], 183–201). We were asked to write a commentary on the Torah portion in which the story of Dinah appeared; however, the translation was provided for us by a third party, putting us in the curious position of writing in our commentary that the word *'innah*, found in the biblical text in translation alongside our commentary as "rape," did not in fact mean rape. The understanding developed by Levitt Kohn and me drew on many other studies since the 1990s that argued for ambiguity in the text's description of Shechem's actions toward Dinah, and likewise questioned the traditional understanding of "rape" here: e.g. Lyn M. Bechtel, "What If Dinah Is Not Raped?," *JSOT* 62 (1994): 19–36; Claudia Camp, "The (E)strange(d) Woman in the Land: Sojourning with Dinah," in her *Wise, Strange and Holy: The Strange Woman and the Making of the Bible* (Sheffield: Sheffield Academic, 2000), Chapter 7; Joseph Fleishman, "Shechem and Dinah—in the Light of Non-Biblical and Biblical Sources," *ZAW* 116 (2004): 12–31; Tikva Frymer-Kensky, "Law and Philosophy: The Case of Sex in the Bible," in her *Studies in Bible and Feminist Criticism* (Philadelphia: The Jewish Publication Society, 2006, 5766), Chapter 16; M. Gruber, "A Re-examination of the Charges against Shechem Son of Hamor," *Beit Mikra Quarterly* 54 (1999): 119–27; Ita Sheres, *Dinah's Rebellion: A Biblical Parable for Our Time* (New York: Crossroad, 1990); Ellen van Wolde, "Does *'Innâ* Denote Rape? A Semantic Analysis of a Controversial Word," *VT* 52 (2002): 528; N. Wyatt, "The Story of Dinah and Shechem," *UF* 22 (1990): 433–58; and more recently, the excellent and thorough discussion in Chapter 3 of Eve Levavi Feinstein's *Sexual Pollution in the Hebrew Bible* (Oxford: Oxford University Press, 2014); and Alison Joseph, "Understanding Genesis 34:2: *'Innâ*," *VT* 66 (2016): 663–68.

[28] *'innah* is used in many places throughout the biblical text in ways that cannot be translated as "rape." In Deut 8:2, it describes God's actions toward Israel in the desert as he makes the slaves wander for forty years; in Lev 16 it is used to describe what the Israelites are to do to their inner-selves on Yom HaKippurim.

presumed to have consented and faces the same capital punishment as her lover, because in the city if she had cried out in protest someone would have heard her. The verb used to describe the action here is the same as in 2 Samuel 13: שכב, "to lie (with)"—English "to lay" works well here too. In Deut 22:24, the law concludes that both the man and the woman must be executed: the woman because she was in the city and no one heard her cry out in protest, and the man on account of the fact that he *'innah*-ed the wife of his neighbor. If the point of this law is that the woman is presumed to have consented, then *'innah* here cannot mean rape.

The law continues: in Deut 22:25, if the same offense takes place in the country, the betrothed virgin is presumed innocent because no one would have heard her protest, and therefore only the man is executed. From the description here and contrast with the previous law, this is clearly a case of non-consensual sex, or rape. The man's sexual act with her is recounted differently in the text of this law from the way in which it is described in the case of sleeping with the woman in town. Rather than simply using the term שכב, Deut 22:25 describes this encounter with the betrothed virgin in the country as "he overpowered (חזק) her and lay with (שכב) her." These are the same terms (חזק and שכב) used to describe Tamar's encounter with Amnon.

The verbal expression in common to both clear instances of non-consensual sex in 2 Samuel 13 and Deut 22:25 is based on the Hebrew root חזק (meaning "strength"). As a verb, this word is often translated "to take hold of" (also possible: "to seize," or "to overpower"). This verb is the one used for non-consensual sex (in our terms, "rape") in Deuteronomy (22:25) as well as in the story of Tamar and Amnon (2 Sam 13:14): not *'innah*. Notably, this expression using the verbal root חזק is *not* used in Genesis 34 in the string of verbs describing what happened to Dinah. So what exactly happened to Dinah, as far as the narrator is concerned? What does *'innah* mean?

From the usage in Deuteronomy (e.g. 22:23–24) and in Genesis 16, one can conclude that *'innah* denotes a downward movement in a social sense, meaning to "debase" or "humiliate" as in Genesis 16, or to lower a person's status, as in Genesis 34; or even to "violate" as in Deut 22:24—but a violation that is not dependent on the woman's consent, and therefore not equivalent to our concept of rape. Dinah's virginity has been violated, regardless of whether she consented: her status is clearly lowered from a virgin in her father's house, able to fetch a virgin's bride-price and be of maximal use to her family's negotiations for alliances through marriage with other kinship groups, to a non-virgin in a stranger's house, no longer of use to her own kin for political purposes. Though an offense to Dinah's family, the fact that Shechem has committed *'innah* on Dinah does not—and cannot—carry with it the psychological and emotional implications for the woman that the contemporary notion of rape suggests. In this particular text, the woman has no voice, and the narrator has no interest in whether or not she consented to the sexual act. In the context of the ancient Near East, by sleeping with someone without her family's consent to marriage, Dinah would have been considered to have been *'innah*-ed whether or not she consented.[29]

If we pay attention to them, scribal linguistic strategies provide social-scientific insights into the culture their narrative was originally intended to address. Modern presentist approaches that read rape into the text infer from, and imbue the story with, different meanings and thereby obscure the worldview of its ancient context. Whether we envision the story's context as that of fathers relating it to sons, or male scribes writing for a male audience, the sociological frameworks of its origin determine the type of rhetorical and even lexical choices scribes make while transmitting and developing narrative traditions. To understand Dinah's story as told here, we should look at the narrative's internal explanations and word choices to describe what has befallen her.

---

[29] See similarly Frymer-Kensky, *Women of the Bible*, 182.

The brothers' motive for deceiving the Shechemites into circumcising themselves only to fall by the brothers' swords, is explained in 34:13: Shechem had defiled (טמא) their sister Dinah. This is a word usually reserved to describe ritual pollution, not sexual behavior. How had Shechem's sexual encounter with Dinah defiled her? The brothers give their answer in the form of a rhetorical question in 34:31: "He should make our sister like a prostitute?"

Rather than focusing on Dinah's consent, the story focuses on the result of her intercourse with Shechem: from her brothers' perspective, she has become טמא, polluted. As noted by Eve Levavi Feinstein and Tikvah Frymer-Kensky, the brothers' exclamation that Shechem treated Dinah as a prostitute is the key to understanding why the narrative uses the term טמא to describe Dinah's state: Shechem had intercourse with Dinah as though she lacked the protection and guardianship of father and brothers, and in so doing, brought shame on Dinah's family.[30] In other words, the problem is one of violating familial, and not personal or bodily, boundaries; or more aptly put, in the case of women in ancient Israel, there was no conceptual difference between the boundaries of her physical body and the social body of her family.

Thus, despite the protests, outcries, and denigrations of a text that would feature the victimization of Jacob's daughter, and the sympathy and support of modern feminist biblical scholars who feel the need to voice Dinah's anger, shame, humiliation, and betrayal, this story is not about the rape of Dinah at all. It is tangentially about the lowering of Dinah's social status as she moves from fulfilling the proper role in the proper place (virgin daughter in her father's house) to a socially ambiguous role with no proper corresponding physical place. But her story serves as a warning pointing to the larger, and overriding issue of the political and ethnic identity of the Israelites in relation to the other people in the land. That is the reason for the story's inclusion in the text, and that is the focus of the recounting. Suspending our judgments about "patriarchy" and what kind of bodily autonomy Dinah *ought* to have, allows us to better understand the context in which the text was written. This was a context in which the bodies of daughters—and of sons, slaves, wives, and even men—were part of a larger entity than the individual. Marriage alliances were forged by the family unit and dominated by fathers and brothers for the good of the family, clan, and tribe. These—and not the individual—were the building blocks of ancient Israelite society. And these corporate concerns are what informed the locution and rhetoric of the scribes who developed this story, and also justified—even necessitated—the inclusion of Genesis 34 in the larger narrative about Israel's lineage and territory.

Being feminist social scientists who allow the ancients to speak for themselves and who do not impose our own modern conceptions of sexual independence and bodily autonomy onto ancient peoples, we need to recognize that there is a fundamental difference between our modern concept of rape and a literary creation which features a sexual and potential marital alliance not consented to by Dinah's family.

In denying the relevance of history, feminist literary criticism is ultimately plagued most deeply by the problem of cultural relativism. Historians—and especially social scientific ones, heavily influenced by the tools and methods of anthropology—are trained not to judge the societies we study. Our purpose is to understand them, as much as possible, in emic terms; with the growing explicit acknowledgment that objectivity is unattainable, and perhaps even undesirable. Historians are not interested in criticizing the past for not having the values of the present; and when feminist biblical scholars do this, they make their work irrelevant—and even antithetical—to the historical task. Historical study of the Bible—as with the study of religion in general, as it has developed in the academy over the last century—defines itself precisely against value-loaded critical readings

---

[30]Frymer-Kensky, "Virginity in the Bible," 89; and Feinstein *Sexual Pollution in the Hebrew Bible*, 76.

of sacred texts, whether laudatory or condemning. The task of a historian is to investigate, not to evaluate.

Feminists in other fields have moved beyond use of the term "patriarchy" for exactly that reason; it is not helpful, and in fact is harmful to understanding the subjects under study.[31] Third-wave feminism rejects the strict dichotomy of male–female, and the strict hierarchy implied by the term "patriarchy," noting instead that power structures are more nuanced, and outsider imposition of capitalist, post-industrialist categories like "patriarchy" are just as contested as the power structures such categories seek to subvert. Feminist historians and other social scientists are interested neither in finding and decrying nor in finding and rectifying male dominance of women in the societies and cultures they study. This however has been, and remains, the central focus of feminist biblical scholarship as it is construed at the Society of Biblical Literature, in published research, and at universities everywhere in syllabi focused on "women in the Hebrew Bible"—both by feminist biblical scholars who consider their work confessional, and by those whose work is (stridently) non-confessional.

Rejecting "patriarchy" is a step toward bringing together feminist literary criticism, feminist historical criticism, mainstream biblical scholarship, *and* feminist social science in other disciplines. Feminism defines itself by its attempt to give voice to the voiceless, be they women, men, slaves, children, or any other category of person. Feminist criticism can do this for the world of the Hebrew Bible; recover or at least reconstruct the voices, stories, histories, of the people who write and who are written, in terms that would be more familiar to that worldview; and *should* do this, should seek the voices of the various corporate bodies and communities within ancient Israel, beyond the hegemonic voices of both selected and selective authors of the biblical texts; *and* beyond the hegemonic voices of the biblical scholars—feminist or not—who read and seek to reify them as other. Giving them our voices—that is, giving voices to women as victims—doesn't tell us anything about ancient Israel and only serves political ends, while undermining the authority of feminist *historical* investigations into ancient Israel.

Continuing to use the term "patriarchy" in all of its connotative premises, can produce only polemics (confessional or non-confessional) about the way the Bible is used today to oppress women; polemics which are then used to inform biblical literary analyses from which are drawn conclusions about history (and the history of patriarchy). This circularity begins with the methodological flaw of reading modern constructions of patriarchy into an ancient text. In Meyers' words, using the term "patriarchy" imposes "contemporary feminist standards (which hope for an elimination of sexist tradition by seeking to promulgate equality between the sexes) to measure the cultural patterns of an ancient society struggling to establish its viability under circumstances radically different from contemporary western conditions."[32] This is not only antithetical to social-scientific inquiry, but to the very nature and purpose of feminist theory and method.

The student in my introductory Hebrew Bible class who remarked on the immorality of the patriarchs in Genesis felt very strongly that her own sense of what was moral was "right" and "true," and she was deeply disturbed that the presumed source of her moral compass, the Bible itself, seemed to disagree. This appears to be the starting point for many feminist biblical scholars as well. However, the basic premise in historical-critical investigation of the Bible should be that the Bible represents the ideals and values of an ancient foreign culture and *not* presentist ones—even if we are motivated in undertaking such investigation by present ideological, theological, or political concerns. A goal in biblical pedagogy in an academic setting should be to help students

---

[31]See Meyers, "Patriarchy."
[32]Meyers, *Rediscovering Eve*, 26.

understand how their senses of what is "right" and "true" are mediated by cultural presuppositions. Likewise, such constructed frameworks inform our understanding of (and categorization according to) gender, class, ethnicity, and other social performances. How we think about and reconstruct the activities and settings of scribes and scribalism is part of this equation. The projection of anachronistic models onto ancient Israelite society invariably impacts the ways in which we conceive of scribal hegemony over texts and the traditions they transmit. If we are historians who seek to understand these figures and their methods, to gain a sense of the processes of composition, compilation, and transmission of the biblical texts within the context of the society from which they emerged, it is crucial for us as scholars and as teachers to think carefully about our categories of analysis—like "patriarchy"—so that we might move beyond imposing contemporary constructions on these ancient texts and the scribes who produced them.

# BIBLIOGRAPHY

Abusch, Tzvi. "Ghost and God: Some Observations on a Babylonian Understanding of Human Nature." Pages 363–83 in *Self, Soul, and Body in Religious Experience*. Edited by Albert I. Baumgarten, Jan Assmann, and Guy G. Stroumsa. Leiden: Brill, 1998.

Achenbach, Reinhard. "Levitische Priester und Leviten im Deuteronomium. Überlegungen zur sog. 'Levitisierung' des Priestertums." *ZAR* 5 (1999): 285–309.

Ackerman, Susan. "Digging up Deborah: Recent Hebrew Bible Scholarship on Gender and the Contribution of Archaeology." *Near Eastern Archaeology* 66 (2003): 172–84.

Aharoni, Yohanan. *Arad Inscriptions*. Jerusalem: Israel Exploration Society, 1981.

———. *Investigations at Lachish: The Sanctuary and Residency*. Lachish 5. Tel Aviv: Institute of Archaeology, 1975.

Aḥituv, Shmuel, and Amihai Mazar. *Echoes from the Past. Hebrew and Cognate Inscriptions from the Biblical Period*. Jerusalem: Carta, 2008.

———. "The Inscriptions from Tel Reḥov and Their Contribution to Study of Script and Writing During the Iron Age IIA." Pages 39–68 in *"See, I Will Bring a Scroll Recounting What Befell Me" (Ps 40:8): Epigraphy and Daily Life—From the Bible to the Talmud Dedicated to the Memory of Professor Hanan Eshel*. Edited by Esther Eshel and Yigal Levin. JAJS 12. Göttingen: Vandenhoeck & Ruprecht, 2014.

———. "A New Moabite Inscription." *IMSA* 2 (2003): 3–10.

Aḥituv, Shmuel, Esther Eshel, and Ze'ev Meshel. "The Inscriptions." Pages 73–142 in *Kuntillet 'Ajrud (Ḥorvat Teman): An Iron Age II Religious Site on the Judah-Sinai Border*. Edited by Ze'ev Meshel and Liora Freud. Jerusalem: Israel Exploration Society, 2012.

Aḥituv, Shmuel, Eithan Klein, and Amir Ganor. "The 'Jerusalem' Papyrus: A Seventh-Century BCE Shipping Certificate." *IEJ* 67 (2017): 168–82.

Aitken, James K. *The Semantics of Blessing and Cursing in Ancient Hebrew*. Dudley, MA: Peeters, 2007.

Albertz, Rainer, James D. Nogalski, and Jakob Wöhrle, eds. *Perspectives on the Formation of the Book of the Twelve: Methodological Foundations—Redactional Processes—Historical Insights*. BZAW 433. Berlin: de Gruyter, 2012.

Albright, W. F. "The Gezer Calendar." *BASOR* 92 (1943): 16–26.

———. "The Phoenician Inscriptions of the Tenth Century B.C. from Byblus." *JAOS* 67 (1947): 153–60.

Alexandre, Yardenna. "A Canaanite-Early Phoenician Inscribed Bronze Bowl in an Iron Age IIA-B Burial Cave at Kefar Veradim, Northern Israel." *Maarav* 13 (2006): 7–41, 129–32.

———. "The 'Hippo' Jar and Other Storage Jars at Hurvat Rosh Zayit." *TA* 22 (1995): 77–88.

Amadasi Guzzo, and Maria Giulia. "'Alphabet insaisissable'. Quelques notes concernant la diffusion de l'écriture consonantique." *Transeuph* 44 (2014): 67–86.

Andersen, Francis I. *Habakkuk: A New Translation with Introduction and Commentary*. AB 25. New York Doubleday, 2001.

Andersen, Francis I., and David Noel Freedman. *Amos: A New Translation with Introduction and Commentary*. AB 24A. New York, Doubleday, 1989.

Andiñach, Pablo R. "The Locusts in the Message of Joel." *VT* 42 (1992): 433–41.

Arnaoutoglou, I. *Ancient Greek Laws: A Sourcebook*, London: Routledge, 1998.

Ash, Paul S. "Solomon's? District? List." *JSOT* 67 (1995): 67–86.

Assis, Elie. *The Book of Joel: A Prophet between Calamity and Hope*. LHBOTS 581. New York: Bloomsbury, 2013.

Athas, George. *The Tel Dan Inscription: A Reappraisal and a New Interpretation*. JSOTSup 360. London: Sheffield Academic, 2003.

Aufrecht, Walter E. *A Corpus of Ammonite Inscriptions*. 2d ed. University Park: Eisenbrauns, 2019.

Avigad, Nahman. *Hebrew Bullae from the Time of Jeremiah: Remnants of a Burnt Archive*. Jerusalem: Israel Exploration Society, 1986.

Avishur, Yitzhak. *Phoenician Inscriptions and the Bible: Select Inscriptions and Studies in Stylistic and Literary Devices Common to the Phoenician Inscriptions and the Bible*. Tel Aviv: Archaeological Center Publication, 2000.

Avrahami, Yael. *The Senses of Scripture: Sensory Perception in the Hebrew Bible*. New York: T&T Clark International, 2012.

Baden, Joel S. *The Promise to the Patriarchs*. Oxford: Oxford University Press, 2013.

**Báez, Fernando. *A Universal History of the Destruction of Books: From Ancient Sumer to Modern Iraq*. Translated by A. MacAdam. New York: Atlas & Co, 2008.**

Baines, John. *Visual and Written Culture in Ancient Egypt*. New York: Oxford University Press, 2007.

Baker, David W. "Scribes as Transmitters of Tradition." Pages 65–77 in *Faith, Tradition & History: Old Testament Historiography in its Near Eastern Context*. Edited by A. R. Millard et al. Winona Lake: Eisenbrauns, 1994.

Bal, Mieke. 1990. "Review of Discovering Eve: Ancient Israelite Women in Context." *JAAR* (1990): 511–13.

Barkay, Gabriel. "Iron Age II–III." Pages 302–73 in *Archaeology of Ancient Israel*. Edited by Ammon Ben-Tor. Raanana: Open University of Jerusalem, 1992.

Barkay, Gabriel, Andrew G. Vaughn, Marilyn J. Lundberg, and Bruce Zuckerman. "The Amulets from Ketef Hinnom: A New Edition and Evaluation." *BASOR* 334 (2004): 41–71.

Barthes, Roland. *S/Z: An Essay*. Translated by Richard Miller. New York: Hill & Wang, 1974.

Barton, John. *Joel and Obadiah: A Commentary*. OTL. Louisville: Westminster John Knox, 2001.

Baurain, C. *Les Grecs et la Méditerranée orientalie: Des siècles obscurs à la fin de l'époque archaïque*. Nouvelle Clio. Paris: Presses Universitaires de France, 1997.

Beattie, A. J. "Some Notes on the Spensithios Decree." *Kadmos* 15 (1975): 8–47.

Bechtel, Lyn M. "What If Dinah Is Not Raped? (Genesis 34)." *JSOT* 19 (1994): 19–36.

Beit-Arieh, Itzhak. "**A Literary Ostracon from** Ḥorvat ʿUza." *TA* 20 (1993): 55–63.

Bekkum, Koert van. "'The Situation Is More Complicated': Archaeology and Text in the Historical Reconstruction of the Iron Age IIA Southern Levant." Pages 215–44 in *Exploring the Narrative: Jerusalem and Jordan in the Bronze and Iron Ages: Papers in Honour of Margreet Steiner*. Edited by Noor Mulder-Hymans et al. LHBOTS 583. London/New York: Bloomsbury T&T Clark, 2014.

Ben Zvi, Ehud. *A Historical-Critical Study of the Book of Zephaniah*. BZAW 198. Berlin: de Gruyter, 1991.

———. "The List of Levitical Cities." *JSOT* 54 (1992): 77–106.

———. "A Sense of Proportion. An Aspect of the Theology of the Chronicler." Pages 160–173 in *History, Literature and Theology in the Book of Chronicles*. Edited by E. Ben Zvi. BibleWorld. London/Oakville: Equinox 2006.

Ben Zvi, Ehud, and Michael H. Floyd, eds. *Writings and Speech in Israelite and Ancient Near Eastern Prophecy*. SymS 10. Atlanta: Society of Biblical Literature, 2000.

Berlin, Adele. *Zephaniah: A New Translation with Introduction and Commentary*. AB 25A. New York: Doubleday, 1994.

Bessac, Jean-Claude. "Les roches de construction d'Ougarit: production, façonnage, mise en ouevre." Pages 111–41 in *Étudies ougaritiques III*. Edited by Valérie Matoian and Michael al-Maqdissi. RSO 21. Leuven: Peeters, 2013.

Beyerlein, Walter. *Herkunft und Geschichte der ältesten Sinaitraditionen*. Tübingen: Mohr Siebeck, 1961.

Bile, M. *Le dialecte Crétois ancien. Étude de la langue des inscriptios receuil des inscriptions postérieures aux IC*. École française d'Athènes. Études Crétoises 27. Paris: Paul Geuthner, 1988.

Blenkinsopp, Joseph. *Isaiah 1–39: A New Translation with Introduction and Commentary*. AB 19. New York: Doubleday, 2000.

——— . "The Sage, the Scribe, and Scribalism in the Chronicler's Work." Pages 307–15 in *The Sage in Israel and the Ancient Near East*. Edited by J. G. Gammie and L. G. Perdue. Winona Lake: Eisenbrauns 1990.

Block, Daniel I. *The Book of Ezekiel: Chapters 1–24*. NICOT. Grand Rapids: Eerdmans, 1997.

Blum, Erhard. "Die altaramäischen Wandinschriften vom Tell Deir 'Alla und ihr institutioneller Kontext." Pages 21–52 in *Materiale Textkulturen: Konzepte – Materialen – Praktiken*. Edited by Thomas Meier et al. Berlin: de Gruyter, 2015.

——— . "Die Kombination I der Wandinschrift vom Tell Deir 'Alla. Vorschläge zur Rekonstruktion mit historisch-kritischen Anmerkungen." Pages 573–601 in *Berührungspunkte: Studien zur Sozial- und Religionsgeschichte Israels und seiner Umwelt. Festschrift für Rainer Albertz zu seinem 65. Geburtstag*. Edited by Ingo Kottsieper et al. AOAT 350. Münster: Ugarit-Verlag, 2008.

——— . "'Versteht du dich nicht auf die Schreibkunst…?' Ein weisheitlicher Dialog über Vergänglichkeit und Verantwortung. Kombination II der Wandinschrift vom Tell Deir 'Alla." Pages 33–53 in *Was ist der Mensch, dass du seiner gedenkst? (Psalm 8,5): Aspekte einer theologischen Anthropologie. Festschrift für Bernd Janowski zum 65. Geburtstag*. Edited by Michaela Bauks et al. Neukirchen-Vluyn: Neukirchener Verlag, 2008.

——— . "Die Wandinschriften 4.2 und 4.6 sowie die Pithos-Inschrift 3.9 aus *Kuntillet 'Aǧrūd*." ZDPV 129 (2013): 21–54.

Blyth, Caroline. "Terrible Silence, Eternal Silence: A Feminist Re-Reading of Dinah's Voicelessness in Genesis 34." *BibInt* 17 (2009): 483–507.

Bolin, Thomas M. *Ecclesiastes and the Riddle of Authorship*. New York: Routledge, 2017.

Bottéro, Jean. *Mesopotamia: Writing, Reasoning, and the Gods*. Translated by Zainab Bahrani and Marcvan de Mieroop. Chicago: University of Chicago Press, 1992.

Boyd, Samuel L., Humphrey H. Hardy II, and Benjamin D. Thomas. "Two New Inscriptions from Zincirli and Its Environs." *BASOR* 356 (2009): 73–80.

Braulik, Georg, *Deuteronomium Teil 1: 1–16,17*. NEB 15. Würzburg: Echter, 1986.

Breasted, James H. *Ancient Records of Egypt: Historical Documents from the Earliest Times to the Persian Conquest*, vol. 4. Chicago: University of Chicago Press, 1906.

Brichto, Herbert Chanan. "Kin, Cult, Land and Afterlife: A Biblical Complex." *HUCA* 44 (1973): 1–54.

Britt, Brian. "Deuteronomy 31–32 as a Textual Memorial." *BibInt* 8 (2000): 358–74.

Brooke, George J. "Levi and the Levites in the Dead Sea Scrolls and the New Testament." Pages 115–39 in *The Dead Sea Scrolls and the New Testament: Essays in Mutual Illumination*. Edited by G. J. Brooke. London: Fortress Press, 2005.

Brosius, Martha, ed. *Ancient Archives and Archival Traditions*. Oxford: Oxford University Press, 2003.

Buck, C. D. *The Greek Dialects: Grammar, Selected Inscriptions, Glossary*. Chicago: University of Chicago Press, 1955.

Budin, Stephanie. "Phallic Fertility in the Ancient Near East and Egypt." Pages 25–38 in *Reproduction: Antiquity to the Present Day*. Edited by N. Hopwood et al. Cambridge: Cambridge University Press, 2018.

Bunimovitz, Shlomo, and Zvi Lederman. "Beth-Shemesh: Culture Conflict on Judah's Frontier." *Biblical Archaeology Review* 23 (1997): 42–49, 75–77.

———. "The Early Israelite Monarchy in the Sorek Valley: Tel Beth-Shemesh and Tel Batash (Timnah) in the 10th and 9th Centuries BCE." Pages 407–28 in *"I Will Speak the Riddles of Ancient Times": Archaeological and Historical Studies in Honor of Amihai Mazar on the Occasion of His Sixtieth Birthday*. Edited by Aren M. Maeir et al. Winona Lake: Eisenbrauns, 2006.

Burkes, Shannon. *Death in Qoheleth and Egyptian Biographies of the Late Period*. Atlanta: Society of Biblical Literature, 1999.

Burlingame, Andrew. "Line Five of the Amman Citadel Inscription: History of Interpretation and a New Proposal." *BASOR* 376 (2016): 63–82.

Byrne, Ryan C. "The Refuge of Scribalism in Iron I Palestine." *BASOR* 345 (2007): 1–31.

Camp, Claudia V. *Wise, Strange and Holy: The Strange Woman and the Making of the Bible* (Sheffield: Sheffield Academic, 2000).

Cancik-Kirschbaum, Eva, and Babette Schnitzlein, eds. *Keilschriftartefakte: Untersuchungen zur Materialität von Keilschriftdokumenten*. BBVO 26. Gladbeck: PeWe Verlag, 2018.

Carasik, Michael. "To See a Sound: A Deuteronomic Rereading of Exodus 20:15." *Prooftexts* 19 (1999): 257–65.

Carawan, E. "What the *Mnemones* Know." Pages 163–84 in *Orality, Literacy, Memory in the Ancient Greek and Roman World*. Mn.S 278. Edited by E. A. Mackay. Leiden: Brill, 2008.

Carlson Hasler, Laura. *Archival Historiography in Jewish Antiquity*. Oxford: Oxford University Press, forthcoming.

Carr, D. M. *The Formation of the Hebrew Bible*. Oxford: Oxford University Press, 2011.

———. *Writing on the Tablet of the Heart: Origins of Scripture and Literature*, Oxford: Oxford University Press, 2005.

Carroll Robert *Jeremiah: A Commentary*. OTL. Philadelphia: Westminster, 1986.

Carstens, Pernille. "The Torah as Canon of Masterpieces: Remembering in Archives." Pages 309–23 in *Cultural Memory in Biblical Exegesis*. Edited by P. Carstens et al. Piscataway, NJ: Gorgias Press, 2012.

Ceccarelli, P. *Ancient Greek Letter Writing: A Cultural History* (600 BC – 150 BC). Oxford: Oxford University Press, 2013.

Certeau, Michel de. *The Practice of Everyday Life*. Translated by S. F. Randall. University of California Press, 1984.

Chapman, Cynthia Ruth. "Modern Terms and Their Ancient Non-Equivalents. Patrilineality and Gender in the Historical Study of the Bible." *HeBAI* 5 (2016): 78–93.

Childs, Brevard S. *Isaiah*. OTL. Louisville: Westminster John Knox, 2001.

Christ, Carol, and Judith Plaskow. *Womanspirit Rising*. San Francisco: Harper & Row, 1979.

Christensen, Duane L. *Nahum: A New Translation with Introduction and Commentary*. AYB 24F. New Haven: Yale University Press, 2009.

Clines, David J. A., ed. *The Dictionary of Classical Hebrew*, vol. 7. Sheffield: Sheffield Academic, 2010.

Coldstream, Nicolas, and Amihai Mazar. "Greek Pottery from Tel Rehov and Iron Age Chronology." *IEJ* 53 (2003): 29–48.

Cook, Edward M. "Olive Pits and Alef-Bets: Notes on the Qeiyafa Ostracon." *Ralph the Sacred River*, March 14, 2010. http://ralphriver.blogspot.com/2010/03/olive-pits-and-alef-bets-notes-on.html.

Cook, Stephen L. *The Social Roots of Biblical Yahwism*. Atlanta: SBL, 2004.

Cooke, G. A. *A Critical and Exegetical Commentary on the Book of Ezekiel*. ICC. Edinburgh: T. & T. Clark, 1936.

Cowley, Arthur E. *Aramaic Papyri of the Fifth Century B.C*. Oxford: Clarendon Press, 1923.

Crawford, S. W. *Rewriting Scripture in Second Temple Times*. Studies in the Dead Sea Scrolls and Related Literature. Grand Rapids: Eerdmans, 2008.

Crenshaw, James L. *Joel: A New Translation with Introduction and Commentary*. AB 24C. New York: Doubleday, 1995.

Crenshaw, James L. *Ecclesiastes: A Commentary*. Philadelphia: Westminster, 1987.

———. "Education in Ancient Israel." *JBL* 104 (1985): 601–15.

Cross, Frank Moore. "Epigraphic Notes on Hebrew Documents of the Eighth–Sixth Centuries B.C.: II. The Murabbaʿât Papyrus and the Letter Found Near Yabneh Yam." *BASOR* 165 (1962): 34–46.

———. "A Fragment of a Monumental Inscription from the City of David." *IEJ* 51 (2001): 44–47.

———. *Leaves from an Epigrapher's Notebook. Collected Papers in Hebrew and West Semitic Palaeography and Epigraphy*. HSS 51. Winona Lake: Eisenbrauns, 2003.

———. "The Origin and Early Evolution of the Alphabet." *Eretz-Israel* 8 (1967): 8*–24*.

———. "A Suggested Reading of the Ḥorvat ʿUza Ostracon." *TA* 20 (1993): 64–65.

Dahmen, Ulrich, *Leviten und Priester im Deuteronomium: Literarkritische und redaktionsgeschichtliche Studien*. BBB 110. Bodenheim: Philo Verlag 1996.

Dajani, R. W. "The Amman Theater Fragment." *ADAJ* 12–13 (1967–68): 65–67.

Daly, Mary. *Beyond God the Father: Toward a Philosophy of Women's Liberation*. Boston: Beacon Press, 1973.

Davies, Philip R. *Scribes and Schools. The Canonizing of the Hebrew Scriptures*. Library of Ancient Israel. Louisville: John Knox Press, 1998.

Davis, Ellen F. *Swallowing the Scroll: Textuality and the Dynamics of Discourse in Ezekiel's Prophecy*. JSOTSup 78. Sheffield: Almond, 1989.

Dearman, J. Andrew. "My Servants the Scribes: Composition and Context in Jeremiah 36." *JBL* 109 (1990): 403–21.

———, ed. *Studies in the Mesha Inscription and Moab*. ABS 2. Atlanta: Scholars Press, 1989.

Demsky, Aaron. "The Jerusalem Ceramic Inscription." Sidebar in "Artifact Found Near Temple Mount Bearing Canaanite Inscription from the Time before King David." *Foundation Stone*, July 7, 2013. http://www.foundationstone.org/mazar/.

———. "Writing in Ancient Israel and Ancient Judaism, Part One: The Biblical Period." Pages 2–20 in *Mikra: Text, Translation, Reading and Interpretation of the Hebrew Bible in Ancient Judaism and Early Christianity*. Minneapolis: Fortress Press, 1990.

Detienne, M. "L'espace de la publicité, ses opérateurs intellectuels dans la cite." Pages 29–81 in *Les savoirs de l'écriture en Grèce ancienn*. Edited by M. Detienne. Cahiers de Philologique 14. Lille: Presses universitaire, 1992.

Devecchi, Elena, Gerfried, G. W. Müller, and Jana Mynářová, eds. *Current Research in Cuneiform Palaeography: Proceedings of the Workshop Organized at the 60th Rencontre Assyriologique Internationale, Warsaw 2014*. Gladbeck: PeWe-Verlag, 2015.

Diels, H., and W. Kranz. *Die Fragmente der Vorsokratiker II*. 6th ed. Berlin: Weidemann, 1952.

Dietrich, Walter. "Die Überführung der Lade nach Jerusalem (2 Sam 6): Geschichten und Geschichte." Pages 191–206 in *Die Samuelbücher im deuteronomistischen Geschichtswerk. Studien zu den Geschichtsüberlieferungen des Alten Testaments II*. BWANT 201. Stuttgart: Kohlhammer 2012.

———. *Nahum Habakkuk Zephaniah*. Translated by Peter Altmann. IECOT. Stuttgart: Kohlhammer, 2016.

Dobbs-Allsopp, F. W. *On Biblical Poetry*. Oxford: Oxford University Press, 2015.

Dobbs-Allsopp, F. W., J. J. M. Roberts, C. L. Seow, and R. E. Whitaker. *Hebrew Inscriptions: Texts from the Biblical Period of the Monarchy with Concordance*. New Haven: Yale University Press, 2005.

Dolansky, Shawna, and Sarah Shectman. "What Is Gendered Historiography and How Do You Do It?" *JHS*, forthcoming.

Donner, Herbert, and Wolfgang Röllig. *Kanaanäische und aramäische Inschriften*. 3 vols. 2d ed. Wiesbaden: Harrassowitz, 1966–69. 5th ed., 2002.

Dorsey, David A. *The Roads and Highways of Ancient Israel*. ASOR Library of Biblical and Near Eastern Archaeology. Baltimore: Johns Hopkins University Press, 1991.

Du Toit, Jacqueline S. *Textual Memory: Ancient Archives, Libraries, and the Hebrew Bible*. Sheffield: Sheffield Phoenix, 2011.

Duhm, Bernard. *Das Buch Jeremia*. Tübingen: Mohr, 1901.

Dummermuth, Friedrich. "Zur deuteronomischen Kulttheologie und ihren Voraussetzungen." *ZAW* 70 (1958): 59–98.

Duru, Refik. *Yesemek: The Largest Sculpture Workshop of the Ancient Near East*. Istanbul: Türsab, 2004.

Dušek, Jan. *Les manuscrits araméens du Wadi Daliyeh et la Samarie vers 450–332 av. J.-C.* CHANE 30. Leiden: Brill, 2007.

Edelman Diana V. "From Prophets to Prophetic Books: The Fixing of the Divine Word." Pages 29–54 in *The Production of Prophecy: Constructing Prophecy and Prophets in Yehud*. Edited by Diana V. Edelman and Ehud Ben Zvi. London: Equinox, 2009.

——— . "Introduction." Pages xi–xxiv in *Remembering Biblical Figures in the Late Persian and Early Hellenistic Periods: Social Memory and Imagination*. Edited by Diana V. Edelman and Ehud Ben Zvi. Oxford: Oxford University Press, 2013.

Edwards, G. P., and R. B. Edwards. "The Meaning and Etymology of *poinikastas*." *Kadmos* 16 (1977): 131–40.

——— . "Red Letters and Phoenician Writing." *Kadmos* 13 (1974): 48–57.

Effenterre, H. van, "Le contrat de travail du scribe Spensitios." *BCH* 97 (1973): 31–46.

——— . "Le statut compare des travailleurs étrangers en Chyphre, Crète et autres lieux à la fin de l'archaisme." Pages 279–93 in *Acts of the International Archaeological Symposium: The Relations between Cyprus and Crete, ca. 2000 – 500 B.C.* Nikosia: Department of Antiquities, 1979.

Eichrodt, Walther. *Ezekiel: A Commentary*. Translated by Cosslett Quin. OTL. Philadelphia: Westminster, 1970.

Elayi, Josette. "Four New Inscribed Phoenician Arrowheads." *Studi Epigrafici e Linguistici* 22 (2005): 35–45.

Erbse, H. *Scholia Graeca in Homeri Iliadem (scholia vetera)* II. Berlin: de Gruyter, 1971.

Erickson, B. "Eleutherna and the Greek World, ca. 600–400 B.C." Pages 199–212 in *Crete Beyond the Palaces: Proceedings of the Crete 2000 Conference*. Edited by L. P. Day, M. S. Mook and J. D. Muhly. Prehistory Monographs 10. Philadelphia: INSTAP Academic Press, 2004.

Eskenazi, Tamara Cohn, and Andrea L. Weiss. *The Torah: A Women's Commentary*. New York: Union of Reform Judaism Press, 2008.

Exum, J. Cheryl. "Second Thoughts about Secondary Characters: Women in Exodus 1.8–2.10." Pages 75–87 in *Feminist Companion to Exodus to Deuteronomy*. Edited by Athalya Brenner. Sheffield: Sheffield Academic, 2000.

Fagels, R., trans. *The Iliad*. London: Penguin, 1990.

Fander, Monica. "Historical-Critical Methods." Pages 205–24 in *Searching the Scriptures: A Feminist Introduction*. Edited by Elisabeth Schüssler Fiorenza. New York: Crossroad, 1993.

Feinstein, Eve Levavi. *Sexual Pollution in the Hebrew Bible*. New York: Oxford University Press, 2014.

Feldmeier, Reinhard, and Herrmann Spieckermann. *Der Gott der Liebe. Eine biblische Gotteslehre*. Topoi Biblischer Theologie / Topics of Biblical Theology 1. Tübingen: Mohr Siebeck, 2011.

Finkelstein, Israel. "Notes on the Historical Setting of Kuntillet 'Ajrud." *Maarav* 20 (2013 [2015]): 13–25.

Finkelstein, Israel, and Benjamin Sass. "The West Semitic Alphabetic Inscriptions, Late Bronze II to Iron IIA: Archeological Context, Distribution and Chronology." *HebAI* 2 (2013): 149–220.

Fischer-Hansen, T., T. H. Nielsen, and C. Ampolo. "Pithekoussai." Pages 285–87 in *An Inventory of Archaic and Classical Poleis: An Investigation Conducted by The Copenhagen Polis Centre for the Danish National Research Foundation*. Edited by M. H. Hansen and T. H. Nielsen. Oxford: Oxford University Press, 2004.

Fishbane, Michael. *Biblical Interpretation in Ancient Israel*. Oxford: Clarendon, 1985.

Fisher, Kevin D. "Investigating Monumental Social Space in Late Bronze Age Cyprus: An Integrative Approach." Pages 167–202 in *Spatial Analysis and Social Spaces*. Edited by Eleftheria Paliou et al. Berlin: de Gruyter, 2014.

Fitzmyer, Joseph A. *The Aramaic Inscriptions of Sefire*. BibOr 19/A. 2d ed. Rome: Pontifical Biblical Institute, 1995.

Fleishman, Joseph. "Shechem and Dinah in the Light of Non-Biblical and Biblical Sources." *ZAW* 116 (2006): 12–32.

Fleming, Daniel *The Legacy of Israel in Judah's Bible*. New York: Cambridge University Press, 2012.

Fornara, C. W. *Translated Documents of Greece and Rome*. Vol. 1, *Archaic Times to the End for the Peloponnesian War*. 2nd ed. Cambridge: Cambridge University Press, 1983.

Fox, Michael V. *Ecclesiastes*. Philadelphia: Jewish Publication Society, 2004.

———. "Frame-Narrative and Composition in the Book of Qohelet." *HUCA* 48 (1977): 83–106.

———. *A Time to Tear Down and a Time to Build Up: A Rereading of Ecclesiastes*. Grand Rapids: Eerdmans, 1999.

———. *Proverbs 1–9: A New Translation with Introduction and Commentary*. AB 18A. New York: Doubleday, 2000.

Fraser, P. M., and E. Matthews. *A Lexicon of Greek Personal Names*. Vol. 1, *The Aegean Islands, Cyprus, Cyrenaica*. Oxford: Clarendon Press, 1987.

Frymer-Kensky, Tikva Simone. *Studies in Bible and Feminist Criticism*. Philadelphia: The Jewish Publication Society, 2010.

Fulco, William J. "The Amman Theater Inscription." *JNES* 38 (1979): 37–38.

Gagarin, M. "The Laws of Crete." Pages 17–29 in *Transferts culturels et droits dans le monde grec et héllenistique. Actes du colloque international (Reims, 14–17 mai 2008)*. Edited by B. Legras. Histoire ancienne et médiévale 110. Paris: Publications du Sorbonne, 2012.

———. "Letters of the Law: Written Texts in Archaic Greek Law." Pages 59–77 in *Written Texts and the Rise of Literate Culture in Ancient Greece*. Edited by H. Yunis. Cambridge: Cambridge University Press, 2003.

———. *Writing Greek Law*. Cambridge: Cambridge University Press, 2008.

Gagarin, M., and P. Perlman. *The Laws of Ancient Crete c. 650–400 BCE*. Oxford: Oxford University Press, 2016.

Gardiner, Alan H. "The House of Life." *Journal of Egyptian Archaeology* 24 (1938): 157–79.

Garfinkel, Yosef, Mitka R. Golub, Haggai Misgav, and Saar Ganor. "The 'Išbaʿal Inscription from Khirbet Qeiyafa." *BASOR* 373 (2015): 217–33.

Gass, Erasmus. *Der Moabiter: Geschichte und Kultur eines ostjordanischen Volkes im 1. Jahrtausend v. Chr.* ADPV 38. Wiesbaden: Harrassowitz, 2009.

———. "New Moabite Inscriptions and Their Historical Relevance." *JNSL* 38 (2012): 45–78.

Geiger, Michaela, *Gottesräume: Die literarische und theologische Konzeption von Raum im Deuteronomium*. BWANT 183. Stuttgart: Kohlhammer 2010.

Gelb, Ignace Jay, ed. *The Assyrian Dictionary of the Oriental Institute of the University of Chicago*. Chicago: The Oriental Institute of the University of Chicago, 1956–2006.

Geoghegan, Jeffrey C. *The Time, Place and Purpose of the Deuteronomistic History: The Evidence of "Until This Day."* BJS. Providence: Brown University, 2006.

Gerber, D. E. *Greek Elegiac Poetry: From the Seventh to the Fifth Centuries BC.* LCL 258. Cambridge, MA: Harvard University Press, 1999.

Gesenius, Wilhelm. *Hebräisches und Aramäisches Handwörterbuch über das Alte Testament.* Edited by H. Zimmern et al. Springer, 1962 (reprint of the 1915 edition).

Gibson, John C. L. *Textbook of Syrian Semitic Inscriptions III: Phoenician Inscriptions Including Inscriptions in the Mixed Dialect of Arslan Tash.* Oxford: Clarendon Press, 1982.

Gitin, Seymour, Trude Dothan, and Joseph Naveh. "A Royal Dedicatory Inscription from Ekron." *IEJ* 47 (1997): 1–16.

Goldenberg, Naomi. *Changing of the God.* Boston: Beacon Press, 1979.

Goodley, A. D. *Herodotus Books V–VII.* LCL 119. Cambridge, MA: Harvard University Press, 1922.

Goody, J. *The Logic of Writing and the Organization of Society: Studies in Literacy, Family, Culture and the State.* Cambridge: Cambridge University Press, 1986.

Gorlin, C. E. "The Spensithios Decree and Archaic Cretan Civil Status." *ZPE* 74 (1988): 159–65.

Grabbe, Lester. *Ezra-Nehemiah.* London/New York: Routledge, 1998.

Gray, George Buchanan. *A Critical and Exegetical Commentary on the Book of Isaiah I–XXXIX.* Vol. 1. ICC. Edinburgh: T. & T. Clark, 1912.

Graybill, Rhiannon. *Are We Not Men: Unstable Masculinity in the Prophets.* Oxford: Oxford University Press, 2016.

Green, Douglas J. *"I Undertook Great Works": The Ideology of Domestic Achievements in West Semitic Royal Inscriptions.* Tübingen: Mohr Siebeck, 2010.

Greenberg, Moshe. *Ezekiel 1–20: A New Translation with Introduction and Commentary.* AB 22. Garden City, NY: Doubleday, 1983.

Grosman, Leore, Avshalom Karasik, Ortal Harush, and Uzy Smilanksy. "Archaeology in Three Dimensions: Computer-Based Methods in Archaeological Research." *Journal of Eastern Mediterranean Archaeology & Heritage Studies* 2 (2014): 48–64.

Gruber, Meyer. "A Re-Examination of the Charges against Shechem Son of Hamor." *Beit Mikra Quarterly* 54 (1999): 119–27.

Gschnitzer, F. "Bemerkungen zum Arbeitsvertrag des Schreibers Spensithios." *ZPE* 13 (1974): 265–75.

Gunkel, Hermann. "Die Lade ein Thronsitz." *Zeitschrift für Missionskunde und Religionswissenschaften* 51 (1906): 1–20.

———. *Genesis.* Translated by M. E. Biddle. Macon, GA: Mercer University Press, 1997.

Hackett, Jo Ann, and Walter E. Aufrecht, eds. **The Balaam Text from Deir ʿAllā.** HSM 31. Chico: Scholars Press, 1984.

———. *"An Eye for Form": Epigraphic Essays in Honor of Frank Moore Cross.* Winona Lake: Eisenbrauns, 2014.

Hadjiev, Tchavdar S. *The Composition and Redaction of the Book of Amos.* BZAW 393. Berlin: de Gruyter, 2009.

———. "Survival, Conversion and Restoration: Reflections on the Redaction History of the Book of Zephaniah." *VT* 61 (2011): 570–81.

Hagedorn, A. C. *Between Moses and Plato. Individual and Society in Deuteronomy and Ancient Greek Law.* FRLANT 204. Göttingen: Vandenhoeck & Ruprecht, 2004.

———. "Wie flucht man im östlichen Mittelmeer? Kulturanthropologische Perspektiven in die *Dirae Teiae* und das Deuteronomium." Pages 117–50 in *Kodifizierung und Legitimierung des Rechts in der Antike und im alten Orient.* Edited by M. Witte and M. T. Fögen. BZAR 5. Wiesbaden: Harrassowitz, 2005.

Hallo, William W. "Isaiah 28:9–13 and the Ugaritic Abecedaries." *JBL* 77 (1958): 324–38.

Hamilton, Gordon J. "From the Seal of a Seer to an Inscribed Game Board: A Catalogue of Eleven Early Alphabetic Inscriptions Recently Discovered in Egypt and Palestine." *The Bible and Interpretation,* February 2010. http://www.bibleinterp.com/PDFs/Seal_of_a_Seer.pdf.

———. "Two Methodological Issues Concerning the Expanded Collection of Early Alphabetic Texts." Pages 127–56 in *Epigraphy, Philology, and the Hebrew Bible: Methodological Perspectives on Philological and Comparative Study of the Hebrew Bible in Honor of Jo Ann Hackett.* Ancient Near Eastern Monographs 12. Atlanta: Society of Biblical Literature Press, 2015.

Haran, Menaḥem. "Book-Scrolls at the Beginning of the Second Temple Period: The Transition from Papyrus to Skins." *HUCA* 54 (1983): 111–22.

———. "Book-Scrolls in Israel in Pre-Exilic Times." *JSS* 33 (1982): 161–73.

———. "Ezekiel, P, and the Priestly School." *VT* 58 (2008): 211–18.

———. "On the Diffusion of Literacy and Schools in Ancient Israel." Pages 81–95 in *Congress Volume: Jerusalem, 1986.* Leiden: Brill, 1988.

Havelock, E. A. *Origins of Western Literacy.* The Ontario Institute for Studies in Education. Monograph Series 14. Toronto: Ontario Institute for Studies in Education, 1976.

Hawke, J. *Writing Authority: Elite Competition and Written Law in Early Greece.* DeKalb: Northern Illinois University Press, 2011.

Hawkins, John David. *Corpus of Hieroglyphic Luwian Inscriptions.* 3 vols. UISK 8. Berlin: de Gruyter, 2000.

Heckl, R. "Mose als Schreiber. Am Ursprung der jüdischen Hermeneutik des Pentateuchs." *ZAR* 19 (2013): 179–234.

Hendel, Ronald S. "Historical Context." Pages 51–83 in *The Book of Genesis: Composition, Redaction, and Interpretation.* Edited by Craig Evans et al. Leiden: Brill, 2012.

———. *Remembering Abraham: Culture, Memory and History in the Hebrew Bible.* New York: Oxford University Press, 2005.

Herzberg, Hans Wilhelm. *Die Samuelbücher übersetzt und erklärt.* ATD 10, 5. Aufl., Göttingen: Vandenhoeck & Ruprecht, 1973.

Herzog, Ze'ev, and Lily Singer-Avitz. "Redefining the Centre: The Emergence of State in Judah." *TA* 31 (2004): 209–44.

———. "Sub-Dividing the Iron Age IIA in Northern Israel: A Suggested Solution to the Chronological Debate." *TA* 33 (2006): 163–95.

*Hesiod: Theogony, Works and Days, Testimonia.* Translated by Glenn W. Most. LCL 57. Cambridge, MA: Harvard University Press, 2006.

Heubeck, A. "Homer und die Schrift." *Archaeologica Homerica* III/10 (1979): 126–84.

Higginbotham, Carolyn R. *Egyptianization and Elite Emulation in Ramesside Palestine: Governance and Accommodation on the Imperial Periphery.* Culture and History of the Ancient Near East 2. Leiden: Brill, 2000.

Hoftijzer, Jean, and Gerrit van der Kooij. *Aramaic Texts from Deir 'Alla.* DMAO 19. Leiden: Brill, 1976.

———. *The Balaam Text from Deir 'Alla Re-evaluated: Proceedings of the International Symposium Held at Leiden, 21–24 August 1989.* Leiden: Brill, 1991.

Hölkeskamp, K.-J. "(In-)Schrift und Monument. Zum Begriff des Gesetzes im Archaischen und Klassischen Griechenland." *ZPE* 132 (2000): 73–96.

Hollis, Susan Tower. "Hathor and Isis in Byblos in the Second and First Millennia BCE." *Journal of Ancient Egyptian Interconnections* 1 (2009): 1–8.

Holloway, Steven W. *Assyrian Empire.* Leiden: Brill, 2002.

Hooks, Bell. "Marginality as a Site of Resistance." Pages 241–43 in *Out There: Marginalization and Contemporary Cultures.* Edited by R. Ferguson. Cambridge: MIT Press, 1990.

Horn, Siegfried H. "The Ammān Citadel Inscription." *BASOR* 193 (1969): 2–13.

Hurowitz, Victor. *I Have Built You an Exalted House: Temple Building in Light of Mesopotamian and Northwest Semitic Writings*. Sheffield: JSOT, 1992.

Hyatt, J. Philip. "The Date and Background of Zephaniah." *JNES* 7 (1948): 25–29.

Ismard, P. *Democracy's Slaves: A Political History of Ancient Greece*. Cambridge, MA: Harvard University Press, 2017.

Jaillard, D. "Memory, Writing, Authority: The Place of the Scribe in Greek Polytheistic Practice (Sixth to Fourth Centuries BCE)." Pages 23–34 in *Writing the Bible: Scribes, Scribalism and Script*. Edited by P. R. Davies and Thomas Römer. BibleWorld. Durham: Acumen, 2013.

Jamieson-Drake, David W. *Scribes and Schools in Monarchic Judah: A Socio-Archaeological Approach*. The Social World of Biblical Antiquity Series 9. JSOTSup 109. Sheffield: Sheffield Academic, 1991.

Janowski, Bernd. "Keruben und Zion. Thesen zur Entstehung der Zionstradition." Pages 231–64 in *Ernten, was man sät*. FS Klaus Koch. Edited by D. R. Daniels et al. Neukirchen-Vluyn: Neukirchener Verlag, 1991.

Japhet, Sara. "Periodization between History and Ideology II: Chronology and Ideology in Ezra-Nehemiah." Pages 491–508 in *Judah and the Judeans in the Persian Period*. Edited by O. Lipschits and M. Oeming. Winona Lake: Eisenbrauns, 2006.

**Jeffery, L. H. "Das Schreiben und die Gedichte Homers." Pages 262–68 in *Das Alphabet. Entstehung und Entwicklung der griechischen Schrift*. Edited by G. Pfohl. Wege der Forschung 88. Darmstadt: Wissenschaftliche Buchgesellschaft, 1968.**

———. *The Local Scripts of Archaic Greece: A Study of the Origin of the Greek Alphabet and Its Development from the Eighth to the Fifth Centuries B.C.* Oxford Monographs on Classical Archaeology. 2nd ed. Oxford: Oxford University Press, 1990.

Jeffery, L. H., and A. Morpurgo-Davies. "ΠΟΙΝΙΚΑΣΤΑΣ and ΠΟΙΝΙΚΑΖΕΝ: BM 1969.4–2.1: A New Archaic Inscription from Crete." *Kadmos* 9 (1970): 118–54.

Jeremias, Jörg. *The Book of Amos: A Commentary*. Translated by Douglas W. Stott. OTL. Louisville: Westminster John Knox, 1999.

Jong, Matthijs J. de. *Isaiah among the Ancient Near Eastern Prophets: A Comparative Study of the Earliest Stages of the Isaiah Tradition and the Neo-Assyrian Prophecies*. VTSup 117. Leiden: Brill, 2007.

Joseph, Alison L. "Understanding Genesis 34:2: 'Innâ." *VT* 66 (2016): 663–68.

Kaiser, Otto. *Isaiah 13–39: A Commentary*. Translated by R. A. Wilson. OTL. Philadelphia: Westminster, 1974.

Kalimi, Issak, *Zur Geschichtsschreibung des Chronisten: Literar-historiographische Abweichungen der Chronik von ihren Paralleltexten in den Samuel- und Königsbüchern*. BZAW 226. Berlin/New York: de Gruyter, 1995.

**Kartveit, Magnar. *Motive und Schichten der Landtheologie in I Chronik 1–9*. CB.OT 28. Stockholm: Almqvist & Wiksell, 1989.**

Katz, Hayah, and Avraham Faust. "The Chronology of the Iron Age IIA in Judah in Light of Tel 'Eton Tomb C3 and Other Assemblages." *BASOR* 371 (2014): 103–27.

Keefe, Alice. "Stepping In / Stepping Out: A Conversation between Ideological and Social Scientific Feminist Approaches to the Bible." *Journal of Religion and Society* 1 (1999): 1–14.

Keel, Othmar, and Amihai Mazar. "Iron Age Seals and Seal Impressions from Tel Rehov." *Eretz-Israel* 29 (2009): 57*–69*.

Kegler, Jürgen, and Matthias Augustin. *Deutsche Synopse zum Chronistischen Geschichtswerk*. BEATAJ 33. Frankfurt am Main: Peter Lang, 1993.

———. *Synopse zum Chronistischen Geschichtswerk*. BEATAJ 1. Frankfurt am Main: Peter Lang, 1991.

Keimer, Kyle H. "The Impact of Ductus on Script Form and Development in Monumental Northwest Semitic Inscriptions." *UF* 46 (2015): 189–212.

Kelm, George L., and Amihai Mazar. "Tel Batash (Timnah) Excavations: Third Preliminary Report, 1984–1989." BASORSup 27 (1991): 47–67.

Kitchen, Kenneth A. "Egyptian Interventions in the Levant in the Iron Age II." Pages 113–32 in *Symbiosis, Symbolism, and the Power of the Past: Canaan, Ancient Israel, and Their Neighbors from the Late Bronze Age through Roman Palaestina. Proceedings of the Centennial Symposium, W.F. Albright Institute of Archaeological Research and American Schools of Oriental Research, Jerusalem, May 29/31, 2000*. Edited by William G. Dever and Seymour Gitin. Winona Lake: Eisenbrauns, 2003.

———. "Establishing Chronology in Pharaonic Egypt and the Ancient Near East: Interlocking Textual Sources Relating to C. 1600–664 BC." Pages 1–18 in *Radiocarbon and the Chronologies of Ancient Egypt*. Edited by Andrew J. Shortland and Christopher Bronk Ramsey. Oxford: Oxbow Books, 2013.

Klemm, Rosemarie. *Stones and Quarries in Ancient Egypt*. London: British Museum, 2008.

Knohl, Israel. *The Sanctuary of Silence: The Priestly Torah and the Holiness School*. Minneapolis: Fortress Augsburg, 1995.

Köckert, Matthias. "Das nahe Wort: Wandlungen des Gesetzesverständnisses in der deuteronomisch-deuteronomistischen Literatur." Pages 47–71 in Köckert, *Leben in Gottes Gegenwart. Studien zum Verständnis des Gesetzes im Alten Testament*. FAT 43. Tübingen: Mohr Siebeck 2004.

Koerner, R. "Beamtenvergehen und deren Bestrafungen nach frühen griechischen Inschriften." *Klio* 69 (1987): 450–98.

———. "Vier frühe Verträge zwischen Gemeinwesen und Privatleuten auf griechischen Inschriften." *Klio* 63 (1981): 179–206.

Koller, Aaron J. *The Semantic Field of Cutting Tools in Biblical Hebrew*. CBQMS 49. Washington, DC: Catholic Biblical Association, 2012.

Kratz, R. G. "Rewriting Torah in the Hebrew Bible and the Dead Sea Scrolls." Pages 273–92 in *Wisdom and Torah: The Reception of "Torah" in the Wisdom Literature of the Second Temple Period*. Edited by B. U. Schiper and D. A. Teeter. JSJSup 163. Leiden/Boston: Brill, 2013.

Krause, Joachim J. "Kuntillet 'Ajrud Inscription 4.3: A Note on the Alleged Exodus Tradition." *VT* 67 (2017): 485–90.

Kristensen, K. R. "Archaic Laws and the Development of Civic Identity in Crete, ca. 650–450 BCE." Pages 141–57 in *Cultural Practices and Material Culture in Archaic and Classical Crete: Proceedings of the International Conference, Mainz, May 20–21, 2011*. Edited by O. Pilz and G. Seelentag. Berlin: de Gruyter, 2014.

———. "Defining 'Legal Place' in Archaic and Early Classical Crete." Pages 31–46 in *Transferts culturels et droits dans le monde grec et héllenistique. Actes du colloque international (Reims, 14–17 mai 2008)*. Edited by B. Legras. Histoire ancienne et médiévale 110. Paris: Publications du Sorbonne, 2012.

Kritzas, Ch. "Φοινικήϊα γράμματα. Νέα Αρχαϊκή Επιγραφή απο τον Έλτυνα." Pages 1–26 in Το γεωμετρικό Νεκροταφείο Ελτύνας. Edited by G. Rhetheomiotakis and M. M. Englezou. Heraklion, 2010.

Kugel, James L. *The Idea of Biblical Poetry: Parallelism and Its History*. New Haven: Yale University Press, 1981.

———. *Traditions of the Bible: A Guide to the Bible as it Was at the Start of the Common Era*. Cambridge, MA: Harvard University Press, 1999.

Kugler, Robert A. "The Priesthood at Qumran. The Evidence of References to Levi and the Levites." Pages 465–79 in *The Provo International Conference on the Dead Sea Scrolls: Technological Innovations, New Texts, and Reformulated Issues*. Edited by D. W. Parry and E. Ulrich. STDJ 30. Leiden: Brill, 1999.

Kuhrt, D. "Art. Thot (Ḏḥwtj)." Pages 497–523 in vol. 6 of *Lexikon der Ägyptologie*. Wiesbaden: Harrassowitz, 1986.

Labahn, Antje, *Levitischer Herrschaftsanspruch zwischen Ausübung und Konstruktion. Studien zum multifunktionalen Levitenbild der Chronik und seiner Identitätsbildung in der Zeit des Zweiten Tempels.* WMANT 131. Neukirchen-Vluyn: Neukirchener Verlag 2012.

Lambert, William G. "Ancestors, Authors, and Canonicity." *JCS* 11 (1957): 1–14.

Lamon, Robert S., and Geoffrey M. Shipton. *Megiddo I: Seasons of 1925–1934, Strata I-V.* Oriental Institute Communications 42. Chicago: University of Chicago Press, 1939.

Lapsley, Jacqueline E. "Introduction: Gender and Method." *HeBAI* 5 (2016): 75–77.

Lauinger, J. "Neo-Assyrian Scribes, 'Esarhaddon's Succession Treaty', and the Dynamics of Textual Mass Production." Pages 285–314 in *Texts and Context: The Circulation and Transmission of Cuneiform Texts in Social Space.* Edited by P. Delnero and J. Lauinger. Studies in Ancient Near Eastern Records 9. Berlin/Boston: de Gruyter, 2015.

Layton Scott C., and Dennis Pardee. "Literary Sources for the History of Palestine and Syria: Old Aramaic Inscriptions." *Biblical Archaeologist* 51 (1983): 172–89.

Le Maitre, R. W., ed. *Igneous Rocks: A Classification and Glossary of Terms.* 2d ed. Cambridge: Cambridge University Press, 2002.

Lehmann, Reinhard G. "Calligraphy and Craftsmanship in the Aḥīrōm Inscription: Considerations on Skilled Linear Flat Writing in Early First Millennium Byblos." *Maarav* 15 (2008): 119–64.

Lemaire, André. "From the Origin of the Alphabet to the Tenth Century B.C.E.: New Documents and New Directions." Pages 1–20 in *New Inscriptions and Seals Relating to the Biblical World.* Edited by Meir Lubetski and Edith Lubetski. Atlanta: Society of Biblical Literature, 2012.

———. *Inscriptions hébraïques, Tome I. Les ostraca.* LAPO 9; Paris: Cerf, 1977.

———. *Les écoles et la formation de la Bible dans l'ancien Israël.* Göttingen: Vandenhoeck and Ruprecht, 1981.

———. "Levantine Literacy ca. 1000–750 B.C.E." Pages 11–45 in *Contextualizing Israel's Sacred Writings. Ancient Literacy, Orality, and Literary Production.* Edited by Brian B. Schmidt. AIL 22. Atlanta: SBL, 2015.

———. "Levantine Literacy ca. 1000–750 BCE." Pages 11–46 in *Contextualizing Israel's Sacred Writing: Ancient Literacy, Orality, and Literary Production.* Edited by Brian B. Schmidt. Atlanta: SBL Press, 2015.

———. "Remarques sur les inscriptions phéniciennes de Kuntillet 'Ajrud." *Semitica* 55 (2013): 83–99.

Lerner, Gerda. *The Creation of Patriarchy.* Oxford: Oxford University Press, 1986.

Leuchter, Mark. "The Aramaic Transition and the Redaction of the Pentateuch." *JBL* 136 (2017): 249–68.

———. "From Levite to Maśkil in the Persian and Hellenistic Eras." Pages 215–32 in *Levites and Priests in Biblical History and Tradition.* Edited by M. Leuchter and J. M. Hutton. SBL.AIIL 9. Atlanta: SBL Press, 2011.

———. "Jehoiakim and the Scribes: A Note on Jer 36, 23." *ZAW* 127 (2015): 320–25.

———. *The Levites and the Boundaries of Israelite Identity.* New York: Oxford University Press, 2017.

Levenson, Jon D. *Resurrection and Restoration of Israel: The Ultimate Victory of the God of Life.* New Haven: Yale University Press, 2006.

Levine, Baruch A. "Levites." Pages 523–32 in vol. 8 of *The Encyclopedia of Religion.* New York: Macmillan, 1987.

Levtow, Nathaniel B. "Text Production and Destruction in Ancient Israel: Ritual and Political Dimensions." Pages 111–39 in *Social Theory and the Study of Israelite Religion.* Edited by Saul Olyan. RBS 71. Atlanta: Society of Biblical Literature, 2012.

Lichtheim, Miriam. *Ancient Egyptian Literature: A Book of Readings.* 2 vols. Berkeley: University of California Press, 1973.

Lilly, Ingrid E. "Rûaḥ Embodied—Job's Internal Disease from the Perspective of Mesopotamian Medicine." Pages 323–36 in *Borders: Terminologies, Ideologies, and Performances*. Edited by Annette Weissenrieder. WUNT 366. Tübingen: Mohr Siebeck, 2016.

Lilly, Ingrid E. *Winds in the Body: A Medical Anthropology of Spirit in the Ancient Near East, Hebrew Bible, and Second Temple Jewish Literature*. Cambridge: Cambridge University Press, forthcoming.

Lipka, Hilary. "Shaved Beards and Bared Buttocks: Shame and the Undermining of Masculine Performance in Biblical Texts." Pages 176–97 in *Being a Man: Negotiating Ancient Constructs of Masculinity*. Edited by Ilona Zsolnay. London: Routledge, 2017.

Lohfink, Norbert, *Das Hauptgebot: Eine Untersuchung literarischer Einleitungsfragen zu Dtn 5–11*. AnBib 20. Rome: Pontificio Instituto Biblico, 1963.

Longman, Tremper III. *Fictional Akkadian Autobiography: A Generic and Comparative Study*. Winona Lake: Eisenbrauns, 1991.

López-Ruiz, Carolina. "Near Eastern Precedents of the 'Orphic' Gold Tablets: The Phoenician Missing Link." *JANER* 15 (2015): 52–91.

——— . "Phoenician and Carthaginian Literature." In *Oxford Handbook of the Phoenician and Punic Mediterranean*. Edited by Carolina López-Ruiz and Brian Doak. Oxford: Oxford University Press, forthcoming.

Löwisch, Ingeborg. *Trauma Begets Genealogy: Gender and Memory in Chronicles*. Sheffield: Sheffield Phoenix, 2015.

Lundberg, Marilyn J. "Editor's Notes: The Aḥiram Inscription." *Maarav* 11 (2004): 81–93.

Lundbom, Jack R. "Baruch, Seraiah, and Scribal Colophons in the Book of Jeremiah." *JSOT* 36 (1986): 89–114.

——— . *Jeremiah 1–20*. AB 21A. New York: Doubleday, 1999.

——— . *Jeremiah 21–36*. AB 21B. New York: Doubleday 2004.

——— . *Jeremiah 37–52*. AB 21C. New York: Doubleday, 2004.

——— . *Jeremiah: A Study in Ancient Hebrew Rhetoric*. Missoula: Scholars Press, 1975.

Macchi, Jean-Daniel, and Thomas Römer. Pages 9–27 in "La formation des livres prophétiques: enjeux et débats *Les recueils prophétiques de la Bible: Origines, milieux, et contexte proche-oriental*. Edited by Jean-Daniel Macchi et al. MdB 64. Geneva: Labor et Fides, 2012.

MacDonald, M. C. A. "Literacy in an Oral Environment." Pages 49–118 in *Writing and Ancient Near Eastern Society: Papers in Honour of Alan R. Millard*. Edited by Piotr Bienkowski et al. LHBOTS 426. New York: T&T Clark, 2005.

MacGinnis, John. *Letter Orders from Sippar and the Administration of the Ebabbara in the Late-Babylonian Period*. Poznań: Bonami, 1995.

——— . "The Use of Writing Boards in the Neo-Babylonian Temple Administration at Sippar." *Iraq* 64 (2002): 217–36.

Maeir, A., and Itzhaq Shai. "Reassessing the Character of the Judahite Kingdom: Archaeological Evidence for Non-Centralized, Kinship-based Components." Pages 323–40 in *From Sha'ar Hagolan to Shaaraim: Essays in Honor of Professor Yossi Garfinkel*. Edited by Saar Ganor et al. Jerusalem: Israel Exploration Society, 2016.

Maeir, A., S. Wimmer, A. Zukerman, and A. Demsky. "A Late Iron Age I/Early Iron Age II Old Canaanite Inscription from Tell eṣ-Ṣâfi/Gath, Israel: Palaeography, Dating, and Historical-Cultural Significance." *BASOR* 351 (2008): 39–71.

Maier, F. G. "Idalion." Pages 1225–26 in *An Inventory of Archaic and Classical Poleis: An Investigation Conducted by The Copenhagen Polis Centre for the Danish National Research Foundation*. Edited by M. H. Hansen and T. H. Nielsen. Oxford: Oxford University Press, 2004.

Malena, Sarah. "Fertile Crossroads: The Growth and Influence of Interregional Exchange in the Southern Levant's Iron Age I-IIA Transition, Examined through Biblical, Epigraphic, and Archaeological Sources." PhD diss., University of California, San Diego, 2015.

Mandell, Alice, and Jeremy D. Smoak. "Reading beyond Literacy, Writing beyond Epigraphy: Multimodality and the Monumental Inscriptions at Ekron and Tel Dan." *Maarav* 22 (2018): 79–112.

———. "Reconsidering the Function of Tomb Inscriptions in Iron Age Judah: Khirbet Beit Lei as a Test Case." *JANER* 16 (2016): 192–245.

Mandell, Alice. "'I Bless You to YHWH and His Asherah'—Writing and Performativity at Kuntillet 'Ajrud." *Maarav* 19 (2012 [2015]): 131–62.

Marom, Nimrud, Amihai Mazar, Noa Raban-Gerstel and Guy Bar-Oz. "Backbone of Society: Evidence for Social and Economic Status of the Iron Age Population of Tel Rehov, Beth-Shean Valley, Israel." *BASOR* 354 (2009): 1–21.

Martin, Dale. *Sex and the Single Savior: Gender and Sexuality in Biblical Interpretation*. Louisville: Westminster John Knox, 2006.

Master, Daniel I. "State Formation Theory and the Kingdom of Ancient Israel." *JNES* 60 (2001): 117–34.

Mastnjak, Nathan. "Jeremiah as Collection: Scrolls, Sheets, and the Problem of Textual Arrangement." *CBQ* 80 (2018): 25–44.

Mays, James Luther. *Amos: A Commentary*. OTL. Philadelphia: Westminster, 1969.

Mazar, Amihai, and Nava Panitz-Cohen. "The Iron Age Chronology Debate: Is the Gap Narrowing? Another Viewpoint." *Near Eastern Archaeology* 74 (2011): 105–11.

———. "It Is the Land of Honey: Beekeeping at Tel Reḥov." *Near Eastern Archaeology* 70 (2007): 202–19.

———. "An Ivory Statuette Depicting an Enthroned Figure from Tel Rehov." Pages 101–10 in *Bilder Als Quellen, Images as Sources: Studies on Ancient Near Eastern Artefacts and the Bible Inspired by the Work of Othmar Keel*. Edited by Susanne Bickel et al. Orbis Biblicus et Orientalis. Fribourg; Göttingen: Academic Press; Vandenhoeck & Ruprecht, 2007.

———. "The Northern Shephelah in the Iron Age: Some Issues in Biblical History and Archaeology." Pages 247–67 in *Scripture and Other Artifacts: Essays on the Bible and Archaeology in Honor of Philip J. King*. Edited by Philip J. King et al. Louisville: Westminster/John Knox Press, 1994.

———. "Reḥob." *The Oxford Encyclopedia of Bible and Archaeology*. Edited by Daniel M. Master et al. New York: Oxford University Press, 2013.

———. "Three 10th–9th Century B.C.E. Inscriptions from *Tēl Reḥōv*." Pages 17–84 in Saxa Loquentur: *Studien zur Archäologie Palälastinas/Israels. Festschrift für Volkmar Fritz*. Edited by Cornelis G. Den Hartog, Ulrich Hübner, and Stefan Münger. AOAT 302. Münster: Ugarit Verlag, 2003.

**Mazar, Eilat, David Ben-Shlomo, and Shmuel Aḥituv. "An Inscribed Pithos from the Ophel, Jerusalem."** *IEJ* 63 (2013): 39–49.

Mazzoni, Stefania. "A Sculptures Quarry at Sikizlar." *AAAS* 26–27 (1986–87): 268–75.

McCormick, C. M. "From Box to Throne: The Development of the Ark in DtrH and P." Pages 175–86 in *Saul in Story and Tradition*. Edited by C. S. Ehrlich and M. C. White. FAT 47. Tübingen: Mohr Siebeck 2006.

McLean, B. H. *An Introduction to Greek Epigraphy of the Hellenistic and Roman Periods from Alexander the Great down to the Reign of Constantine*. Ann Arbor: University of Michigan, 2002.

Mendel-Geberovich, Anat. "Literacy: Biblical Hebrew." *EHLL* 2 (2013): 552–58.

———. רשימות בממצא האפיגרפי בישראל ובשכנותיה מימי הבית הראשון. PhD diss., Hebrew University of Jerusalem, 2014.

———. "Who Wrote the Aḥiqam Ostracon from Ḥorvat 'Uza?" *IEJ* 61 (2011): 54–67.

Mettinger, Tryggve N. D. *The Dethronement of Sabaoth: Studies in the Shem and Kabod Theologies.* CBOT 18. Lund: C. W. K. Gleerup, 1982.

Meyers, Carol. *Discovering Eve: Ancient Israelite Women in Context.* Oxford: Oxford University Press, 1988.

———. "Gender Roles and Genesis 3:16 Revisited." Pages 118–41 in *The Word of the Lord Shall Go Forth: Essays in Honor of David Noel Freedman on His Sixtieth Birthday.* Edited by Carol L. Meyers and Michael Patrick O'Connor. Winona Lake: Eisenbrauns, 1983.

———. "Material Remains and Social Relations: Women's Culture in Agrarian Households of the Iron Age." Pages 425–44 in *Symbiosis, Symbolism, and the Power of the Past: Canaan, Ancient Israel, and Their Neighbors from the Late Bronze Age through Roman Palaestina.* William Dever and Seymour Gitin. Winona Lake: Eisenbrauns, 2003.

———. "Procreation, Production, and Protection: Male–Female Balance in Early Israel." *Journal of the American Academy of Religion* (1983): 489–514.

———. *Rediscovering Eve: Ancient Israelite Women in Context.* Oxford: Oxford University Press, 2012.

Milik, J. T. "17. Palimpseste: Lettres, liste de personnes (VIII$^e$ [sic] siècle avant J.-C.)." Pages 93–100 in *Les Grottes de Murabba'ât.* DJD 2. Oxford: Clarendon, 1961.

Millard, A. "The Tablets in the Ark." Pages 254–266 in *Reading the Law: Studies in Honour of Gordon J. Wenham.* Edited by G. J. McConville and K. Möller. LHBOTS 461. New York: T&T Clark, 2007.

Millard, Alan. "The Ostracon from the Days of David Found at Khirbet Qeiyafa." *Tyndale Bulletin* 62, no. 1 (2011).

Miller, Robert D. "Shamanism in Early Israel." Pages 309–42 in *Wiener Zeitschrift für die Kunde des Morgenlandes* 101. Edited by Claudia Römer. Vienna, 2011.

Misgav, Haggai, Yosef Garfinkel, and Saar Ganor. "The Ostracon." Pages 243–57 in *Khirbet Qeiyafa.* Vol. 1, *Excavation Report 2007–2008.* Edited by Yosef Garfinkel and Saar Ganor. Jerusalem: Israel Exploration Society; Institute of Archaeology, Hebrew University of Jerusalem, 2009.

Momigliano, Arnaldo. *The Classical Foundations of Modern Historiography.* Sather Classical Lectures 54. Berkeley: University of California Press, 1990.

Montanari, F. *The Brill Dictionary of Ancient Greek.* Leiden/Boston: Brill, 2015.

Montet, P. *La Nécropole Royale de Tanis.* Vol. 1, *Les Constructions et le Tombeau d'Osorkon II à Tanis.* Paris, 1947.

Mowinckel, Sigmund. *Der Komposition des Buches Jeremia.* Kristiania: Dybwad, 1914.

Mroczek, Eva. *The Literary Imagination in Jewish Antiquity.* Oxford: Oxford University Press, 2016.

———. "Thinking Digitally about the Dead Sea Scrolls: Book History Before and Beyond the Book." *Book History* 14 (2011): 241–69.

Münger, Stefan, and Thomas E. Levy. "The Iron Age Egyptian Amulet Assemblage." Pages 741–65 in *New Insights into the Iron Age Archaeology of Edom, Southern Jordan: Surveys, Excavations and Research from the University of California, San Diego & Department of Antiquities of Jordan, Edom Lowlands Regional Archaeology Project (ELRAP).* Edited by Thomas E. Levy et al. Monumenta Archaeologica 35. Los Angeles: The Cotsen Institute of Archaeology Press, 2014.

Murphy, Roland E. "A Fragment of an Early Moabite Inscription from Dibon." *BASOR* 125 (1952): 20–23.

Na'aman, Nadav. "The Inscriptions of Kuntillet 'Ajrud Through the Lens of Historical Research." *UF* 43 (2011 [2012]): 300–24.

———. "Literacy in the Negev in the Late Monarchical Period." Pages 47–70 in *Contextualizing Israel's Sacred Writings: Ancient Literacy, Orality, and Literary Production.* Edited by Brian B. Schmidt. AIL 22. Atlanta: SBL, 2015.

———. "A New Outlook at Kuntillet 'Ajrud and Its Inscriptions." *Maarav* 20 (2013 [2015]): 39–51.

———. "Royal Inscriptions and the Histories of Joash and Ahaz, Kings of Judah." *VT* 48 (1998): 333–49.

———. "A Sapiential Composition from Ḥorvat ʿUza." *HeBAI* 2 (2013): 221–33.

———. "The Temple Library of Jerusalem and the Composition of the Book of Kings." Pages 129–52 in *Congress Volume Leiden 2004*. Leiden/Boston: Brill, 2006.

Nagy, Gregory. "Hesiod and the Ancient Biographical Traditions." Pages 271–311 in *Brill's Companion to Hesiod*. Edited by Franco Montanari et al. Leiden: Brill, 2009.

Najman, Hindy. "Ethical Reading: The Transformation of the Text and the Self." *JTS* 68 (2017): 507–29.

Naveh, Joseph. "A Fragment of an Ancient Hebrew Inscription from the Ophel." *IEJ* 32 (1982): 195–98.

———. "Hebrew and Aramaic Inscriptions." Pages 1–14 in *Excavations at the City of David 1978–1985 Directed by Yigal Shiloh. Volume VI. Inscriptions*. Edited by Donald T. Ariel. Qedem 41. Jerusalem: Hebrew University of Jerusalem, 2000.

Neef, Heinz-Dieter. "Art. Levitenstädte." *Calwer Bibellexikon* 2 (2003): 828.

Nelson, Richard D. *Joshua: A Commentary*. Louisville: Westminster John Knox, 1997.

Niditch, Susan. *Oral World and Written Word: Orality and Literacy in Ancient Israel*. LAI. London: SPCK, 1997.

Nies, James Buchanan, ed. *Babylonian Inscriptions in the Collection of James B. Nies*. New Haven: Yale University Press, 1917.

Nissinen, Martti. "How Prophecy Became Literature." *SJOT* 19 (2005): 153–72.

———. *Prophets and Prophecy in the Ancient Near East*. WAW 12. Atlanta: Society of Biblical Literature, 2003.

———. *References to Prophecy in Neo-Assyrian Sources*. SAAS 7. Helsinki: University of Helsinki Press, 1998.

———. "Since When Do Prophets Write?" Pages 585–606 in *In the Footsteps of Sherlock Holmes: Studies in the Biblical Text in Honour of Anneli Aejmelaeus*. Edited by Kristin de Troyer et al. CBET 72. Leuven: Peeters, 2014.

Nogalski, James D. *Reading and Hearing the Book of the Twelve*. Edited by Marvin A. Sweeney and James D. Nogalski. SymS12. Atlanta: Society of Biblical Literature, 2000.

Olson, Ryan S. *Tragedy, Authority, and Trickery: The Poetics of Embedded Letters in Josephus*. Washington, DC: Center for Hellenic Studies, 2010.

Osborne, James F. "Monuments and Monumentality." Pages 1–19 in *Approaching Monumentality in Archaeology*. Edited by James F. Osborne. Albany: SUNY, 2014.

———. "Monuments of the Hittite and Neo-Assyrian Empires During the Late Bronze and Iron Ages." Pages 87–105 in *Mercury's Wings: Exploring Modes of Communication in the Ancient World*. Edited by F. S. Naiden and Richard J. A. Talbert. Oxford: Oxford University Press, 2017.

Osborne, James F., and Geoffrey D. Summers. "Visibility Graph Analysis and Monumentality in the Iron Age City at Kerkenes in Central Turkey." *Journal of Field Archaeology* 39 (2014): 292–309.

Osborne, R. *Greece in the Making 1200–479 BCE*. Routledge History of the Ancient World. London: Routledge, 1996.

Otto, E. "Mose, der erste Schriftgelehrte. Deuteronomium 1,5 in der Fabel des Pentateuch." Pages 273–84 in *L'Ecrit er l'Esprit. Etudes d'histoire du texte et de théologie biblique en hommage à Adrian Schenker*. Edited by D. Böhler et al. OBO 214. Göttingen: Vandenhoeck & Ruprecht, 2005.

Otto, Eckart. "Die post-deuteronomistische Levitisierung des Deuteronomiums. Zu einem Buch von Ulrich Dahmen." *ZAR* 5 (1999): 277–284.

Pardee, Dennis. "Moabite Compositions." Pages 89–91 in *The Context of Scripture*. Vol. 4, *Supplements*. Edited by K. Lawson Younger. Leiden: Brill, 2017.

———. "A New Aramaic Inscription from Zincirli." *BASOR* 356 (2009): 51–71.

Parker, Heather Dana Davis. "The Levant Comes of Age: The Ninth Century BCE through Script Traditions." PhD diss. The Johns Hopkins University, 2013.
Parker, Simon B. "Did the Authors of the Books of Kings Make Use of Royal Inscriptions?" *VT* 50 (2000): 357–78.
Parkinson, Richard B., and Stephen Quirke. *Papyrus*. Austin: University of Texas Press, 1995.
Parpola, Simo. *Assyrian Prophecies*. SAA 9. Helsinki: Helsinki University Press, 1997.
Pat-El, Na'ama. "Israelian Hebrew: A Re-Evaluation." *VT* 67 (2017): 227–63.
Paul, Shalom M. *Amos: A Commentary on the Book of Amos*. Edited by Frank Moore Cross. Hermeneia. Minneapolis: Fortress, 1991.
Payton, Robert. "The Ulu Burun Writing-Board Set." *AnSt* 41 (1991): 99–106.
Pébarthe, C. "Spensithios, scribe ou archiviste public? Réflexions sur les usages publics de l'écriture en Crète à l'époque archaïque." *Temporalités* 3 (2006): 37–55.
Peckham, J. B. *Phoenicia: Episodes from the Ancient Mediterranean*. Winona Lake: Eisenbrauns, 2014.
Pedersen, Johannes. *Israel: Its Life and Culture*. Vols. 1 and 2. London: Oxford University Press, 1926, 1940.
Pedersén, Olof. *Archives and Libraries in the Ancient Near East: 1500–300 BC*. Bethesda, MD: CDL Press, 1998.
Perdue, Leo G. *Proverbs*. Louisville: John Knox, 2000.
Perlitt, Lothar, *Bundestheologie im Alten Testament*. WMANT 36. Neukirchen-Vluyn: Neukirchener Verlag 1969.
Perlman, P. "Crete." Pages 1144–95 in *An Inventory of Archaic and Classical Poleis: An Investigation Conducted by The Copenhagen Polis Centre for the Danish National Research Foundation*. Edited by M. H. Hansen and T. H. Nielsen. Oxford: Oxford University Press, 2004.
Person, Raymond F. *The Deuteronomic School: History, Social Setting and Literature*. Studies in Biblical Literature 2. Atlanta: Society of Biblical Literature, 2002.
Peters, John Durham. *Marvelous Clouds: Toward a Philosophy of Elemental Media*. Chicago: University of Chicago Press, 2015.
Pierce, Laurie E. "Materials of Writing and Materiality of Knowledge." Pages 167–79 in *Gazing on the Deep: Ancient Near Eastern and Other Studies in Honor of Tzvi Abusch*. Edited by Jeffrey Stackert et al. Bethesda: CDL, 2010.
Plato. *Laches, Protagoras, Meno, Euthydemus*. Translated by W. R. M. Lamb. LCL. London: Heinemann, 1924.
Polak, Frank M. "Style Is More than the Person: Sociolinguistics, Literary Culture, and the Distinction between Written and Oral Narrative." Pages 38–103 in *Biblical Hebrew: Studies in Chronology and Typology*. Edited by Ian Young. JSOTSup 369. London: T&T Clark, 2003.
Pomponio, F., and U. Seidl. "Art. Nabû A–B." Pages 16–29 in *Reallexikon der Assyriologie und Vorderasiatischen Archäologie* 9. Berlin/New York: de Gruyter, 1998–2001.
Porten, Bezalel, and Ada Yardeni. *Textbook of Aramaic Documents from Ancient Egypt*. 4 vols. Jerusalem: Hebrew University, 1986–99.
Porzig, Peter. *Die Lade Jahwes im Alten Testament und in den Texten vom Toten Meer*. BZAW 397. Berlin: de Gruyter, 2009.
Posner, Ernst. *Archive in the Ancient World*. Cambridge, MA: Harvard University Press, 1972.
Pounder, R. L. "The Origin of θιοί as Inscription-Heading." Pages 243–50 in *Studies Presented to Sterling Dow on his Eightieth Birthday*. Edited by K. J. Rigsby. Greek Roman and Byzantine Monographs 10. Durham: Duke University Press, 1984.
Powell, B. B. *Writing and the Origins of Greek Literature*. Cambridge: Cambridge University Press, 2002.
Preuss, Horst Dietrich. *Deuteronomium*. EdF 164. Darmstadt: Wissenschaftliche Buchgesellschaft, 1982.
Quick, Laura. *Deuteronomy 28 and the Aramaic Curse Tradition*. Oxford: Oxford University Press, 2018.

Quinn, Josephine. *In Search of the Phoenicians*. Princeton: Princeton University Press, 2018.
Rad, Gerhard von, "Beginnings of Historical Writing in Ancient Israel." Pages 125–53 in *From Genesis to Chronicles*. Minneapolis: Fortress Press, 2005 (original 1944).
——— . *Studies in Deuteronomy*. London: SCM, 1953.
——— . "Zelt und Lade." Pages 109–29 in von Rad, *Gesammelte Studien zum Alten Testament*. ThB 8. Munich: Kaiser, 1958.
Radford Ruether, Rosemary. *Goddesses and the Divine Feminine: A Western Religious History*. Berkeley: University of California Press, 2006.
Rainey, Anson F., and R. Steven Notley. *The Sacred Bridge: Carta's Atlas of the Biblical World*. Jerusalem: Carta, 2006.
Raubitschek, A. E. "The Cretan Inscription BM 1969.4-2.1: A Supplementary Note." *Kadmos* 9 (1970): 155–56.
Reade, Julian. "The Manufacture, Evaluation, and Conservation of Clay Tablets Inscribed in Cuneiform: Traditional Problems and Solutions." *Iraq* 79 (2017): 163–202.
Reed, Annette Yoshiko. "Textuality between Death and Memory: The Prehistory and Formation of the Parabiblical Testament." *JQR* 104 (2014): 381–412.
Reed, William L., and Fred V. Winnett. "A Fragment of an Early Moabite Inscription from Kerak." *BASOR* 172 (1963): 1–9.
Reich, Ronny, and Eli Shukron. "A Fragmentary Palaeo-Hebrew Inscription from the City of David, Jerusalem." *IEJ* 58 (2008): 48–50.
Reich, Ronny, Eli Shukron, and Omri Lernau. "Recent Discoveries in the City of David, Jerusalem." *IEJ* 57 (2007): 153–69.
Reinhartz, Adele. "Margins, Methods, and Metaphors: Reflections on A Feminist Companion to the Hebrew Bible." *Prooftexts* 20 (2000): 43–60.
Reisner, George Andrew, Clarence Stanley Fisher, and David Gordon Lyon. *Harvard Excavations at Samaria, 1908–1910*. Cambridge, MA: Harvard University Press, 1924.
Rendsburg, Gary A. "No Stelae, No Queens: Two Issues Concerning the Kings of Israel and Judah." Pages 95–107 in *The Archaeology of Difference. Gender, Ethnicity, Class and the "Other" in Antiquity. Studies in Honor of Eric M. Meyers*. Edited by Douglas R. Edwards and C. Thomas McCullough. AASOR 60–61. Boston: ASOR, 2007.
Renz, Johannes, and Wolfgang Röllig. *Handbuch der althebräischen Epigraphik*. 4 vols. Darmstadt: Wissenschaftliche Buchgesellschaft, 1995–2003.
Rhodes, P. J., and D. M. Lewis. *The Decrees of the Greek States*. Oxford: Clarendon Press, 1997.
Richards, Thomas. *The Imperial Archive: Knowledge and the Fantasy of Empire*. London: Verso, 1993.
Richelle, Matthieu. "Elusive Scrolls: Could Any Hebrew Literature Have Been Written Prior to the Eighth Century BCE?" *VT* 66 (2016): 556–94.
——— . "Quelques Nouvelles Lectures Sur L'ostracon de Khirbet Qeiyafa." *Semitica* 57 (2015): 147–62.
Ridgway, D. "Phoenicians and Greeks in the West: A View from Pithekoussai." Pages 35–46 in *The Archaeology of Greek Colonisation: Essays Dedicated to Sir John Boardman*. Edited by G. R. Tsetskhladze and F. De Angelis. Oxford: Oxford University Committee for Archaeology, 1994.
Rindge, Matthew. "Mortality and Enjoyment: The Interplay of Death and Possessions in Qoheleth." *CBQ* 73 (2011): 265–80.
Roberts, J. J. M. *Nahum, Habakkuk, and Zephaniah: A Commentary*. OTL. Louisville: Westminster John Knox, 1991.
Rogerson, J. W. *Old Testament Criticism in the 19th Century: England and Germany*. Minneapolis: Fortress Press, 1985.
Rollston, Chris A. "The Dating of the Early Royal Byblian Phoenician Inscriptions: A Response to Benjamin Sass." *Maarav* 15, no. 1 (2008): 57–93.

———. "The Phoenician Script of the Tel Zayit Abecedary and Putative Evidence for Israelite Literacy." Pages 61–96 in *Literate Culture and Tenth-Century Canaan: The Tel Zayit Abecedary in Context*. Edited by Ron E. Tappy and P. Kyle McCarter. Winona Lake: Eisenbrauns, 2008.

———. "The Putative Authenticity of the New 'Jerusalem' Papyrus Inscription: Methodological Caution as a Desideratum." Pages 319–28 in *Rethinking Israel. Studies in the History and Archaeology of Ancient Israel in Honor of Israel Finkelstein*. Edited by Oded Lipschits et al. Winona Lake: Eisenbrauns, 2017.

———. "Scribal Curriculum during the First Temple Period: Epigraphic Hebrew and Biblical Evidence." Pages 71–102 in *Contextualizing Israel's Sacred Writings. Ancient Literacy, Orality, and Literary Production*. Edited by Brian B. Schmidt. AIL 22. Atlanta: SBL, 2015.

———. "Scribal Education in Ancient Israel: The Old Hebrew Epigraphic Evidence." *BASOR* 344 (2006): 47–74.

———. "The Script of Hebrew Ostraca of the Iron Age: 8th–6th Centuries BCE." PhD diss., The Johns Hopkins University, 1999.

———. *Writing and Literacy in the World of Ancient Israel: Epigraphic Evidence from the Iron Age*. Atlanta: Society of Biblical Literature, 2010.

Rom-Shiloni, Dalit. *Exclusive Inclusivity: Identity Conflicts Between the Exiles and the People Who Remained (6th–5th Centuries BCE)*. LHBOTS 543. New York: Bloomsbury, 2013.

———. "How can you say, 'I am not defiled…'?" (Jeremiah 2:20–25): Allusions to Priestly Legal Traditions in the Poetry of Jeremiah." *JBL* 133 (2014): 757–75.

Rose, Martin, *5. Mose 12–25 Einführung und Gesetze / 5. Mose 1–11 und 26–34 Rahmenstücke zum Gesetzeskorpus*. ZBK.AT 5.1 / 5.2. Zurich: Züricher Verlagshaus 1994.

Roth, Martha T. *Law Collections from Mesopotamia and Asia Minor*. WAWSBL 6. Atlanta: Scholars Press, 1995.

Rottzoll, Dirk U. *Studien zur Redaktion und Komposition des Amosbuchs*. BZAW 243. Berlin: de Gruyter, 1996.

Rudnig, Thilo A. *Davids Thron: Redaktionskritische Studien zur Geschichte von der Thronnachfolge Davids*. BZAW 358. Berlin: de Gruyter 2006.

Russell, John Malcolm. *Sennacherib's Palace without Rival at Nineveh*. Chicago: University of Chicago, 1991.

Ruzé, F. "Au début de l'écriture politique: Le pouvoir de l'écrit dans la cite." Pages 82–94 in *Les savoirs de l'écriture en Grèce ancienne*. Edited by M. Detienne. Cahiers de Philologique 14. Lille: Presses Universitaire, 1992.

Safrai, Zeev, and Avi Sasson. *Quarrying and Quarries in the Land of Israel in the Period of the Mishnah and Talmud*. Elkanah: Eretz Heifetz, 2001 (Hebrew).

Said, Edward W. *Culture and Imperialism*. New York: Vintage Books, 1994.

Samuel, Harald. *Von Priestern zum Patriarchen: Levi und die Leviten im Alten Testament*. BZAW 448. Berlin/Boston: de Gruyter 2014).

Sanders, Seth L. "The Appetites of the Dead: West Semitic Linguistic and Ritual Aspects of the Katumuwa Stele." *BASOR* 369 (2013): 35–55.

———. *From Adapa to Enoch*. FAT; Tübingen: Mohr Siebeck, 2017.

———. "From People to Public in the Iron Age Levant." Pages 191–211 in *Organization, Representation, and Symbols of Power in the Ancient Near East: Proceedings of the 54th Rencontre Assyriologique Internationale at Würzburg 20–25 July 2008*. Edited by Gernot Wilhelm. Winona Lake: Eisenbrauns, 2012.

———. *The Invention of Hebrew*. Urbana: University of Illinois Press, 2009.

———. "Writing and Early Iron Age Israel: Before National Scripts, Beyond Nations and States." Pages 97–112 in *Literate Culture and Tenth-Century Canaan: The Tel Zayit Abecedary in Context*. Edited by Ron E. Tappy and P. Kyle McCarter. Winona Lake: Eisenbrauns, 2008.

Sass, Benjamin, and Israel Finkelstein. *The Alphabet at the Turn of the Millennium: The West Semitic Alphabet Ca. 1150–850 BCE: The Antiquity of the Arabian, Greek and Phrygian Alphabets*. Tel Aviv: Emery and Claire Yass Publications in Archaeology, 2005.

———. "The Emergence of Monumental West Semitic Alphabetic Writing, with an Emphasis on Byblos." *Semitica* 59 (2017): 109–41.

———. "The Swan-Song of Proto-Canaanite in the Ninth Century BCE in Light of an Alphabetic Inscription from Megiddo." *Semitica et Classica* 9 (2016): 19–42.

———. "Wenamun and His Levant – 1075 B.C. or 925 B.C.?" *Egypt and the Levant* 12 (2002): 247–55.

Sasson, Jack M. "The Lord of Hosts, Seated over the Cherubs." Pages 227–34 in *Rethinking the Foundations: Historiography in the Ancient World and in the Bible: Essays in Honour of J. Van Seters*. Edited by S. L. McKenzie and T. Römer in collab. with H. H. Schmid. BZAW 294. Berlin: de Gruyter, 2000.

Schade, Aaron. "The Syntax and Literary Structure of the Phoenician Inscription of Yeḥimilk." *Maarav* 13 (2006): 119–22.

Schaper, Joachim. "Anthropologie des Schreibens als Theologie des Schreibens. Ein medienarchäologischer Gang durch das Buch Exodus." Pages 281–96 in *Metatexte. Erzählungen von schrifttragenden Artefakten in der alttestamentlichen und mittelalterlichen Literatur*. Edited by F. E. Focken and M. R. Ott. Materiale Textkulturen 15. Berlin/Boston: de Gruyter, 2016.

———. "On Writing and Reciting in Jeremiah 36." Pages 137–47 in *Prophecy in the Book of Jeremiah*. Edited by Hans M. Barstad and Reinhard G. Kratz. BZAW 388. Berlin: de Gruyter, 2009.

———. "'Scriptural Turn' und Monotheismus: Anmerkungen zu einer (nicht ganz neuen) These." Pages 275–91 in *Die Textualisierung der Religion*. Edited by J. Schaper. FAT 62. Tübingen: Mohr Siebeck, 2009.

———. "A Theology of Writing: The Oral and the Written, God as Scribe, and the Book of Deuteronomy." Pages 97–119 in *Anthropology and Biblical Studies. Avenues of Approach*. Edited by L. J. Lawrence and M. I. Aguilar. Leiden: deo Publishing, 2004.

Schart, Aaron. "Combining Prophetic Oracles in Mari Letters and Jeremiah 36." *JANES* 23 (1995): 75–93.

Schloen, David, and Amir Fink. "New Excavations at Zincirli Höyük in Turkey (Ancient Sam'al) and the Discovery of an Inscribed Mortuary Stele." *BASOR* 356 (2009): 1–13.

Schmid, Konrad. "Hintere Propheten (Nebiim)." Pages 303–401 in *Grundinformation Altes Testament*. Edited by Jan Christian Gertz. Göttingen: Vandenhoeck & Ruprecht, 2006.

Schmidt, Brian B., ed. *Contextualizing Israel's Sacred Writings: Ancient Literacy, Orality, and Literary Production*. AIL 22. Atlanta: SBL, 2015.

———. *The Materiality of Power: Explorations in the Social History of Early Israelite Magic*. FAT 105. Tübingen: Mohr Siebeck, 2016.

Schmitt, G. "Levitenstädte." *ZDPV* 111 (1995): 28–48.

Schmitz, Philip C. "The Phoenician Papyrus from Tal Virtù, Malta." Pages 61–71 in *"What Mean These Stones?" (Joshua 4:6, 21): Essays on Texts, Philology, and Archaeology in Honour of Anthony J. Frendo*. Edited by Dennis Mizzi et al. ANESSup 50; Leuven: Peeters, 2017.

Schniedewind, William M. *How the Bible Became a Book: The Textualization of Ancient Israel*. Cambridge: Cambridge University Press, 2004.

———. "Scribal Education in Ancient Israel and Judah into the Persian Period." Pages 11–28 in *Second Temple Jewish Paideia in Context*. Edited by Jason M. Zurawski and Gabriele Boccaccini. BZNW 228. Berlin: de Gruyter, 2017.

———. "Sociolinguistic Reflections on the Letter of a 'Literate' Soldier (Lachish 3)." *Zeitschrift für Althebraistik* 13 (2000): 157–67.

———. "Understanding Scribal Education in Ancient Israel: A View from Kuntillet 'Ajrud." *Maarav* 21 (2014 [2017]): 271–93.

Scholz, Susanne. *Rape Plots: A Feminist Cultural Study of Genesis 34*. Peter Lang, 2002.

———. "'Tandoor Reindeer' and the Limitations of Historical Criticism." Pages 47–69 in *Her Master's Tools? Feminist and Post-Colonial Engagements of Historical-Critical Discourse*. Edited by C. Vander Stichele and T. Penner. Atlanta: SBL, 2005.

Schüssler Fiorenza, Elisabeth. "Remembering the Past in Creating the Future: Historical-Critical Scholarship and Feminist Biblical Interpretation." Pages 43–63 in *Feminist Perspectives on Biblical Scholarship*. Edited by Adela Yarbro Collins. Atlanta: Scholars Press, 1985.

Schweitzer, Steven J. *Reading Utopia in Chronicles*. LHBOTS 442. New York/London: T & T Clark, 2007.

Seelentag, G. *Das archaische Kreta: Institutionalisierung im frühen Griechenland*. Klio Beihefte 24. Berlin/Boston: de Gruyter, 2015.

———. "Regeln für den Kosmos. Prominenzrollen und Institutionen im archaischen Kreta." *Chiron* 39 (2009): 65–99.

Seeligmann, Isac L. "Anfänge der Midraschexegese in der Chronik." Pages 31–54 in Seeligmann, *Gesammelte Studien zur Hebräischen Bibel*. FAT 41. Tübingen: Mohr Siebeck 2004.

Seow, C. L. *Ecclesiastes: A New Translation with Introduction and Commentary*. AB 18C. New York: Doubleday, 1997.

Shear, I. M. "Bellerophon Tablets from the Mycenaean World? A Tale of Seven Bronze Hinges." *Journal of Hellenic Studies* 118 (1998): 187–89.

Shectman, Sarah. *Women in the Pentateuch: A Feminist and Source-Critical Analysis*. Sheffield: Sheffield Phoenix, 2009.

Sheres, Ita. *Dinah's Rebellion: A Biblical Parable for Our Time*. New York: Crossroad, 1990.

Shoham, Yair. "Hebrew Bullae." Pages 29–57 in *Excavations at the City of David 1978–1985 Directed by Yigal Shiloh*. Vol. 6, *Inscriptions*. Edited by Donald T. Ariel. Qedem 41. Jerusalem: Hebrew University of Jerusalem, 2000.

Shortland, Andrew. "Shishak, King of Egypt: The Challenges of Egyptian Calendrical Chronology in the Iron Age." Pages 43–54 in *The Bible and Radiocarbon Dating: Archaeology, Text and Science*. Edited by Thomas E. Levy and T. Higham. London/Oakville: Equinox, 2005.

Sickenger, James P. "Literacy, Documents, and Archives in the Ancient Athenian Democracy." *The American Archivist* 62 (2002): 229–46.

Singer, Itamar. "Egyptians, Canaanites, and Philistines in the Period of the Emergence of Israel." Pages 282–338 in *From Nomadism to Monarchy: Archaeological and Historical Aspects of Early Israel*. Jerusalem: Biblical Archaeology Society, 1994.

Sjöberg, Ake W. "The Old Babylonian Edubba." Pages 159–79 in *Sumerological Studies in Honor of Thorkild Jacobsen*. Edited by Stephen J. Lieberman. University of Chicago Assyriological Studies 20. Chicago: University of Chicago Press, 1974.

Skornik, Jordan. "Paradigms and Possibilities: On Literary Prophecy and the Hebrew Bible." PhD diss., University of Chicago, 2018.

Smith Mark S., and Wayne T. Pitard. *The Ugaritic Baal Cycle*. Vol. 2. VTSup 114. Leiden: Brill, 2009.

Smith, H. W. *Aeschylus I*. LCL 145. Cambridge, MA: Harvard University Press, 1922.

Smoak, Jeremy D. "From Temple to Text: Text as Ritual Space and the Composition of Numbers 6:24-26." *JHS* 17 (2017): 1–26.

———. "Inscribing Temple Space: The Ekron Dedication as Monumental Text." *JNES* 76 (2017): 319–36.

———. *The Priestly Blessing in Inscription and Scripture: The Early History of Numbers 6:24–26*. New York: Oxford University Press, 2016.

Sonnet, J.-P. *The Book Within the Book: Writing in Deuteronomy*. Biblical Interpretation Series 14. Leiden: Brill, 1997.

Spivak, Gayatri. "Can the Subaltern Speak?" Pages 271–313 in *Marxism and the Interpretation of Culture*. Edited by Cary Nelson and Lawrence Grossberg. Urbana: University of Illinois Press, 1988.

Stager, Lawrence E. "The Patrimonial Kingdom of Solomon." Pages 63–73 in *Symbiosis, Symbolism and the Power of the Past*. Edited by W. G. Dever and S. Gitin. Winona Lake: Eisenbrauns, 2003.

Steck, Odil Hannes, *Israel und das gewaltsame Geschick der Propheten: Untersuchungen zur Überlieferung des deuteronomistischen Geschichtsbildes im Alten Testament, Spätjudentum und Urchristentum*. WMANT 23. Neukirchen: Neukirchener Verlag, 1967.

Steindorff, Georg. "The Statuette of an Egyptian Commissioner in Syria." *Journal of Egyptian Archaeology* 25 (1939): 30–33, plate VII.

Steiner, Richard C. *Disembodied Souls: The Nefesh in Israel and Kindred Spirits in the Ancient Near East, With an Appendix on the Katumuwa Inscription*. ANEM 11. Atlanta: SBL Press, 2015.

Steiner, Richard. "Bishlam's Archival Search Report in Nehemiah's Archive: Multiple Introductions and Reverse Chronological Order as Clues to the Origin of the Aramaic Letters in Ezra 4–6." *JBL* 125 (2006): 641–85.

Stenstrom, Hannah. "Historical-Critical Approaches and the Emancipation of Women: Unfulfilled Promises and Remaining Possibilities." Pages 31–45 in *Her Master's Tools? Feminist and Post-Colonial Engagements of Historical-Critical Discourse*. Edited by C. Vander Stichele and T. Penner. Atlanta: SBL, 2005.

Stoebe, Hans Joachim, *Das erste Buch Samuelis*. KAT VIII.1. Gütersloh: Gütersloher Verlagshaus, 1973.

———. *Das zweite Buch Samuelis*. KAT VIII.2. Gütersloh: Gütersloher Verlagshaus, 1994.

Stökl, Jonathan. *Prophecy in the Ancient Near East: A Philological and Sociological Comparison*. CHANE 56. Leiden: Brill, 2012.

Stoler, Ann Laura. *Along the Archival Grain: Epistemic Anxieties and Colonial Common Sense*. Princeton, NJ: Princeton University Press, 2010.

Stolper, Matthew. *Entrepreneurs and Empire: The Murašû Archive, the Murašû Firm, and Persian Rule in Babylonia*. Leiden: Nederlands Historisch-Archaeologisch Instituut te Istanbul, 1985.

Struble, Eudora J., and Virginia Rimmer Herrmann. "An Eternal Feast at Sam'al: The New Iron Age Mortuary Stele from Zincirli in Context." *BASOR* 356 (2009): 15–49.

Sukenik, Eleazar L. "Note on a Fragment of an Israelite Stele found at Samaria." *PEFQS* (1936): 156.

Summers, Geoffrey D., and Erol Özen. "The Hittite Stone and Sculpture Quarry at Karakız Karabası and Hapis Boğazı in the District of Sorgun, Yozgat, Central Anatolia." *AJA* 116 (2012): 507–19.

Suriano, Matthew J. "Breaking Bread with the Dead: Katumuwa's Stele, Hosea 9:4, and the Early History of the Soul." *JAOS* 134 (2014): 385–405.

———. "The Formulaic Epilogue for a King in the Book of Kings in Light of Royal Funerary Rites in Ancient Israel and the Levant." PhD diss., University of California, Los Angeles, 2008.

———. *A History of Death in the Hebrew Bible*. Oxford: Oxford University Press, 2018.

———. "Kingship and *Carpe Diem*, Between Gilgamesh and Qoheleth." *VT* 67 (2017): 285–306.

Sweeney, Marvin S. *Zephaniah: A Commentary*. Edited by Paul D. Hanson. Hermeneia. Minneapolis: Fortress, 2003.

Symington, Dorit. "Late Bronze Age Writing-Boards and Their Uses: Textual Evidence from Anatolia and Syria." *AnSt* 41 (1991): 111–23.

Tallet, Pierre. *Les papyrus de la mer Rouge. 1, Le "journal de Merer" (Papyrus Jar A et B)*. MIFAO 136. Cairo: Institut français d'archéologie orientale, 2017.

Talstra, Eep. "Deuteronomy 31: Confusion or Conclusion? The Story of Moses' Threefold Succession." Pages 87–110 in *Deuteronomy and Deuteronomic Literature*. Festschrift C. H. W. Brekelmans. Edited by M. Vervenne and J. Lust. BETL 133. Leuven: Leuven University Press, 1997.

Tappy, Ron E., P. Kyle McCarter, Marilyn J. Lundberg, and Bruce Zuckerman. "An Abecedary of the Mid-Tenth Century B.C.E. from the Judaean Shephelah." *BASOR* 344 (2006): 5–46.
Taylor, John. "The Third Intermediate Period (1069–664 BCE)." Pages 330–68 in *The Oxford History of Ancient Egypt*. Edited by Ian Shaw. Oxford: Oxford University Press, 2002.
Teeter, D. A. *Scribal Laws: Exegetical Variation in the Textual Transmission of Biblical Law in the Late Second Temple Period*. FAT 92. Tübingen: Mohr Siebeck, 2014.
Thiselton, Anthony. "The Supposed Power of Words in the Biblical Writings." *JTS* 25 (1974): 283–99.
Thomas, R. (1992), *Literacy and Orality in Ancient Greece*. Key Themes in Ancient History. Cambridge: Cambridge University Press, 1992.
———. "Writing, Reading, Public and Private Literacies. Functional Literacy and Democratic Literacy in Greece." Pages 13–45 in *Ancient Literacies: The Culture of Reading in Greece and Rome*. Edited by W. A. Johnson and H. N. Parker Oxford: Oxford University Press, 2009.
Thompson, John A. "Joel's Locusts in the Light of Near Eastern Parallels." *JNES* 14 (1955): 52–55.
Tinney, Steve. "Texts, Tablets and Teaching: Scribal Education at Nippur and Ur." *Expedition* 40 (1998): 40–50.
Torczyner, Harry. *The Lachish Letters*. Lachish 1. London: Oxford University Press, 1938.
Torrey, C. C. *Ezra Studies*. Chicago: University of Chicago Press, 1910.
"Translation, Walter's Art Gallery." http://art.thewalters.org/viewwoa.aspx?id=33246.
Trible, Phyllis. "Depatriarchalizing in Biblical Interpretation." *Journal of the American Academy of Religion* 41 (1973): 30–48.
———. *God and the Rhetoric of Sexuality*. Fortress Press (1978).
———. "Eve and Adam: Genesis 2–3 Re-Read." *Andover Newton Quarterly* 13 (1973): 251–58.
**Tropper, Josef. *Die Inschriften von Zincirli*. ALASP 6. Münster: Ugarit-Verlag, 1993.**
Toorn, Karel van der. "From the Mouth of the Prophet: The Literary Fixation of Jeremiah's Prophecies in the Context of the Ancient Near East." Pages 191–202 in *Inspired Speech: Prophecy in the Ancient Near East: Essays in Honour of Herbert B. Huffmon*. Edited by John Kaltner and Louis Stulman. JSOTSup 378. London: T&T Clark, 2004.
———. "Mesopotamian Prophecy between Immanence and Transcendence." Pages in 71–87 in *Prophecy in Its Near Eastern Context: Mesopotamian, Biblical, and Arabian Perspectives*. Edited by Martti Nissinen. SymS 13. Atlanta: Society of Biblical Literature, 2000.
———. *Scribal Culture and the Making of the Hebrew Bible*. Cambridge, MA: Harvard University Press, 2007.
Van Selms, A. "Isaiah 28:9–13: An Attempt to Give a New Interpretation." *ZAW* 85 (1973): 332–39.
Van Wolde, Ellen. "Does 'innâ Denote Rape? A Semantic Analysis of a Controversial Word." *VT* 52 (2002): 528–44.
Vanderhooft, David S. "The Edomite Dialect and Script: A Review of the Evidence." Pages 137–57 in *You Shall Not Abhor an Edomite, for He Is Your Brother: Edom and Seir in History and Tradition*. Edited by Diana V. Edelman. ABS 3. Atlanta: Scholars Press, 1995.
———. "Iron Age Moabite, Hebrew, and Edomite Monumental Scripts." Pages 107–26 in *"An Eye for Form": Epigraphic Essays in Honor of Frank Moore Cross*. Edited by Jo Ann Hackett and Walter E. Aufrecht. Winona Lake: Eisenbrauns, 2014.
Vanstiphout, H. L. J. "On the Old Babylonian Eduba Curriculum." Pages 1–16 in *Centers of Learning: Learning and Location in Pre-Modern Europe and the Near East*. Edited by Jan Willem Drijvers and Alasdair A. MacDonald. Brill's Studies in Intellectual History 61. Leiden: Brill, 1995.
Vaux, Roland de. "Historique des découvertes." Pages 3–8 in *Les Grottes de Murabba'ât*. DJD 2. Oxford: Clarendon, 1961.
Vayntrub, Jacqueline. "Before Authorship: Solomon and Prov. 1:1." *Biblical Interpretation* 26 (2018): 182–206.

——— . "The Book of Proverbs and the Idea of Ancient Israelite Education." *ZAW* 128 (2016): 96–114.

——— . "Proverbs and the Limits of Poetry." PhD diss., Chicago: University of Chicago, 2015.

——— . "Transmission and Mortal Anxiety in the Tale of Aqhat." In *Like 'Ilu Are You Wise: Studies in Northwest Semitic Languages and Literature in Honor of Dennis G. Pardee*. Edited by H. H. Hardy, J. Lam, and E. Reymond. Chicago: Oriental Institute Publications, forthcoming.

Veijola, Timo, *Das 5. Buch Mose Deuteronomium: Kapitel 1,1–16,17*. ATD 8,1. Göttingen: Vandenhoeck & Ruprecht 2004.

Viviers, D. "La cité de Datalla et l'expansion territorial de Lyktos en Crète centrale." *BCH* 118 (1994): 229–59.

Voutrias, E. "The Introduction of the Alphabet." Pages 266–76 in *A History of Ancient Greek: From the Beginning to Late Antiquity*. Edited by A.-F. Christidis. Cambridge: Cambridge University Press, 2007.

Wallace, S. *Ancient Crete: From Successful Collapse to Democracy's Alternatives, Twelfth to Fifth Centuries BC*. Cambridge: Cambridge University Press, 2010.

Wearne, Gareth. "'Guard it on your tongue!' The Second Rubric in the Deir 'Alla Plaster Texts as an Instruction for the Oral Performance of the Narrative." Pages 125–42 in *Registers and Modes of Communication in the Ancient Near East: Getting the Message Across*. Edited by Kyle H. Keimer and Gillan Davis. London: Routledge, 2018.

——— . "The Plaster Texts from Kuntillet 'Ajrud and Deir 'Alla: An Inductive Approach to the Emergence of Northwest Semitic Literary Texts in the First Millennium B.C.E." PhD diss., Macquarie University, 2015.

Weaver, Mary Jo. "Who Is the Goddess and Where Does She Get Us?" *Journal of Feminist Studies* 5 (1989): 49–64.

Weeks, Stuart. "Literacy, Orality, and Literature in Israel." Pages 465–78 in *On Stone and Scroll: Essays in Honour of Graham Ivor Davies*. Edited by James K. Aitken, Katharine J. Dell, and Brian A. Mastin. BZAW 420. Berlin: de Gruyter, 2011.

Weinfeld, Moshe, *Deuteronomy and the Deuteronomic School*. Oxford: Clarendon, 1972.

Weippert, Manfred. "Assyrische Prophetien der Zeit Asarhaddons und Assurbanipals." Pages 71–115 in *Assyrian Royal Inscriptions: New Horizons in Literary, Ideological, and Historical Analysis: Papers of a Symposium Held in Cetona (Siena) June 26–28, 1980*. Edited by F. M. Fales. OAC 17. Rome: Istituto per l'Oriente, 1981.

——— . "'Das Frühere, siehe, ist eingetroffen…': über Selbstzitate im altorientalischen Prophetenspruch." Pages 147–69 in *Oracles et prophéties dans l'Antique: Acts du Colloque de Strasbourg 15–17 juin 1995*. Edited by Jean-Georges Heintz. Travaux du centre de recherche sur le Proche-Orient et la Grèce antiques 15. Paris: de Boccard, 1997.

——— . "'König, fürchte dich nicht!' Assyrische Prophetie im 7. Jahrhundert v. Chr." *Or* 71 (2002): 1–54.

Westermann, Claus. *Genesis 12–36. A Commentary*. Translated by John J. Scullion. Minneapolis: Augsburg, 1984.

Whisenant, Jessica. "Let the Stones Speak! Document Production by Iron Age West Semitic Scribal Institutions and the Question of Biblical Sources." Pages 133–60 in *Contextualizing Israel's Sacred Writings: Ancient Literacy, Orality, and Literary Production*. Edited by Brian B. Schmidt. AIL 22. Atlanta: SBL, 2015.

Whitley, J. "Cretan Laws and Cretan Literacy." *AJA* 101 (1997): 635–61.

Wilamowitz-Moellendorff, U. von, *Die Ilias und Homer*, 2nd ed. Berlin: Weidemann, 1920.

Wildberger, Hans. *Isaiah 13–27*. Translated by Thomas H. Trapp. CC. Minneapolis: Fortress, 1997.

Willetts, R. F. "The Cretan Inscription BM 1969.4–2.1: Further Provisional Comments." *Kadmos* 11 (1972): 96–98.

Williams, Donald L. "The Date of Zephaniah." *JBL* 82 (1963): 77–88.

Williams, Ronald J. "Scribal Training in Ancient Egypt." *JAOS* (1972): 214–21.
Wilson, Ian. "Merely a Container? The Ark in Deuteronomy." Pages 212–49 in *Temple and Worship in Biblical Israel*. Edited by J. Day. LHBOTS 422. New York: T&T Clark 2007.
Wilson, J.-P. "Literacy." Pages 542–63 in *A Companion to Archaic Greece*, Blackwell Companions to the Ancient World. Edited by K. A. Raaflaub and H. van Wees. Malden: Wiley-Blackwell, 2013.
Wilson, Robert R. "Orality and Writing in the Creation of Exilic Prophetic Literature." Pages 83–96 in *Worship, Women, and War: Essays in Honor of Susan Niditch*. Edited by John J. Collins et al. BJS 357. Providence: Brown University, 2015.
Wirbelauer, E. "Eine Frage der Telekommunikation? Die Griechen und ihre Schrift im 9.–7. Jahrhundert v. Chr." Pages 187–206 in *Griechische Archaik: Interne Entwicklungen – Externe Impulse*. Edited by R. Rollinger and C. Ulf. Berlin: Akademie Verlag, 2005.
Wolf, F. A. *Prolegomena to Homer (1795): Translated with Introduction and Notes by Anthony Grafton, Glenn W. Most, and James E.G. Zetzel*. Princeton: Princeton University Press, 1985.
Wolff, Hans Walter. *Joel and Amos: A Commentary on the Books of the Prophets Joel and Amos*. Edited by S. Dean McBride Jr. Translated by Waldemar Janzen, S. Dean McBride Jr., and Charles a Muenchow. Hermeneia. Philadelphia: Fortress, 1977.
Woodard, R. D. "*Phoinikēia Grammata*: An Alphabet for the Greek Language." Pages 25–46 in *A Companion to the Ancient Greek Language*. Blackwell Companions to the Ancient World. Edited by E. J. Bakker. Malden: Blackwell, 2010.
Würthwein, Ernst. *Das erste Buch der Könige: Kapitel 1–16 übersetzt und erklärt*. ATD 11.1. Göttingen: Vandenhoeck & Ruprecht 1977.
Wyatt, Nick. "The Story of Dinah and Shechem." *UF* 22 (1990): 433–58.
Yardeni, Ada. "Further Observations on the Ostracon." Pages 259–60 in *Khirbet Qeiyafa*. Vol. 1, *Excavation Report 2007–2008*. Edited by Yosef Garfinkel and Saar Ganor. Jerusalem: Israel Exploration Society; Institute of Archaeology, Hebrew University of Jerusalem, 2009.
———. *The National Hebrew Script up to the Babylonian Exile*. Jerusalem: Carta, forthcoming.
Young, Ian M. "Israelite Literacy: Interpreting the Evidence." *VT* 48 (1998): 239–53, 408–22.
Zahn, M. M. "Innerbiblical Exegesis – The View from beyond the Bible." Pages 107–20 in *The Formation of the Pentateuch: Bridging the Academic Cultures of Europe Israel, and North America*. Edited by J. C. Gertz et al. FAT 111. Tübingen: Mohr Siebeck, 2016.
Zhakevich, Philip. "The Tools of an Israelite Scribe: A Semantic Study of the Terms Signifying the Tools and Materials of Writing in Biblical Hebrew." PhD diss., University of Texas at Austin, 2015.
Zimmerli, Walther. *Ezekiel 1: A Commentary on the Book of the Prophet Ezekiel, Chapters 1–24*. Translated by Ronald E. Clements. Hermeneia. Philadelphia: Fortress, 1979.
———. *Ezekiel 2: A Commentary on the Book of the Prophet Ezekiel, Chapters 25–48*. by James D. Martin. Hermeneia. Minneapolis: Fortress, 1983.
Zimmermann, Frank. "The Aramaic Provenance of Qohelet." *JQR* 36 (1945): 17–45.
Zsolnay, Ilona. *Being a Man: Negotiating Ancient Constructs of Masculinity*. Routledge, 2016.

# INDEX OF REFERENCES

Hebrew Bible/
Old Testament
*Genesis*
14:21       81
16          133, 144,
            145
24:1–9      83
27          79, 82, 83
27:4        79
27:19       79
27:22       79
27:33       80
27:39       80
34          143, 145,
            146
34:2        144
34:13       146
34:31       146
48:10–49:33 83
49          82, 83
50:24–25    83

*Exodus*
5           69
5:6         69
5:10        69
5:15        69
16:33–34    71
25:20       111
40:34–38    111

*Leviticus*
16:23       71

*Numbers*
5:23        70
6:24–26     7, 38
11:16       69
16:2        111
17:4        71
17:7        71
22–24       37
23–24       82

*Deuteronomy*
1:15        69
4:13        110, 116,
            117
4:44        110
4:45        110, 116
5           116
5:1         110, 116
5:2         110

5:3         116
5:6–21      110
6:1         110, 116
8:2         144
9:7–12      111
9:9–11      116
9:9–10      107
9:9         110, 116, 117
9:10        110, 116
9:11        110, 116, 117
9:15        110, 116, 117
10:1–5      111, 114, 116
10:1–4      114
10:2        107, 110, 116
10:5–7      114
10:5        107, 110
10:6–7      114
10:6        114
10:8–9      114, 120
10:8        107, 113–15, 120, 121
10:9        114
10:10–11    114
12:12       120
14:27       120
16:18       69
17:9        113
17:18–19    74
17:18       113
18:1        113, 120
18:7        113
18:18       95
20:5        69
21:5        113, 115, 120
22          144
22:23–24    145
22:23       144
22:24       145
22:25       145
24:8        113
26:4        71
27          112
27:9        113
27:14       113
31          112, 114–16
31:9        107, 115, 116, 121
31:22       115
31:24–26    115, 121
31:24       116
31:25–26    116
31:25       107, 113, 115
31:26       107, 110, 116, 118
31:27       115
32:8        136

33          82, 83

*Joshua*
3–6         108
3           112
3:2–3       112
3:2         69
3:3         108, 112, 121
8           112
8:30–35     112
8:33        69, 108, 112, 121
21          108
21:16       108
23          83
23:2        69

*Judges*
8:13–17     69

*1 Samuel*
3:20        72
4:1–7:1     108
4:1         108
4:3–5       117
4:3         108
4:5         108
4:7–8       117
5:1         108
5:8         108
5:10        108
6:11        108
6:14–15     108
6:14        108
6:15        9, 107–109, 111, 112,
            121
6:21        109
7:1–2       109
7:6         72
7:9–10      72
7:16        72
8:4         72
10:10       88
10:25       71, 72
13          145
24:14       88
25          27

*2 Samuel*
5:24        108
6           118
6:13        118
8:16–18     21
11:1        74

# INDEX OF REFERENCES

| | | | | | |
|---|---|---|---|---|---|
| 12:1 | 95 | *1 Chronicles* | | 6:2 | 127 |
| 13 | 144 | 1–9 | 129 | 7:12 | 42 |
| 13:14 | 144, 145 | 6:44 | 108 | 7:21 | 42 |
| 15 | 108 | 15 | 112, 118 | | |
| 15:17–21 | 109 | 15:2 | 118 | *Nehemiah* | |
| 15:24–30 | 109 | 15:12 | 118 | 13:13 | 42 |
| 15:24 | 9, 107, 109–12, 121 | 15:14 | 118 | | |
| 15:25 | 109, 110 | 15:15 | 118, 120 | *Job* | |
| 15:29 | 109, 110 | 15:25–29 | 118 | 19:21–24 | 91 |
| 19 | 27 | 15:26 | 118 | 31:35 | 91 |
| 20:23–26 | 21 | 15:27 | 118 | 32:11 | 91 |
| 23:1–7 | 83 | 16:4 | 118 | | |
| | | 16:6 | 118 | *Proverbs* | |
| *1 Kings* | | 16:37 | 118 | 1:1 | 86 |
| 2:1–9 | 83 | 16:41 | 118 | 5:13 | 77 |
| 3:15 | 117 | 17:1 | 118 | 10:1 | 86 |
| 4 | 14 | 22:19 | 118 | 22:17–24:33 | 67 |
| 4:9 | 20 | 28:2 | 71, 118 | 25–29 | 91 |
| 5:12 | 86 | 28:18 | 118 | 25:1 | 86, 91 |
| 6:19 | 117 | 29:29 | 72 | 25:2 | 91 |
| 8 | 108, 117, 118 | | | | |
| 8:1–13 | 111, 112 | *2 Chronicles* | | *Ecclesiastes* | |
| 8:1–4 | 111 | 4:8 | 71 | 1:1 | 86 |
| 8:1 | 111, 117 | 5:2 | 118 | 1:2 | 85 |
| 8:3 | 111 | 5:4 | 118 | 1:12 | 86, 87 |
| 8:4 | 9, 107, 110–12, 120, 121 | 5:7 | 118 | 2:18–19 | 89 |
| | | 6:10–11 | 118 | 2:21 | 89 |
| 8:5 | 111 | 6:11 | 118 | 2:24 | 81 |
| 8:6 | 111, 117 | 9:29 | 72 | 2:26 | 90 |
| 8:7–8 | 111, 120 | 12:15 | 72 | 4:8 | 81 |
| 8:8 | 111 | 13:22 | 72 | 6:2 | 81 |
| 8:9 | 71, 107, 110–12, 116 | 17:7–9 | 118 | 6:3 | 81 |
| 8:10–11 | 111 | 20:14 | 118 | 6:7 | 80, 81 |
| 8:12–13 | 111 | 20:34 | 72 | 7:1 | 92 |
| 11:41 | 86 | 21:12 | 6, 72 | 7:28 | 81 |
| 12:31 | 112 | 23:14 | 118 | 12:8 | 85 |
| 16 | 20 | 25:1–7 | 118 | 12:9–14 | 85, 88 |
| 17:1 | 95 | 26:22 | 72, 137 | 12:9–10 | 90, 91 |
| 19:19–21 | 73 | 32:32 | 72 | 12:10 | 85, 90 |
| 22:19 | 95 | 33:19 | 72 | 12:12 | 85 |
| | | 35:3 | 118 | | |
| *2 Kings* | | 35:4 | 74 | *Song of Songs* | |
| 1:16 | 95 | 35:15 | 118 | 1:1 | 86 |
| 2:1–18 | 73 | | | | |
| 6:1–7 | 73, 77 | *Ezra* | | *Isaiah* | |
| 6:3 | 73 | 4 | 128 | 1–39 | 105 |
| 9 | 20 | 4:1–5 | 128 | 1:8 | 72 |
| 10:1 | 74 | 4:6–11 | 128 | 6 | 137 |
| 13:14–19 | 83 | 4:7 | 128 | 8:1 | 95 |
| 19:1 | 72, 76 | 4:8–11 | 128 | 8:16–22 | 73, 77 |
| 20:20 | 68 | 4:8 | 42 | 8:16 | 73 |
| 22–23 | 65 | 4:9 | 42 | 10:1 | 63 |
| 22 | 64, 66, 69, 71, 73, 74, 76–78 | 4:11 | 128 | 10:5–10 | 103 |
| | | 4:12 | 128 | 15–16 | 99, 101 |
| 22:8–13 | 69 | 4:16 | 128 | 15:1–16:12 | 100 |
| 22:8 | 76 | 4:17–24 | 127 | 15:5 | 99 |
| 22:10 | 70, 76 | 4:17 | 42 | 16:4 | 99 |
| 22:12 | 76 | 4:21 | 128 | 16:13–14 | 99, 100 |
| 22:14–20 | 72 | 4:23–24 | 128 | 24–27 | 105 |
| 22:16 | 70 | 4:23 | 42 | 28:7–13 | 73 |
| 23:1–2 | 75 | 5:17 | 127 | 28:9–10 | 73 |
| 23:2 | 73, 74, 76 | 6:1–5 | 127 | 30:8 | 72, 95 |
| 25:7 | 100 | 6:1 | 127 | 37–38 | 137 |

*Isaiah* (cont.)

| | |
|---|---|
| 38:8 | 74 |
| 39:8 | 95 |
| 50:4–5 | 73 |
| 54:13 | 73 |

*Jeremiah*

| | |
|---|---|
| 7:27 | 95 |
| 8:8 | 64, 69, 77 |
| 9:21 | 95 |
| 11:3 | 95 |
| 13:12 | 95 |
| 14:17 | 95 |
| 16:11 | 95 |
| 18:11 | 95 |
| 19:3 | 95 |
| 19:11 | 95 |
| 19:14 | 95 |
| 20:8 | 95 |
| 21:3 | 95 |
| 21:8 | 95 |
| 22:2 | 95 |
| 23:16 | 95 |
| 25:2 | 95 |
| 25:3 | 95 |
| 25:27 | 95 |
| 25:28 | 95 |
| 25:30 | 95 |
| 26:2 | 95 |
| 26:4 | 95 |
| 26:7 | 95 |
| 26:8 | 95 |
| 26:16 | 95 |
| 27:12 | 95 |
| 27:16 | 95 |
| 28 | 20 |
| 28:11 | 95 |
| 28:13 | 95 |
| 29 | 6 |
| 29:24 | 95 |
| 30:2 | 95 |
| 32:6 | 95 |
| 32:12–13 | 75 |
| 32:12 | 75 |
| 32:16 | 75 |
| 34:2 | 95 |
| 34:6 | 95 |
| 35:13 | 95 |
| 35:18 | 95 |
| 36 | 7, 64, 66, 69, 71, 74, 76–78, 99 |
| 36:1–4 | 74 |
| 36:2 | 72, 76, 95 |
| 36:4–6 | 95 |
| 36:4 | 72, 76 |
| 36:10 | 71 |
| 36:11 | 75 |
| 36:12 | 71 |
| 36:13 | 75 |
| 36:16–22 | 76 |
| 36:17–18 | 76, 95 |
| 36:18 | 76 |
| 36:20 | 71 |
| 36:27–28 | 76 |
| 36:27 | 76 |
| 36:28–32 | 99 |
| 36:28 | 76, 95 |
| 36:32 | 76, 95 |
| 38:1 | 95 |
| 38:4 | 95 |
| 38:17 | 95 |
| 39:16 | 95 |
| 43:1 | 95 |
| 43:10 | 95 |
| 44:16 | 95 |
| 44:20 | 95 |
| 44:24 | 95 |
| 45:1 | 95 |
| 51:59–60 | 76 |
| 51:59 | 72, 75 |
| 51:60 | 72, 95 |

*Ezekiel*

| | |
|---|---|
| 1:3 | 72 |
| 2 | 89 |
| 2:4 | 95 |
| 2:7 | 95 |
| 2:8–3:3 | 70 |
| 2:9–3:1 | 6 |
| 2:10 | 70 |
| 3:1 | 95 |
| 3:11 | 95 |
| 3:27 | 95 |
| 4:1 | 71 |
| 6:3 | 95 |
| 8:11 | 75 |
| 11:16 | 95 |
| 11:17 | 95 |
| 11:25 | 95 |
| 12 | 100, 101 |
| 12:10 | 95 |
| 12:11 | 95 |
| 12:12 | 100 |
| 12:19 | 95 |
| 12:23 | 95 |
| 12:28 | 95 |
| 13:18 | 95 |
| 14:4 | 95 |
| 14:6 | 95 |
| 17:3 | 95 |
| 17:9 | 95 |
| 17:12 | 95 |
| 19:2 | 95 |
| 20:3 | 95 |
| 20:5 | 95 |
| 20:27 | 95 |
| 20:30 | 95 |
| 21:3 | 95 |
| 21:8 | 95 |
| 21:14 | 95 |
| 21:33 | 95 |
| 22:3 | 95 |
| 24:2 | 71, 95 |
| 24:3 | 95 |
| 24:18 | 95 |
| 24:21 | 95 |
| 25:3 | 95 |
| 26:7–14 | 101, 104 |
| 27:3 | 95 |
| 28:2 | 95 |
| 28:12 | 95 |
| 28:22 | 95 |
| 29:3 | 95 |
| 29:17–21 | 101, 104 |
| 30:2 | 95 |
| 31:2 | 95 |
| 32:2 | 95 |
| 33:2 | 95 |
| 33:10 | 95 |
| 33:11 | 95 |
| 33:12 | 95 |
| 33:25 | 95 |
| 33:27 | 95 |
| 34:2 | 95 |
| 35:3 | 95 |
| 36:1 | 95 |
| 36:3 | 95 |
| 36:6 | 95 |
| 36:22 | 95 |
| 37:4 | 95 |
| 37:16 | 71, 95 |
| 37:19 | 95 |
| 37:20 | 71 |
| 37:21 | 95 |
| 38–39 | 105 |
| 38:3 | 95 |
| 38:24 | 95 |
| 39:1 | 95 |
| 39:17 | 95 |
| 43:11 | 95 |
| 44:6 | 95 |

*Joel*

| | |
|---|---|
| 1:4 | 103 |
| 2:2 | 103 |
| 3:2 Eng. | 104 |
| 4:2 | 104 |

*Amos*

| | |
|---|---|
| 1:3 | 102 |
| 1:6 | 102 |
| 2:1 | 102 |
| 7:8 | 95 |
| 7:14 | 72 |

*Jonah*

| | |
|---|---|
| 3:4 | 95 |

*Nahum*

| | |
|---|---|
| 1:1 | 103 |
| 1:2 | 103 |
| 1:8 | 103 |
| 1:9 | 103 |
| 1:15 Eng. | 103 |
| 2:1 | 103 |
| 2:2 Eng. | 103 |

# INDEX OF REFERENCES

| | |
|---|---|
| 3:1 | 103 |
| 3:7 | 103 |
| 3:8 | 103 |
| 3:18 | 103 |

*Habakkuk*

| | |
|---|---|
| 1:6 | 103 |
| 2:2 | 72, 77, 95 |
| 2:5 | 80 |
| 3 | 103, 105 |

*Zephaniah*

| | |
|---|---|
| 2:4 | 103 |
| 2:8 | 103 |
| 2:12 | 103 |
| 3:8–10 | 105 |

*Haggai*

| | |
|---|---|
| 1:13 | 95 |
| 2:2 | 95 |
| 2:21 | 95 |

*Zechariah*

| | |
|---|---|
| 1–8 | 104 |
| 1:3 | 95 |
| 5:1–2 | 6 |
| 6:12 | 95 |
| 7:5 | 95 |
| 13:3 | 95 |

APOCRYPHA
*Tobit*

| | |
|---|---|
| 14:3–11 | 83 |

*1 Maccabees*

| | |
|---|---|
| 2:49–69 | 83 |

*2 Maccabees*

| | |
|---|---|
| 2:29–31 | 125 |

PSEUDEPIGRAPHA
*Jubilees*

| | |
|---|---|
| 31:15 | 119 |
| 45:16 | 119 |

*Testament of Levi*

| | |
|---|---|
| 2:2 | 119 |
| 2:10 | 119 |
| 8:17 | 119 |
| 9:6 | 119 |
| 13:1–7 | 119 |

*Testament of Reuben*

| | |
|---|---|
| 6:8 | 119 |
| 6:10 | 119 |

DEAD SEA SCROLLS
4Q159

| | |
|---|---|
| Frg. 5 | 119 |

4Q175

| | |
|---|---|
| 14–18 | 119 |

CLASSICAL AND ANCIENT CHRISTIAN LITERATURE
Aeschylus
*Prometheus Bound*

| | |
|---|---|
| 454–461 | 45 |

Aischylos

| | |
|---|---|
| fr. 705 | 43 |

*Septem*

| | |
|---|---|
| 646 | 43 |

Aristotle
*Politics*

| | |
|---|---|
| 1272a | 51 |
| 1321b | 50 |

| | |
|---|---|
| fr. 501 | 44 |

*Critias*

| | |
|---|---|
| fr. B2.9 = fr. B2.10 | 44 |

Herodotus
*Histories*

| | |
|---|---|
| 5.58 | 44 |
| 6.60 | 48 |

Hesiod
*Theogony*

| | |
|---|---|
| 10 | 87 |
| 31 | 87 |
| 39 | 87 |
| 43 | 87 |
| 65 | 87 |
| 67 | 87 |
| 97 | 87 |

Homer
*Iliad*

| | |
|---|---|
| 11.388 | 43 |
| 13.552–554 | 43 |
| 17.598–600 | 43 |
| 4.139 | 43 |
| 6.166–170 | 42 |
| 7.175–189 | 42, 43 |
| 9.485–622 | 49 |

*Odyssey*

| | |
|---|---|
| 1.141 | 42 |
| 4.57 | 42 |
| 12.67 | 42 |
| 22.279–280 | 43 |
| 24.229 | 43 |

Plato
*Protagoras*

| | |
|---|---|
| 341a–e | 92 |
| 347e–348a | 92 |

OSTRACA, PAPYRI AND TABLETS
*Lachish Letter*

| | |
|---|---|
| 3 | 67–69 |

ANCIENT NEAR EASTERN AND MEDITERRANEAN TEXTS AND SOURCES
*AHw*

| | |
|---|---|
| 1028 | 97 |

*BIN*

| | |
|---|---|
| 4 126:9 | 88 |

*BM*

| | |
|---|---|
| A 1–21 | 46, 47 |
| B 1–17 | 46, 47 |
| B 6–11 | 51 |
| B 11–17 | 45 |
| inv. 1969.4–2.1 | 45 |

*CAD*

| | |
|---|---|
| R 62–66 | 95 |
| S 171–72 | 97 |

*CCT*

| | |
|---|---|
| 2 45a:12 | 88 |

*FrGrHist*

| | |
|---|---|
| III 458 fr. 6 | 45 |
| III 468 fr. 1.74 | 45 |

*Herr*

| | |
|---|---|
| 110 | 42 |

*IC*

| | |
|---|---|
| I.x.2 = *Nomima* II.80 | 51 |
| I xvi 26 | 47 |
| I xvi 32 | 47 |
| II. xii.11 = *Nomima* I.14 | 50 |
| IV 13 e2 = *Nomima* I.1 | 49 |
| IV.14 p-g2 = *Nomima* I.82 | 51 |
| IV 42B | 50 |
| IV 43 Ba.Bb | 47 |
| IV 51 | 47 |
| IV 64 | 47, 49 |
| IV 64 = *Nomima* I.8 | 48 |
| IV 65 | 47 |
| IV 72 l.1 | 47 |
| IV 72 IX.32 | 50 |
| IV 72 X.42–43 | 47 |
| IV 72 XI.10-17 = *Nomima* II.40 | 51 |
| IV 78 | 47 |
| IV 80 | 47 |
| IV 87 | 50 |
| IV 87.8 = *Nomima* I.97 | 51 |
| XI.16 | 50 |
| XI.52–55 | 50 |

*IE*
| | |
|---|---|
| I.1 | 53 |
| I.8 | 54 |
| I.10 | 54 |
| I.17 | 53 |
| I.24 | 54 |
| I.27 | 54 |

*IG*
| | |
|---|---|
| VII 2789 | 47 |
| VII 2809 | 47 |
| VII 2811-2818 | 47 |
| VII 2820 | 47 |
| VII | 47 |
| XII/2.96 | 49 |
| XII/2.97 3083 | 49 |

*KAI*
| | |
|---|---|
| 4 | 32 |
| 7 | 32 |
| 9 | 32 |
| 10 | 32 |
| 24 | 84 |
| 181 | 31 |
| 201 | 31 |
| 202 | 31, 84 |
| 214–21 | 31 |
| 216 | 84 |
| 222–24 | 31 |
| 266 | 35 |

*KTU*
| | |
|---|---|
| 1.6 VI | 70 |

*Kuntillet 'Ajrud*
| | |
|---|---|
| 4.3 | 38 |

*Laws of Hammurabi*
| | |
|---|---|
| i. 27–49 | 84 |
| xlviii 95–xlix 17 | 84 |

*LSCG*
| | |
|---|---|
| 49 | 47 |
| 96 | 47 |
| 92 | 47 |
| 102 | 47 |

*ML*
| | |
|---|---|
| 32 | 50 |

*Nomima*
| | |
|---|---|
| I.14 | 50 |
| I.22 | 52 |
| I.22 = *SEG* 27.631 | 47 |
| I.23 | 52 |
| I.23 = *SEG* 29.402 = *IvO* 2 | 52 |
| I.31 = *ICS* 217 | 53 |
| I.104 = ML 30 | 49 |
| I.105 D19–21 | 49 |

*RÉS*
| | |
|---|---|
| 1791 | 34 |

*SAA*
| | |
|---|---|
| 1 and 2 (= WAW 12 68–83) | 96 |
| 8 552 | 97 |
| 9 1–3 (= WAW 12 68–88) | 96, 98 |
| 9 1.4 (= WAW 12 71) | 98 |
| 9 3 (= WAW 12 84–88) | 96 |
| 9 3.3 (= WAW 12 86) | 98 |
| 9 4 (= WAW 12 89) | 96 |
| 9 5–8 (= WAW 12 90–93) | 96 |
| 9 7 (= WAW 12 92) | 98 |
| 10 111 (= WAW 106) | 97 |
| 10 352 | 95 |
| 16 59 (= WAW 12 115) | 97 |
| 16 60 (= WAW 12 116):10'–11' | 98 |

*TAD*
| | |
|---|---|
| A1.1 | 35 |
| B2.4 line 16 | 48 |
| B3.1 line 20 | 48 |
| C3.1 | 35 |
| C3.2 | 35 |

*WAW*
| | |
|---|---|
| 12 1–50 | 96 |
| 12 1:3 | 95 |
| 12 1:29 | 95 |
| 12 1:42 | 95 |
| 12 1:47 | 95 |
| 12 1:61 | 95 |
| 12 2:4 | 95 |
| 12 2:17 | 95 |
| 12 3:9 | 95 |
| 12 4:20 | 95 |
| 12 7:9 | 95 |
| 12 7:20 | 95 |
| 12 9:43 | 95 |
| 12 16:17 | 95 |
| 12 16:25 | 95 |
| 12 16:33 | 95 |
| 12 18:14 | 95 |
| 12 19:7 | 95 |
| 12 20:10 | 95 |
| 12 21:9 | 95 |
| 12 24:7 | 95 |
| 12 25:17 | 95 |
| 12 30:24 | 95 |
| 12 31:20 | 95 |
| 12 32:21 | 95 |
| 12 34:8' | 95 |
| 12 38:8 | 95 |
| 12 48:29–42 | 95 |
| 12 109 | 95 |

# INDEX OF AUTHORS

Abusch, T. 80
Achenbach, R. 120
Ackerman, S. 135, 136
Aharoni, Y. 35, 36
Aḥituv, S. 15, 16, 20, 22, 23, 29, 31, 32, 35, 37, 38
Aitken, J. K. 80
Albertz, R. 104
Albright, W. F. 16, 24
Alexandre, Y. 16, 23
Ampolo, C. 44, 56
Andersen, F. I. 102, 103
**Andiñach**, P. R. 103
Arico, A. F. 31
Arnaoutoglou, I. 54, 55
Ash, P. 22
Assis, E. 103, 104
Athas, G. 31, 33, 34
Aufrecht, W. E. 29, 31, 32
Augustin, M. 112
Avigad, N. 36, 42, 55
Avishur, Y. 24

Baden, J. 79, 82
Báez, F. 131
Baines, J. 67, 73
Baker, D. W. 1
Bal, M. 139
Barkay, G. 38, 67, 68
Barthes, R. 102
Barton, J. 103, 104
Baurain, C. 43, 55
Beattie, A. J. 48, 49, 55
Bechtel, L. 144
Beit-Arieh, I. 38
Bekkum, K. van 20
Ben Zvi, E. 96, 102, 108, 118
Ben-Shlomo, D. 16
Berlin, A. 102
Bessac, J.-C. 33
Bile, M. 45, 56
Blenkinsopp, J. 100, 105, 118
Block, D. I. 100
Blum, E. 37
Blyth, C. 143
Bolin, T. M. 86
Bottéro, J. 81
Braulik, G. 114
Breasted, J. H. 25
Brichto, H. C. 84, 89
Britt, B. 115
Brooke, G. J. 119
Brosius, M. 126, 127
Buck, C. D. 52, 56

Bunimovitz, S. 17, 20
Burkes, S. 82
Burlingame, A. R. 29, 32
Byrne, R. C. 6, 15, 21

Camp, C. 144
Cancik-Kirschbaum, E. 30
Carawan, E. 56
Carr, D. M. 1, 4–6, 37, 41, 56, 64–67, 70, 73, 96
Carroll, R. 2, 30
Carstens, P. 126
Ceccarelli, P. 44, 45, 49, 56
Certeau, M. de 125, 131
Chapman, C. 136
Childs, B. S. 100
Christ, C. P. 134
Christensen, D. L. 103
Clines, D. J. A. 87
Coldstream, N. 22
Cook, E. M. 17, 19
Cook, S. L. 6
Cooke, G. A. 100
Cowley, A. E. 127
Crawford, S. W. 41, 56
Crenshaw, J. L. 73, 87, 103, 104
Cross, F. M. 20, 32, 35, 38

Dahmen, U. 114, 120
Dajani, R. W. 31
Daly, M. 134
Davies, P. 1, 118, 119
Davis, E. F. 101
Dearman, J. A. 31, 75
Demsky, A. 20, 30, 67
Detienne, M. 45, 56
Devecchi, E. 30
Diels, H. 44, 56
Dietrich, W. 102, 103, 107, 118
Dittenberger, K. 41
Dobbs-Allsopp, D. W. 16, 20, 29, 31, 32, 38
Dolansky, S. 133
Donner, H. 29
Dorsey, D. A. 19, 20
Dothan, T. 32
Du Toit, J. S. 127
Duhm, B. 2
Dummermuth, F. 117, 120
Duru, R. 33
Dušek, J. 34

Edelman, D. V. 5, 95, 96
Edwards, G. P. 49, 56
Edwards, R. B. 49, 56

Effenterre, H. van 41, 52, 53, 56
Eichrodt, W. 100, 105
Elayi, J. 17
Engelmann, H. 41
Erbse, H. 43, 56
Erickson, B. 50, 56
Eshel, E. 37
Exum, J. C. 135

Fagels, R. 42, 56
Fander, M. 137, 138
Faust, A. 13
Feinstein, E. L. 144
Feldmeier, R. 110
Fink, A. 81
Finkelstein, I. 15–17, 24, 37
Fischer-Hansen, T. 44, 56
Fishbane, M. 101
Fisher, K. D. 34
Fitzmyer, J. A. 31
Fleishman, J. 144
Fleming, D. 3, 6
Floyd, M. H. 96
Fornara, C. W. 56
Fox, M. V. 82, 83, 87, 92
Fraser, P. M. 47, 56
Freedman, D. N. 102
Frymer-Kensky, T. 144–46
Fulco, W. J. 31

Gagarin, M. 42, 45, 47–52, 55, 56
Ganor, S. 16, 17, 35
Gardiner, A. H. 67
Garfinkel, Y. 16, 17
Gass, E. 29, 31
Geiger, M. 114
Geoghegan, J. C. 3
Gerber, D. E. 56
Gesenius, W. 108, 111
Gibson, J. C. L. 24, 25
Gitin, S. 32
Gogel, S. L. 42, 56
Goodley, A. D. 44, 57
Goody, J. 41, 57
Gorlin, C. E. 48, 57
Grabbe, L. L. 127, 128
Gray, G. B. 100
Graybill, R. 82, 89
Green, D. J. 84
Greenberg, M. 100
Grosman, L. 23
Gruber, M. 144
Gschnitzer, F. 51, 57
Guarducci, M. 41
Gunkel, H. 83, 117
Guzzo, M. G. A. 32

Hackett, J. A. 29, 37
Hadjiev, T. S. 102
Hagedorn, A. C. 42, 49, 57
Hallo, W. W. 73
Hamilton, G. J. 15, 17, 20, 21
Haran, M. 35, 63, 67

Hasler, L. C. 127
Havelock, E. A. 41, 57
Hawke, J. 48, 53, 57
Hawkins, J. D. 32
Heckl, R. 41, 57
Heidel, A. 67
Hendel, R. S. 5, 136
Hermann, V. 84
Herzberg, H. W. 109, 110
Herzog, Z. 13
Heubeck, A. 42, 57
Higginbotham, C. R. 27
Hoftijzer, J. 37
Hogue, T. 31
Hölkeskamp, K.-J. 53, 57
Hollis, J. H. 25
Holloway, S. W. 127
hooks, b. 143
Horn, S. H. 32
Hurowitz, V. 130
Hyatt, J. P. 102

Ismard, P. 48, 53, 57

Jaillard, D. 45, 57
Jamieson-Drake, D. W. 4, 14, 19, 22
Janowski, B. 117
Japhet, S. 128
Jeffery, L. H. 42, 44, 45, 48, 52, 57
Jeremias, J. 102
Joffe, A. H. 27
Jong, M. de 96–98
Joseph, A. 144

Kaiser, O. 100, 105
Kalimi, I. 112
Kartveit, M. 108
Keefe, A. 138
Keel, O. 14
Kegler, J. 112
Keimer, K. H. 32, 34
Kelm, G. L. 16
Kitchen, K. 25
Klein, E. 35
Klemm, R. 33
Knohl, I. 63
Köckert, M. 110, 115
Koerner, R. 48, 51, 52, 57
Kohn, R. L. 144
Koller, A. J. 30, 33
Kooij, G. van der 37
Kranz, W. 44, 56
Kratz, R. G. 42, 55, 57
Krause, J. J. 38
Kristensen, K. R. 42, 48, 49, 58
Kritzas, Ch. 49, 58
Kugel, J. L. 83, 92
Kugler, R. A. 119
Kuhrt, D. 58

Labahn, A. 113, 118, 119
Lamb, W. R. M. 92
Lambert, W. G. 70

# INDEX OF AUTHORS

Lamon, R. S.  25
Lapsley, J.  136
Lauinger, J.  41, 58
Layton, S. C.  73
Le Maitre, R. W.  31
Lederman, Z.  17, 20
Lehmann, R. G.  30
Lemaire, A.  14, 17, 35, 38, 63, 67, 73
Lernau, O.  36
Lerner, G.  134
Leuchter, M.  1, 3, 4, 7, 65, 121
Levine, B. J.  119
Levtow, N. B.  99
Levy, T. E.  26
Lewis, D. M.  41, 54, 58
Lichtheim, M.  26, 88
Lilly, I. E.  89
Lipka, H.  139
Lohfink, N.  114
Longman III, T.  82
López-Ruiz, C.  36, 38
Loquentur, S.  20
Löwisch, I.  126, 129
Lundberg, M. J.  24
Lundbom, J. R.  2

MacDonald, M. C. A.  64, 67, 70
MacGinnis, J.  33, 127
Macchi, J.-D.  96
Maier, A.  4, 17, 53
Maier, F. G.  58
Malena, S.  13, 19
Mandell, A.  29, 31–34, 37
Marom, N.  23
Martin, D.  131
Masson, O.  41
Master, D. I.  4
Mastnjak, N.  35
Matthews, E.  47, 56
Mays, J. L.  102
Mazar, A.  13–16, 20, 22, 23
Mazar, E.  16
Mazzoni, S.  33
McCormick, C. M.  111, 116
McLean, B. H.  33, 34
Meiggs, R.  41
Mendel-Geberovich, A.  30, 38
Merkelbach, R.  41
Meshel, Z.  37
Mettinger, T. N. D.  117
Meyers, C.  133, 137, 139–41, 147
Milik, J. T.  35
Millard, A.  21, 114
Miller, R. D.  6
Misgav, H.  16, 17
Momigliano, A.  128
Montanari, F.  44, 58
Montet, P.  25
Morpurgo-Davies, A.  45, 48, 57
Most, G. W.  87
Mowinckel, S.  2
Mroczek, E.  83, 126, 129, 130
Müller, G. G. W.  30

Münger, S.  26
Murphy, R. E.  31
Mynárova, J.  30

Na'aman, N.  35–38, 130
Nagy, G.  87
Najman, H.  130
Naveh, J.  32
Neef, H.-D.  108
Nelson, R. D.  112
Niditch, S.  65, 67, 68, 96, 99
Nielsen, T. H.  44, 56
Nissinen, M.  95–99
Nogalski, J. D.  104
Notley, R. S.  25

Olson, R.  129
Osborne, J. F.  31, 32, 34, 44
Osborne, R.  58
Otto, E.  41, 58, 120
Özen, E.  33

Panitz-Cohen, N.  23
Pardee, D.  31, 73, 81, 84
Parker, D. D.  30
Parker, H. D. D.  31
Parker, S. B.  36
Parkinson, R. B.  35
Parpola, T.  96, 97
Pat-El, N.  32
Paul, S. M.  102
Payton, R.  33
Peckham, J. B.  49, 58
Pedersen, J.  80
Pedersén, O.  126, 127
Perdue, J. L.  87
Perlitt, L.  110, 115, 117
Perlman, P.  45, 47–52, 56, 58
Person, R. E.  63
Peters, J. D.  129, 130
Pierce, L. E.  30
Pitard, W. T.  70
Plaskow, J.  134
Polak, F. M.  5
Pomponio, F.  41, 58
Porten, B.  34
Porzig, P.  109, 112, 114–17, 120
Posner, E.  126
Pounder, R. L.  47, 58
Powell, B. B.  43, 58
Preuss, H. D.  110, 114, 115
Purgold, W.  41

Quick, L.  5
Quinn, J.  36
Quirke, S.  35

Rad, G. von  3, 4, 109
Radford Ruether, R.  134
Rainey, A. F.  25
Raubitschek, A. E.  50, 58
Reade, J.  30
Reed, A. Y.  83

Reed, W. L. 31
Reich, R. 33, 36
Reinhartz, A. 138
Reisner, G. A. 35
Rendsburg, G. A. 33
Renz, J. 29, 31, 32, 35
Rhodes, P. J. 54, 58
Richards, T. 127
Richelle, M. 4, 14, 19
Richey, M. 32
Richter, S. L. 117
Ridgway, D. 44, 58
Rindge, M. 83, 85
Roberts, J. J. M. 102, 103, 105
Rogerson, J. W. 2
Röllig, W. 29, 31, 32, 35
Rollston, C. A. 15, 17, 21, 24, 29, 30, 32, 34, 35, 63, 67
Rom-Shiloni, D. 5, 104
Römer, T. 96
Rose, M. 113, 115, 117
Roth, M. T. 84
Rottzoll, D. U. 102
Rudnig, T. A. 109
Russell, J. M. 33
Ruzé, F. 41, 45, 48, 54, 58

Safrai, Z. 33
Said, E. W. 127
Samuel, H. 108, 109, 111–16
Sanders, S. L. 4, 6, 7, 14, 15, 21, 23, 84
Sass, B. 15–17, 24, 26, 32
Sasson, A. 33
Sasson, J. M. 108, 109
Schade, A. 24
Schaper, J. 41, 58, 60, 99, 125
Schart, A. 96, 98
Schloen, D. 81
Schmid, K. 96
Schmidt, B. B. 29, 96
Schmitt, G. 108
Schmitz, P. C. 38
Schniedewind, W. 5, 30, 37, 38, 67, 68, 71, 92, 96, 126, 129, 130, 136
Schnitzlein, B. 30
Scholz, S. 138, 143
Schüssler Fiorenza, E. 138
Schweitzer, S. J. 119
Seelentag, G. 48–52, 55, 60
Seeligmann, I. L. 109
Seidl, U. 41, 58
Seitz, R. 114
Selms, A. van 73
Seow, C. L. 87, 90
Shai, I. 4
Shear, I. M. 42, 60
Shectman, S. 135, 136
Shipton, G. M. 25
Shoham, Y. 36
Shortland, A. 25
Shukron, E. 33, 36
Sickenger, J. P. 127
Singer, I. 25
Singer-Avitz, L. 13

Sjöberg, W. 66
Skornik, J. 37
Smith, M. S. 70
Smoak, J. D. 29, 31–34, 38, 39, 126, 129
Smyth, H. W. 45, 60
Sokolowski, F. 41
Sonnet, J.-P. 41, 60
Speickermann, H. 110
Spivak, G. C. 142
Stager, L. E. 4
Steck, H. 109
Steindorf, G. 25
Steiner, R. C. 80, 81, 128
Stenstrom, H. 137
Stoebe, H. J. 109, 110
Stökl, J. 97, 98
Stoler, A. L. 127
Stolper, M. 127
Struble, E. 84
Sukenik, E. L. 32
Summers, G. D. 33, 34
Suriano, M. J. 24, 31, 81–84, 88
Sweeney, M. A. 102, 104
Symington, D. 33

Tallet, P. 35
Talstra, E. 114–16
Tappy, R. E. 17
Taylor, J. 25
Teeter, D. A. 41, 60
Thiselton, A. 80
Thomas, B. D. 31
Thomas, R. 43, 60
Thompson, J. A. 103
Tinney, S. 66
Toorn, K. van der 1, 2, 38, 41, 60, 64–67, 70, 71, 75, 96–99, 126, 130, 136
Torczyner, H. 35
Torrey, C. C. 128
Trible, P. 134
Tropper, J. 31

Vanderhooft, D. S. 29, 32
Vanstiphout, H. L. J. 66
Vaux, R. de 35
Vayntrub, J. 79, 80, 83, 86–90
Veijola, T. 114, 120
Viviers, D. 45, 60
Voutrias, E. 43, 44, 60

Wallace, S. 49, 60
Washburn, J. 31
Wearne, G. 37, 38
Weaver, M. 134
Weeks, S. 96
Weinfeld, M. 3, 63, 110, 117
Weippert, M. 96, 98
Wente Jr., E. F. 26
Westermann, C. 80
Whisenant, J. 35
Whitley, J. 55, 60
Wilamowitz-Moellendorff, U. von 43, 60
Wildberger, H. 100, 105

Willetts, R. F.  55, 60
Williams, D. L.  102
Williams, R. J.  64, 66, 73
Wilson, I.  114, 117
Wilson, J.-P.  43, 60
Wilson, R. R.  99
Winnett, F. V.  31
Wirbelauer, E.  43, 44, 49, 60
Wöhrle, J.  104
Wolde, E. van  144
Wolf, F. A.  43, 60
Wolff, H. W.  102, 104
Woodard, R. D.  43, 49, 60
Würthwein, E.  111
Wyatt, N.  144

Yardeni, A.  16, 30, 34
Yehuda, E. B.  87
Young, I. M.  4, 6, 67, 70, 72
Younger, Jr., K. L.  84

Zahn, M. M.  41, 60
Zhakevich, P.  30, 34
Zimmerli, W.  100, 105
Zimmerman, F.  87
Zsolnay, I.  136

www.ingramcontent.com/pod-product-compliance
Lightning Source LLC
Chambersburg PA
CBHW080539300426
44111CB00017B/2798